ICARO MODERNO
255

Michele Palermo

Eagles over Gazala
The air battles in North Africa, May-June 1942

IBN Editore

Aviolibri Records no. 13

Copyright © IBN Istituto Bibliografico Napoleone 2014
Via dei Marsi, 57 - 00185 Roma (Italy)
tel. 06 4469828 - Fax 06 4452275
e-mail: info@ibneditore.it

www.ibneditore.it

First Published 2014

ISBN (10) 88-7565-168-X
ISBN (13) 9788875651688

All right reserved. No part of this book may be reproduced or transmitted in any form or by any means, electronic or mechanical, including photocopying, recording, scanning or by any information storage and retrieval system, on the internet or elsewhere, without permission from the Publisher in writing.

Printed in Italy

Front Cover - Artwork by Marco Manni.

Rear Cover - The wreck of Kittyhawk IA, ET574 of 260 Squadron, as discovered on 12th February 2012, by an Italo-Egyptian team of researchers, led by the Italian surgeon Daniele Moretto of the ARIDO association. On 28th June 1942 the plane, coded HS-B and piloted by F.Lt. Sgt. Dennis Copping had left L.G.09 to fly to a Repair Maintenance Unit. The pilot set the wrong course, crashed in the Desert and went missing.

SUMMARY

Foreword p. 7

Chapter 1	Introduction	p. 9
Chapter 2	Orders of battle	p. 17
Chapter 3	The preparations (22-25 May)	p. 21
Chapter 4	The launching of the operations (26-30 May)	p. 35
Chapter 5	'The Cauldron' and Bir Hakeim (31 May-10 June)	p. 69
Chapter 6	Knightsbridge (11-18 June)	p. 129
Chapter 7	Tobruk and Egypt (19-30 June)	p. 179
Chapter 8	Conclusions	p. 215
Appendix 1	From Sidi El Barrani to El Alamein 1940-1942, a Strategic overview (Ernico Cernuschi)	p. 229
Appendix 2	Performances of aircraft (Michele M. Gaetani)	p. 233
Appendix 3	Availability of aircraft	p. 242
Appendix 4	Sorties	p. 249
Appendix 5	Losses	p. 255
Appendix 6	Serial numbers of Macchi C.202s	p. 269
Appendix 7	Investigation of Fighter Squadrons' Results in the Western Desert as at 29th July 1942.	p. 273
Appendix 8	Naval Warfare and Intelligence along the North African Coasts, January - June 1942. (Enrico Cernuschi)	p. 275

Glossary p. 285
Sources p. 287
Acknowledgements p. 291
Index of names p. 293

FOREWORD

The events of the air war over the desert during World War II have been covered by a fair number of studies, mostly in the English language. The works range from author Roderick Owen's pioneering 'The Desert Air Force' (1948) to the classic 'Fighters over the Desert' by Christopher Shores and Hans Ring.

All of these works have contributed over the years to a better understanding of that air campaign. However, out of necessity, they only give a partial view of the events that is generally linked to the nationality of the authors.

The accuracy of the data provided in these studies was also affected by the fact that, in the immediate years after the war's end, much of the official documentation was kept secret or made available only to the authors of the so-called 'official histories' published by the air forces of the involved countries. Consequently, a complete historical reconstruction that draws directly from the analysis of the official documents from all the contenders, therefore allowing the reader to have a clear and complete picture of the actual course of events, has always been missing. Now that the official records have finally been made available to the researchers, new struggles have emerged. Attempts to provide such a framework clashed with the difficulty of describing with the right degree of precision the complexity of multiple aerial combats between contenders of half a dozen different air forces that often overlap in space and time. This problem has only been overcome through using a fair level of approximation or through limiting the scope of the study to a specific unit or air force.

Michele Palermo, in his work, finally offers us this long-awaited, fully-detailed reconstruction, covering short time intervals in multiple volumes, in a way that allows him to describe the events with the greatest possible accuracy.

The present volume deals with the so called 'Battle of Gazala' a period that has been of great importance for the war in North Africa as it rose from a seemingly stale situation. The Axis army was near to reaching Alexandria and the Suez Canal, which would be a significant blow to British Empire. At last, however, as the Author will unfold in detail in his next books, the Commonwealth was able to turn the tide and push back Rommel to Tripoli.

Thanks to his in-depth research approach, Michele Palermo is able to shed new light on many aspects of this important air campaign. He covers broader themes, such as the impact on the operations of the air forces and the balance of power between the contenders, but also included are more specific topics, such as the contribution of SAAF and the other forces of the Dominions to the Commonwealth effort, or the actual results obtained by the super-ace Marseille.

The air war over the Mediterranean is too often described as a clash between two contenders only, namely the Commonwealth air forces and the Luftwaffe. Readers already familiar with the history of this confrontation will finally be able to appreciate in full the significant contribution of the Regia Aeronautica. Aside from the review of the performance of the Allied and Luftwaffe pilots, the author examines in detail how the Italians truly fared in combat through analyzing the outcomes of the engagements: it becomes clear that the Italians consistently shot down more planes than they lost throughout the campaign and were in no way inferior to their adversaries. This conclusion defies the historical debate of their competence, declaring once and for all that pronouncements of the Italians' 'lack of determination or stamina' are merely a remnant of war time propaganda.

All the above is backed by interesting digressions, useful and timely summary tables and by what is probably the best chapter dealing with the technical aspects of the aircraft involved, ever provided in a study of this kind, making even more precious this innovative work. Published seventy-one years after the battle of Gazala, this updated and original book will become the necessary starting point for a proper understanding of the critical air campaign that led to the battle of El Alamein.

Ludovico Slongo

Chapter 1
INTRODUCTION

The Backdrop

By May the two armed forces had been confronting each other over the Ain El Gazala front for three months. They both had the same objective: to accumulate sufficient resources to unleash the next move against the enemy.
They were both ready, or nearly, but this time, instead of a repeat of Crusader, the Axis was to move first.
Comfortable in the knowledge that he had an adequate quantity of vehicles and supplies available to him in comparison to the enemy's, Rommel prepared his plan with the approval of the Italian High Command.
It was a simple plan, easy to implement and based on two simultaneous actions: a frontal attack by the Italian XXI and X Corps from the north between the coast and Mteifel El Kebir with the intent to engage the defensive formation of the Commonwealth, and an encircling manoeuvre by the armoured and motorised units (XX Corps, DAK and 90th Division) to the south of Bir Hakeim. In this way, it was believed possible that the main body of the 8th Army would be crushed within two days. Tobruk would then immediately be besieged and the right moment and manner to attack would be evaluated.
The Commonwealth Army included the 13th Corps, which was stationed along the front line for about forty kilometres between Gazala and Bir B. Belafarit, and the 30th Corps, which was stationed over a wide strip to the south and east for the protection of the southern flank. The remaining forces were placed in depth to protect Tobruk.
The Commonwealth's armoured forces included a total of 850 tanks at the front (divided between light, medium, and infantry support) in addition to 120 of all types kept ready in reserve. Axis operational tanks in their turn included 333 Panzers (53 *Mk.IIs*, 242 *Mk.IIIs* and 38 *Mk.IVs*, a small number of the latter with more powerful guns) and 228 medium-sized Italian tanks (*M13s* and *M14s*).
The Axis had 90,000 men that faced 100,000 of the Commonwealth.
The artillery was in favour of the Commonwealth by a ratio of 2:1. However, concerning anti-tank guns, the Axis was superior.
The operations began as planned, but not all of the forces were available for the encircling manoeuvre from the south. This was because Bir Hakeim proved to be a much harder nut to crack than expected. Therefore, the stronghold was besieged by only a part of the attacking forces. Still, the main body of the Italian-German armoured forces attacked the Commonwealth formation from behind and a series of important battles unfolded.
Finally, during the first week of June, the battle in 'the Cauldron' was won and Bir Hakeim fell on the 10th. As a consequence, all of the Commonwealth formations had to fall back into the Knightsbridge zone. There they were attacked and routed after a week of clashes. At this point the 8th Army was well and truly in a crisis and began its retreat to El Alamein.
In those same days, the air and sea battle in the Mediterranean took place with the double attempt made by two convoys to supply Malta, one from Gibraltar and one from Alessandria. The latter, called 'Operation Vigorous', involved the opposing air forces in North Africa.

Vickers Wellingtons escorted by a Spitfire; other theatre (San Diego Air and Space Museum)

Only the stronghold of Tobruk remained in the hands of the Commonwealth in Libya, but it was no longer the fortress it had been. After only two days of fighting, its garrison was forced to surrender. By then the way to Egypt was open and the pursuit of the surviving Commonwealth forces only stopped at the bottleneck of El Alamein.
In the end, therefore, the Axis' plan had succeeded, but not within the planned timescale and with the consequence of a diminished offensive capability.

Opposing Air Forces

Commonwealth air forces (A.H.Q. Egypt and A.H.Q. Western Desert)

In North Africa, the Commonwealth Air Force Commands had in their strengths a little over 2,100 airplanes of all types. And yet, less than 43% of them were serviceable, amounting to fewer than 900.
About 120 of these were *Blenheims* (100) and *Marylands* (20) that were practically never used in offensive operations anymore. Another several dozen of various aircrafts were located in Sudan and Southern Egypt.
There were eleven squadrons of *Hurricanes* with about 275 serviceable aircrafts, ten of which were operational and five of which were in the front line. There were therefore about 130 *Hurricanes* operating in the battle.
All six *Kittyhawk* (about 160 aircrafts) and three *Tomahawk* (about 60) Squadrons were front line units.

The remaining bomber squadrons were also totally operational (*Wellingtons*, *Bostons* and *Baltimores*). As a good number of planes were 'serviceable within fourteen days', more planes would become available to replace losses. In total, the Commonwealth had about 400 fighters and 170 bombers that were combat ready at the beginning of the offensive.

It seems strange that so many operationally effective planes were not used, but this would have had the effect of increasing logistical problems. We only need to think of the circumnavigation of Africa for supplies.

Luftwaffe (Fl. Fü. Afrika and X. Fl. Kps)

III./JG 27 had again been transferred from Sicily to reinforce the offensive and so the number of planes ready for action rose to about ninety *Bf.109F*s as well as to about fifteen *Bf.109 F* fighter-bombers. This brought the availability of single-engined fighters to about 150 aircrafts, of which somewhat more than 100 were combat ready.

There was only a Staffel of LG 1 (eleven *Ju.88s*) based in Africa (subordinate to Fl. Fü. Afrika). However, the units based in Greece and Crete (subordinate to X. Fl. Kps), which totaled over 120 *Ju.88s* and *He.111s* (over 70 combat ready), would be able to take part in operations, operating from Athens.

As always, there was a considerable number of *Stukas* available — about 100 aircrafts at the beginning of June (about 70 estimated combat ready).

Even if their numbers were small, the *Bf.110s* continued to be present as reconnaissance and ground strafing planes.

Messerschmitt Bf.110 escorting Ju.52 transports (San Diego Air and Space Museum)

S.M.82 transports in Sicily (Archivio di Stato)

Regia Aeronautica (V Squadra Aerea)

Concerning front line units, the Italian fighter component was by May 1942 based exclusively on *C.202s*, even though its strength had not been much reinforced in comparison with the previous periods (four groups were present instead of three). This amounted to about 110 planes, of which about 80 were combat ready. Instead, the ground attack component was very much reinforced by transferring the obsolete fighter types into it, and also presumably because it was considered more effective and efficient than level bombing, and the strength of level bombers had been reduced to only about ten combat-ready aircrafts. The Italian ground attack force was composed of *C.200s* of 2° Stormo (about 45 were combat ready) and *CR.42* fighter-bombers of 50° Stormo (about forty of which were combat ready). The torpedo-bomber component was also far from negligible, with twenty-three dedicated *S.79s* being combat ready. The remaining level bomber units were also used for reconnaissance while the torpedo *S.79s* were also used as convoy escort planes. Rear area protection of the supply centres of Tripoli and Benghazi was provided by two groups of *G.50s* and *CR.42s* and one of *C.200s*, respectively.

Therefore, as for front line combat ready aircrafts, about 400 Commonwealth fighters were opposed by about 180 *Bf.109s* and *C.202s*, a substantial decrease in superiority compared to the start of 'Operation Crusader'. A part of the Commonwealth fighter force was used for ground attack, but these were fundamentally of the same type as the others used as pure fighters. In addition to pure fighters, about 100 Italian and German single engined fighter aircrafts were used only for ground attack. Some thirty *Bf.110s* were also available for reconnaissance and ground-attack.

About 140 Commonwealth bombers of various types were opposed by about 90 Axis long-range bombers in North Africa and Greece, most of them German, and about *70 Stukas*.

The numerical superiority of the Commonwealth fighters was at least partially compensated for by the better performance of the *Bf.109s* and *C.202s*.

We have to highlight the situation of aircraft replacements. The Commonwealth had a number of planes in the backlines (Appendix 3) that in few days could be delivered to the units. The Luftwaffe had to fly replacements from Greece and the Regia Aeronautica from Italy. But while the flow of replacements enabled the Commonwealth to balance the losses, German and Italian fighter units had their strength constantly reduced. It is a fact that only two C.202s were replaced during the period.

It is well known that Hitler was not keen to weaken the Russian front on behalf of Rommel. At the same time Italian aircraft production, in particular of C.202s, was not sufficient to supply the African front together with the Malta front.

The Planes

The innovations regarding the Commonwealth forces were significant.

The *Tomahawk IIB* (*P-40C*) was gradually replaced by the *Kittyhawk IA* (*P-40E*); the *Hurricane I* practically disappeared. Therefore, *Mark IIA* and *B* (with eight and twelve .303 guns, respectively) were present together with *Mark IIC* armed with four 20 mm cannons. Finally *Mark IID* started to become operational with 40 mm anti-tank guns. It should be noted that in most of the units, the armament of *Mark IIC* was reduced to only two guns as it seemed that the plane tended to stall when its guns were firing. Unfortunately the pilots' opinions do not appear frequently; nevertheless, it would appear that they were not exactly satisfied with what was all the same a powerful weapon. A study of the motivations that led the operational units to accept such modifications would be well worthwhile; it seems as if the operational units and the aircraft developers were frequently in disagreement about what was appropriate armament. Something similar had happened in the Regia Aeronautica with the removal of the *C.202*'s wing guns.

It should be noted that most of the units armed with *Hurricanes* and *Kittyhawks* were supplied with planes equipped with racks to transport bombs; therefore, they were fitted out for the role of fighter-bombers.

The Commonwealth had a Wing (239) with three squadrons armed with *Kittybombers* that could carry a 500-pound bomb, indicating that lessons had been learned from the experience of No. 80 Squadron which first flew Hurribombers in CRUSADER. These units were used in a double role even when involved in the very same action. Finally, the *Spitfire* began to appear.

As for the light bombers, the *Maryland* disappeared except in the strategic reconnaissance role, and the *Baltimore* was introduced to flank the *Boston* as a light bomber representing the backbone of the bomber force. The first American-operated *B-24 Liberator* made its appearance and supported the RAF bombers. The RAF *Wellington* medium sized bombers were supported in their night-time campaign by *Blenheim* light bombers, which by then were deemed to be obsolete in daylight action compared to the American light bombers, due to their inferior speed and armament. There were not any significant innovations for the Germans, who in the main operated the same planes as during "Crusader". There were however two German Staffel (Squadrons) of *Bf.109 F4/Zs*; these could carry a 250 kg bomb or four 50 kg ones.

The Italians did not introduce any new planes. The *Macchi C.202* was confirmed in its role as the only front line interceptor fighter while the *C.200* was in the main battle zone relegated to the role of ground attack aircraft along with the *CR.42*. The latter, armed with two 50 kg wing bombs and two machine guns, would in fact replace the *Stuka* in the Italian air force.

In total the Italians placed as many as four groups divided between *CR.42s* and *C.200s* in the field, including the rear area air defense units covering Benghazi and Tripoli.

We are somewhat puzzled by the comparison between the characteristics of the Italian ground attack planes and those of their Allies and their enemies: the bomb loads were very smaller and the fire power from the guns was four times less powerful than that of the American fighters or that of the German. This made a lot of difference on firing at targets on the ground. This is not to mention the difference in engine power. The difference with the *Hurricane IID* is still more astonishing. Nevertheless, it should be highlighted that the radial engines were much less vulnerable than the in-line liquid cooled ones.

The *C.200s* and *G.50s* of the second line continued to carry out the role of interceptors and, numerically more important, of protection for the convoys and the important logistical bases.

The traditional bombing role the Regia Aeronautica had was continually being reduced, possibly to reduce logistical load in the theatre.

Quality and Availability of the Sources

In terms of availability, unfortunately, the height of the air war in Africa corresponded with the period in which the worst documentation was available. The documentation of several Commonwealth units has been lost and that which is available is often incomplete. This is, at least in part, due to the logistical crisis brought on by the intense air battles and the retreat itself. Further, the documentation continued to suffer from poor standardization and evident gaps. In short, the SAAF documentation is generally more than reasonable and that of the RAAF is also acceptable. In addition there are very good diaries of the 73 and 213 Squadrons, but they fall far short in other RAF units and in particular the 33, 260 and 274 Squadrons. 243 Wing's diary was examined to make up for the short-coming, even though, obviously, the higher one rises in the hierarchy, the fewer details there are. It is interesting to note that the losses were not mentioned in the diary itself. Fortunately, a considerable number of gaps have been filled thanks to the 'Report on operations during the withdrawal from Cyrenaica, 26 May- 6 July 1942' (AIR 23/6481), provided by Andreas Biermann.

The daily operational reports transmitted to the R.A. by Oberbefehlshaber Süd (OBS, High Command South) were used for the Luftwaffe. However, they were less detailed than in 1941 and often not at all clear. These are specified for the benefit of the reader. The rest is drawn from several publications (see the bibliography), giving precedence to the most recent ones.

So as not to be left out, there are also more gaps in the Italian documents. The diaries of 4° Stormo, the key unit of the period, were lost. The only exception was the diary of 84[a] Squadriglia, which nevertheless is not the original one but has been reconstructed.

In terms of quality, in particular relating to claims, the R.A. as the other air forces reported enemy aircraft credited as shot down or probably shot down. It seems however that the damaged enemy aircraft should have been noted as effectively machine-gunned but this must have been somewhat confusing, because in most cases pilots only reported the enemy planes that were merely shot at, with no regard for effectiveness of the attack.

It has to be noted, however, that all achievements reported in any document or diary (such as destroyed/shot down, probably shot down, damaged) can be considered officially credited.

Another problem in terms of quality is that of the recognition of the enemy planes: *Hurricanes*, *P-40s*, and *Spitfires* were too often confused, making it hard to work out "who did what." Nevertheless, the Commonwealth documentation allows us to clear up most of the cases. For the *Bf.109* and *C.202*, however, things are very different. In the diaries of many Commonwealth units these two aircrafts are systematically seen together. This factor has led to some authors being convinced that this was a carefully planned tactic: the Italians, who were good at aerobatics, would joust with their enemies, scattering the formations, while the Germans, who were good marksmen, picked them off one by one. And yet, there is not the slightest evidence to uphold this theory. Therefore, except in some well-documented cases, the Macchis flew on their own account. On the other hand, their performances were similar and their number large enough, and so the need to create operational complications cannot even be understood. It had been different some months before when the *C.200s* and *G.50s* took responsibility for providing close cover of the German bombers, in particular the *Stukas*, while the *Bf.109Fs* did guard duty up high. In that period, the fighter formations were actually mixed over the desert as well as over Malta, but this is well documented from specific orders and clearly reported in the diaries. Moreover, the requirements in that theater were very different.

It has to be kept in mind that the Commonwealth adopted from March the Daylight Saving Time so their time was one hour ahead of Axis time.

Chapter 2
ORDERS OF BATTLE

BRITISH COMMONWEALTH (R.A.F. Middle East Command)

MAIN FRONT LINE UNITS

Fighters
- 233 Wing: 2 SAAF (*Kittyhawks*), 4 SAAF (*Tomahawks*), 5 SAAF (*Tomahawks*), 260 Sqn. (*Kittyhawks*); Gambut 2 (L.G.115).
- 239 Wing (fighters and fighter-bombers, *Kittyhawks*): 3 RAAF, 112, 250 SAAF, 450 Sqn.; Gambut 1 (L.G.102).
- 243 Wing: 33 (*Hurricane IIAs and Bs*), Gambut Main; 73 (*Hurricane IIA-B-Cs*), Gambut Main; 80 Sqn. (*Hurricane IICs*), Gambut Main; 213 Sqn. (*Hurricane IICs*), Gambut West; 274 (*Hurricane IIA-Bs*), Gambut Main; 145 (*Spitfire VC*), Gambut Main;
- 238 Sqn. (*Hurricane Is*) S. Haneish (102) Gambut M.
- 252 and 272 Sqn. (*Beaufighters*), coastal fighters, Qasaba (L.G.10).

Bombers
- 3 SAAF Wing: 12 SAAF Sqn. (Boston III), 24 SAAF Sqn. (Boston III), 223 Sqn. (Baltimore II).
- 231 Wing: 37 Sqn. (Wellington IC), Gabriya (L.G.09); 70 Sqn. (Wellington IC), Qotafiya (L.G.104); 108 Sqn. (Wellington IC), Gabriya (L.G.09).
- 236 Wing: 104 Sqn. and 148 Sqn. (Wellington II), Daba (L.G.106).
- 238 Wing: 38 Sqn. and 40 Sqn. (Wellington Ic), Shallufa (40 Sqn. also torpedo bombers).
- 39 Sqn. (Beaufort I and IIs), torpedo bombers, Sidi Barrani (L.G.5).
- 14 Sqn. (Blenheim IVs)

Reconnaissance
- 40 SAAF and 208 Sqn. (*Hurricanes I-IIs* and *Tomahawks*), army cooperation, Sidi Azeiz, El Adem.
- 2 Photo Reconnaissance Unit (P.R.U.) Heliopolis, detachment at Gambut (*Spitfire IVs*)
- 60 SAAF Sqn. (*Marylands*), Heliopolis
- 1437 Flt. (*Marylands* and *Baltimores*), strategical reconnaissance.

MAIN UNITS BEHIND THE FRONT LINE

Fighters
- 227 Sqn. (*Beaufighters*) nightfighters, Gianacalis.
- 335 (Hellenic) Sqn. (*Hurricane Is*) Qotafiya (L.G.20).
- 805 FAA Sqn. (*Martlets*) Qotafiya (L.G.20).
- 889 FAA Sqn. (*Fulmar IIs*) Fuka Sat. (L.G.16).
- Alsace (Free French) Sqn. (*Hurricane Is*), Fuka Sat. (L.G.16).

- 94 Sqn. (*Kittyhawks*) Mariut.
- 1 SAAF Sqn. (*Hurricane IIA-Bs*), Port Said.
- 5 SAAF Sqn. (*Tomahawks*), Sidi Hineish (L.G.115).
- 69 Sqn. (*Beaufighters*) Abu Sueir N. (Night-fighters).

Others
- Fleet Air Arm's Squadrons: 815, 821, 826 (*Swordfishes* and *Albacores*).
- 230 Sqn. (*Sunderlands*), general reconnaissance, Aboukir.
- 459 Sqn. (*Hudson IIIs*), general reconnaissance, Burg El Arab (L.G.40).
- 249 Transport Wing: 117 Sqn. (*D.C.IIs*), Bilbeis; 216 Sqn. (*Bombays*), Khanka.
- 1 General Reconnaissance Unit (G.R.U.) (*Wellingtons*), Ismailia
- 162 Sqn. (*Wellingtons*), RCM and RDF, Bilbeis.
- 267 Sqn. Various Transports.

LUFTWAFFE (Fl. Fü. Afrika)

Fighters
In view of the spring's offensive III./JG 27 was again transferred from Sicily, so combat ready *Bf.109 F* totalled about 90 planes, plus about fifteen *Bf.109 F* fighter-bombers.

- I./JG 27 (*Bf.109 F-4s*) Tmimi, end of June Sidi Barrani, then Fuka.
- II./JG 27 (*Bf.109 F-4s*) Tmimi, end of June Sidi Barrani, then Fuka.
- III./JG 27 (*Bf.109 F-4s*) Tmimi, end of June Sidi Barrani, then Bir El Astas (Marsa Matruh).
- III./JG 53 (*Bf.109 F-4*), Martuba (26 May), Gazala, end of June Sidi Barrani.
- Jabo./JG 27 (*Bf.109 F-4/Bs*) Martuba.
- Jabo./JG 53 (*Bf.109 F-4/Bs*) Martuba (26 May).
- 7./ZG 26 (*Bf.110 D-3s*) Derna.
- 2./NJG 2 (*Ju.88 C-6s*, night-fighters) Derna.
- I./NJG 2 (*Ju.88 C-6s*, night-fighters) Iraklion from June.

Bombers
- I./St.G 3 (*Ju.87 R-2s, R-2 trops, R-4s*; *Bf.110s, He.111s*) Derna-South, Tmimi, Bu Hania.
- I./St.G 4 (*Ju.87s*), from June.
- I./St.G 5 (*Ju.87s*), from June.
- 12./LG 1 (*Ju.88 A-4s*), Barce
- I./LG 1 (*Ju.88 A-4s*), Iraklion (X. Fl. Kps).
- II./ LG 1 (*Ju.88 A-4s*), Iraklion from June (X. Fl. Kps).
- I. / KG 54 (*Ju.88s*), Eleusis from June.
- II./KG 100 (*He.111 H-6s*), Kalamaki (X. Fl. Kps).

Reconnaissance
- 4.(H)/12 (*Bf.110 C-4s, Bf.109 Fs, Hs.126s*) Tactical Reconnaissance, Martuba.
- 1.(F)/121 (*Ju.88 D-1s, Bf.109 Fs*) Long-range Reconnaissance, Derna.

REGIA AERONAUTICA (V Squadra Aerea)

Fighters
- 1° St. C.T. (*C.202s*): 6° Gr., 79ª, 81ª e 88ª Sq.; 17° Gr., 71ª, 72ª e 80ª Sq.; Martuba 4; from middle June remains only 88ª Sq.
- 4° St. C.T. (*C.202s*): 9° Gr. C.T. 73ª, 96ª e 97ª Sq.; 10° Gr. 84ª, 90ª, 91ª Sq.; Martuba 4; from the end of June Sidi El Barrani, then Fuka.

Assalto (ground attack)
- 50° St. (*CR.42*-bombers): 158° Gr. (236ª, 387ª, 388ª Sq.), 159° Gr. (389ª Sq., 390ª Sq., 391ª Sq.), El Fetheia (Derna) 30.5; Sidi El Barrani 29.6.
- 2° St. (*C.200s*) Martuba 5: 8° Gr. (92ª, 93ª, 94ª Sq.); 13° Gr. (77ª, 78ª, 82ª Sq.), from 24.6 Ain El Gazala,
- 3° Gr. (153ª, 154ª, 155ª Sq.; *CR.42s*) Martuba 5, up to 31ˢᵗ May.

Bombers and Reconnaissance
- 35° St. (*Cant.Z.1007bis*): 86° Gr. (190ª and 191ª Sq.); 95° Gr. (230a and 231ª Sq.) Barce and Derna.

UNITS BEHIND THE FRONT LINE
Fighters
- 150° Gr. C.T. (363ª, 364ª e 365ª Sq.; *C.200s*), Bengasi.
- 160° Gr. C.T. (375ª, 393ª e 394ª Sq.; *G.50s* and *CR.42s*), Tripoli.
- 12° Gr. C.T. (159ª, 160ª, 165ª Sq.; *G.50s*) Tripoli.

Torpedo Bombers
- 131° Gr. (279ª and 284ª Sq.); 133° Gr. 174ª Sq. and 175ª Sq.); (*S.79s*) Bengasi K.2.

Transports
- 145° Gr. (604ª and 610ª Sq.) (*S.81s, S.82s, S.73s, Ca.133s, S.75s*). A flight of *S.82s* was equipped as night-bombers.

Reconnaissance
- 196ª Sq. R.S.M. (*Cant.Z.501s*)
- 145ª Sq. R.S.M. (*Cant.Z.501s*)
- 103ª Sq. (*Ca.311s*)
- 118ª Sq. (*Ca.311s*)
- 123ª Sq. (*Ca.311s*)
- 24ª Sq. (*Ca.311s*)
- 33ª Sq. (*Ca.311s*)

Aviazione Presidio Coloniale (A.P.C. - Colonial Aviation)
- 1° Gr. A.P.C. (*Ca.309s*)
- 12ª Sq. A.P.C. (*Ca.309s*)

Chapter 3
THE PREPARATIONS (22-25 May)

In the days before the offense, the flying activity of both sides increased to a high level. In particular, the pounding of Axis aerodromes by 3 SAAF Bomber Wing's attack formations began, heavily escorted by 233 and 239 Fighter Wings.

22 May 42

A) Nine *Bostons* of 24 SAAF were off from Baheira heading for Martuba (7.20-9.25). Over Gambut, they met with the fighter escort, which was particularly strong on this occasion: eight *Kittyhawks* of 450 Squadron provided top cover at 14,000 feet (three planes turned back because of engine trouble); nine *Kittyhawks* of 112 Squadron acted as medium cover at 12000 feet; and twelve *Kittyhawks* of 250 Squadron were close cover.
Twelve *Kittyhawks* of 3 RAAF were on a "freelance bomber escort" (two returned because of engine trouble); eight *Kittyhawks* of 260 Squadron and twelve *Tomahawks* of 4 SAAF took off a little later on a diversionary sweep to cover the return of the bombers.

At 8.43, bombs were dropped over the objective from an altitude of 14000 feet and four Bostons were slightly damaged by anti-aircraft fire. 24 SAAF was again able to report that two *Bf.109s* were shot down by fighters: one to the south of Martuba 3 in a head-to-head attack, and one in the sea in the Gulf of Bomba. A *Tomahawk* crashed in area (S) P5620 as well as a second unidentified fighter (S) P5244.

450 Squadron reported that it was attacked by two *Bf.109s* after crossing the coast, three miles south of Ras El Tin. A *Kittyhawk*, presumably that of Sgt. Williams (AK717), was shot down and caught fire upon hitting the ground. F.Lt. Rose (AK998) set off in pursuit of a *Bf.109* and claimed a probable victory. The dropping of bombs over Martuba 5 was seen and caused two substantial fires; and then, five miles to the south of the target, a *Kittyhawk* was seen to come down helplessly in a spin.

Formation of 3 SAAF Bostons and Baltimores. An escorting P-40 can also be seen (Bouwer)

On the south-west route for the return, six enemy planes were seen taking off with four more soon after from the airfields to the south of Martuba. On the return, a *Kittyhawk* crash-landed due to enemy action; presumably its pilot was Sgt. Young (AL131), while Sgt. Quirk (AK634) went missing. F.Lt. Rose force-landed at Gambut main.

3 RAAF was flying in two sections of six and four, in fluid pairs, when it was attacked three times by four *Bf.109s*, two of which were destroyed by Gibbs and Barr.

F.Lt. Barr (AL199) was leading the section of four:

> "...at 11000' about 1500' above the bombers on their port. Me.109s were reported at 9 o'clock, 2000' above. When we were about 15 miles E of Bomba 2 109s attacked one section and 2 more attacked mine from 6 o'clock. I went down after one after Sgt. Kildey had given it a good burst and had got in a good astern attack when I had to evade an attack from behind. No results observed. ...saw one 109 climbing up in a spiral about 1000' below. I dived on it and kept on it from beam to astern in a steep turn. It then rolled over and fell away on its' back. I was attacked again and pulled away and did not observe results. Height about 4000'. As my guns had stopped firing, I returned to base and got front wheels down with auxiliary pump, damaging tail wheel and cowls in the landing. Own casualties: 3 rounds hit starboard side cutting the hydraulic line and puncturing the tyre. Another hit the voltage regulator. Enemy casualties: 1 Me.109 probable."

112 Squadron reported that it had been attacked by five *Bf.109s* before reaching the coast about ten miles north of Bomba. There were no individual instances of combat but on the way home from the target, F.O. Knoll (AK.908) engaged a *Bf.109* and was attacked from the rear and damaged, while F.O. Gundry (AK787) went missing.

250 Squadron reported seeing two and three squadrons of enemy aircraft on different occasions. S.L. Judd (AL157) stated:

> "...On approaching Ras El Tin...one 109F attacked the section flying on the right of the Bostons without damaging any of our AC. The other escorting Squadrons were observed to be having combats with numerous 109s. On the return journey various 109s some fairly near to the rear of the Bombers, but I did not see any attack. This Squadron remained in position (one flight 3 AC on either side)."

F.Lt. Waddy (AK846):

> "...After dropping the bombs the Bostons turned left and as we approached Tmimi, I observed one Me.109F, camouflaged light brown, with white spinner and white wing tips, flying on our starboard side, at the same height, about 1000 yards away. I called up and warned the formation to watch him. He suddenly pulled up above the formation turning slightly to the right and then made a rear quarter attack on a straggling Kitty. I started a right hand side turn to stop the attack, which he broke off and climbed away. I then saw him take the same position related to the formation as at first. ...as soon as I saw him pull up again to the right I went into a steep left hand turn and as he made his attack on the other Kitty again I met him head on and fired a good burst which hit him. He banked to the right and broke beneath me and then I saw the pilot bale out. The Kitty he attacked appeared to me to be hit but I only saw it dive away and could not see it again."

Kittyhawk of 112 Sqn. (Aviation Heritage Museum of Western Australia)

Sgt. Seabrook (AK704) also hit a *Bf.109* but only Waddy's was confirmed. The pilot seen by Waddy must have been P.O. Rogerson (AL116), who was badly hit and crash-landed at Gambut.

260 Squadron witnessed the attack on the top cover and afterwards sighted and engaged four *Bf.109s* and two *Macchis*. Sgt. Carlisle fired at one of them, which made a half-roll and dived away with black smoke coming from it, but no claim was made. 4 SAAF failed to meet any enemy aircraft.

Four Schwarms of JG 27 had departed just after 7.00: one of 1./JG 27, on air-raid warning; one of 2./JG 27, also on air-raid warning; one of 4./JG 27 on free sweep; and one of III./JG 27, details lacking. II Gruppe was still at Martuba and about to be transferred to Tmimi. Eight P-40s were credited shot down:
Oblt. Franzisket (1./JG 27), 20 km E of Derna (7.41);
Fw. Steinhausen (1./JG 27), 20 km S of Martuba (7.50); a second one was damaged;
Lt. Arnold Stahlschmidt (2./JG 27), SW of Tmimi (7.50);
Lt. von Lieres u. Wilkau of (2./JG 27), S of Tmimi (7.51);
Ofw. Bendert (2) (4./JG 27), 30 km E of Tmimi (7.33); 2-3 km N of Ain El Gazala, 30-50 m (7.45);
Uffz. Steis (4./JG 27), 30 km E of Tmimi (7.36);
Ofw. Rosenburg (9./JG 27), 10 km S of Martuba, height 4500 m (7.55).
Initially Bendert's second claim over the sea was not confirmed. There are also two more claims of I./JG 27 that were not confirmed.
During the day, Uffz. Sdun (8./JG 27, *Bf.109* W.Nr. 10102) was shot down by enemy fighters and was wounded, possibly a victim of Waddy.

The first to attack must have been four *Bf.109s* of 4./JG 27 which clashed with 450 Squadron and 3 RAAF shooting down Williams. The *Bf.109s* of the other two groups subsequently intervened.

Six *Macchis* of 17° Gruppo (two of 71ª Sq. and four of 72ª Sq.) also took off on warning (7.45-8.25) to intercept the bomber's raid over Martuba 5. Only Cap. Tomaselli (C.O.), at an altitude of 5000 m, managed to reach and damage a *Boston* (160 rounds). The action must have taken place during the return of the bombers; nevertheless, none of their pilots reported any attacks. 1° Stormo complained because the alarm was given too late.

Simultaneously, five *Baltimores* of 223 Squadron (7.01-8.48) attacked Derna (8.06, 18000 feet). Therefore the *Boston* escort also had to cover the Baltimores. It seems that German fighters took off when this raid was picked up by radar, while the Italians took off on the raid of 24 SAAF.

This attack caused the death of an Italian airman in addition to wounding three others. Two *CR.42s* were put out of use and two *CR.42s* were badly damaged. Eight *C.200s*, three *CR.42s* and one *Ca.311* were also slightly damaged. On the German side, one *Ju.87* was destroyed and a second was damaged.

B) Serg. Magg. Benati (*C.202*, 79ª Sq., 6° Gruppo) scrambled from Benghazi due to the sighting of a reconnaissance aircraft (10.05-10.45). After about twenty-five minutes of flying, it reached a Maryland at an altitude of 7500 m, 30 km from the coast. Eventually, thanks to radio contact, Benati managed to shoot it down into the sea (600 rounds). No evidence has been found to confirm this action, however.

Sgt/P. Alexopulos (335 Hellenic Squadron, *Hurricane* I Z.4101) was off at 11.40 on a false alarm over a convoy. Probably owing to engine failure he ditched near the ships but the plane sank almost immediately and he was not seen again.

Night of 22-23

Wellington IC BB484X (F.Sgt. Ward) of 38 Squadron was laying mines off Benghazi when it was badly damaged by anti-aircraft fire and crashed in the desert; one of the crew was killed. At Berka *Ju.88 A-4* W.Nr. 5728 was destroyed due to the bombing.

During a bombing on Martuba, an Italian airman was seriously wounded and a *C.200* (M.M. 7678, 77ª Sq., 13° Gr.) was destroyed.

Ju.88 A-4 W.Nr. 5603, L1 + LN (5./L.G.1) was lost over the aerodrome of Abu Haggag, probably shot down by AA. Fw. Scharnowsky was KIA while the rest of the crew was taken prisoner.

23 May

A) 80 Squadron provided a cover patrol for *Kittyhawks* being refuelled at El Adem (8.15-9.45). It was jumped by six *Bf.109s* and in the ensuing dogfight, F.Sgt. Scott (BE339) and Sgt. Howard (BM974) were shot down. Both were seen to crash in flames near Tobruk. Sgt. Mc Cormack (BN354) was also hit but managed to land at El Adem (Cat.II). The *Hurricane IICs* hardly managed to fire a few rounds (60 Ball, 25 HE). 274 Squadron was also present in the mission but it had probably already landed at the time of the German attack.

A Schwarm of 5./JG 27 on a fighter sweep claimed three P-40s:

S.M.82 transports of 609ª Sq. (Archivio di Stato)

Fw. Reuter, 10 km NW of El Adem (8.35);
Lt. Jenisch (2) 10 km NW of El Adem (8.36) and 5 km NE of El Adem (8.39).

B) F.O. Sowrey (BN128) and Sgt. Stephenson (BM981) of 213 Squadron shot down a *Ju.88* (Idku, 9.25-10.25). The results were dramatic according to Stephenson (Red II):

> "...after another attack from Red I, I saw the starboard engine burst into flames. I gave him another burst and then saw flames inside the cockpit, whilst debris was flung around everywhere. The crew threw a dinghy out and the AC tried to gain height, but as I delivered my final attack, it blew up, rolled over, then half rolled and dived straight into the sea. No sign of survivors..."

The fury against a previously condemned enemy is difficult to explain. At that time there was the usual activity of reconnaissance *Ju.88s* and Oblt. Obernhuber with all his crew went missing (II./KLG 1, *Ju.88 A-4*, W.Nr. 5633 L1 + BP).

C) Five *C.202s* (81ª Sq., 6° Gruppo), commanded by Cap. Baldini, scrambled to intercept a formation of enemy bombers and fighters in the sky over the airfield (9.25-10.20).
No more than four *Macchis* managed to reach the enemy at an altitude of 6500 m over Gazala and clashed two times with an indeterminate number of *Hurricanes* and *P-40s*. It seems that only two pilots arrived within firing range: the first one was Serg. Magg. Morosi, who declared that after a long pursuit he shot down a *Hurricane* which fell into the sea, (430); the second one was Palazzeschi, who fired at another *Hurricane* (150).

It would appear that some *Bf.109s* of II./JG 27 also took off on warning from Tmimi, which claimed as many as five P-40s:
Oblt. Rödel (2) (Stab II./JG 27), 10 km N of Ras El Tin (9.40); 40 km NE of Ras El Tin, 200 m (9.47);
Ofhr. Kientsch (2) (Stab II./JG 27), 10 km NE of Ras El Tin, 5000 m (9.40); 3 km NE of Ain El Gazala (9.55);
Ofw. Bendert (4./JG 27), 5 km S of Ain El Gazala (10.05).
The long time intervals between the single claims might make us think of separate clashes and that Bendert scrambled at a different time (9.42-10.18).

Again 24 SAAF with nine *Bostons* was headed to Derna (9.15-11.10) with a large escort: eleven *Kittyhawks* of 2 SAAF as top cover (one carried out an emergency landing straight after take-off and a second returned a little later); ten *Tomahawks* of 4 SAAF as medium cover (9.35-11.15); ten *Tomahawks* of 5 SAAF as close cover; and 112, 250 , and 260 Squadrons were indirectly covering the attack formation.

At 10.15, the bombers crossed the coast at an altitude of 12000 feet, still gaining height. At 10.25, they had reached an altitude of 14000 feet over Derna and started bombing, observing three direct hits on the Stukas. Then they sighted five enemy aircraft take off from Martuba main, while five fighters were flying over Derna main at 1000 feet.

2 SAAF was flying at 18000 feet and two minutes after the bombs had been dropped, twelve *Bf.109 Fs* attacked the *Kittyhawks* from 15000 feet, breaking into sections and delivering stern attacks. The Squadron was compelled to initiate a defensive action by turning towards the enemy, having a quick burst, and turning back towards the bombers. At 10.40 the enemy broke away climbing. 2 SAAF noted that the enemy had been unable to penetrate the fighter screen and so all the aircraft returned safely.

Lt. Bryant (AK963) was lagging behind the formation when he was attacked by four *Bf.109s* for twenty minutes. He was shot (Cat.II) but was able to return safely home.

On the way out, two pilots saw a *Hurricane* shot down by a *Bf.109* (possibly one of 80 Squadron) (rounds: 0.5-1975).

Only one 4 SAAF Squadron pilot managed to fire at an attacking fighter. Furthermore, 4 SAAF reported that, notwithstanding the heavy anti-aircraft fire, the formation did not sustain any damage. And what is more, the bombardment, carried out between 13000 and 14000 feet, did not turn out to be accurate. Instead 5 SAAF would not have been involved.

Twelve *Kittyhawk Is* of 250 Squadron had to cover the return of the bombers. As many as six of these broke off from the mission because of high water temperature and low oil pressure. The remaining aircraft were attacked by about five *Bf.109s* coming down from a much higher altitude. Only Sgt. Webster (AL162 LD-I) suffered, however, when his plane was hit but not badly.

Also, 112 Squadron was flying over Gazala in order to protect the return of the bombers, when some *Bf.109*s were spotted. However, according to the war diary these would risk to attack the Kittyhawk. Obviously it must have been a humorous statement considering that the opponents never showed lack of courage and most of all the performances of the *Bf.109* were so superior to those of the Kittyhawk that it made no sense to avoid the attack.

Finally, seven *Kittyhawks* of 260 Squadron (9.35-11.00) accompanied the bombers to an altitude of 13000 feet up to Martuba. And then while these proceeded to Derna, they came down to attack the airfields in a diversionary action. At the same time they engaged a Bf.110 and damaged it.

Baltimore (Bouwer)

We can consider that overall there were about ten attacking fighters and so they were insufficient to get through to the bombers. In fact, they actually only clashed with the top cover.

D) During the day, 33 Squadron was over Tobruk employed in the escort of convoys. It is not known at what time, but presumably during the second mission over Tobruk, the two covering *Hurricane IIBs* were attacked by four *Bf.109s*. F.Lt. Desmond Wade (5654) was shot down and lost his life; his plane was seen slipping into the sea. The "Daily Resume of Air Operations" stated that two C.202s attacked two *Hurricanes* one of which was shot down into the sea. In its turn, Sgt. Laflamme's plane (BG917) was badly damaged, even if it was able to come back to base. At the end of his first mission, Sgt. Belec's (*Hurricane* BG884 RS-G) overturned on landing.

Therefore it is possible that this unit had been involved in the previous action against the *Macchis*, but it is also possible that it had clashed with 5./JG 27, which claimed three P-40s: Fw. Reuter (2), 2 km NE of Tobruk (over the sea, 11.13); 10 km E of Tobruk (11.16); Uffz. Gierster, 5 km SE of Tobruk (11.05).

Also 2./JG 27 headed to Tobruk, after an alarm warning (10.35-11.35). Of this unit Uffz. Beckmann claimed another Hurricane but it was not confirmed.

33 Squadron had been equipped with the *Hurricane IIBs* which, besides keeping the wing tanks, were armed with twelve .303 calibre guns.

E) At 10.32, a formation of four Baltimores of 223 Squadron also took off to attack the main airfield of Derna (probably during this raid was destroyed *Ju.87 R-4/Trop*, W.Nr. 6241 of 3./St.G.3). As there had been a delay of thirty minutes, the escort of 3 RAAF and 450 Squadron did not meet up with it, and this will prove very costly for the bombers. After the bombs were dropped from 18000 feet at 11.55, the planes were intercepted by three *Bf.109s* near Ras El Tin at an altitude of 15000 feet at 12.00:

"The first attack was made on one ac that was lagging behind. The pilot finding that the rear gunner was unable to use his rear guns on account of stoppage went down to sea level and successfully evaded them, returning to base badly shot up. He landed with his wheels down but the ac was classed Cat.II. The remainder of the formation then subjected to continual attacks and as the rear guns on all ac also jammed, the enemy, finding they had no opposition, closed in within 75 to 50 yards range and attacked from the rear. …they succeeded in flying as far as Tobruk, two of them spun in from height, killing both crews instantaneously. The remaining machine belly landed being badly shot up and was classified Cat.II."

But nevertheless they managed to claim the destruction of a *Bf.109* with the guns fixed in the tail. AG708 (F.O. Bangley) and l'AG717 (Sgt. Horsfield) were shot down in flames with the loss of the entire crew. AG703 (P.O. Leake) was forced to make an emergency landing at Bir El Gobi while AG762 (Sgt. Mc Clure) returned at 12.25. The latter plane had been hit by 400 rounds and was SOC. Alltogether five members the crews were wounded.

This time the 223 Squadron had been particularly unfortunate because it came across two Schwarms of 3./JG 27 (take-off at 10.35), led by the two most dangerous enemy pilots: Marseille and Homuth. All four bombers were claimed destroyed to the south of Tobruk:
Oblt. Marseille (2), 3 km SE of the port of Tobruk (11.05, 11.06);
Ofw. Mentnich, SE of the port of Tobruk (11.08);
Hptm. Homuth shot down a plane north of Fort Acroma (11.18) after a tenacious pursuit, so it was probably AG762. Some sources reported that Homuth claimed it was damaged.

Following the disastrous raid 223 Squadron was withdrawn for a few days and an immediate inquire was instituted into the cause of the .300 rear gun stoppages. No solution was found so the gun so it was substituted with the .303 Browning.

F) Twenty miles south of Tmimi, seven *Kittyhawks* of 450 Squadron were acting as the escort for two *Hurricane Is* of 40 SAAF on a reconnaissance mission when they ran into four *Bf.109s* and possibly C.202s. In the ensuing clash, Sgt. Mc Burney (AK998) and Sgt. Nursey (AK606) claimed a *Bf.109* each. And then the formation was scattered and they returned separately. Some motor transports were strafed.
Col. Biden (40 SAAF, 17.05-18.30) claimed a probable *C.202*.

"Whilst on a tac/r, with Capt. Blauuw, escorted by 7 Kittyhawks of 450 and 250 Sqns. (not reported), the formation was attacked by 6+ EA near Segnali. During my initial turn, I saw one AC crash into the ground in flames, and as I completed my turn to the East, I saw a Macchi 202 on the tail of a Kitty. I pulled my aircraft into a steep climb and fired a full deflection shot, and continued firing until I was about 40' from the AC. I saw my tracer and incendiary entering the AC at the cockpit. At this stage my AC spun to the right and I lost contact. As I was heading for the ground, I saw an AC going down with white smoke issuing from it. I then led the fighters into a dust cloud and evaded the enemy."

Uffz. Gierster (5./JG 27) claimed a P-40, 15 km south east of Gadd El Ahma, 600 m (16.52), but his plane was then hit and he was forced to parachute out; he saved himself even if he was slightly wounded (*Bf.109* W.Nr. 7390 sw.5+).

It is interesting to note that during the day, the Germans claimed to have shot down twelve fighters in total. However, we are only able to confirm the shooting down of three of them.

Kittyhawk squadron (Aviation Heritage Museum of Western Australia)

The discrepancy would seem to be explained (the probable excess of claims aside) by the lack of detail or incompleteness of some diaries of the Commonwealth units. On this day the CWGC reports the death of F.Sgt. Stammers of 33 Sqn.

Night of 23-24

Three *Ju.88s* attacked the landing grounds of Gambut (19.00-23.30); one aircraft force-landed (OBS).

Martuba was bombed: four *C.200s* were badly damaged and six others slightly.

24 May

A) S.Ten. Ferrari (*C.200*, 364ª Sq., 150° Gruppo) was on a standing patrol over Benghazi Harbor (13.10-15.10) when he intercepted and hit a Beaufighter. The latter was chased but was able to get away, possibly thanks to its higher speed (rounds: 360).

Lt. Scheid lost his life with his crew for unknown reasons during a transfer from Tripoli to Benghazi (III./Z.G.26, Bf.110 F-2 W.Nr. 4543, 3U + BD). A connection with the previous attack cannot be excluded.

Ju.52 W.Nr. 6809 (K.Gr.z.b.V. 102) was destroyed following an accident (100%).
Ju.88 A-4 W.Nr. 5727 (IV./L.G.1), crash-landed at Martuba due to lack of fuel (70%). A member of the crew lost his life.

1° Stormo Command tent at Martuba (Ufficio Storico SMA)

Night of 24-25

Ten *Ju.88s* attacked Bir El Abd aerodrome (2000-2312), two aircraft were set on fire, and many night-fighters were seen above Marsa Matruh. *Ju.88 A-4* W.Nr. 5553, L1+GH, went missing (Lt. Hetterich).
Eight *Ju.88s* of LG 1 made a glide approach down to 300 m. over the aerodrome. One aircraft was driven off by fighters. Some fighters were attacking down to less than 300 m (ULTRA).

Martuba was bombed: an Italian airman was slightly wounded and two *C.202s* were burned out (M.M.7888, 71ª Sq.; M.M.7911, 97ª Sq.).

Martuba, 1° Stormo field mess (Ufficio Storico SMA)

25 May

A) Ten *Hurricanes* of 80 Squadron (7.50-9.05) escorted two reconnaissance aircraft of 40 SAAF Squadron. 2 *Hurricanes* were to act as No. 2 to the latter at 1000 feet; 4 were to cover them at 2000 feet; and the remaining 4 were to be top cover. Possibly due to haze, the formation lost contact and Sgt. Comfort (80 Squadron, BN413) and Lt. Nicol (40 SAAF) were shot down over Tmimi, while Comfort was flying as wingman for Nichols.

These should have been victims of 5./JG 27, whose pilot claimed two P-40s, 20 km east of Tmimi: Lt. Jenisch shot down one in flames (7.25) and Fw. Niederhöfer forced a second one into an emergency landing (7.27).

B) Ten *C.202s* of 6° Gruppo (four of 79^a Sq. and six of 88^a Sq.), commanded by Magg. Larcher, were on a free sweep between Gazala and Bir Hakeim (16.20-17.40). The *Macchis* were south-east of Gazala (16.45, 5000 m) when a formation of about twenty enemy fighters composed by P-40s and *Spitfires* was spotted at a lower altitude. Making the most of their superior height, the *Macchis* launched the attack, scattering the enemy formation and following it a long way over its territory. Finally they were credited with as many as nine P-40s shot down and thirteen divided between P-40s and *Spitfires* machine-gunned (3600 rounds):
M.llo Baschirotto (88^a Sq.) shot down two P-40s;
M.llo Stabile (88^a Sq.) shot down two P-40s and fired at two more (570 rounds); his plane was in its turn hit, but not badly, by eight bullets;
Cap. Camarda (79^a Sq.) shot down a P-40 and fired at two more (124 rounds);
Ten. Civetta (88^a Sq.) shot down a P-40;
S. Ten. Sgorbati (88^a Sq.) shot down a P-40;
S. Ten. Ferrazza (79^a Sq.) shot down a P-40;
and Serg. Magg. Paroli (79^a Sq.) shot down a P-40.

It seems the *Macchis* came across twelve *Hurricane IIs* of 274 Squadron, which had scrambled from Tobruk (17.05-17.40, the times do not match exactly) and were then directed over Gazala at an altitude of 12000 feet. They were to intercept four enemy aircraft that had been spotted. The British pilots claimed a *Bf.109* was probably destroyed and that two more were damaged (F.Lt. Keefer and P.O. Samuels, Sgt. Neil, respectively). In turn, F.Lt. Playford's fighter was hit and the pilot, slightly wounded, was forced to land the aircraft on its belly ("Desert Flyer"). F.Sgt. Parbury had to make an emergency landing two miles west of the base, reportedly for fuel exhaustion. It returned in the evening, and it was possible that he could have been hit.

It appears that it was quite a clash, also taking into account that the *Macchis* fired 3600 rounds, and that was a considerable amount of ammunitions for the light armament of the Italian planes. Nevertheless, the actual results were poor when compared with the huge number of claims. The estimate made by the pilots of the 6° Gruppo on the number of planes encountered would make us think of the possible presence of a second enemy unit. It would probably have been equipped with P-40s (260 Squadron was also present in the area, but it did not report encountering the enemy).

Bostons and *Kittybombers* attacked Tmimi and several hits were claimed. *Bf.109 F-4/Trop* (4./J.G.27 W.Nr. 10044) was destroyed (100%); *Bf.109 F-4/Trop* (4./J.G.27 W.Nr. 8432) was damaged (25%).

Night of 25-26

C) F.O. Pain (73 Squadron, *Hurricane* BN157, 20.25-21.30) took off on a reconnaissance mission and strafed Tmimi aerodrome. At 21.10, he ran into a *C.200* over Tmimi and damaged it (80 Ball, 88 HE/Inc). *Albacores* cooperated, dropping flares.

P.O. Beaumont (73 Squadron, *Hurricane* BD774) did not return from a night attack on anti-aircraft positions at Bomba (22.50).

D) F.O. Selby (73 Squadron, *Hurricane* BM975, 21.55-23.30) attacked one of two *CR.42s* that were strafing east-north-east of Gambut and shot one down. Nine *CR.42s* of 155ª Sq. (3° Gruppo) bombed and strafed Gambut (23.30-2.30). Serg. Magg. Modesti went missing and was initially believed killed, but he was in fact taken prisoner. The timing does not match but it seems that the latter fell victim of Selby.

Six *Ju.88s* attacked the landing grounds and roads east of Tobruk up to Bir Azeiz (21.57-2.43); one aircraft was lost. Twelve *Ju.88s* attacked the landing grounds of Hanascia and Bir El Area (3.00-5.04); Lt. Riedlberger (I./N.J.G.2, *Ju.88 C-2* W.Nr. 833, R4 + DL, 100 %) was shot down by Flak west of Bardia and lost his life.

Martuba was bombed: one *C.202* was burned out (M.M.7904), a second one badly damaged, and two others slightly damaged (all of 88ª Sq.). Probably in the same action were damaged two *Bf.109 F-4/Trops* : W.Nr. 10191 (Stab/J.G.27, 50 %); W.Nr. 8557 (9./J.G.27, 40 %).

DATE		AXIS TIME	CLAIMS									CASUALTIES						UNITS INVOLVED
			COMM.			GERMAN			ITALIAN			COMM.		GER.		ITA.		
			S	P	D	S	P	D	S	P	M	S	D	S	D	S	D	
22	A	6.20-8.25	3A	1A	1A	8A		1A			1B	5A		1A				I,II,III/JG 27, 17° Gr, 24SAAF, 450, 250, 260, 112, 3 RAAF Sqn
	B	10.05-10.45							1B									6°Gr, reconnaissance?
23	A	7.15-8.45				3A						2A	1A					80 Sqn, II/JG 27
	B	9.25-10.25	1B											1B				213 Sqn, II/KLG 1
	C	9.25-10.20				5A			1A		1A			2A				6°Gr, II/JG27, 2 SAAF, 4 SAAF, 250, 260 Sqn.
	D	11.05-11.13				3A						1A	1A					33 Sqn, II/JG 27
	E	9.32-11.25				4B						4B						I/JG 27, 223 Sqn
	F	16.05-17.30	2A	1A		1A								1A				II/JG 27, 40 SAAF, 450 Sqn
24	A	13.10-15.10								1A	2							150° Gr, Beaufighter?
25	A	6.50-8.05				2A						2A						II/JG27, 40 SAAF, 80 Sqn
	B	16.20-17.40		1A	2A				9A		13A	1A						6°Gr, 274 Sqn
	C	19.15-20.45			1A													73 Sqn, C.200?
	D	0.20-1.40?	1A													1A		73 Sqn, 3° Gr.
	TOT		1B, 6A			4B, 22A			1B, 10A			4B, 11A		1B, 2A		1A		

LEGENDA

S - SHOT DOWN   P - PROBABLE   D - DAMAGED   M - MACHINE GUNNED
A - SINGLE ENGINE FIGHTER   A2 - TWIN ENGINE FIGHTER   B - BOMBER   Bs - STUKA   T - OTHER TYPES

Chapter 4
LAUNCHING OF THE OPERATIONS (26-30 May)

At 14.00 on May 26th, the Italian X and XXI Corps launched a frontal attack on the central Gazala positions after heavy artillery fire. At about 21.00 and under the cover of darkness, all of the armoured and mobile elements (the Africa Korps, the Italian XX Corps, and the German 90th Light Afrika Division) began a brilliant but risky flanking manoeuvre around the southern end of the Allied lines. They put their trust in the enemy's own minefields to protect their flank and rear.

On May 27th, the Ariete Armoured Division was the first to encounter the enemy south of Bir Hakeim, engaging the 3rd Indian Motor Brigade (7th Armoured Division) at 6.40. The former suffered losses but overran the Indian Brigade. And then, at 8.00, Ariete attacked Bir Hakeim defended by the 1st Free French, but failed to take the position and sustained heavy losses from the fire of the French 75 mm guns. Bir Hakeim proved to be a bigger problem than Rommel had anticipated, having significantly underestimated the resistance it would offer.

At 7.20 the 15th Panzer Division launched the attack on the 4th Armoured Brigade (7th Armoured Division) at full speed. Heavy losses were inflicted but also significant casualties were suffered. The 4th Armoured Brigade then withdrew towards El Adem. The effectiveness of the newly arrived Grant tanks (armed with 75 mm guns) seems to have surprised the enemy. Then there was the turn of the 21st Panzer Division (8.00) against the 22nd Armoured Brigade. The latter retreated in disorder to the north east, having sustained considerable losses.

At the same time, while the Axis was advancing on its far right, the 90th Light Afrika engaged the 7th Motorised Brigade at Retma and forced it to withdraw east toward Bir el Gubi. Resuming their advance towards El Adem, the 90th Light Afrika came upon the advanced HQ of the 7th Armoured Division near Bir Beuidin in the mid-morning, dispersing it and capturing its commander, Messervy. However, he managed to escape afterwards. This disruption meant that the division remained without effective command for the next two days.

By late morning, the Axis armoured units had advanced more than 25 miles north. And yet, when the battle seemed won at 14.00, the 2nd and 22nd Armoured Brigades (1st Armoured Division) jumped on the 21st and 15th Panzer Divisions. Heavy losses were sustained on both sides.

The 4th Armoured Brigade was also sent to El Adem and the 90th Light Afrika was driven back to the south west.

During the day, the Trieste Division began working through the minefields north of Bir Hakeim to open a way for the supplies. The southern route was too long and dangerous. At the same time, the Ariete Division was working on the eastern side of the minefields north of Bir Hakeim.

In the evening, the situation for the Axis was not ideal at all: the troops were positioned between the extensive minefields, had encountered stiff British resistance, and were cut off from their own supply lines. The next day, General Norrie launched the 1st Army Tank and 2nd Armoured Brigades into an attack in an effort to encircle Rommel at Bir El Harmat. The Ariete Division was engaged without success and the two Brigades had to withdraw.

At this point, 420 Commonwealth tanks were facing 150 German and 90 Italian tanks, a challenging situation for the Axis.

On the morning of the 29th, Norrie attacked again to push the enemy against the fortified positions of the 150th Infantry. Again the 2nd Brigade engaged the 15th Panzer Division at 11.00 with uncertain outcome and soon the 21st Panzer Division entered the fray together with a part of the Ariete Division. At noon, the 22nd Brigade also arrived in support and attacked the Ariete Division, but again with no results.

The 4th Armoured Brigade eventually arrived in the evening, but the 90th Light Afrika was able to stop it.

The fighting did not have an outcome also in part due to heavy sandstorms.

The supply situation for Rommel improved because a path was opened through the minefields north of Bir Hakeim.

During the day, Gen. Crüwell, commander of Afrika Korps, was shot down in his Storch and taken prisoner. Kesselring, who was curiously in Africa for an inspection, was temporarily appointed to substitute for him. On the morning of the 30th, again the 2nd and 22nd Brigades attacked the Ariete but their positions were not taken. The Italian artillery, equipped with 88 mm German guns, was crucial in stopping the British tanks.

26 May

4 SAAF reported the heaviest night attack; one plane was badly damaged.

At dawn, 59 *Macchi*s of 1° and 4° Stormo made a massive attack on Gambut, aiming to cripple the enemy front line fighter force. While 1° St. remained in coverage, 4° St. dived down to strafe the lined up *Kittyhawk*s: Commonwealth fighters were lined up, so ten were claimed to be burned out and fifteen damaged. Only 250 Squadron declared the damage of three *Kittyhawk*s (two heavily). 4 SAAF reported the attack of six *Macchi*s (erroneously on the 27th) but with no damage. 73 Squadron also reported an attack of low flying *Bf.109s*.

It seems strange that such a massive attack inflicted so few casualties and it appears possible that 112 Squadron, based in the Martuba complex, was also strafed. The book "Shark Squadron" lists 17 *Kittyhawk*s in charge in May that a month later in June were no longer in charge of the unit. No account exists to explain this change. 6 of these (AK637, AK680, AK766, AK777, AK906, and AK908) were present in the days prior to the 26th. Perhaps 112 Squadron aircraft were lined up together with 250 Squadron (unit of the same Wing) but the attack was not reported.

In any case, the Commonwealth fighters' activity in the day seems to have been lower than in the previous days.

A) 12 *Kittyhawks* of 3 RAAF scrambled over El Adem (6.55-7.45) to intercept enemy aircraft presumably directed on Gambut. They were flying at 11000 feet when contact established E of El Adem with four *Ju.88s* with top cover of six *Bf.109s*. The enemy formation was at 12500. One flight engaged the enemy fighters, while the remainder made for the bombers. Sgt. Clabburn (AL145) claimed a *Ju.88* damaged and S.L. Gibbs (AK874) claimed a probable *Bf.109*. And then the latter attacked a *Ju.88* but was shot down by the rear gunner: he baled out with the engine on fire, but struck the tailplane with the parachute entangled and landed badly, breaking his ankle and leg. However the enemy bombers were able to reach Gambut and damage two fighters on the ground.

Formation of Macchis of 96ª Sq. (Gentilli)

In the meantime nine *Hurricanes* of 33 Squadron were up on local patrol (7.20-8.55). Four of them came across the *Ju.88* that was previously damaged and P.O. Inglesby together with Sgt. Belleau shot it down. The crew was reported captured.

The only possible corroboration found is the attack on Gambut and Abiar Zaid aerodromes by nine *Ju.88s* (2.24-7.15, OBS).

At 9.00, P.O. Samuel (274 Squadron) was hit by anti-aircraft fire and crash-landed during an escort to reconnaissance aircraft.

B) Eight *Kittybombers* of 112 Squadron attacked Tmimi (14.00-15.00) escorted by 450 Squadron. P.O. Knapik (112 Squadron, AK682) was shot down. Dyson (450 Squadron) spotted a *C.202* that was attacking a fighter-bomber before leaving the coast, and so he engaged it without observing results other than a cloud of dust on the ground.

It seems they were engaged by a formation of four *Messerschmitts* of 5./JG 27 that scrambled over Gazala:
Fw. Reuter shot down a *Kittyhawk*, causing it to crash on the edge of his airfield and somersault (2 km north-east of Ain El Gazala, 13.35). Reuter was then pursued by six *Kittyhawks* and hit by seventeen strikes.
Lt. Jenish damaged a second *Kittyhawk*.

C) 260 Squadron was on an interception patrol (15.20-16.30). The eight *Kittyhawks* were cruising near Gazala at 10000 feet when they sighted two pairs of *Bf.109s*: one below at 9000, the other above at 12000. In the ensuing combat F.Lt. Waddy carryed out a head on attack against an enemy fighter, closing from 200 to 75 yds and claimed it probably destroyed. However, an unnamed Sergeant of 260 Squadron was injured (aircraft Cat.II).

The only informations available are that 2 and 4./JG 27 were on a free sweep around that time, the former west of Tobruk.

Eight *C.200s* of 8° Gruppo attacked motor transports in the Mteifel El Chebir area (16.35-17.40); Serg.Magg. Antonicelli (M.M.5271) was hit by anti-aircraft fire and force-landed behind Axis lines (AC badly damaged).

Seventy-two *Ju.87s* attacked artillery at Gazala; one aircraft was shot down by Flak (OBS). Overall four Ju.87s were lost to enemy fire during the day: *Ju.87 D-1* W.Nr. 2059 (III./St.G.3), by A.A. near Gazala; Lt. Bruchner (III./St.G.3), KIA near Gazala; Lt. Jänicke (1./St.G.3, *Ju.87 R-4/Trop* W. Nr. 6333, S7 + BH), KIA by Flak near Tmimi; Uffz. Kochner (7./St.G.3, *Ju.87 D-1* W.Nr. 2076, S7 + JM), missing near Gazala.

F.Sgt. Russell (250 Squadron, *Kittyhawk* AL130) crashed during take-off and was killed.

Ju.52 W.Nr. 7109 (Transportstaffel XI.Fl.K.) reportedly was shot down by fighters over Crete (100%). No corroborotion has been found.

Night of 26-27

F) There was intense activity by 73 Squadron. F.Lt. Scade (BN165, 21.45-23.14, 1500 feet) described:

> "...at 22.30, after attempting to shoot down 3 Ju.88s, I finally managed to do a front quarter attack on a fourth Ju.88. He immediately went into a dive through the cloud to the ground where it gave the appearance of attempting to jettison bombs and then burst into flames... 43 Ball, 14 HE/Inc."

S.L. Joyce (BN156, 21.45-23.15, 2000 feet) claimed a *Ju.88* destroyed at 22.55.
It was just after take-off that F.O. Selby (BN975, 4.15-5.45) saw a *Ju.88* firing with his front and rear gun at 300 feet. He opened fire and damaged it.
    Fifteen *Ju.88s* attacked tents south-east of Marsa Matruh. The railway was hit in several places (19.40-23.47); two aircraft were lost.
Twelve *Ju.88s*, which were flying at a height of 450 m, attacked vehicles on the roads in the El Gobi, El Adem, Sidi Azeiz area (19.29-0.04); one aircraft was lost.
Six *Ju.88s* attacked traffic on roads in the El Gobi-Sidi Omar, El Gobi-Tobruk area near Bardia. They strafed Hanascia landing ground, and the railway near Bir Nazem (1.00-5.38); one aircraft was lost (OBS).
Fw. Wittland (IV./L.G.1, *Ju.88 A-4* W.Nr. 5617, L1 + EW, 100 %) was shot down by Flak near Hanascia and taken prisoner with all his crew.
Three more crews went missing: Lt. Liersch (K.Fl.Gr.606 F, *Ju.88 A-4* W.Nr. 140227, 7T + IK) near Pl.Qu.8751; Oblt. Riba (I./L.G.1, *Ju.88 A-4* W.Nr. 5615, L1 + RL) near Hanascia; Fw. Liebsch (I./L.G.1, *Ju.88 A-4* W.Nr. 140215, L1 + QK) near Bir el Gobi.
Two of these bombers were probably victims of 73 Squadron.

Uffz. Konrad (III./Z.G.26, *Bf.110 E-2* W.Nr. 4419, 100 %) was hit by friendly anti-aircraft fire just after take-off (21.47) and force-landed behind the Axis lines (OBS).

Martuba was bombed; one *C.202* was burned out (M.M.7726, 72^a Sq.); and two others (81^a Sq.) were badly damaged.

Heavy damage on a Macchi of 88ª Sq. (Gentilli)

27 May

A) Fifteen *C.202s* (6° Gruppo: three of 79ª Sq., three of 81ª Sq. and four of 88ª Sq.; 6.10-7.20; 17° Gruppo: two of 71ª Sq. and three of 80ª Sq.; 6.15-7.15), led by Magg. Larcher, escorted fourteen *C.200s* of 13° Gruppo, attacking motor vehicles on Via Balbia to the east of Gazala.

Notwithstanding the mist, 6° Gruppo made out and was able to attack about fifteen enemy fighters, identified as '*P-40s*' and '*P-46s*', at an altitude of 4500 m to the south of Gazala (after 6.30). It was declared that these fled, but not before having lost three planes; twelve more were machine-gunned.

M.llo Stabile (88ª Sq.) shot down a *P-40* and fired at two more (300 rounds);
Cap. Ocarso (88ª Sq.) shot down a *P-40*;
M.llo Bordin (88ª Sq.) shot down a *P-40*;
Cap. Giacomelli (81ª Sq.) fired at five *P-40s*, damaging one of them;
Cap. Camarda (79ª Sq.) damaged a *P-40* (280 rounds);
Ten. Falchi (81ª Sq.) fired at five *P-40s*;
Magg. Larcher fired at two *P-40s*;
S.Ten. Ferrazza (79ª Sq., 200 rounds);
Serg. Saiani (79ª Sq., 180 rounds).

17° Gruppo was in its turn credited with three victories and another three machine-gunned: Ten. Talamini (80ª Sq.) shot down a *P-40* and fired at three other enemy planes (200 rounds); Serg. Magg. Andrich (80ª Sq., M.M.7892) shot down a *P-40* (150 rounds); and Serg. Magg. Host (80ª Sq., M.M.7752) shot down a *P-40* (200 rounds).
The last two pilots returned with damaged aircraft, Host's badly (strangely by cannon fire). In total, the *Macchis* fired 2730 rounds.
The pursuit could not be continued because the Italian planes were at the limit of their range. It appears that the two pilots of 71ª Sq. didn't participate in the battle and probably remained as cover, also because in the meantime the *C.200s* were strafing; moreover, the latter witnessed the shooting down of an enemy plane by the escort. As many as six *C.200s* were hit and Serg. Magg. Poggi (M.M.5253, engine damaged) had to land away from the airfield.

Twelve *Kittyhawks* of 2 SAAF were on an interception patrol over Gazala (6.45-8.25). Maj. Human was leading the formation. At 7.45, while they were flying at 10000 feet over Gazala, twelve *Bf.109s* and *C.202s* were seen; these attacked from above in small groups coming out of the sun. A general dogfight ensued, and most pilots were able to open fire at the enemy aircraft. The Squadron came back in "dribs and drabs," Burdon, Ruiter, and Smith having had a running battle to El Adem. But a lack of fuel prevented them from mixing with the enemy. Smith fired a few bursts with no results. In total, 2350 rounds from 0.50 guns were fired. Human (AL186 DB-G) claimed to have destroyed a *Bf.109*:

> "...A 109F approached from head on but decided to turn away, half way through by doing a diving turn to the right I was able to close in quickly and gave him three bursts from quarter stern. He turned on his back and spun down in an inverted position with smoke pouring from his AC. I followed to low level and saw AC burning on the ground (0.50, 500 rounds)."

Lt. Reynolds (AK747 DB-L) claimed to have damaged a *C202*, possibly Host's:

> "...I noticed a Mc202 jump one of our machines and as I came in on him he turned away, enabling me to give him two bursts from quarter stern. Smoke poured freely from the E and it spun down, giving me the impression that it was out of control. One Mc202 was probably destroyed. .50, 95 rounds."

Lt. Allen (AK642 DB-T):

> "...I turned into two Me109s which were attacking us. One dived away, and the second climbed up. I took a full deflection shot at a diving aircraft (109 or Macchi) but missed. And on looking round saw a 109 on my tail firing. I rolled and pulling out spun. The Me overshot me, presented me with a 30 degree deflection which I was able to hold for some time. He flew through the bursts which struck aft the pilot's cockpit, and on the tail plane and I saw pieces disintegrate. Force landed at El Adem owing to lack of fuel. One Me109 damaged. .50-240 rounds."

Lt. Paddon (AL138 DB-R) and Ford (AK904 DB-H) did not return and were reported shot down 10 miles south of Gazala. Major Human claimed the destruction of a *Bf.109* while another two pilots claimed a probable *C.202* and a damaged *Bf.109*.
The comparison of the rounds fired is interesting, considered there were about the same number of aircraft: the *Macchis* fired a greater number of rounds despite a rate of fire about four times slower.

At 5.00, about twelve *Hurricane IICs* of 229 Squadron took off from Malta heading for Egypt. Three of them were lost before reaching their destination. F.Sgt. Ganes ran out of fuel, crash-landed, and was taken prisoner.
P.O. Lee (BE642) came across about six *Ju.87s* before crash-landing because of running out of fuel. He attacked them and had to contend with heavy return fire from the rear gunners.
Sgt. Wilcox (Z4005) was shot down along the coast by a *Macchi*; it was almost certainly in the context of the above mentioned clash.

Between 5.21 and 8.14, *Bf.109s* carried out eleven escort flights for reconnaissance aircraft. In one of these missions Fw. Krenzke of 6./JG 27 claimed a *P-40* 20 km to the south of Ain El Gazala at 6.55; therefore, it cannot be ruled out that he shot down one of the two *Kittyhawks*.

Sgt. Wilcox's Hurricane IIC (229 Squadron, Z4005), shot down on his way back from Malta (Gentilli)

B) Ten *Bf.110s*, based at Derna, were on a mission (8.10-10.20), presumably a ground attack (OBS). Four of the planes belonged to 7./ZG 26 and were led by Oblt. Wehmeyer. They clashed with twenty *P-40s* and claimed three, all by 7./ZG 26:
Oblt. Wehmeyer (8.52);
Uffz. Nietzke (8.54);
and Fw. Wein (8.56).
This was countered with the loss of two *Bf.110s*: Uffz. Frickmann and his gunner, was shot down over Ela-Da and became POW (*C-5* W.Nr. 2195, 3U + MR, 100%); *E-2* W.Nr. 2384, 80%. Other source states that the latter was shot down by friendly Flak over Martuba.
The *Bf.110s* were probably escorted by six *Bf.109s* of III./JG 53: *"6.53-9.21 34 109s free sweep, scramble, bomber escort, clash with twenty P-40s two P-40s shot down. Another clash with numerous P-40s, two probably shot down"* (OBS). There must be some mix up with the claims because only two were claimed by the Bf.109s, of which only the first one was confirmed: Ofw. Stumpf (9./JG 53), 3 km SE of El Adem (9.10); and Fw. Herkenhoff (9./JG 53), 4 km SE of El Adem (9.11).
Also 2./JG 27 was present in the same area at the same time.

Twelve *Tomahawks* of 5 SAAF scrambled from Gambut 2 to intercept enemy planes (9.30-10.20); Major Frost was leading the formation. This consisted of three fluid flights, each formed by two fluid pairs in line abreast with 200 yard intervals. White Flight was leading 1000 feet below top flight and slightly ahead.

When the enemy formation was sighted, Blue Section was instructed to act as top cover while White and Red Sections would attack the bombers, identified as ten *Do.215s* escorted by ten *Bf.109s*. The *Tomahawks* (9.50, fifteen miles south-west of El Adem, 14000 feet) dived to attack: the leading section of Red Flight was mostly engaged with *Bf.109s*, while the rest engaged the bombers that went into a defensive circle (rounds: .50-1280, .303-3674).

Lt. Morgan (AN354 GL-X) attacked the bombers, giving three bursts. But he had to break away because a *Bf.109* shot his tail planes to pieces (Cat.I; rounds: .5-400, .303-1000).

2/Lt. Golding (AN468 GL-J) attacked the bombers:

> "I closed at about 50 yards on the second bomber and fired three fairly long bursts, all of which hit the aircraft. There was no return fire after the first burst. ...tracers flying past me on both sides and I therefore turned steeply.... One Do.215 damaged. .50-20, .303-40"

Lt. Van der Spuy (AK533 GL-Y):

> "I did a quarter stern attack on one of the rear bombers and noticed black smoke coming from the starboard engine. I then did a head on attack from slightly below on another bomber. After the second burst my plane was thrown violently on its back and spun down at great speed. After righting it at 5000......returned to base" One Do215 damaged. Slight damage by several bullet holes on my plane. .50-100, .303-4000."

Capt. Hewitson (Red Section, AK448 GL-H):

> "... Me109s seen coming toward us 2000 feet below on port side ... as I went to attack with my No.2 I saw five 109s attacking us from port side. I turned towards them and did a head on attack on the leading AC. I then delivered a head on attack on the second 109 which broke away. The first 109 then tried a stern quarter attack on me from the left and broke away in a slight climbing turn to the left, exposing the whole of his belly to my fire ... Pilot baled out. One 109 shot down. .50-40, .303-140."

Lt. Morrison (AK421 GL-Z) attacked the bombers in echelon starboard formation. He hit one that was in the rear and saw smoke pouring out from its starboard engine. It then dived to the ground with one crew member baling out. Morrison was then attacked by a *Bf.109* and was damaged (Cat.I, rounds: .50-20, .303-34).

Major Frost (AK195 GL-W) attacked the last bomber and fired a burst from astern at close range. His starboard engine caught fire and large pieces flew off while the enemy aircraft rolled over and crashed to the ground with no one bailing out. As he turned, his port elevator and wing tip were shot away by cannon shells (aircraft Cat.II, rounds: .50-60, .303-280).

Lt. Muir *(AN262 GL-C)* correctly identified the *Bf.110s*, whith a main formation in echelon starboard. He attacked one from the quarter stern slightly above but had to break away because of the returning fire. Then he made the mistake of attacking a second one head on, seeing six guns firing at him. Afterwards he lost contact. In his report he claimed one *Bf.110* damaged and the rear gunner probably killed. .50-60, .303-160 rounds expended.

Lt. Finlayson (AN427 GL-D) crash-landed at base (Cat.II).

It appears that the South Africans managed to make just one pass against the *Bf.110s*, and so these must have been defended well enough by the escort, which among other things had the

Bf.110 (Gentilli)

advantage of altitude. The second clash mentioned in the OBS report must have involved 4 SAAF, but should be considered an error in the times.

Twelve *Tomahawks* of 4 SAAF scrambled to make for Bir Hakeim (10.50-12.15). They were attacked by three *Bf.109s*, one of which shot off the tail of Lt. Woodliffe's aircraft, compelling him to make an emergency landing near El Adem.

2/Lt Woodliffe (AK or AM414 KJ-L):

"...Suddenly I saw Lt. Lang and Lt. Warden turn sharply away... (RT was out of order). Endeavoured to turn after Lt. Warden but became detached from him. I straightened out and bullet holes appeared in my wings. Immediately did a steep turn to the right, but caught a sight of the enemy. My engine began to ''miss'' and smoke appeared in the cockpit. I immediately turned towards our lines and started to dive to the deck in a spiral....again noticed bullet holes appearing in the AC and flames and black smoke appeared from the engine....I pumped the wheels down and managed to land the AC with both wheels punctured ... near El Adem where the engine fire burned itself out." (Cat.II).

Lt. Warden (AN379 KJ-X):

"...I lost my leader Lt. Langerman and turned to meet the second attack when I found that Lt. Woodliffe had not turned fast enough and one 109 was on his tail. I turned in towards this 109 giving him about a 2 sec. frontal burst from 300 yards. He immediately pulled over and the second 109 attacked me putting a cannon shell through the wing. I turned in towards him but he declined to fight. I did another...turn just in time to see the other 109 do another attack on Woodliffe. I pulled in towards him and gave a small burst from 400 yards to get him off Woodliffe's tail. He pulled away....I had to turn to meet another attack...This 109 pulled away and I continued to circle with the remaining 109s... One then left and the other jumped me. I turned and gave him a long ¼ frontal burst from 300 yards to about 100 yards and had to sweep past his tail to avoid colliding. ….saw ...white smoke coming out from the fuselage...."

Two *Bf.109s* were claimed damaged and Warden's own aircraft was hit (Cat.II).
The total rounds expended were: .50-850, .303-1300+400. Therefore, the latter should be the second clash of III./JG 53, reported by OBS.

Seven *C.202s* of 84ª Sq., during a surveillance sweep between Acroma and El Adem (12.40-14.00), participated in the strafing of motor vehicles together with *CR.42s*. It resulted in two motor vehicles catching fire.

Eight *Bf.110s* attacked motor vehicles in the El Adem area (12.55-1405, OBS) and one of them (3U + ET, 9./ZG 26) was hit by flak over Tobruk and shot down: Staffelkapitän Oblt. Bergfleth and Fw. Schupfner were killed.

3 RAAF and 112 Squadron were busy on ground attack missions.
Four *Kittyhawks* of 3 RAAF were attacking columns (13.45-15.00) when Sgt. Thomas was hit by flak and force-landed. Two aircraft of 3 RAAF were on another bombing mission (16.05 -17.05) when Sgt. Clabburn (AK806) was shot down by anti-aircraft. He returned the day after.

Heavy landing of a Bf.199 F of II./JG 27 (Gentilli)

Caudron Goeland (Gentilli)

C) Four *Kittyhawks* of 112 Squadron were also on a ground attack mission (15.15-16.50) when F.Lt. Dickinson (AL122) was shot down. No encounters with enemy fighters were reported but the loss could be credited to Lt. Körner of 2./JG 27 who claimed a *P-40* south of Gambut (15.30).

D) Twelve *Bostons* of 12 SAAF were off to attack 200-300 motor transports and tank carriers (14.48-16.15).
Eleven *Kittyhawks* of 450 Squadron were on escort (15.25-16.33, two returned because of engine trouble). During the return flight, they were attacked by three *Bf.109s*, one of which badly damaged Sgt. Oakley's *Kittyhawk* (which probably didn't return to base, AL184 Cat.II). The *Messerschmitt* was in its turn hit by Sgt. Shillabeer (AK787) and the pilot baled out near Sidi Rezegh.

It is possible that they clashed with a Schwarm of 5./JG 27 escorting two *Bf.109*E reconnaissance planes in the early afternoon. The latter were involved in a fight with eight *Kittyhawks*. On the way home they should have run into 450 Squadron. Fw. Reuter (*Bf.109* W.Nr. 7369 rt. 6+) was shot down between Tobruk and El Adem. He was flying a not fully efficient aircraft because his personal mount had been damaged the day before; he baled out and was taken prisoner. He was credited with twenty-one victories (it seems that this mission and loss was not reported by OBS).

The aircraft that was shot down should also have been seen by F.Lt. Brown of 112 Squadron at 16.20 (with some difference in the times).

The bombers reported one direct hit and four or five fires. Two aircraft were hit by anti-aircraft fire: one belly landed and the other was slightly holed. The result was the damaging of two aircraft of that unit; presumably they were *Boston III* AL773, damaged (Cat.II) and AL759, which was salvaged on 3 June.

E) Nineteen *C.200s* of 8° Gruppo had to strafe armoured vehicles in the Acroma-El Masar area. Top cover was provided by eight *C.202s* of 17° Gruppo (five of 71ª Sq., two of 72ª Sq., one of which returned earlier because of engine trouble, and three of 80ª Sq.) led by Ten. Ligugnana (16.35-17.35). While the *C.202s* were at an altitude of 4500 m, a formation of about fifteen *P-40s* tried to prevent the ground attack of the *C.200s*. The pilots of 17° Gruppo launched the attack, hitting eleven enemy planes. Three of these were believed to have been shot down:
M.llo Stella (71ª Sq.) probably shot down a *P-40*, and fired at two more; his plane was in its turn hit in the cooling system area and so he had to land it at Timini (M.M.7863, engine to be replaced);
Ten. Marchi (80ª Sq.), a *P-40* probable (512 rounds);
Serg.Magg. Ermo (71° Sq.), a *P-40* probable;
Ten. Ligugnana (71ª Sq.), fired at two *P-40s*;
Ten. Morandi (71ª Sq.), fired at a *P-40*;
Ten. Carini fired 132 rounds. In total they fired 1192 rounds.

Meanwhile, many *C.200s* were hit by anti-aircraft fire and Cap. Cecchet of 8° Gruppo (M.M.8331) was forced to land away from the airfield within friendly lines.

Six *Tomahawk IIBs* of 5 SAAF had scrambled between Tobruk and Gazala (17.25-18.45). The *Tomahawks* were searching for seven enemy aircraft when they were attacked. 2/Lt. Stevens (AN263 GL-V) was jumped by a *Bf.109* at 15000 feet over Tobruk and hit; he recalled:

> "I was jumped by a Me.109. My cockpit was filled with smoke anf flames, and I thought my machine was on fire, and after trying to open my hood, which would not budge, I tried to jettison it. Eventually I managed to open it, and when the smoke cleared, I was relieved to notice that I wasn't on fire. I then had a good look about the sky to try and locate the rest of the Squadron and also any sign of enemy AC. I then noticed that my engine was overheating. I throttled right back, and started gliding in an easterly direction, watching my tail all the time. My engine would not cool off, and at 2000 feet, I noticed a lot of tracks and I decided to land on one of them, which I did without damaging the AC. I then tried to contact out R/T controlling station without any results ... I noticed three soldiers approaching ... and told me "hands up"... "

Stevens was taken prisoner but after a few hours he found himself taken in the midst of a tank battle and managed to escape, returning the next day.

Seven *Tomahawks* of 4 SAAF were also over Bir Hakeim (17.45-19.00) when they sighted two *Macchis*. Capt. Bayley was jumped by one of them while he was alone, but *"the Macchi would not stay to fight"* ('Springbok Fighter Victory').

F) Between 15.40 and 19.35, fifty-eight *Bf.109s* escorted bombers and made free sweeps;

there was a clash with five *P-40s* and two were shot down. These were claimed by 5./JG 27: Fw. Krenke, 15 Km E of Bir Hakeim (16.40); and Lt. Jenish, S of El Adem (17.10).

They would have met up with four *Kittyhawk*s of 3 RAAF that were attacking motor vehicles five miles south of Bir Hakeim (16.50-18.20), during which time Sgt. Norman (AL183) was lost (even if the unit's diary did not report clashes with enemy planes).

G) 274 Squadron scrambled (18.15-19.20) and intercepted approximately twelve *Ju.87s* and four *Bf.109s* to the south of Tobruk: F.Sgt. Neil claimed one *Ju.87* destroyed, Sgt. Walsh one *Bf.109* damaged, and P.O. Samuel one *Ju.87* damaged.

Between 13.00 and 19.35, thirty *Ju.87s* attacked the roads in the Tobruk area. They clashed with thirty *P-40s* and *Hurricanes* (OBS) but no losses were mentioned. Probably the unit encountered was III./St.G 3 (15.55-17.15).

Lt. Grimes of 40 SAAF was hit by anti-aircraft fire during a reconnaissance mission and force-landed at Gambut.

Sgt. Sands (73 Squadron, *Hurricane IIC* BN282) was missing during a flight from El Adem to Gambut.

2 SAAF and 4 SAAF were moved to L.G.115 for the night for fear of paratrooper landings. They landed when it was nearly dark and three aircraft of the former were damaged upon landing; it is possible that they were AM743 DB-I, AK642 DB-T and AL133 DB-Y.

Night of 27-28

CR.42s of 3° Gruppo bombed and strafed the area between Gazala and Acroma (20.30-23.30); Cap. Tovazzi (154ª Sq.) went missing.

Six *He.111s* carried out several disrupting attacks on Fuka (18.52-4.37); Uffz. Schneider (II./K.G.100, He.111 H-6 W.Nr. 7218, 6N + CJ). The pilot and part of the crew were POW, others went missing.

Also Ofw. Naiß (I./N.J.G.2, *Ju.88 C-6* W.Nr. 360190, R4 + EL) was shot down in area Omar-Bir el Gobi-Tobruk, with the loss of the entire crew. It is presumed this occurred during the same night.

28 May

Five *Baltimores* of 223 Squadron attacked Martuba 3 from 18000' (6.00-9.00); six enemy fighters were seen but no interception was made.

The attack is reported by V Squadra at 7.20: a *C.202* (M.M.7810, 90ª Sq.) was burned out and four others were slightly damaged.

A) Two *Hurricanes* were claimed destroyed by 4./JG 27, 25 km east of Bir Hakeim: Oblt. Vögl (8.45); and Ofw. Schultze (8.46). No corroboration has been found.

B) On a free sweep east of Gambut, a Schwarm of 1./JG 27 with auxiliary tanks clashed with four *Hurricanes*, one of which was claimed by Fw. Steinhausen, 5 km north of Gasr El Ahrid (10.00).

They clashed with four *Hurricane IICs* of 80 Squadron (10.30-12.20) on standing patrol over their base (9.35-11.00). They were divided into two sections when *4 Bf.109s* were seen at 13000 ft coming out of the sun. One of these dived on F.Sgt. Wintersdorff (BE706), who was seen spinning and smoking (he was shot down east of Samhit, approximately 12 miles from base). Sgt. Sykes (BE567) *"tallyhoed"* and fired a short burst but was out of range. Also, a second *Hurricane* was shot up (Green 2, Cat. II) but returned to base with the pilot unhurt. Rounds: Ball 80, He/Inc 80.

C) 5 SAAF was off on a patrol over Gazala with eight *Tomahawks* (10.45-12.25). They sighted nine *Ju.87* bombers over the sea with eight fighters about 2000 feet above, and so they turned to gain height and saw the enemy formation turn over the land. After witnessing briefly the bombers dropping their bombs, they then saw instead the escort in two lots of three *Bf.109s*. Frost attacked one from astern and closed in to a short distance: he saw large pieces fall off, and then the plane was also attacked by Slater and Martin. It crashed in flames near Tmimi.
Maj. Frost (AK or AN434 GL-F; .50-120, .303-250);
Lt. Slater (AN433 GL-B; 0.50-130, 0.303-300);
2/Lt. Martin (AM401 GL-I, 0.50-140, 0.303-250).

It must have been a *Bf.109E* reconnaissance aircraft that was on a mission together with *Stukas*. It was then that Fw. Lange (4.(H)/12, W.Nr. 3489) was shot down over Komar east and lost his life.

During a free sweep (9.40-11.15), Lucchini returned alone ahead of time because an undercarriage wheel was not completely retracted, causing cooling problems. Even though he was attacked by ten *P-40s*, with his aircraft slightly damaged, he managed to extricate himself and fired at an enemy fighter before returning (this episode was not reported in his log book). It is possible that Lucchini also came across 5 SAAF.

D) Ten. Polizzy of 79ª Sq., 6° Gruppo broke away from the formation while returning from a mission (10.25-11.35) and intercepted and attacked a formation of five *Bostons* north of Acroma. He declared to have shot down one and to have damaged a second one (700 rounds fired). There is no confirmation for this action.

E) Four *Kittyhawks* of 260 Squadron were off on a free sweep in the El Adem-Acroma-Gazala area (11.50-12.40). They sighted and engaged two *Bf.109* Fs and F.Lt. Hindle damaged one.

F) Four *Macchis* of 81ª Sq., 6° Gruppo together with four *Bf.109s* (among which Oblt. Schultz's), led by Ten. Palazzeschi, were on a free sweep between Acroma and El Adem (11.35-13.00). The two pairs of planes, in echelon right, reached the operating zone at an altitude of 3000 m at 11.55 when they saw and attacked an enemy formation of fifteen *Bostons*

Macchi of 81ª Sq. (Gentilli)

escorted by fifteen *P-40s*. Three *P-40s* were shot down and four machine-gunned. M.llo Collovini shot down one *P-40* individually and a second one shared with Schultz; he recalled:

> "... I discovered a large formation of enemy bombers escorted by fighters. I wiggled my wings to give the alarm and, a moment later, we attacked them like lightnings. I met two Curtiss P.40 head on along with the pilot that was flying in front of me. One of them opened fire and then overturned. I dived on him in hot pursuit and from a few meters I hit him with a short burst of fire. The enemy plane overturned again and hit the ground inverted. I was able to see just the tail coming out of the cloud of dust. Immediately after I climbed again because I could see, over my head, the enemy formation in a complete turmoil. On my right another Curtiss was diving, trying to escape. I jumped him and started firing. A German Messerschmitt joined me and opened fire on the British. The fire was very accurate and shortly after the English plane overturned and caught fire on hitting the ground. It was an awesome sight ... Back at base the German command was contacted to know the report of the German pilot who took part in the shooting down. Later that evening I heard that the allied comrade told his interpreter that the victory had been shared between us. It was the truth and I appreciated his honesty."

Ten. Palazzeschi shot down a *P-40*;
Ten. Falchi fired at three *P-40s*.
In total 590 rounds were expended.
Schultz was credited with a *P-40* shot down in the El Adem area (12.20).

   The Axis fighters must have run into the formation of twelve *Bostons* (nine of 24 SAAF and three of 12 SAAF, 12.30-13.50) on their way to bomb motor vehicles at the front. Close cover consisted of twelve *Kittyhawks* of 450 (12.50-14.00) while nine *Kittyhawks* of 250 Squadron were top cover.

Kittybomber (Aviation Heritage Museum of Western Australia)

24 SAAF was in loose vic formation when it dropped forty-three 250 lb bombs on more than 200 tanks and motor transports. All bombs fell in the target area but the vehicles were well dispersed so the results could not have been optimal. The crews of the bombers saw first four Stukas to be dive-bombing south of the road (pin point 390438). Then twelve more Stukas were also dive-bombing, with a heavy barrage put up by Commonwealth's aircraft against them. One *Bf.109 F* was seen going down in flames and then to crash into the ground (pin point 408415). Six more *Bf.109 E* (often the *Macchi* was misidentified with the *Bf.109 E*) were seen, and one of them was fired upon by one of our air gunners, but no results were observed. But the bombers were only slightly involved in the clash between the enemy fighters and the escort.

After several attacks on a large motorized column six miles south of Gazala on the way home, 250 Squadron was attacked by four to six fighters including *Bf.109 Fs* and either *C.200s* or G.50s. Sgt. Ovenstone (AK877) was attacked by a *Bf.109*, which dived on him, and was shot down in flames. P.O. Cable (AK921) and another pilot engaged with no results, and anyway the enemy was kept away from the bombers. A second *Kittyhawk* was damaged by a cannon shell. It seems that 250 Squadron had to straggle behind because the bombers were getting away too slowly.

The pilots of 450 Squadron spotted four *Stukas* and four *Bf.109s* acting as escort and were present at the shooting down of Ovenstone six miles north-west of El Adem.
An aircraft of 24 SAAF returned ahead of time because of problems with the motor pump. Before landing, the pilot disposed of the bombs by dropping them into the sea just to the north of Baheria, causing the immediate intervention of the anti-aircraft battery that damaged his plane.
Considering that Ovenstone was the only loss, it cannot be established who can effectively be credited with the victory.

At 14.30, F.Lt. Dikinson (112 Squadron, AK829) was on a ground attack together with another

C.200s of 92ª Sq., 8° Gr. (Ufficio Storico SMA)

three aircraft (14.00-14.55) when he was again shot down. This time, however, he lost his life; presumably he was hit by anti-aircraft fire, even if five enemy fighters were spotted at 8000 feet.

G) Two aircraft of 7./JG 27 were on patrol: Uffz. Gruber claimed to have shot down a *P-40* 8 km north of Fort Acroma (14.05).

H) In the afternoon, ten *Hurricanes* of 33 Squadron scrambled to intercept an attack by *Stukas* in the Acroma area (14.25-16.07, one *Hurricane* returned early). At first six *Bf.109s* surprised the squadron and damaged two aircraft. Afterwards between El Adem and 25 miles west, the *Hurricanes* came across a formation of five *Stukas* escorted by eight/ten *Bf.109s* and C.202s. A dogfight developed and F.O. Wade claimed a *C.202* and a *Ju.87* while Sgt. Lyons went missing.

They came up against a formation of *Stukas* escorted by seven Bf.109s of II./JG 27. That day the German dive-bombers had carried out ninety sorties over Acroma. These were escorted by seven *Bf.109s* of II./JG 27. Two *P-40s* were claimed by the *Messerschmitts*: Obgefr. Vanderweert (6./JG 27), 30 km SW of El Adem (14.45); and Lt. Doyé (Stab II./JG 27), 11 km SE of El Adem (14.55).

I) Five *Macchi C.200s* of 94ª Sq. (8° Gruppo, 14.35-15.35) were on a ground attack when they engaged and fired at two *P-40s* that were strafing Axis troops. Serg.Magg. Bottazzi (M.M.6674) was shot down. The diary notes that it was not able to establish if he was hit in battle or by anti-aircraft fire.

Lt. Webb (*Tomahawk* 312, 40 SAAF) was on a reconnaissance mission at an altitude of 1500 feet between the Acroma-El Armat main road (15.20-16.10) when he was engaged by four *Macchis* and claimed one probable victory (Bottazzi). His plane was, in its turn, damaged on the tail but he continued on the mission and returned safely.

J) Lt. Pare (AN383 GL-N, 16.20-17.25) and Lt. Sommerville of 5 SAAF were off on a reconnaissance mission:

"While circling over a concentration of tanks and motor transports at 16.55 at 2000 ft. 3 109s attacked from astern. Their approach was unobserved until they were approximately 500 yards astern when Lt. Sommerville shouted "Duck" over the RT. Cannon shells struck the right wing and aileron, elevator and set fire to the fuselage tank....I baled out at approximately. 800 ft." He returned safely.

A Rotte of Stab II./JG 27 was escorting a *Bf.110* in a reconnaissance mission over El Adem when it came up against the two *Tomahawks*. Oblt. Schulz claimed a *P-40* 15 km east of El Adem (16.12).
During a strafing (19.05-20.10), Lt. Ismay (2 SAAF, AK747 DB-L) was hit by anti-aircraft fire and crash-landed.

Capt. Nel (40 SAAF, Tomahawk 312) was attacked by six enemy aircraft, during a reconnaissance mission in area El Adem - Gazala (19.40-20.20), but after a couple of minutes they desisted.
2./JG 27 was escorting Stukas in the same time and place, but it also matches time and place of Schultz's action.

Lt. Simon (4./JG 27, W.Nr. 8436) crashed during a test flight at Tmimi and lost his life.

Lt. Schroer (Stab I./JG 27) had to force-land his plane at Tmimi because of engine failure (15.05). A *Bf.109* of 9./JG 53 (W.Nr. 10108) was shot down by flak over Dohar Bahia.

Uffz. Jordan (*Fi.156* W.Nr. 5601, NN + GB) lost his life for unkown reasons. It can be noted that the day before a *Hs.126* was claimed by an undetermined Commonwealth aircraft.

During the day a pilot of 9./J.G.53 (Bf.109 F-4/Trop W.Nr.10108) was shot down by Flak over Dohar-Bahia. The plane was destroyed but the pilot returned safely.

223 Squadron was withdrawn from operations during the day because of problems with the .3 calibre Browning defensive guns. It was made clear that the order concerned missions without escort (!): this meant that the unit was a kind of sacrificial lamb, as was shown by its heavy losses.

Night of 28-29

K) *Hurricane IICs* of 73 Squadron were very busy.
Sgt. Wiseman (BM988) was flying at 3000 feet at 23.00 when he damaged a *Ju.88* (160 rounds).
P.O. Fraser (BE570) was flying at 2000 feet at 3.25 when he damaged a *Ju.88* that was strafing the coast road; he was able to fire only 20 rounds because his cannons jammed.
Sgt. Jones (BN402) was flying at 500-700 feet at 4.50 when he damaged a *Ju.88*; after one second, the two starboard cannons ceased firing.
F.Lt. Scade (BN165, 4.45-6.30) was flying at 1000 feet at 5.25:
"Saw tracers coming from AC strafing Bardia/Tobruk road. Chased it and eventually got a visual of a Ju.88 at 500'. ...Closed to within 150 yards and fired. EA turned violently and dived to 100'. I

fired again from close range....saw a violent explosion....my cannons jammed.... 65 Ball, 32 HE.Inc."
Then Scade, who was flying at 500 feet at 5.30, damaged another Ju.88.

Capt. McDougall (BN415, 0.45-6.25) was flying at 1000 feet when he attacked three *Ju.88s* at 4.30, 4.45, and 5.15. The first two were claimed damaged, while the third was destroyed (60 Ball, 30 HE); only two cannons were working. Problems with the cannons were far from being solved.

Martuba was attacked: a *C.202* was burned out (M.M.7796, 91ª Sq.) and others were slightly damaged.

29 May

Gen. Cruewell was shot down in his Storch and was taken prisoner.

A) Twelve *Hurricane IICs* of 80 Squadron were flying at 6000 feet on a sweep over El Adem, Acroma and Bir Hakeim (6.30-8.00). Mc Cormack returned earlier because of engine trouble (it is not clear if he crash-landed). S.L. West (BE564), together with Sgt. Handysides (Yellow 1, BE705), saw four *Bf.109s* behind and at the same level flying south-west. The two pilots said tallyho and turned round against the enemy: as the *Messerschmitts* climbed steeply, Law fired a short burst at 100 yards, but only his starboard cannons were working so it was impossible for him to aim. Law then came down to 300 feet and found two more *Bf.109s*, and so he took evasive action and returned to base. Handysides came away from the formation and returned to base. Sgt. Hughes (BN413) was attacked from behind and damaged, and so he also returned to base (6 Ball).
P.O. Pearson (BM991, Cat.III), F.Sgt. Campbell (BN354, Cat.II), Sgt. Swire (BE396, Cat.III), and Sgt. Sykes (BN547, Cat.II) were all hit and force-landed.
The unit was heavily punished; perhaps this was also because the *Hurricanes* were almost completely unable to fire back due to the poor functioning of the 20 mm guns.

Seven *Kittyhawks* of 2 SAAF were also on an attacking mission between El Adem-Acroma-Bir Hakeim (6.45-8.05) when their pilots sighted ten *Bf.109s*. They were apparently protecting an enemy column that stretched back for twenty miles. Three of these enemy fighters continued to attack as far as Tobruk (7.25-7.45). Lt.Brown (AK870) was shot down and baled out, but his parachute did not open; he was on his first mission. It was noted that the enemy would not have stayed to fight (total rounds: .50-1040).

Six *Bf.109s* of II./JG 27 and six of III./JG 53 were on a free sweep, the former over Mteifel El Chebir and the latter between El Adem and Acroma. Enemy planes were encountered and three were shot down:
Ofw. Krenzke (6./JG 27), *Hurricane* (6.10, this could not be confirmed because of a lack of witnesses);
Lt. Munzert (9./JG 53), *Hurricane* (6.13);
and Ofw. Kronschnabel (9./JG 53), *P-40* (6.30).

In examining the times, it would seem that both the units had encountered 80 Squadron, against which they claimed only two victories. This was possibly because they only saw two *Hurricanes* force-land.

Subsequently at least 9./JG 53 had encountered 2 SAAF (when Kronschnabel shot down Brown).
The next day 80 Sqn., battered by the recent losses, was sent eastward to L.G.121 for a rest.

B) During the day, one hundred eight *Ju.87s* bombed concentrations of motor transports and tanks at El Adem, Gazala, Bir El Gobi and Acroma; two of them force-landed in enemy territory (OBS): Staffelkapitän Hptm. Drescher (4./St.G.3, *D-1* W.Nr. 2469), force-landed at Gazala and was taken prisoner; Oblt. Olfermann (4./St.G.3, *D-1* W.Nr. 2450), was KIA with the rest of the crews.
In one of the first missions, the escort was provided by seven *Bf.109s* of 2./JG 27 (7.02-8.12) along with 6 of III./JG 27. The former engaged about ten *P-40s* and claimed to have shot three down:
Lt. Stahlschmidt, N of Fort Acroma (7.49);
Hptm. Maack, W of Tobruk (7.50);
and Lt. Körner, W of Tobruk (7.52).
Lt. Von Fritsch (9./JG 27, W.Nr. 8575, ge. 5 +, 100%) was hit and crash-landed on the coast in the area of Borde Bu Hasna, near Gazala, and was taken prisoner.
Ten *Kittyhawks* of 450 Squadron were on patrol at 7000 feet over Acroma (7.50-9.10) when they were attacked by two *Bf.109s* without results. Shortly afterwards two more joined in, but the attack was broken off. And then the formation was ordered to patrol 20 miles north of El Adem to intercept an enemy formation. While re-forming they were again attacked by three *Bf.109s* for three minutes; this attack was also broken off, however. At this time the *Stukas* were bombing at Pin Point 394440 and then headed north-west. 450 Squadron pursued and overtook them 20 miles east of Gazala: one section dived to engage two miles north of the coast (it is not clear if they engaged only the *Stukas*), while the other section engaged four *Bf.109s* for four minutes (it is not clear why the escort was alone so far from the bombers and why only four *Bf.109s* were noted).
Sgt. Mc.Burnie (AK987) destroyed a *Bf.109* (Von Fritsch) and shared a *Ju.87* with Sgt. Jenkins (AK789) over Gazala; Sgt. Nursey (AK606) destroyed a *Stuka*.
Sgt. Packer (AL163) was killed 10 miles west of Gazala.
Sgt. Dean (AK979) and Sgt. Shaw (AK998) were missing.
During the clash a large formation of thirty aircraft, probably Italian, was sighted 4/5000 feet above and six miles to the east.

It is not clear how the German escort was organized. Perhaps 2./JG 27 was top cover and arrived late, engaging the Australians toward the end of the clash. It seems that the number of escort fighters was the

Serg.Magg. Martinoli, 73ª Sq. (Ufficio Storico SMA)

Fi.156 'Storch' (Gentilli)

same as the *Kittyhawks*. Therefore, the former were not in the position to put up an adequate defence, even if they exacted a considerable toll shooting down three Australian pilots.

Five *CR.42s* of 158° Gruppo bombed enemy batteries south-east of Gasr El Regem (10.30-12.15): one aircraft force-landed behind Axis lines after being hit by anti-aircraft.

During a sweep of 274 Squadron (12.10-13.15) one *Hurricane* pilot turned back earlier. After the mission, the rest of the Squadron went back to base and there was no trace of the former pilot who was posted missing. He must have been P.O. Bell who returned to the Squadron four days later, the 3rd of June.

C) Magg. Larsimont Pergameni was leading eight aircraft of 9° Gruppo on a free sweep (five of 73^a Sq. and three of 97^a Sq.; 14.40-16.05). The visibility was much reduced because of the sand swept up by the wind. While the formation was crossing over Acroma at an altitude of 4000 m toward 15.00, a patrol of about a dozen *P-40s* was spotted at a lower altitude: its pilots noticed their presence and tried to increase altitude by turning towards the *Macchis*, which launched the attack. Three enemy fighters were credited as shot down along with two probable victories and seven machine-gunned down (2773 rounds):
Serg.Magg. Martinoli (73° Sq.) shot down a *P-40* and machine-gunned two others;
Serg. Guerci (73^a Sq.) shot down a *P-40*;
The third was credited to all the pilots of 97^a Sq. taking part in the action (among whom was S.Ten. Querci).
S.Ten. Massa (73^a Sq., M.M.7824) did not return; he had only been with the unit for three months.

Nine *Tomahawks* of 5 SAAF (15.40-16.55) were on patrol possibly with eleven *Hurricanes* of 274 Squadron (15.40-17.20).

Tomahawk of 5 SAAF Squadron (Bouwer)

Frost (5 SAAF) stated:

"16.00 10000 8 or 9 EA were seen diving out of the sun. They were 109E, F and 202. Turned to face them and general dogfight followed. 109 staying above and doing dive attacks, while Macchis came down and fought. Good burst with little deflection at a Macchi (Massa) which climbed past me. EA turned over and started burning. Was seen to crash by other pilots. .50 20, 303 40." At 16.20, the enemy broke off and headed west.

Lt. Lindberg reported (AK366 GL-O):

At 10000 feet "... When I observed the EA I attempted a head on attack on one below me, but overshot. I then went into a steep turn and saw a Me.109 climbing steeply to the north from below me with a Tomahawk close behind. I approached and the 109 pulled over on its back giving the impression of being out of control. While he was at the top of the stall turn he presented a deflection target well within range, so I opened fire. I lost him as he went down, but saw an AC burst into flames as it hit the ground a few seconds later (Massa). Shortly after this I saw a Macchi 202 on the tail of a Tomahawk about 1500' below, I dived and the Macchi pulled away from his target into a gentle climbing turn to the left. When I got within range I allowed plenty of deflection and opened fire. I saw incendiary ammo. bursting in his airscrew disc and on the port wing. At about 50 yards range I saw an AC coming up on my right towards me, so I broke off the attack. One Macchi 202 damaged (.50-400, .303-1200)"

Hewitson (AK448 GL-H), at 10000 feet:

"... Saw bombs bursting in sea near Gazala and when approaching to investigate 8 or 9 EA attacked out of the sun. General dogfight followed and while diving down to escape a Bf.109 I noticed another 109 F on the tail of a Tomahawk at 50 ft. I came in and attacked the 109 F from above astern, pulled away and delivered another attack after which the 109 pulled away and climbed to about 1500 ft. during which time I was firing from astern at about 200 yards. Black smoke was seen coming out from behind the Me.109 and it seemed to stall at that height. I was then attacked by another Me.109 and the result of the first combat was not observed. One Me.109F damaged (.50-100, .303-150)"

Lt. Saunders (AM495 GL-T):

"... I dived very fast on the tail of a Macchi 202 and opened fire holding it to very short range. I saw pieces coming off and pulled up over the top of him and turned but saw him diving very fast going west ... One Macchi 202 damaged (.50-100, .303-400)".

Lt. Slater's plane (AN433) of 5 SAAF was attacked three times from the rear by a *Bf.109*: he was hit, the engine failed, and a landing was made six miles south of Tobruk (Cat.II, then SOC — perhaps it wasn't salvaged).
Bidwell's engine cut off twice during the combat.
(Total rounds: 0.50-1827; 0.303-6318).

274 Squadron did not see any enemy aircraft, but Sgt. Dodds, who returned early, came across four *Bf.109s* and claimed one damaged.
It would appear that another two *Kittyhawks* had been slightly damaged (*"RAF Casualties Middle East"* and M865).
The Italians had the advantage of height and reported that their adversaries had to succumb to their initiative throughout the air-combat; this must have been intense, especially considering that 2773 rounds were fired.
During a mission (17.15-18.25), 24 SAAF witnessed a *Kittyhawk* making an emergency landing in zone 410480 (El Adem).

Lt. Webb (40 SAAF, *Tomahawk* 445) approached some aircraft at 2/2500 feet thinking that they were his escort, not noticing that they were actually *Stukas* (17.00-17.35). Upon realizing what they were, he got behind them and fired two bursts at the leader, one at approximately 200 yards. Expecting to be attacked by top cover he left the bombers and continued his mission.

At 17.26, Sgt. Devlin (450 Squadron, AK981) crashed during take-off and was killed.

Obfw. Schulze of 4./JG 27 crash-landed east of Tmimi because of engine failure during a *Stuka* escort (10.50-11.50, *Bf.109* Wk.n. 7356, 30%). Otto Schultz picked him up with a Storch.

<u>Night of 29-30</u>

D) At 21.00, eight *Bostons* of 24 SAAF attacked Derna. One of these was attacked by a night fighter but the gunner Sgt. Oberholster managed to shoot it down in flames with two bursts and watched it fall into the sea. The plane Z2176L (Lt. Murrow) went missing; it had presumably been shot down by Oblt. Wehmeyer. The pilot of 7./ZG 26 claimed a *Wellington* at 20.34. A second *Boston* (AL673W) was hit by anti-aircraft fire and had to return with only one engine working. Upon landing, however, the second one also failed and therefore it crashed. Wehmeyer, along with another three pilots, also made an attack on concentrations of motor vehicles to the west of Tobruk (19.35-20.52).

148 Squadron also lost two aircraft — but this time it was due to accidents.

Macchis of 71ª Sq.; in the back a Cant.Z.1007bis (Archivio di Stato)

30 May

A) Four *Bf.109s* of I./JG 27 were on a free sweep (5.33-6.33): they came across enemy fighters and Marseille claimed a *Kittyhawk*, 1 km north-west of El Adem (6.05).
   Ten *Kittyhawk*s of 250 Squadron (6.55-7.40) were top cover for ten planes of 450 Squadron that was on a reconnaissance-strafe mission over the Bir Hakeim area. Top cover was split up, however, by an attack of five/six *Bf.109s* out of the sun north-west of El Adem.
P.O. Cable (AK921) fired a good burst at one;
Sgt. Buckland (AK704) was shot down and the plane caught fire 10 miles west of Tobruk — he baled out but the parachute did not open;
Sgt. Cairns (AL157) was shot up;
and Sgt. McWilliam's plane (AL162) engine seized when commencing a dive on a *Bf.109* — he force-landed on a minefield but remained unscathed.

Oblt. Pufahl (7./JG 53) was on an escort for *Bf.110s* (6.10) when his plane was shot down by mistake by a *Ju.88*; he had come upon it by chance and crash-landed south of Gazala (*Bf.109* W.Nr.10126, 100%).

B) Eight *Macchis* of 17° Gruppo (three of 71ª Sq., two of 72ª Sq. and three of 80ª Sq.) were on a free sweep in the Bir Harmat (9.50-11.05) area. They were led by Cap. Baruffi (71ª Sq.). Climbing to an altitude of 4500 m, they intercepted a formation of *P-40s* that was trying to

attack *Stukas* that were bombing armoured vehicles north-east of Bir Harmat. They were credited with four *P-40s* shot down and another six machine-gunned (total rounds: 1164):
Ten. Carini (72ª Sq.) shot down a *P-40*;
The other three *P-40s* were shared between the eight pilots. M.llo Giuseppe Magli (72ª Sq., M.M.7735) didn't return and was posthumously promoted Sottotenente. Other pilots were: Ten. Morandi (71ª Sq.), M.llo Lui (71ª Sq.), Ten. Marchi (80ª Sq., 80 rounds), Ten. Ghiglia (80ª Sq., 154 rounds) and Serg.Magg. Andrich (80ª Sq., 470 rounds).

The action had probably involved nine *Kittyhawks* of 2 SAAF on a reconnaissance mission to identify targets for the *Bostons* (10.20-12.10). At 11.00, Lt.s Allen and McLeod landed at El Adem because of engine trouble. The *Kittyhawks*, which had to fly low at an altitude of 800 feet, reported the attack by five *Macchi C.202s* at 11.45 and were caught at a disadvantage. The *Macchis* were sighted in a loose formation at 2000 feet down sun, *"gambolling about in rough line astern in typical Italian fashion."* The usual dive and zoom tactics were employed. Lt. Berrangé stated (AK735 DB-E, 11.45):

> "I heard duck on the R/T and did a steep turn to the left. As I looped round I saw 2 Macchis completing attacks and climbing into the sky. I then completed my turn through about 270 degrees and then noticed a Macchi coming in low from the East to attack our 3 AC below. I pushed my stick forward as he came in and fired two short bursts which went in front of him, then fired a long burst and saw my bullets converging on him. He immediately pulled up vertically, smoke came from him as he got to the top of his climb, when he stalled, went on his back and dived into the ground where he burst into flames. .50. 180."

Lt. Smith nearly collided with another *Macchi*.
Lt. Harrison (AK841 DB-K) was hit and losing control of his aircraft but managed to regain it; he crash-landed on its belly and was taken prisoner. During the fight, the enemy ground forces fired with MG (total rounds: 50-570).

C) Four *Bf.109s* of I./JG 27 were on a freelance over the Mteifel-Harmat area. They attacked enemy fighters that were flying low; Fw. Keppler (1./JG 27) shot down a *Kittyhawk* south-east

24 SAAF Bostons on landing (Bouwer)

of Sidi Rezegh (11.30) and damaged a second one.

The reason is not known for Uffz. Zimmermann's (1./JG 27,W.Nr. 8654, 40%) force-landing on Via Balbia 12 km north of Tmimi.

Two *Kittyhawks* of 250 Squadron together with eight more of 450 Squadron were top cover for four others of 3 RAAF and six *Kittybombers* of 112 Squadron on a sweep (12.05-13.00). Sgt. Stewart reported (250 Squadron, AK779):

> "As P.O. Gregory (my No.1) got into position to attack another group of vehicles, a 109E dived in between and followed him down in a turn. I fired at this machine but only two of my guns worked and these ceased to fire after about 10 rounds. Whilst I was trying to reload my guns I was fired at by a 109E and received two bullet holes."

Also the Kittyhawks of 450 Squadron dived down to strafe and claimed several vehicles destroyed. A *Bf.109* attacked Dyson but without results. A second plane was also attacked, presumably Halliday's; it force-landed wheels down (pin point 390361), presumably Keppler's victim. Halliday's aircraft was only slightly damaged and returned to operations soon after.

Lt. Webb (40 SAAF, *Tomahawk II* 913) sustained a surprise attack over Knightsbridge (12.00-13.00) by a *Bf.109*. Luckily he was able to dodge the first burst and get away. He was also aided by his own AA.

Probably Webb was involved against I./JG 27.

In the afternoon the *Stuka* attacks were limited because of a lack of fighter escort.

Four *Kittyhawks* of 112 Squadron were bombing from 14.20 to 15.15; at 14.50, Sgt. Burney (AK770) was shot down in his plane, presumably as a result of anti-aircraft fire. Escort was provided by four aircraft of 450 Squadron.

D) At 14.15, nine *Bostons* of 12 SAAF took off for an action 10 miles north of Segnali. Eight *Kittyhawks* of 260 Squadron were top cover (14.45-15.55) with two more of 2 SAAF as close cover (14.45-16.00). It appears that 24 SAAF, which was to accompany it, left late because of a misunderstanding and therefore the escort was reduced in number.

260 Squadron reported to have clashed with two *Bf.109s* and two *Macchis* (there were probably only German fighters) and were being attacked continuously, both on the outward flight and on the return one on the road for El Adem. It claimed to have damaged a plane but suffered heavy losses. F.Lt. Wylie was shot down on the way to the target and lost his life; P.O. Hale baled out on leaving the target but went missing; and F.Sgt. Copping managed to get back to base but crash-landed. F.Sgt. Edwards noted that the two planes shot down had been engaged by aggressive *Macchi* pilots and that Hale had been strafed while coming down with his parachute. A *Bf.109* was claimed damaged by Edwards.

2 SAAF reported that at 15.25 (?), four *Bf.109s* broke through top cover and shot down 2/Lt. Fulton (AK735 DB-E) at Rotunda Ualeb; the pilot was taken prisoner.

The adversaries should have been four pilots of Stab I./JG 27 on a free sweep (13.50-15.00). These claimed four *P-40s*:

Oblt. Sinner, Bir El-Hamat (14.05);

Lt. Schroer, NE of Bir Hakheim (14.05);

Fw. Kaiser (2), E of Bir Hakeim (14.07); and SE of Bir El Harma, 500 m (14.09).

The Germans would have shot down the aircraft in the first phase of the attack and then continued on to pursue the enemy formation.

E) Nine *Bostons* of 24 SAAF attacked motor transports in the Segnali area (14.45-16.00). They had a reduced escort: ten *Tomahawks* of 5 SAAF were middle cover (15.05-16.10, one returned earlier) while two other *Tomahawks* of 4 SAAF were close cover (15.05-16.10).
It was at about 15.45, after they had dropped their bombs and were flying at an altitude of 10000 feet south-west of Acroma, when eight *Bf.109s* in sections of four in line astern delivered a diving attack out of the sun from 13000 feet.
Lt. Whyte (5 SAAF, AN354 GL-X) claimed a probable victory: *"...I sighted a Me.109 F attacking a Tomahawk. The EA pulled up and came down head-on to me. I pulled up and gave it a long burst. The EA became obscured by white fumes and went down in a glide... 50: 40, .303: 90."*

4 SAAF limited itself to reporting the attack of a further ten *Bf.109s*, which nevertheless did not manage to reach the bombers. Two or more enemy planes were seen coming down, out of control. The bombers' crews observed ten fires in the area recently bombed by 12 SAAF and reported that a *Kittyhawk*, not belonging to its own escort, was shot down behind its own lines, the pilot having baled out safely. Three bombers were slightly holed by anti-aircraft fire.

Serg.Magg. Borreo (88ª Sq.) back from a mission, earlier period (Gentilli)

The enemies should have been pilots of III./JG 53 (about eight); it is recorded that the Schwarm of 8./JG 53 ran across *Bostons* with fighter escort, which were accompanied by fighter-bombers. Three *P-40s* were claimed:
Ofw. Stumpf (9./JG 53, 14.25);
Hptm. Belser (8./JG 53), 30 km SE of Carzella, 1500 m (14.35);
and Lt. Quaritsch (8./JG 53, 14.58).

Apart from errors with the times, only the latter ties in with 24 SAAF's diary. The first two would have been coherent with the pursuit of 12 SAAF's formation; nevertheless in that case, only four *Messerschmitts* had been spotted.

During the day, *Bf.109 F-4/Trop* W.Nr. 10024 of Stab III./JG 53 was wrecked upon landing at Martuba (60%). It cannot be excluded that it was damaged in the above reported combat.

F) Nine *C.202s* of 6° Gruppo (three of 79ª Sq., four of 81ª Sq. and two of 88ª Sq.), led by Cap. Giacomelli, were on a free sweep between Bir Harmat and Bir Hakeim, 90 km inside enemy territory (14.40-16.05). Once they reached an altitude of 5000 m to the south of Acroma at 15.10, a big enemy formation was spotted despite the presence of mist. It was perhaps as a result of the bad visibility that three pilots of 79ª Sq. were separated and didn't participate in the clash. Giacomelli gave the signal to attack and a lively air-combat followed. Three *P-40s* and a *Hurricane* were shot down while four *P-40s* were machine-gunned:
Cap. Giacomelli (81ª Sq.) and Serg. Magg. Meneghetti (81ª Sq.) shared a *P-40* shot down;
Ten. Palazzeschi (81ª Sq.) shot down a *P-40*;
Serg.Magg. Borreo (88ª Sq.) shot down a *P-40* and fired at a second one;
Serg. Bartesaghi (88ª Sq.) shot down a *Hurricane* and fired at a second one.
Serg.Magg. Nello Meneghetti (M.M.7881) did not return to base. He was posthumously promoted Maresciallo.
81ª Sq. fired 1670 rounds and 88ª Sq. fired 1110.

The *Macchis* should have run into six *Kittyhawks* of 250 Squadron (15.50-16.55). The latter were the escort for four *Kittybombers* of 3 RAAF (15.55-16.50) and were heading north of Bir Hakeim. Three planes of 112 and three more of 450 (15.55-16.45) were also attacking nearby so probably the four Squadrons were in the same formation.
250 Squadron also participated in the strafing and so the squadrons alternated in the actions of ground attack and providing cover.

3 RAAF reported to have been attacked by four *Bf.109s* and lost F.Lt. Barr (AK889) and Sgt. MacDiarmid (AL153), the former returned while the latter was killed. Two pilots of 250 Squadron in their turn engaged some of the six *Bf.109s* encountered, hitting two, but Sgt. Devlin (AK648) was also hit and came down seven miles south-east of Acroma, losing his life. Sgt. Stewart (250 Squadron, AK790) was strafing vehicles with his No.1 (P.O. Gregory) when *"a 109E dived in between and followed him down in a turn. I fired at this machine but only two of my guns worked and these ceased to fire after about 10 rounds. Whilst I was trying to reload I was fired at by a 109E and received two bullet holes."*
Sgt. Hannaford (250 Squadron, AK884):

> "I started to climb due North, and at 1000 ft ran into a fight where three other Kittyhawks were being attacked by 109s. A 109 made an attack on an aircraft below me, and I managed to get a

good burst into his fuselage from underneath. I saw my burst open up a hole in his fuselage and pieces fly from it. I was then attacked by 109s, but they spoilt one other attack and I took a scare shot at one of them. Just after this I noticed what I thought to be two Kittyhawks crash into the deck in flames. I noticed one of them going down with only one wing, spiralling in the horizontal plane and it burst into flames as it hit the deck. The other I merely saw it crash and burst into flames. In the mean time one of the 109s left me, but the other continued to make attacks on me. I was not able to get a shot at him, as I was only at about 300 ft. He followed and made attacks on me almost to El Adem, where the AA opened up and scared him off."

P.O. Twemlow (250 Squadron, AK921):

"...I then turned right to do another run but saw 2 109Fs coming down on the machines above me. Immediately climbed and one of the enemy aircraft came down and attacked a machine in front of me. I was unable to get into range, but fired a short burst in front of him as he pulled up again. The other 109 I had previously seen then attacked me and after turning into him he also climbed away. I then climbed into a position level with the first 109 (about 1500 ft.) when he dived on another Kittyhawk I dived after him, fired three bursts, of somewhat more than a second, and hits in each case were seen, but, however, had no effect evidently as the 109 climbed away again. I was attacked by two more 109s which had been giving top cover to the others. Three other Kittyhawks were then also involved in a general dogfight but no damage to either side was observed by me. During these engagements there were another two 109s above, but they did not come down."

After the bombing 3 RAAF was climbing up to cover 250 Squadron, pairs of *Bf.109*s attacked from above. Barr confirms:

"After dive bombing and strafing enemy positions near Knightsbridge, my section of four was climbing up to act as top cover while 6 of 250 Sqn. strafed. I reported Ea 2000 ft. above in the

3 RAAF Squadrons' Kittyhawks (Aviation Heritage Museum of Western Australia)

sun and 2 109s dived down for an astern attack which was evaded. They climbed away and the other two attacked shooting down my No.2 (Sgt. McDiarmid) I got a short burst from front quarter with no observed result. I turned into a dive attack from a 109 (Meneghetti) as he went by I fired a 2 second burst from dead astern beneath. He dived towards the ground. I was hit from astern and took evading action. I was then half flung over on my back at about 50' by what I thought to be an AA fire blast. I came out but the propeller hit the ground and a few hundred yards further I crash-landed at point 385411. Capt. Waters MO of the Royal Gloucestershire Brigade, reported that an aircraft (not recognized) crashed at Bir El Tamar a few minutes before my landing, but his Sergeant thought it was a 109. Pin point 375412 approximately.
The other 4 109s did not attack, but swept round in a large circle. 15 Ju87s then arrived and dive bombed the area and made off quickly to the west. They dived from about 2500 down to 1500 feet only. The 8 109s appeared to be clearing the area prior to the attack by Ju87s which were covered by only 2 109s."

Twemlow and Hannaford also destroyed 3 motor transports and damaged a six-wheeler.

A Kittyhawk of the second formation was reported missing after having engaged a *Bf.109*. This matches well with the loss of Jenkins of 450 Squadron who was reported missing during the day but returned later.

The second pair of enemy planes must have been that of Giacomelli and Meneghetti, who shot down McDiarmid. Barr then in his turn shot down Meneghetti.
The *Macchis* were benefitted by the low altitude of the adversaries 239 Wing was constantly being employed on risky missions and was made to pay dearly for this. Nevertheless, they managed to shoot down a *Macchi* on this occasion. In particular 450 Squadron flew seven missions during the day (34 sorties) and in most of them it came across enemy fighters.

Lt. Grimes (40 SAAF, *Tomahawk* 913) was off on a reconnaissance mission in area El Adem - Knightsbridge (16.25-16.55). At 16.30, he was attacked at 1000 feet by two enemy fighters that dived out of the sun. He banked slightly to the left and climbed up beneath one but his guns would not work. He turned over an area where there was Commonwealth's anti-aircraft but the enemies still were not driven off. He continued his evasive action by steep turning and making his way eastwards until the enemy aircraft abandoned the attack.
This report matched Bartesaghi's claim well.

G) A Schwarm of 4./JG 27 was out on a free-lance (15.40-16.16). There were four claims:
Ofw. Bendert, P-40, East of Fort Acroma (16.03);
Oblt. Vögl (3), 2 P-40s, SW of Tobruk (16.05, 16.18); Hurricane, NE of Bir El Harmat (16.08).

H) Lt. Harder (7./JG 53) claimed a *P-40* at 16.17. There is no confirmation for the last two actions. The only hypothesis that can be taken into account relates to 274 Squadron, which had been in action with six aircraft since 16.15. It was on a free sweep over El Adem, Bir Hakeim, and Tobruk. This unit reported to have had no casualties but this term was usually used following a clash with the enemy.
In August, some pilots of 4./JG 27 would be accused of falsifying air-combats and victories.

Fifteen *C.200s* of 13° Gruppo strafed motor transports in the Gaer El Regem-Bir En Neghia area in three waves (15.20-16.40). Serg.Magg. Giuseppe Allevot (78ª Sq., M.M.8300) was shot down by anti-aircraft fire and killed.

I) At 17.15, nine *Bostons* of 12 SAAF were off again. Ten *Tomahawks* of 4 SAAF were close cover (17.30-18.45), four *Kittyhawks* of 2 SAAF (17.25-18.15) were top cover (8000 feet), and two were medium (7000 feet). Two *Tomahawks* of 5 SAAF were also a part of the escort (17.25-18.25).

The *Kittyhawks* of 2 SAAF were attacked by four *Bf.109s*, which were escorting six *Stukas*, at about 18.00 just before and just after the *Bostons* bombed enemy vehicles around Knightsbridge.

Maj. Human (AL186 DB-G):

> "...saw a 109F attacking from above at a quarter stern. I started a medium turn to the right, which was converted into a steep climbing turn as he got within range. As soon as he passed underneath me I whipped round to the left and got in a good burst as he tried to turn right towards me. I saw him flick on his back....the machine hit the ground. .50: 100."

Lt. Allen (AK975 DB-O) dropped out of the formation after losing control of the plane. Once he regained it, he flew over enemy lines and caught a Ju.52 parked on the ground and strafed it (.50- 200).

At 18.00, Lt. Saunders (5 SAAF, AM495 GL-T) was shot down and taken prisoner. Simultaneously Lt. Burdon landed because of engine trouble.

4 SAAF notes that in the outward flight, they came across a formation of *Ju.87s* that disposed of its bombs right over its own troops. Then, it headed back home followed by its escort. The South African pilots saw a *Bf.109*, a *Kittyhawk,* and a *Tomahawk* of 5 SAAF coming down out of control. Two bombers were holed by intense anti-aircraft fire.

At 16.20, four planes of II./JG 27 were on a freelance. Oblt. Boerngen of 5./JG 27 claimed a *P-40* south-east of Fort Acroma (17.05).

J) Three *Kittyhawks* of 450 Squadron (17.45-18.30) along with three of 3 RAAF and three of 250 Squadron escorted four fighter-bombers of 112 Squadron.

As the formation was approaching the target (375415), two *Bf.109s* attacked it: the aircraft of 112 Squadron jettisoned their bombs and turned home covered by part of the escort. F.Sgts McBurnie (AL206) and Nursey (AL200) of 450 Squadron engaged the attackers without result. The former, flying low to the ground, was then shot down and crash-landed seventeen miles south of Gambut, receiving sligh injuries. He then got out of the plane while the *Bf.109* was strafing it (Cat.III). Nursey went missing.

250 Squadron reported the attack of three *Bf.109s* that were coming out of the sun; Sgt. Troke (AK884) fired a burst with no results.

At 16.25, six *Bf.109s* of I./JG 27 were off to escort *Stukas*. They engaged enemy fighters and claimed two:

Lt. von Lieres u. Wilkau (2./JG 27), *P-40*, 30 km east of El Adem (17.02);
and Hptm. Maack (2./JG 27), *Kittyhawk*, east of Sidi Rezegh (17.08).

Two other *Bf.109s* crash-landed during the day: Fw. Hillgruber's plane (7./JG 27) belly-landed south of Tmimi because of engine failure; *Bf.109 F-4/Trop* 8736 (9./JG 27) force-landed east of Harmat (100%) but it is not known why; it cannot be ruled out that in one or both cases this was due to enemy action.

C.202 of 81ª Sq. (Archivio di Stato)

At 17.45, P.O. Rawlingson (208 Squadron) was detailed for a photographic reconnaissance: he was engaged by a *Bf.109* and had a chance to fire a four or five second burst at him: no claims were submitted and no damages were sustained.

Night of 30-31

K) Serg. Host scrambled on a *CR.42*: he engaged enemy bombers in air-combat observing hits on one of them.
On the 29th at Martuba, Ten. Talamini and Serg. Magg. Host (80ª Sq., 17° Gruppo) formed a section of night fighters mounted on *CR.42s* received from 3° Gruppo, which was transferred back to Italy.

Two pilots of 73 Squadron who were on night intruder patrols with their *Hurricanes* did not return: Sgt. Atherly (MB975) got lost but safely force-landed; Sgt. Barrie (BM388, 3.15) lost his life.

DATE	AXIS TIME	CLAIMS COMM.			CLAIMS GER.			CLAIMS ITA.			CASUALTIES COMM.		CASUALTIES GER.		CASUALTIES ITA.		UNITS INVOLVED
		S	P	D	S	P	D	S	P	M	S	D	S	D	S	D	
26	A 5.55-6.45	1B		1B	1B						1A						3 RAAF, 33 Sqn, Ju.88?, Bf.109s?
	B 13.00-14.00				1A						1A			1A			5./JG 27, 112, 450 Sqn
	C 14.20-15.30		1A								1A						260, I/JG 27?
	D 20.45-22.14	2B		1B										2B			73 Sqn, Ju.88s?
27	A 6.10-7.20	1A	2A	1A	1A			6A	3A		3A					2A	"6°Gr, 17°Gr; 6./JG 27; 2 SAAF, 229 Sqn"
	B 8.10-10.20	2A2 1A		3A2 3A	5A	4A					2A	1A	2A2				"ZG 26, III/JG 53; 5 SAAF, 4 SAAF Sqn"
	C 14.15-15.50				1A						1A						I/JG 27, 112 Sqn
	D 14.25-15.33	1A									1A		1A				II/JG 27, 450 Sqn
	E 16.35-17.20								3A	8A	1A					1A	17° Gr, 5 SAAF
	F 16.40-17.10						2A				1A						II/JG 27, 3 RAAF Sqn
	G 17.15-18.20	1Bs		1Bs 1A													274 Sqn, St.G 3, Bf.109?
28	A 8.45-8.46						2A										II/JG 27,?
	B 9.30-11.20						1A				1A						I/JG 27, 80 Sqn
	C 9.45-11.25	1A						1A					1A			1A	4(H)/12, 10° Gr, 5 SAAF Sqn
	D 10.25-11.35							1B	1B								6° Gr, 12 SAAF Sqn?
	E 10.50-11.40			1A													260 Sqn., Bf.109s?
	F 11.35-13.00	2A		1A				2,5A		4A	1A		1A				6° Gr, II/JG 27, 12, 24 SAAF, 250, 450 Sqn
	G 13.30-14.30						1A										III/JG 27, ?
	H 13.25-15.07						2A				1A		2A				II/JG 27, 33 Sqn
	I 14.35-15.20		1A											1A			8° Gr, 40 SAAF Sqn

DATE	AXIS TIME	CLAIMS COMM			CLAIMS GER			CLAIMS ITA			CASUALTIES COMM		CASUALTIES GER		CASUALTIES ITA		UNITS INVOLVED
		S	P	D	S	P	D	S	P	M	S	D	S	D	S	D	
28	J 15.20-16.25				1A						1A						5 SAAF, II/JG 27
	K 22.00-5.30	1B		4B													73 Sqn, German night bombers
29	A 6.10-6.30				3A						5A						I/JG 27, III/JG 53, 80, 2 SAAF Sqn
	B 7.02-8.12	2Bs 1A			3A						3A		2Bs 1A				I/JG 27, II/JG 27, II/St.G 3, 450 Sqn
	C 14.40-16.05	1A		4A				3A	2A	7A	1A			1A			9° Gr, 5 SAAF
	D 19.35-20.52	1A2			1B						1B						7/ZG 26, 24 SAAF Sqn
30	A 5.33-6.05				1A						1A						I/JG 27, 250 Sqn
	B 9.50-11.05	1A						4A			1A			1A			17° Gr, 2 SAAF Sqn.
	C 11.05-12.00				1A		1A						2A				I/JG 27, 250, 450, 40 SAAF Sqn
	D 13.50-14.09				1A	4A					4A						I/JG 27, III/JG 53?, 12 SAAF, 260, 2 SAAF Sqn
	E 14.25-14.58		1A		3A												I/JG 27, III/JG 53?, 24 SAAF, 4 SAAF, 5 SAAF Sqn
	F 14.40-16.05			2A				4A		4A	4A	1A		1A			6°, 3 RAAF, 250 Sqn. 450, 40 SAAF Sqn
	G 15.40-16.18				4A												II/JG 27, 274 Sqn?
	H 16.17-?				1A												III/JG 53, 274 Sqn?
	I 16.20-17.05	1A			1A						1A						II/JG 27, 2, 5 Sqn
	J 16.25-17.08				2A						2A						I/JG 27, 112, 250, 450
	K 2.30-4.15									3B							17° Gr,?
	TOT	4B 3Bs 3A2 10A			2B 41A			1B 19A			1B 36A		2B 2Bs 2A2 3A		4A		

LEGENDA

S - SHOT DOWN   P - PROBABLE   D - DAMAGED   M - MACHINE GUNNED

A - SINGLE ENGINE FIGHTER   A2 - TWIN ENGINE FIGHTER   B - BOMBER   Bs - STUKA   T - OTHER TYPES

Chapter 5
'THE CAULDRON' AND BIR HAKEIM (31 May-10 June)

The supply situation of Rommel's army improved because a second link-up was formed with elements of the Italian X Corps which were clearing two routes through the minefields from the west. In the early morning, the Commonwealth positions at Sidi Muftah were attacked. After heavy fighting, the British 150th Infantry Brigade, with a part of the 1st Army Tank Brigade, surrendered. Heavy losses were also sustained by the Trieste Division.

On the night of June 1st, the 90th Light Afrika and Trieste Divisions were sent south to renew the attack on Bir Hakeim. Once again the assault failed: the struggle to reduce the box at Bir Hakeim would continue for another ten days.

On the 2nd of June, considerable losses were inflicted on the 4th Armoured Brigade by the 21th Panzer Division.

Ritchie finally led the Eighth Army on an attack of the Axis positions entrenched in 'The Cauldron.' At 2.00 on June 5th, 'Operation Aberdeen' began, but it seems that the Axis armoured forces had been considerably underestimated.

The heavy artillery fire was not well aimed because the Ariete Division's positions had been moved slightly back. The 9th and 10th Indian Brigades along with the 4th Royal Tank Brigade were followed by the 22nd Armoured Brigade, attacking from the east. The 32nd Army Tank Brigade attacked from the north.

All of the attacks were stopped by heavy anti-tank artillery fire. The 32nd Army Tank Brigade lost fifty of their seventy tanks. It was then that the 21st and 15th Panzer Divisions went on the counterattack: the former to the north against the Indian Brigades and the 22nd Armoured Brigade, the latter to the south overrunning the Headquarters of the 5th Indian Division and 7th Armoured Division. The battle was lost: the 8th Army withdrew, covered by the 2nd, 4th, and the remains of the 22nd Armoured Brigades. The latter had lost sixty tanks.

Meanwhile, the 7th Motor Brigade and the 29th Indian Infantry Brigade were harassing the Axis lines of communication.

On the 8th, another strong attack of the 4th Armoured Brigade against the Ariete Division's positions did not have success.

At this point, attention was concentrated on Bir Hakeim and the defences were finally cracked on

SAAF Tomahawk; "Kom terug","Come back" (Bouwer)

June 10th. The French troops were ordered to evacuate during the night; about 2,700 out of the original garrison of 3,600 were able to withdraw through gaps in the line.

And so, during this period most air battles took place over Bir Hakeim: German bombers pounded the stronghold; the Commonwealth fighter units exacted a heavy toll on them in the first period, mainly caused by the insufficient protection provided by the German escort.

After a few days, Axis fighters gained air superiority over Bir Hakeim and air attacks took place without any more losses.

31 May

A) Seven planes of 4 and 6./JG 27 took off (5.40) to escort *Stukas* (included III./St.G. 3: 5.25-6.25) to attack enemy tanks 20 km S of Acroma. After the bombing and on the way back south-west of Acroma, they clashed with five *Hurricanes*. Eleven *P-40s* entered the fight shortly afterwards. Four enemy fighters were claimed by the Schwarm of 4./JG 27:

Oblt. Vögl (2), SW of Fort Acroma (6.15); 2 km NE of Mteifel El Chebir, 2000 m (6.20);
Fw. Stigler, SW of Fort Acroma (6.23);
and Fw. Heidel, W of Acroma, 1700 m (6.24).

Further, all of the aircraft of 6./JG 27 were shot down. Three of the unit's most experienced pilots came down with them: Oblt. Fluder (C.O.), Ofwb. Erich Krenzke, and Fw. Gromotka; this was a great blow. Later it turned out that Fluder (*Bf.109* W.Nr. 8660 ge.3+, 100%) had been killed, while Krenzke (*Bf.109* W.Nr. 8774 ge.9+, 100%), uninjured, was made prisoner. Gromotka (*Bf.109* W.Nr. 8548 ge.4+, 100%) was luckier and came down on friendly territory, able to report back to Tmimi the next day.

Eleven *Tomahawks* of 5 SAAF were on a free sweep over Gazala-Bir Hakeim (6.25-7.50). The Commonwealth pilots had been informed of both the approach of bandits and that *Stukas* were bombing Acroma. And so, at 6.55 and at an altitude of 10000 feet, they turned their planes east. They met with ten *Ju.87s* protected by twelve *Bf.109s* and *C.202s* (there are major doubts about this, however). Four of these planes were close cover, four more 2000 feet above as medium, and another four 3000 feet further above as top cover. The latter were at 10000 feet, the same level as the *Tomahawks*. Major Frost (AM385, GL-W, .50-400, .303-380) ordered Blue Flight to attack the top cover and Red Flight the medium cover. He himself attacked the bombers with his flight of three. Frost and Lt. Morgan (AN354, GL-X; .50-40, .303-160) fired at the rear *Stuka* from astern: the aircraft glided away and was claimed a probable victory. Frost then warded off a *Bf.109* before he and Lt. Sommerville (AN431 GL-S; .50-120, .303-180) attacked a lagging *Stuka* and damaged it. 2/Lt. Martin (AM401 GL-I, Blue 4) banked in behind a *Bf.109* at the same altitude, firing from 300 yards and then following him in a steep dive; at 200 yards he fired two more bursts, seeing pieces falling off from the starboard wing and yellow-brown smoke coming from the wing root. Then he cleared his tail, losing sight of it (a probable victory was claimed; .50-220, .303-1200). Capt. Duncan (AK523 GL-R) shot down a *Bf.109* while Hewitson attacked another without results. At 7.10 the enemy broke away (total rounds: .50-2420, .303-8010).

It seems more likely that there were some other *Messerschmitts* escorting *Stukas*, as 5 SAAF estimated; seven would have been too few.

6./JG 27 was probably top cover, clashing with the Blue Section; Duncan and Martin claimed to

have made victims of two of them. 4./JG 27 was probably medium or close cover.
The Germans certainly suffered heavy losses, but nevertheless the *Stukas* did not sustain considerable damage. Therefore it is possible that in some way the three pilots sacrificed themselves to protect the *Stukas*.
Oblt. Sinner took over command of 6./JG 27.

B) Twelve *Bf.109s* of I./JG 27 (7.00-8.00) and III./JG 53 were the escort for twelve *Ju.87s* heading for Bir El Harmat (6.58). They encountered some *P-40s* and claimed to have shot down ten:
Fw. Steinhausen (1./JG 27) (2) N of Bir Hakeim (7.25, 7.35);
Marseille (3), 5 km W of Bir El Harmat (7.26); 8 km W of Bir El Harmat (7.28); 10 km SW of Fort Acroma (7.34);
Ofw. Mentnich (3./JG 27), W of Bir El Harmat (7.30);
Lt. von Lieres u. Wilkau (2./JG 27), SW of Fort Acroma (7.32);
Lt. Müller (8./JG 53) (2), (7.25); 10 km SSW of Tobruk, 10 m (7.35);
and Hptm. Belser (8./JG 53, 7.42).

Marseille, the star of Africa (Gentilli)

Twelve *Tomahawks* of 4 SAAF scrambled to head for Gazala (7.50-8.50) where they intercepted twelve *Ju.87s* together with twelve *Bf.109s* and *Macchis*; they claimed to have shot down two *Ju.87s*, probably a *Ju.87* and a *Bf.109*, as well as to have damaged a *C.202*.
The SAAF formation was divided into three sections, one of which (Lt. Murray) was top cover.
Major Moodie attacked the *Stukas* but smoke from his guns entered his cockpit, and so he had to break off from the fight.
Capt. Bayly (AN242 KJ-P) damaged a *Ju.87* but his plane was hit on the supercharger and he therefore had to crash-land.
Lt. Murray (AH988 KJ-Q) engaged an enemy aircraft which was reported to be a *Macchi*. It was climbing up from the *Stukas* with five others. Murray damaged it with a full deflection shot and then he engaged a second enemy aircraft. Two other pilots of his section were engaged.
Lt. Lane (AN248 KJ-K) was flying at an altitude of 11000 feet 25 miles south of Gazala at 8.20:

"EA reported 2 o'clock below. Flew straight at top cover. There appeared to be more than 10 109s and Macchi 202s. I mixed with these … Fired a burst at an enemy fighter (2 secs, at approx 200 yards), avoided several and attacked a Macchi 202 from above and behind. I flicked as for a spin while firing and tightening a turn. Recovered immediately but was diving vertically. I smelled glycol and could see no Stukas, so flew back along the ground..."

Lt. Hankok (AH914 KJ-T), Lt. Jackson (AK509), and 2/Lt.Marillier (AN360) were shot down. Only Hankok returned. Lt. Woodliffe (AM406) was wounded but returned.
These pilots complained that their formation wasn't large enough for a mission of the type and that they were against better performing planes than theirs. Doubtless a more numerous cover would have led to fewer losses.

4 SAAF Squadron Tomahawk (Bouwer)

This action was identical to the previous one but had much different results. In fact, 4 SAAF suffered heavy losses, even if these were half of those claimed. However, they were dealing with the top German pilots. This time the Allied pilots were able to submit claims of *Stukas* shot down. This indicates that they would have been protected less effectively than in the previous action.
Two *Ju.87s* were shot by enemy fighters during the day over El Adem: Uffz. Kretschmar (I./St.G.3) was KIA; Uffz. Daminger (1./St.G.3, *Ju.87 R-4/Trop* W.Nr. 6230) crash landed but returned safely. They match the claims, but it possible that one them was shot down by 260 Squadron later in the day.
Finally it should be noted that the South African pilots almost systematically reported the presence of *Macchis* together with *Bf.109s*. This indicates how difficult it was to tell the difference between the two models.

C) S.Ten. Bagnoli (82ª Sq., 17° Gruppo) was late in leaving to escort *CR.42s* of 50° Stormo on an attack on enemy armoured vehicles at Bir Harmat (10.50-11.50). He was separated from the formation when he spotted and attacked a patrol of five *P-40s*, hitting two of them (160 rounds). No confirmation has been found for this action.

D) Twelve planes of 260 Squadron (13.15-14.35) were the escort for six *Bostons* of 24 SAAF (13.15) on an attack on Italian troops retreating in the Segnali area. Six aircraft of 2 SAAF Squadron were medium cover (13.15-14.35) and had probably witnessed the clashes from a distance.

The *Kittyhawks* of 260 Squadron were attacked by four *Bf.109s* on the way out and back. Sgt. Veysey was hit and was seen gliding towards the ground sixteen miles south of Knightsbridge; unfortunately he landed in a minefield and was killed. Sgt. Sheppard's plane was hit in the oleo-system and crashed upon landing. Hindle was shot up (Cat.I). Later they ran into eight *Ju.87s*: one was shot down, two were claimed probables and a fourth was damaged, all by Waddy. It is possible they shot down one of Stukas noted in the clash with 4 SAAF.
6° Gruppo was escorting Stukas and CR.42s, nonetheless, they did not mention encounters with the enemy.

Five *CR.42s* of 50° Stormo bombed and strafed south west of Acroma (13.15-15.15): Serg. Facchini (387ª Sq.) was hit at the fuel tank valve and force-landed within Axis lines. The plane was repaired on the spot and returned.

Three *Tomahawks* of 4 SAAF along with eight of 5 SAAF were the escort on a reconnaissance mission (16.15-17.50): they clashed with three *Bf.109s* without any visible results.

E) Cap. Viglione led nine planes of 9° Gruppo (seven of 96ª Sq. and two of 97ª Sq.) on a free sweep over Bir El Harmat-Bir Hakeim (17.15-18.25). It was over Bir El Harmat that about twenty enemy aircraft split between *Spitfires*, *Hurricanes,* and *P-40s* were spotted around 17.40. They were attacking *Stukas* after they had dropped their bombs. The *Macchis* intervened and engaged the enemy in a violent air-combat so that the *Stukas* were disengaged. The Italian pilots were credited with the destruction of a Spitfire, a *P-40*, and two *Hurricanes* in addition to two *P-40s* and two *Hurricanes* as probables. Others were fired at:
Ten. Annoni (96ª Sq.) shot down a *P-40*;
Cap. Viglione (96ª Sq.) probably shot down a *Hurricane* and fired at two.

C.202 of 4° St. and Stuka (Gentilli)

The remaining pilots were credited with the other three fighters shot down and three probable victories (total rounds: 1050).

Informations on German side are very scarce: three *Ju.87s* attacked motor vehicles over Acroma (17.05-18.30) and one was lost (possibly Uffz. Krieger, KIA, 3./St.G.3, *R-2/Trop* W.Nr. 5995, S7 + GL, shot down in the area).

Eighteen *Ju.87* and ten *Bf.110s* attacked concentrations of enemy vehicles between Acroma - Tobruk and Hakeim stronghold (OBS). 2./JG 27 escorted Stukas over Acroma (17.47-19.00).

Ten *Hurricane IICs* of 33 Squadron (probably top cover) together with five others of 274 Squadron were on a free sweep between Acroma, El Adem, and Bir Hakeim (18.00-19.25). They came across a formation of fifteen *Ju.87s* and at least twelve *Bf.109s*. 274 Squadron attacked the *Stukas*; the *Hurricanes* were in their turn attacked by *Bf.109s*: Sgt. Bruckshaw damaged a *Stuka* while P.O. Ismay was shot down and lost his life. In his turn, 33 Squadron was attacked by the escort and Sgt. Swan claimed a *Bf.109* damaged while P.O. Woods' *Hurricane* was slightly damaged. It is not clear if the *Stuka* had been shot down by Bruckshaw or by anti-aircraft fire.

F) Eighteen *Ju.87s* and ten *Bf.110s* attacked motor vehicles in the Acroma-Tobruk-Bir Hakeim area (17.30-19.45, OBS); twelve *Bf.109s* of II./JG 27 (18.38-19.38) and four of III./JG 53 were the escort.

Enemy planes were encountered and five *P-40s* were claimed shot down:
Oblt. Schulz (Stab II./JG 27) (2), 20 km SE of El Adem, 500 m (18.57); 15 km SW of El Adem (19.00);
Major Gerlitz (Stab III./JG 53), El Adem, 1000 m (19.08);
Oblt. Pufahl (7./JG 53), (18.50);
and Lt. Harder (7./JG 53), (18.52).
On his return flight, Schulz would also have damaged a *P-40* that was attacking a *Bf.110*.

The clash that took place was one of the most demanding actions of the Commonwealth fighters.

239 Wing (24 planes) and 233 Wing (26 planes) together, under the command of W.C. Beresford, were sent to chase Rommel. They consisted of all of the available planes of as many as eight squadrons.

Four *Kittybombers* of 3 RAAF and eight of 112 Squadron (18.45-20.15) were off to attack targets at pin-point 375415; ten *Kittyhawks* of 450 Squadron were top cover and three of 250 Squadron were medium cover. Three aircraft of 450 Squadron returned because of engine trouble while two others did not even take off; also, one of 250 Squadron had returned earlier.

The large number of planes of 450 Squadron that returned ahead of time because of engine trouble would seem to indicate that the efficiency of the aircraft was starting to decline.

The whole of 233 Wing provided the rest of the escort for the *Kittybombers* (eight *Kittyhawks* of 2 SAAF, 19.25-20.30; four *Tomahawks* of 4 SAAF; eight *Tomahawks* of 5 SAAF; six *Kittyhawks* of 260). It is probable that such a mass of fighters was subdivided into more formations, even if they were adjoining ones.

Suddenly 450 Squadron, acting as top cover of a main formation of twenty-four Kitties and Tommies at 6000 feet, was ordered to return to base. But then the order was changed for it to join the formation of 233 Wing. About 10 miles west of El Adem, they saw four *Kittyhawks* 1000 feet above (perhaps the four aircraft of 4 SAAF) being attacked by two enemy aircraft diving on them.

A Kittyhawk and the usual dust cloud (Aviation Heritage Museum of Western Australia)

The leader did a turnabout and pulled up with another aircraft to attack the two enemy aircraft. Sgt. Dyson (AL170) also attacked three times but without result. One *Kittyhawk* was seen to go down. Sgt. Lindsay (AL190) destroyed a *Bf.109* and then his plane was set on fire. Lt. Thomson (AK787) went missing while Sgt. Law (AK897) force-landed 25 miles south-west of El Adem due to engine trouble.

3 RAAF proceeded to bomb the target and one aircraft was hit by anti-aircraft fire. P.O. Mitchell (112 Squadron, AK999) was shot down at 19.45. He was probably also a victim of anti-aircraft fire because in this confused combat, losses were much greater than claims and only 450 Squadron (out of the entire Wing) reported air combats.

2 SAAF was top cover with 260 Squadron when ten *Bf.109s* and *C.202s* were encountered (19.55).

Lt. de Waal (2 SAAF, AL176) was shot up and crashed upon landing (CAT.II).

Capt. Smith: *"Ran into Macchis, 109s W of El Adem; shambles! Got in a good poop at a Macchi from abeam – no time to see any results."*

260 Squadron damaged a *Bf.109* but F.Lt. Hindle went missing after he had been seen in combat with four *Bf.109s*. Meanwhile, F.Sgt. Carlisle was hit and crashed upon landing (Cat.II).

4 SAAF reported the attack of more than fifteen *Bf.109s*; Capt. Copeland was shot down but returned.

5 SAAF reported the attack of more than twelve *Bf.109s* and *C.202s* 20 miles south-west of El Adem.

The engine of Lt. Grobler's plane cut out during the engagement and so he returned home.

Lt. Thorhill-Cook (AM420? GL-L) was flying at 5000 feet south west of El Adem at 20.00:

"Observed a number of EA believed no less than 12 about 10000' flying in open line abreast. Lost sight of them, when someone shouted 'Duck'. All our AC seemed to Duck. The escort was broken up and our machines began milling with 109s diving down amongst them. I saw a 109F on the tail of another of our AC. I closed with him and gave him a short burst from a fine quarter. My shots seemed to go into the engine. I noticed fairly thick black and whitish smoke come down from the engine and the machine seemed to spiral down at a low speed. I could not see if he went in. One 109 probably destroyed. .50-100, .303 340"

Maj. Duncan (AK523 GL-R) destroyed a *Bf.109* and then crashed about 10 miles south west of El Adem (20.00). He was probably shot down, and on the day of his promotion.
2/Lt. Martin (AM401 GL-I) damaged a *Bf.109* (1420 rds).
Maj. Frost (AM385 GL-W) shared a *Stuka* probably destroyed with Lt. Morgan (AN354 GL-X) and a second one damaged with Lt. Sommerville (AN 431 GL-S).
The undercarriage of Morgan's plane collapsed upon landing at 19.40.
Overall, the claims were 2 *Bf.109* destroyed, one probable and 2 damaged; one *Ju.87* probable and one damaged.
2 SAAF reported:

"General Rommel was supposed to have landed in the forward areas. The whole Wing was scrambled to escort Kittybombers who were to bomb the area he was supposed to be in. The show turned out to be a shambles as the order was given at such short notice but none of the Squadrons knew exactly what their duty was. We were attacked by 109's, a most unsatisfactory defensive circle was formed and five aircraft from the Wing were shot down. All pilots from this Squadron returned safely from this operation."

The accounts are rather critical about the haphazard way in which the mission was planned and conducted. It was considered a miracle that only five aircraft were lost. Perhaps, however, this criticism is excessive as the action had probably been ordered at the last moment. Further, it should be underlined that very rarely did more than one wing operate together. Nevertheless, the losses were heavy and in the end as many as eight planes were put out of action. The clash must have taken place when the *Stukas* were already on their way back because most of the Commonwealth fighter pilots just limited themselves to spotting them.
Given the times, the action would not have involved the Italian plane., Nevertheless, even if there is an error in those times, all other elements lead to the conclusion that a single clash took place involving also the *Macchis* and the *Hurricanes*.

Serg. Magg. Ernesto Taddia on board *C.200*, M.M.8294, of 13° Gruppo crashed during a test flight and was killed.

Hudson V8997 of 459 RAAF Squadron crashed on the edge of L.G.40 with the loss of all seven members of the crew.

O.B.S. reported the loss of a single *Ju.87* during the day. In fact it seems that losses (100% damage) due to enemy action totalled to five. The two remaining were lost to anti-aircraft over El Adem: Fw. Kirner and Gefr. Mayer both KIA and belonging to I./St.G.3.

Night of 31-1

G) At 22.30, Ten. Talamini (80ª Sq., 17° Gruppo) scrambled on board a *CR.42* and intercepted a *Wellington*. He claimed to have shot it down after firing 350 rounds. The enemy plane was seen going ablaze upon hitting the ground. He then noticed three other enemy aircraft but because the guns were not working well he had to stop his chase.

Thirteen *Wellingtons* of 148 Squadron, which had taken off from A.L.G.106, were in action over Derna. F.O. Astell's and Sgt. Ross' aircraft did not return. The former had been shot down while the latter had had to land at L.G.05 due to the heavy punishment taken over Derna.

F.O. Astell and crew stated (*Wellington* II AD653R):

"...Whilst circuiting at about 0030 about 2 miles E. of L.G., height 3000', our AC was attacked by a single-engined monoplane [therefore more probably it should have been Talamini]. Crew did not see EA approach, who attacked them from starboard quarter and below. First indication crew had was that they saw tracers going through starboard wing. As a result of this attack, hydraulics rear turret and rudder control were U/S and a fire started in the fuselage somewhere near the bed. Captain jettisoned the balance of bombs and turned for home whilst the navigator was busy extinguishing the fire. About two minutes later when heading for Martuba, EA attacked a second time from starboard quarter and below, starting a second fire in starboard wing and in the engine nacelle, hit the starboard airscrew and the rear gunner ammunition tank setting it on fire. Hit the WO who was

Images of Wellington IC DV648 crash-landed (Archivio di Stato)

operating beam guns in leg with cannon shell and hit second pilot in right arm. By this time AC was losing height rapidly and Captain ordered crew to bale out. WO and rear gunner baled out of escape hatch, second pilot owing to his wounded condition had to have his parachute put on by navigator and baled out through the door. Just before second pilot baled out, EA attacked on the port quarter and two cannon shells exploded on instrument panel and pitot head shot off making instruments US. The navigator let front gunner out of his turret who baled out immediately but it is not certain if AC had sufficient height for his parachute to open. By this time AC was well alight from navigator's cabin backwards and on starboard wing. It was too late for captain and navigator to bale out and AC crash landed at 00.45 about 1.5 miles S of Martuba L.G.s. ..."

After having destroyed the IFF, they headed for home. F.O. Astell and Sgt. Mackintosh made it back while the rest of the crew was taken prisoner.

Also Serg.Magg. Host scrambled and engaged enemy bombers; he shot at three different aircraft, claiming hits on one.

A *Wellington* was also claimed by Oblt. Wehmeyer of 7./ZG 26 (23.10).
Considering the damage, Sgt. Ross' *Wellington* should have been victim of the latter.

Eight *Ju.88s* of I./KG 54 attacked enemy concentrations in the El Adem-Sidi Rezegh area (1.00-6.05); one aircraft went missing (Fw. Kirner, *A-4* W.Nr. 3678, B3-AH).

During night flying practice, a *Beaufort* of 39 Squadron crashed: two died and three were wounded.

1 June

On the first three days of June dust storms severely limited air operations, in particular on the Commonwealth side.

A) In the first scramble of the day from Edku, Lt. Pride (1 SAAF, Z5348 AX-M) damaged a *Ju.88* that emitted a cloud of white smoke. The attack took place at an altitude of 18000 feet, thirty miles north-west of Dikheila at 8.06 (.303: 75 Inc, 75 Ball, 180 AP).

B) Lt.s Le Roux (BE177) and Salmon (BG971) of 1 SAAF (from Port Said) were on patrol over a large tanker of 15000 tons (7.45-9.00) when a Savoia made a low level attack on it. A torpedo was released but passed between the stern of the large vessel and the bow of a smaller tanker, causing no damage. The two pilots immediately peeled off and attacked, getting in a few short bursts each. However, the enemy aircraft got away at an altitude of 50 feet; it was chased for five miles.

Lt. Pride's Hurricane IIB (AX-M Z5348) of 1 SAAF Sqn. (Bouwer)

While they were away, a second torpedo bomber nipped in on the unescorted ships but also in this case the torpedo passed below the ship, exploding beyond it.
It did not seem wise to chase the first torpedo bomber and therefore leaving the ships unprotected.

They were two *S.M.79* torpedo-bombers of 205ª Sq. (Rhodes) led by Ten. Cella that attacked a steamer at 7.35. They claimed a probable hit because they could not observe the results as they were being attacked by enemy fighters.

F.O. Brown (208 Squadron, *Hurricane* I V7821), who was on a reconnaissance mission, was engaged by four *Bf.109s* but returned unscathed (8.45-10.10).

C) At 16.20 (landing 18.00), four *Tomahawk* IIBs of 4 SAAF and six of 5 SAAF took off to escort *Kittybombers* over Knightsbridge. At 17.30, 5 SAAF sighted five *Bf.109s*, two of which were acting as top cover.
2/Lt. Golding reported (5 SAAF, AN468 GL-J) that he:

> "Sighted three Me.109Fs below and at least two above (17.05, 12000'). Climbed after top two but dropped back and rejoined formation. After this the Mes would not come in to fight and we spent some time circling in towards them. Sighted a109 about 1500 ft. below. Dived straight down to it. The pilot of the 109 took no action until I was well into my dive. He then flicked over and also went into a steep dive. I found myself right on his tail and gaining swiftly with the initial speed of my dive, I got in a short burst at about 250 yards and closing in to about 100 yards got in two more bursts. Each time I fired pieces flew off, and the last burst shot bits off his cockpit. At this stage my airspeed was over 400 mph. So I started pulling out, levelling out at about 200 ft above the ground. I tried to turn and had a quick look back seeing a big cloud of dust behind me. .50- 60, .303-200. One 109 destroyed, confirmed by Lt. Ironside."

On the way back, Lt. Murray (4 SAAF, AK998) was jumped by two *Bf.109s* and was shot up; he then crash-landed near El Adem.
Ofw. Stumpf, part of a Schwarm of 9./JG53, claimed to have shot down a plane at 16.30; it must have been Murray's. 5 SAAF could also have possibly come across the planes of this Schwarm. There is no corroboration for Golding's claim.

D) The *Spitfires* were on their first day of operational missions in North Africa. Two aircraft of 145 Squadron were top cover at 24000 feet for the *Hurricanes* of 274 and 33 Squadron, all on a free sweep in the El Adem-Hakeim area (17.35-18.25). This was a new pattern in the tactics of the RAF Wings. The high altitude-flying *Spitfires* would act as extra top cover to the traditional two squadrons of *Hurricanes* and they would cause problems to the opposite fighters' formations.
F.Lt. Sabourin (A326) and Sgt. James (L324) intercepted a *Ju.88* at a slightly higher altitude and left it with smoke pouring from one engine.
274 Squadron reported the attack by four *Bf.109s*, one of which was damaged by Sgt. Eagle.

Again German documents note only that 2./JG 27 was escorting Stukas over Mteifel El Kebir (17.03-17.58).

Five *C.200s* of 13° Gruppo attacked motor transports north-west of Mteilim (17.20-18.50). Serg.

Borgis (78ª Sq., M.M.5312) was hit by anti-aircraft fire and belly-landed in enemy territory. He was taken prisoner.

E) In the evening, six *Kittyhawks* of 3 RAAF Squadron (18.25-20.20) with five others of 112 Squadron acting as top cover (two had returned earlier) scrambled to intercept enemy aircraft. The formation, led by S.L. Barr, caught up with ten *Bf.109s*, four *Ju.88s,* and four *Bf.110s* 17 miles south-south-east of Gazala. 112 Squadron was first engaged by the escort (reported to be six), and then P.O. Edwards (AK907) and F.Lt. Leu (AK985) damaged one *Ju.88* each. However, P.O. Wilson (AL196) went missing and Edwards force-landed safely a few miles from El Adem at 20.15.

The Australians also engaged the enemy. Barr's section attacked the *Bf.110s* and Barr himself (AL178 CV-W) damaged one in a frontal quarter attack. He then delivered a diving attack from port quarter astern on a *Bf.109*, which caught fire, without attempting any evasive action (it was claimed as a probable victory). By then, Sgt. Neill 112 Squadron (AL148 CV-F) was able to fire three short bursts at the same aircraft about 50 feet below him, after avoiding a *Bf.109* with two complete climbing turns. He saw it hit the ground, smoke pouring from it.

P.O. Cowards (AK992 CV-V) dived on a *Bf.109* below him, claiming it badly damaged. He then evaded a second *Bf.109* that was attacking him. He saw a *Bf.109* crash-land at high speed.

Sgts. Finlayson (AK 745) and Boardman (AK818) each claimed a *Bf.109* damaged.

Sgt. Alderson (AK 729) was slightly wounded and the aircraft was Cat.II.

In total, 3 RAAF claimed two *Bf.109s* shot down, one *Bf.109* probable, two *Bf.109s,* and one *Bf.110* damaged.

The Australians had the impression that German fighters did not press home their attacks.

The German attack formation was composed of four *Bf.110s* of III./ZG 26 and four *Ju.88s* of I./KG 54; the escort was provided by *Bf.109s* of 3./JG 27 and III./JG 53. These claimed as many as five *P-40s* and a Spitfire shot down:

Fw. Pöttgen (3./JG 27), NW of Gadd El Ahmar (19.05);
Marseille, 20 km ENE of El Cheimar (19.15);
Lt. Hesse (7./JG 53, 18.35);
Lt. Stecher (7./JG 53, 18.55);
Lt. Klager (7./JG 53, 18.58);
Lt. Quaritsch (8./JG 53), Spitfire, Meitfel El Chebir, 1500 m (18.53). It was possibly during this clash that Lt. Quaritsch's plane (*Bf.109* W.Nr. 10134) was hit by Neill and shot down. The pilot managed to crash-land it behind the Axis lines. Three *Bf.110s* were shot down by anti-aircraft fire over Gazala with the loss of all of the crews: Lt. Wehmeyer (Staffelkapitän, C-5 W.Nr. 2233, 3U + HR), Oblt. Bittner (*F-2* W.Nr. 4548, 3U + US); Ofw. Otto Polenz (*F-2* W.Nr. 4570, 3U + BS).

Pöttgen, Marseille's wingman, finally made his first official claim in over 100 combat missions; up to that day he must have been too busy protecting his leader.

The OBS report would make us think that there had only been only four confirmed victories in this action: between 15.00 and 19.35, thirty-one *Bf.109s* were on a free sweep and a ground attack. Three *P-40s* were shot down and one more was forced to make an emergency landing.

During the day *Ju.87 D-3* W.Nr. 2365 (S7 + CM, II./St.G.3) was shot down by anti-aircraft over Gazala and the crew went missing (Uffz. Holler).

Two *Bf.109s* of Stab/J.G.27 were damaged by bombing: W.Nr. 8509 (50%); W.Nr. 10146 (10%). Several German aircraft were subjected to accidents suffering damage: *E-7* W.Nr. 1469 (4.(H)/12),Tmimi, 45%; *F-4/Trop* W.Nr. 7346 (I./JG 27), Martuba, 80%; *F-4/Trop* W.Nr. 10151 (I./JG 27), Tmimi, 30%; *F-4/Trop* W.Nr. 8731 (6./JG 27), Tmimi, 30%; *Ju.87 D-1* W.Nr. 2127 (III./St.G.3), Derna-Beda Littoria, 40%.

Night of 1-2

F) At 1.48, S.L. Ward of 73 Squadron attacked and damaged a *Ju.88* over Gasr El Arid. He saw the enemy aircraft against the moonlight and managed return fire (107 Ball, 53 HE/Inc).

'RAF Casualties Middle East' reported the loss of a *Hurricane*, two *Kittyhawks*, and a *Tomahawk*, besides the damaging of three *Kittyhawks*. Therefore, it appears that there was something missing concerning losses in the Commonwealth units' diaries.

2 June

Sgt. Glynn of 80 Squadron did not return from a reconnaissance mission over the sea in which he was searching for a *Wellington* (the case is not known) thirty miles north of Bardia (13.15-15.10).

Tomahawk workshop (Bouwer)

A) Two *Hurribombers* of 274 Squadron were off at 16.10 for a sortie over the Cauldron. F.Lt. Moriarty was attacked by three *Bf.109s* and was shot down over Gazala and killed. F.Sgt. was stuck in a sandstorm and had to force land, but returned with his plane the day after.
Moriarty must have been the victim of Ofw. Alfred Schulze of 4./JG 27 made his only claim for a shot down *P-40*, which occurred 5 km south-west of Ain El Gazala (16.22).

Hptm. von Kühlwetter (*Bf.110E-3* W.Nr. 4433, 4.(H)/12) was on a reconnaissance mission over Gazala (18.35-19.35) when he was hit by anti-aircraft fire. All crew went missing.

Night of 2-3

Four *Bostons* of 24 SAAF attacked Derna (3.20) and were aimed at by two night fighters, but they managed to get away.

3 June

A) Two *Bf.109s* of 5./JG 27 covered *Bf.110s* over Bir Hakeim (5.30). They were attacked by three enemy aircraft; Lt. Jenisch (W.Nr. 8677, 100%) was hit and crash-landed 15 km north-west of Bir Hakeim and was strafed on the ground but came away safely.

They ran into the ten *Hurricanes* of 33 Squadron while off on a reconnnaissance sweep North of Hakeim (6.40-7.35) reporting the encounter with 2 *Bf.109s* and one *Bf.110*. A *Hurricane*'s pilot attacked the twin-engined fighter but without observing results. Information is lacking but it can be presumed that Jenisch was shot down by the *Hurricanes*.

B) Cap. Giacomelli led a free sweep of eight *Macchis* of 6° Gruppo (four of 79ª Sq. and four of 81ª Sq.) over the Bir Hakeim-Bir El Harmat area (6.20-7.30).
A formation of enemy fighters that was heading towards Axis lines and estimated to be more than double the number of Italian aircraft was intercepted at an altitude of 4000 m to the south-west of El Adem at 6.45. It was attacked and made to flee; three *P-40s* were credited shot down, one probable, and as many as ten machine-gunned, two of which were damaged (1410 rounds):
Serg. Magg. Benati (79ª Sq.) shot down a *P-40* (110 rounds);
Cap. Baldini (81ª Sq.) shot down a *P-40*;
S.Ten Ganda (81ª Sq.) shot down a *P-40*;

Marseille back from a mission (Gentilli)

M.llo Baldelli (81ª Sq.) fired at three *P-40s*, hitting two of them;
Cap. Giacomelli (81ª Sq.) fired at three *P-40s*;
Ten. Cattaneo (79ª Sq.) fired at a *P-40* (200 rounds);
Serg. Magg. Paroli (79ª Sq.) fired at a *P-40* (60 rounds);
Serg. Saiani (79ª Sq.) fired at a *P-40* (62 rounds).
81ª Sq. expended 960 rounds.
The *Macchis* returned undamaged.

They must have clashed with nine *Tomahawks* of 4 SAAF (6.55-8.20) and ten others of 5 SAAF that had taken off to intercept *Ju.87s* above Bir Hakeim. The South Africans spotted at least fifteen enemy aircraft divided between *Bf.109s* and *Macchi C.202s* at an altitude of 8000 feet, but only one of them attacked, hitting and slightly damaging W.C. Beresford's aircraft (AM406?) at 7.45.

Cecil Golding of 5 SAAF (Le Roux)

Lt. Robottom (8000 feet) attacked a *Macchi* from quarter astern, firing two-second bursts: the enemy aircraft fell away and no results were observed (rounds: .50-250, .303-850).

Lt. McGregor (AK524, Cat.II) did not return. He had to make an emergency landing because his plane's engine seized after being hit (SAAF sources).

5 SAAF merely noted the encounter with fourteen *Bf.109s*; no results were observed.

C) Six *Bf.109s* of JG 27 (11.32-12.52) and six of III./JG 53 were escorting *Stukas* of 3./St.G.3 on an attack of Bir Hakeim. JG 27 engaged about fifteen *P-40s* while III./JG 53 engaged six *P-40s*. Ten enemy fighters were claimed shot down, six of them by Marseille alone:
Marseille (6) from 3 to 10 km west of Bir Hakeim (between 12.22 and 12.33);
Uffz. Gierster (5./JG 27), 10 km east of Bir Hakeim (12.23);
Lt. Klager (7./JG 53, 12.20);
and Hptm. Belser (8./JG 53) (2), (12.25 and 12.28).

During the day, OBS reported 95 sorties of *Stukas* over Bir Hakeim in 9 waves. Four bombers (*R-2/Trop*) were lost; Staffelkapitän Hptm. Spangenberg (2/St.G 3, W.Nr. 5967, S7 + FK) was shot down by flak over Gazala; the other three reportedly were shot down by enemy fighters during this mission over Bir Hakeim: Uffz. Nusswitz (missing, 1./St.G.3, W.Nr. 6015, S7 + OH); Uffz. Schneider (missing,1./St.G.3, W.Nr. 5869, S7 + HH); Lt. Deibel (prisoner, 3./St.G.3 W.Nr. 6666, S7 + FL).

Seven *Kittyhawks* of 2 SAAF (12.15-13.35), led by Maj. Human, were top cover for eight *Tomahawks* of 5 SAAF (12.15-14.45). One had returned earlier on a free sweep between El Adem, Bir Hakeim, and Gazala. W.C. Beresford led the formation. Two more aircraft of 5 SAAF had collided upon taking off because of reduced visibility owing to the sand being swept up by the planes (AK366 and AN431). 2 SAAF was assailed by two enemy planes coming through a gap in the clouds from an altitude of 11000 feet, five miles to the north-west of Bir Hakeim; they were identified as *C.202s*. A brief engagement followed and Lt. Mc Master (B) gave the enemy planes a good going over with several bursts, claiming one damaged (260 rounds).
But the formation was broken and the 5 SAAF planes proceeded without top cover. Some of the best Commonwealth pilots were a part of this formation.

The pilots of 5 SAAF spotted twelve *Ju.87s* while they were starting to bomb at an altitude of 7000 feet near Bir Hakeim at 13.15. They were escorted by twenty planes divided between *Bf.109s* and *C.202s* at an altitude of 8000 feet. The *Tomahawks* charged the *Stukas* but were in their turn attacked by the escorting fighters: a bloodbath followed with ten *Ju.87s* and a *Bf.109* claimed shot down against the loss of five of their own aircraft.
Capt. Botha (AK448 GL-H) attacked the *Stukas* and was credited with 3.5 of them destroyed (one shared with Beresford):

> "...My leader pulled away from me and when I caught up with him I saw him giving one burst. As nothing happened when the Stuka pulled away to the left I closed from quarter astern and gave him a good burst. He burst into flames and went down. I then picked up one on the left of the formation and gave him a burst and he went down in flames. I then looked behind and saw a 109 diving down to attack and I escaped by going underneath the Stukas. I pulled to the left and then went to the right to get behind them. I picked another, gave him a burst and he also went down in flames. The next one I closed in from underneath gave a squirt and pulled up. The pilot pulled his stick back and we nearly collided and I failed to see what happened to him. By this time the EA were very low and split up. I again pulled out to the left and up to gain height. This time I selected one in the centre. After giving him a second burst, smoke came out and he burst into flames. I then ran out of ammunition. Had to land on account of engine heating. Waited a bit and took off again. 0.50: 700, .303: 2000."

The Germans might have thought that his plane had been shot down as it landed in the desert. Botha was immediately awarded with a DFC.
Maj. Frost (AN247 GL-K) and Lt. Gaymans (AN345 GL-M) were credited with a *Ju.87* each.
W.C. Beresford was credited with 1.5 *Ju.87*.
2/Lt. Golding (AN468 GL-J) was hit after he had damaged a *Stuka* that went down smoking. His *Tomahawk* shuddered at the impact and the stick was yanked out of his hands. The rudder wires snapped and the oxygen bottle exploded. He crash-landed behind the *Ju.87* that he had just shot down. Soon afterwards, Capt. Morrison (AK421 GL-Z), his No.1, crashed near him and was followed thirty seconds later by Lt. Muir. Golding and Morrison ran to the burning *Stuka* and pulled the pilot out despite the wounds to their legs. Unfortunately, the gunner was already dead. Not long later, they saw another *Tomahawk* dive to the ground and explode, almost certainly Capt. Pare's (DFC) plane (AN384 GL-V). He was killed after having shot down a *Ju.87*.
Morrison shared a *Stuka* with another pilot.
Lt. Muir (AN262 GL-C) destroyed a *Stuka* and was then shot down, but ended up safe in hospital; 2/Lt. Martin (AM401 GL-I) was also shot down, but was safe.
One of the *Stukas* shot down was that of Lt. Hans Deibel of 3./St.G.3, who was able to bale out and was taken prisoner. However, his gunner, Willy Luberich, was killed.
Later, Deibel recounted his last mission (http://cecilgolding.yolasite.com): at mid-day they were above Bir Hakeim once again. They were expecting the usual strong defensive fire and were flying in squadron formation, carrying a 250 kg bomb and four 50 kg bombs under the wings. The heavier bomb had the 'Dinort-stick' screwed (to trigger the explosion one tenth of a second sooner, Oberst Dinort was Inspekteur of Stukaflieger).
Before diving there were several things to do: the dive brakes had to be lowered, the oil cooler closed, and the ignition switched off. Therefore Deibel pushed the plane forward and dived, but just as he was about to release the bombs, another plane moved from the right and almost in front

of him, smoking severely. It must have been hit because the pilot carried on diving, forcing Deibel to throw himself out of the way at the last moment. This made Deibel lag behind the formation, becoming an easy prey for fighters.

In fact, a *Tomahawk* came out of the sun towards them. At first Willy (his gunner) did not see it and shouted: "*Jäger links!*" But it was too late, and so when Diebl pulled the plane to the left, they flew straight into his fire burst. The rule was to turn towards the enemy, but in this case turning to the right would have meant remaining in the fighter's gun sight much longer. Therefore Diebl just crossed his flight path very briefly; unfortunately the burst was long enough to be deadly: after being hit with a crushing noise, flames came out from the right petrol tank, investing the instrument panel. Willy gave a terrible shout and Diebl could not hold the plane any longer because the flames from the engine were burning his face. Willy screamed once more, and all of a sudden it was quiet except for the wind whistling outside: he had been hit by the enemy's fire. Diebl's sleeves were burning as he hit the release button and pulled the safety rope off the roof and was torn from the plane by the slipstream. He landed in no man's land and was shot at by both the French and the Germans before being taken prisoner. Afterwards he met Golding.

Hans Deibl (Le Roux)

The stalking of 2 SAAF by the two presumed *C.202s* (it is difficult to determine if they were actually *Macchis*, for from what remains of the sparse documentation of 4° Stormo, it appears that there were actions but no encounters with the enemy) would have fatal consequences for 5 SAAF. It appears improbable that 5 SAAF would have dashed unconsciously against the *Stukas*, so it is thought that the South Africans were divided into two sections as usual, one of which should have been top cover. And yet, most South Africans made claims on the *Stukas*, and so it seems that they all attacked the *Stukas*, practically undisturbed in the first phase of the clash. However, the South African attack would have been extremely hazardous given the number of escorting *Messerschmitts*. At the same time, it is difficult to understand why the Germans did not manage to protect the bombers effectively. Everything would be much easier to explain if some other Commonwealth squadrons had participated together with 5 SAAF, but even this appears improbable seeing that there was already 2 SAAF.

It seems likely that the four *Stukas* lost have to be credited to 5 SAAF.

After this combat, Marseille achieved great fame; Pöttgen, his wingman, remembered:

> "All six of the British planes flew at an altitude of about 800 metres. I was flying behind Marseille, and had my work cut out covering him and at the same time counting the adversaries shot down by him and taking note of the places where they crashed. All the aircraft were shot down while he was banking. Marseille had an extraordinary sense and feeling and knew exactly when to press the trigger while turning. As soon as he opened fire, it just remained to watch the rounds hit the enemy plane. The hit marks started on the cowling and continued through the fuselage to end at the cockpit. For all six victories Marseille expended a total of only 10 rounds of 2 cm cannon and 360 rounds of MG 17."

Some authors noted that the victories were achieved while the *Tomahawks* were flying in a 'Lufbery.'

But it is clear enough that at least three of them were hit while they were intent on firing at *Stukas*. It has also been said that not all victories could be assigned to Marseille. This is certainly true, but it must be highlighted that this is not the only case in which only part of those victories can be corroborated.

D) Four *Spitfires* of 145 Squadron were on patrol (16.05-17.00). They were flying at 22500 feet when they spotted four *Bf.109*s far below at 15000 feet. The Spitfires dived on them and S.L. Overton managed to hit one of them with a five second burst. It cannot be excluded they ran into the Stuka's escort of 2./JG 27 (Hakeim, 14.55-15.42).

During the day a *Bf.110* (8./Z.G.26 F-2 W.Nr. 4562) was heavily damaged by anti-aircraft over Gazala (80%).

Night of 3-4

Wellington II Z8385 of 104 Squadron attacked the landing ground at Tmimi (22.45). On the way back, an engine failed, causing the aircraft to struggle back to L.G.121. It was unable to land at L.G.05 because it was under attack. Upon landing, the second engine also cut out and the aircraft crash-landed.

4 June

At about 6.00, P.O. Abram (39 Squadron, *Beaufort* N1024), while searching for an enemy convoy, was attacked by an aircraft believed to be a *C.200* (33° 42' N, 21° 53' E). The torpedo-bomber took evasive action and returned fire before heading back to Sidi Barrani.
    The attacking AC was not indeed a fighter but another torpedo-bomber: the *S.M.79* of Ten. De Michelis (174ª Sq.) on the way to escort Convoy *Giuliani*. At 5.15, flying at low height (300 m), a *Beaufort* was sighted and pursued for 15 minutes. It was shot at and hit with the front 12.7 fixed machine gun, but without observable results. The convoy was reported stopped with *Giuliani* low on the stern.

Finally, the weather improved and so began another day of heavy air activity over the French bastion of Bir Hakeim. In the morning there were two German bombardments.
The first was the work of ten *Stukas* of II./St.G 3 (6.30-8.08) with the escort of I./JG 27 (6.49-8.15). Lt. Hübel (II./St.G.3, *Ju.87 D-1* W.Nr. 2465, S7 + KM) was shot down by anti-aircraft fire and went missing with his gunner.
A) The second followed soon afterwards: twelve *Ju.87*s of I./St.G 3 attacked to the north of Bir Hakeim (7.05-8.45) (OBS). The escort should have consisted of about a dozen planes of II./JG 27, seeing that the practice was to have the same number of fighters as bombers. The *Messerschmitts* would have run into eight *P-40s*, claiming two shot down:
Oblt. Rödel (Stab II./JG 27), 3 km SE of Bir Hakeim, 4500 m (8.15);
and Ofhr. Kientsch (Stab II./JG 27), 10 km SW of Mteifel Chebir (8.20).
And yet, as many as five *Ju.87s* were lost to enemy fighters. Gruppenkommandeur Hptm. Eppen

C.202 M.M.7798 of 90ª Sq., Sicily in May (Archivio di Stato)

(I./St.G.3, *R-2* W.Nr. 6146, S7 + AB, Bir Hakeim) lost his life with his gunner; Uffz. Horst (1./St.G.3, *R-2/Trop* W.Nr. 6163, S7 + NH, Bir Hakeim) survived; Lt. Herritsch (2./St.G.3, *R-4/Trop* W.Nr. 6306, S7 + GK); *Ju.87 R-4* W.Nr. 6205 (2./St.G.3, 60%) crashed at Derna-South due to battle damage, the gunner lost his life; Uffz. Brandt (3./St.G.3, *R-2* W.Nr. 6043) was shot down over Gadda El Ahmir and lost his life. *Ju.87 R-2*, a sixth *Ju.87 R-2* of I./St.G.3 was damaged (10%) and force landed at Tmimi.

Magg. Maddalena led a formation of nine *Macchis* of 10° Gruppo (three from each Squadriglia) on a free sweep over Bir Hakeim (7.45-8.50). Presumably this was in combination with the attack of the *Stukas*. The formation must have consisted of two sections: one at 3500 metres led by Maddalena himself and one as top cover at 4000 metres, led by Ten. Mandolini (91ª Sq.). At 8.05, they were over the target when they spotted about fifteen *P-40s* 200 metres further down. Their pilots had apparently been unaware of their presence and so the *Macchis* dived on them. The pilots of 91ª Sq. clashed with seven *P-40s*. In total the Italian pilots were credited with five enemy planes shot down, three probable victories, and seven machine-gunned (2550 rounds fired):
Ten. Mandolini (91ª Sq.) shot down two *P-40s* and fired at two more (550 rounds);
Ten. Bondi (91ª Sq.) shot down a *P-40*;
M.llo Bignami (84ª Sq.) shot down a *P-40*;
Cap. Piccolomini (90ª Sq.) probably shot down a *P-40* and fired at two more;
S.Ten. Bertolaso (91ª Sq.) probably shot down a *P-40* (110 rounds);
Serg. Barbera (84ª Sq.) probably shot down a *P-40* and fired at three more;
Maddalena fired at three *P-40s*.
A *Macchi* returned hit.
Bertolaso remembered after the war:

> "The 4th of June, finally, if we can say this, I had my baptism of fire. I was with Mandolini and Bondi, and we got ready to go on the by then usual free sweep over the front. We were flying at 6,000 metres

and after flying around the area a bit, Mandolini told us to be ready. I looked around and in the distance I saw a certain number of black dots as they got nearer they seemed more and more distinct. They showed their tails to us and the shapes appeared similar to the Messerschmitt 109s with which I had done mock fighting in Sicily... Mandolini without much ado turned and left me there alone. My first thought was that of finding my companions but while I was roaming about, I saw three aircraft behind me and I had the clear impression that I had had it. I immediately recognized the red noses of the British Spitfires and I had no doubt that in the space of a few moments they would fire. I then tried to get clear and with some very tight turns, I managed to lose sight of them. In next to no time, while I still didn't really know what to do, I saw some P-40s lower down making a circuit. As I had the advantage of altitude, I decided without much conviction to take aim and fired at two of them, then sneaking off towards Martuba. When I arrived I found that my companions were all already at home! I had fired 110 rounds and to my surprise I had been credited with a P-40, probably shot down."

Bertolaso's account makes us think that certain units were not strict in assigning victories.

W.C. Beresford led the whole of 233 Wing to intercept *Stukas* on the way to Bir Hakeim: five *Kittyhawk*s of 260 Squadron were top cover (8.30-9.50); eight *Kittyhawk*s of 2 SAAF were medium cover (8.25-9.43); seven *Tomahawks* of 5 SAAF (8.25-9.55) were below 2 SAAF; and seven *Tomahawks* of 4 SAAF (8.20-9.50) were at the bottom of the formation. Not long before, 274 (7.45) and 33 Squadrons had also been detailed for a mission in the same area.

Only 260 Squadron reported the clash with five *Bf.109s*, of which there were no positive results.

The pilots of 2 SAAF, led by Maj. Human, were at an altitude of 11000 feet when they observed the explosion of bombs (without seeing the bombers). They came down and at 9.10 at 8000 ft, they were attacked by four *Bf.109s* coming down from a higher altitude without any apparent formation. A dog-fight followed.

Lt. De Waal (AL126 DB-L) claimed an enemy plane shot down and a second damaged (720 rounds):

"I saw a 109F to port about 1000 feet below me and climbing. I peeled off, and got up speed, and started climbing after him. I closed rapidly and gave him a short burst at about 250 yards. He heeled over and I watched him go down. I looked away for a brief while and when I looked again I saw him go straight in and burst into flames."

The remaining three *Bf.109s* continued to attack during the return flight and at a certain point only two were seen.

Lt. Burdon (AK611 DB-B) stated:

"...I saw two Kittyhawks attacked to port. I peeled off to port and as the 109 climbed up I managed to get in a full deflection shot, a burst of about three seconds, the result of which was white smoke pouring from the 109. This being confirmed (damaged) later. After my first burst another 109 climbed up to attack. We engaged head on; I pulled the tit and not one gun fired. The 109 must have realized this, so gave me all he had. My engine burst into flames. I eventually slipped down, and crash-landed (9.25 near El Adem, burned Cat.III), my under cart would not function. I did not bale out as I was approximately 800/1000' and thought this too low." He managed to get away from the aircraft before it burst into flames.

Lt. Freewen returned because of engine trouble at 9.25. Total rounds expended: 1820.

Crash-landed Stuka (San Diego Air and Space Museum)

At 9.15, 4 SAAF, led by W.C. Beresford, spotted twelve *Ju.87s* and dashed into the attack, diving to an altitude of 500 feet. They trusted in the cover given by the other squadrons.
Capt. Morphew (AN393) saw puffs of his bullets impacting on the fuselage of at least one *Ju.87*; he thought he had shot it down but did not claim it. Then he headed home because of engine trouble and was attacked by four *Bf.109s*. He struggled with them at about 200 feet and managed to get bursts in on two occasions when the *Messerschmitts* overshot him: he was amazed at their bad shooting. After ten minutes, however, he was badly hit and made a crash-landing. He was then strafed by two *Bf.109s* and taken prisoner by an Italian patrol.
2/Lt. Lawler (AN461) was also shot down and taken prisoner.
While Lt. Lane (AN460) was attacking the *Stukas*, he was hit by return fire and was compelled to force-land. P.O. Keefer of 274 Squadron picked him up with his *Hurricane*.
Capt. Bayly (AM418 KJ-S) was credited with a *Ju.87* destroyed and a second damaged:

> "...Attacked from out of the sun and caught up with the Stukas at about 1000' heading west. I attacked one Stuka from above and behind which was lagging and saw my shots splinter his canopy. He appeared to lose control and fell back considerably. Stuka was seen to be badly damaged. My next attack was across the formation from the north. I made a full deflection attack fired early and saw the latter shots strike the engine which emitted flames and black smoke. Then the airscrew slowed down jerkily as I passed over him. ...the AC appeared to be losing height. I turned west again caught up with the fight got a number of bursts but saw no convincing results."

Maj. Hewitson (AN452 KJ-M) was credited with a *Ju.87* destroyed:

> "...Caught up with the Stukas about 15 miles west of Bir Hakeim and delivered attacks on two near Stukas one of which was hit in the engine and force-landed. I was then attacked by one 109F which I avoided. He flew past me and I delivered an attack from dead astern. No results observed. At end

Maj. Jack Frost, 5 SAAF Squadron, on the left (Bouwer)

of fight only 4 or 5 Stukas were left in the formation. On the way home two of us fought a running fight with two 109s which eventually left us as we crossed into our territory."

Lt. Cohen (KJ-N) was credited with a *Ju.87* damaged:

"...Pulled off with rest of section into 12+ Stukas heading north-west after releasing bombs. Got in a long burst on one aircraft from ¼ astern and then overshot him. I did a steep turn and attacked the same ac again from ¼ frontal and then saw wisps of black smoke coming from underneath the fuselage. At this stage one of my cannons jammed and I did a few beam attacks on several other Stukas without observing any direct result. I then had to wrath off as my ammunition supply was exhausted. I made for home in the company of three ac of 5 SAAF. We were attacked by two Me.109s and in trying to evade them I lost the other three ac. I was then attacked continuously for 10 mins by one Me.109 but was not able to return his fire although I was able to outmanoeuvre him every time he attacked. He eventually broke away...."

Lt. Wheeler (AN428 KJ-K?) was credited with a *Ju.87* probable:

"...Got on the tail of one Stuka and gave him about four bursts. In the final attack I saw something break off which I thought came off the tail unit. At the same time black smoke started coming from below the root of the wings...."

5 SAAF flew above 4 SAAF at 8000 feet. They saw more than ten *Stukas* that were giving a

pounding. They tagged onto 4 SAAF in the attack on the German bombers when they were close to the ground, having just dropped their bombs. The enemy was pursued well into its territory before the engagement was broken off. Major Frost (AM385 GL-W) reported:

> "...Stukas were seen diving. They released their bombs and carried on the dive right down to ground level. We followed the 4 Sqn. to the attack. I fired at and hit a 109 just above the Stukas without result. I then closed on a Ju.387 from the rear, gave one burst and he burst into flames and crashed. I then closed on another from the starboard quarter. He then turned towards me and I got in a burst with deflection. I then got very close to him, gave him another burst and he went down to the ground. I gave him another burst and set the AC alight. I then closed on another Stuka, gave him a good burst from astern and he went down and crash landed. Three Ju.87s destroyed."

Lt. Thorhill Cook (AN313 GL-X) and Lt. Whyte (AN313 GL-W) shared a fourth *Ju.87*. They were flying low on the way back when they were both hit by anti-aircraft fire. The former was shot down and lost his life in the explosion of his aircraft while the latter had his aircraft badly damaged.
Maj. Meaker (AN388 GL-N) was shot down by the return fire of a *Ju.87* behind enemy lines and was picked up by Lt. Horne. It is believed that he set fire to his aircraft.
In total, six *Ju.87s* were claimed destroyed, one probable, and two damaged. The pilots of 5 SAAF never mentioned the German escort in their diaries.

Again 274 and 33 Squadron were on patrol West of Bir Hakeim (7.40-8.55). Three *Bf.109*s dived on the formation but were avoided. Then a further four *Bf.109*s with two C.202s carried out a single attack on the *Hurricanes* without causing any damage.

As we have seen, 233 Wing was stepped at four different altitudes. It seems that 260 Squadron and 2 SAAF had drifted off some way from the other two squadrons. In fact, they did not mention *Stukas*, and so two different clashes must have taken place, at least in the first phase. Therefore the two above-mentioned units must have run into the enemy fighters before the attack on the *Stukas* by 4 and 5 SAAF.
In their turn, 4 and 5 SAAF attacked the *Stukas* without mentioning the number of escorting fighters, as if they had not initially noticed their presence (reports were always very strict about the number of enemy AC encountered). Subsequently 4 SAAF clashed with the escort and strangely 5 SAAF continued not to mention it. The *Stukas* had probably remained alone for most of the attack; therefore, it seems that for the second day in succession the *Messerschmitts* had not managed to protect them adequately. This was perhaps also because of the scarcity of the escort itself; it certainly was not a good result.
In view of the claims and the number of planes encountered, it seems that the Germans engaged only 4 SAAF.

Cap. Franco Lucchini, C.O. of 84ª Sq. (Ufficio Storico SMA)

10° Gruppo's formation was divided into two sections as usual: one at 4000 m (with 91ª Sq.) and the other at 3000 m (with 90ª Sq.).

In effect these reported the clash with fifteen enemy fighters without noticing the *Stukas*, and so the section of *Macchis* of 91ª Sq., covering at an altitude of 4000 m., must have clashed with the five planes of 260 Squadron. The lower one (Piccolomini) would have clashed with 2 SAAF (even the times agree perfectly). Subsequently, the latter would have been able to encounter 4 SAAF at the end of the attack on the *Stukas*; in particular, the presumed time and the way in which Morphew was shot down would incline us towards the *Macchis*.

Considering the high number of claims submitted by fighter pilots, it seems unlikely that Lane and Meaker had both been shot down by return fire from the *Stukas* and Thorhill Cook by anti-aircraft fire. What is more, there is no mention of claims by *Stuka* pilots in the OBS report. Therefore, it cannot be ruled out that in one or more cases they had been shot down by an enemy fighter without this being seen, as this had happened in other cases.

Ten *CR.42s* of 50° Stormo bombed and strafed motor transports in the Bir Hakeim area (12.05-14.30). Ten. Eugenio Antonelli (C.O. 391ª Sq., M.M.8528) was hit by a cannon shell and crashed in flames 300 m east of Bir Hakeim; no parachute was seen. Serg. Faresi (391ª Sq., M.M.8545), following an error in the route and out of fuel, crash-landed near Beda Littoria, wrecking the plane and sustaining injury.

B) Cap. Lucchini led seven *C.202s* of 10° Gruppo (three of 84ª Sq., two of 90ª Sq., and two of 91ª Sq.) on a free sweep over Bir Hakeim (13.00-14.30). Three of these returned ahead of time.

C.202 of 84ª Sq., Sicily in May (Archivio di Stato)

CR.42s bombers of 388ª Sq. (Gentilli)

At 13.20, they spotted an enemy fighter formation of about thirty aircraft split between *Hurricanes* and *P-40s* at an altitude of 5500 m (they were at 3500). As they were not seen by the enemy, they managed to climb up in altitude and attack them from an advantageous position. They were credited with the shooting down of two *P-40s*, four *Hurricanes*, and five *P-40s*. Three *Hurricanes* were also machine-gunned (2240 rounds fired).
Cap. Lucchini (84ª Sq.) shot down a *P-40* and fired at four;
Serg. Perdoni (84° Sq.) shot down a *P-40*.

The Macchis came across twenty four *Hurricanes* of 33 and 274 Squadron again in action on the front. In addition two Spitfires were protecting the formation at high level but returned early. 33 Squadron, on top cover, was attacked by 4/5 *C.202s* and *Bf.109s*; several pilots managed bursts at them but no claims were made. P.O. Rolls was hit but suffered no serious damage.

This time Italian claims appear excessive; it would seem improbable that only four *Macchis* had been able to do so much damage. Even if the number of rounds fired seems to be high, it should be taken into consideration that every *Macchi* had 800 rounds available.

C) Nine *CR.42s* of 50° Stormo (five of 388ª Sq. and four of 390ª Sq., 159° Gruppo) attacked enemy armoured and motorized forces in the immediate vicinity of Bir Hakeim's stronghold (15.50-17.50). Nine *Macchis* of 17° Gruppo (four of 72ª Sq. and five of 80ª Sq.) provided the top cover (16.00-17.25) and were led by Cap. Nioi. Once the bombs had been dropped and the strafing completed, the Fiats of 388ª Sq. that were coming out of the dive were attacked by enemy fighters. Six *Spitfires* and eight *P-40s* were seen (exactly the number of the counterpart). Serg. Magg. Francesco Marcati (390ª Sq., M.M.8572) and Serg. Magg. Bartolozzi (388ª Sq., M.M.5059) were shot down; the former did not bale out and lost his life, but the latter baled out safely and was taken prisoner. Another two were hit by anti-aircraft fire.
The *Macchis* of 17° Gruppo in their turn intervened to protect the *CR.42s*.
The pilots of 72ª Sq. damaged three enemy aircraft (250 rounds);

Cap. Nioi (80ª Sq., 150 rounds) and M.llo Castellani (80ª Sq., 60 rounds) fired at three aircraft, observing hits on one of them.

Also, *C.202s* of 96ª Sq. were present in the area on a free sweep (16.10-17.45) but they would not have run into the enemy.

The whole of 233 Wing scrambled for another *Stuka* party over Bir Hakeim (17.20-18.40).

Six *Kittyhawks* of 260 Squadron clashed with four *CR.42s* protected by six *Bf.109s* or *Macchi C.202s* and claimed the shooting down of a *CR.42* (F.O. Waddy) and the damaging of a second.

Eight *Tomahawks* of 5 SAAF (17.20-18.40) came across six *CR.42s* and two *Bf.109s* at 18.00. *"Capt. Botha (AK448 GL-H) was after a CR.42 when he was forced to avoid four of own AC all filling the atmosphere with lead. The CR 42 did a slow roll off the top of the four and Capt. Botha shot him down in flames."*

4 Squadron was covering 5 SAAF with four *Tomahawks*.
Lt. Ironside (KJ-M) reported three *CR.42s* and a *Bf.109* jettisoning their bombs: he observed a *CR.42* but while attempting to turn into it he was attacked by a *Bf.109 F*. On out-turning this, he then saw a *CR.42* being attacked by three other fighters. As they broke away, he fired a two-second burst and then a three-second burst at it from quarter astern, *"and a red flash was seen in the cockpit, it had the appearance of a red Very Light."* Part of the right side of the engine cowling broke off. On banking round he saw an aircraft burning on the ground.

Lt. Paterson (AN462 KJ-K?):

> "...Met up with 3+ CR.42s which jettisoned their bombs. At least 5 of us fired at one of these. I was last to fire and saw it go down afterwards. In own opinion, I must have killed the pilot. I was rather discouraged by others when I said that, so I made no claim" ('Springbok Fighter Victory').

Therefore, it is quite feasible that pilots from 4, 5 and 260 Squadrons had all fired at the same *CR.42*.

2 SAAF did not report anything.

Four *Kittyhawks* of 112 Squadron were out on bombing mission (17.35-18.35); P.O. Atkinson (AL219) did not return. He was probably hit by anti-aircraft fire.

23 *Ju.88s* attacked enemy positions and troop concentrations 2 km north-east of Bir Hakeim (18.09-21.31). The anti-aircraft fire was not intense but accurate: one aircraft was lost.

A *Fi.156* went missing while searching for lost crews (OBS).

Additional losses were recorded by the Luftwaffe as follows:
Lt. Blume (I./L.G.1, *Ju.88 A-4* W.Nr. 0217, L1 + WL) was shot down over Bir Hakeim and lost his life, while some of the crew were taken prisoners;
Bf.109 F-4/Trop W.Nr. 10140 (Stab II./JG 27 or III./JG 27) was hit by flak over Tmimi (40%).
Bf.109 F-4/Trop W.Nr. 10198 (8./JG 27) was shot down over Bir Hakeim (100%). It seems it was the one reported in the afternoon by OBS, possibly because of anti-aircraft fire.
Ju.88 A-4 W.Nr. 142029, Stab I./L.G.1, damaged tire, Martuba (40%).
Bf.109 F-4/Trop W.Nr. 10042 (8./JG 27), damaged tire, Martuba (80%).
Bf.109 F-4 W.Nr. 7382, Martuba, technical defects (20%).

Night of 4-5

A *Boston* of 24 SAAF (4.25-6.35) was attacked by a night fighter. The bomber evaded the attack, manoeuvring and firing back 100 rounds.

5 June

A) Eight *C.202s* of 71ª Sq. (17° Gruppo), led by Cap. Baruffi, were again on a free sweep in the Bir Hakeim area (5.00-6.15). About twenty *P-40s* were encountered and engaged in air-combat. Six of them were credited as shot down and one probable.
Cap. Vicentini shot down a *P-40*;
Ten. Vatta shot down a *P-40* (340 rounds);
Ten. Morandi shot down a *P-40* (470 rounds);
M.llo Lui shot down a *P-40*;
Serg. Buogo was credited with a probable victory.
The last two victories were assigned to all eight pilots. The remaining three pilots were Cap. Baruffi, Ten. Cappellini, and Ten. Bacchi (40 rounds). In total 2500 rounds were expended and no damage was sustained.

The enemies were twelve *Hurricanes* of 274 Squadron that were on a sweep over Bir Hakeim (6.15-7.17); they came up against the Macchis (reportedly six *Bf.109s* and *C.202s*) twelve miles north-north-east of Bir Hakeim: F.Sgt. Neil and Sgt. Dodds claimed one *Bf.109* damaged each and did not sustain any casualties.

During a reconnaissance carried out by 33, 274 and 145 Squadrons (9.45-11.30), a *Hurricane* was jumped by two *Bf.109s* with no results.

B) A Schwarm of 5./JG 27 was on a frei Jagd east of Bir Hakeim (11.15-12.15); three *P-40s* were claimed:
Fw. Niederhöfer (2), 5 km W of Fort Acroma (11.00); 1 km NE of El Adem (11.40);
and Oblt. Boerngen, 20 km NE of Mteifl Chebir (11.51).
There are some doubts about the first claim: it is not consistent with the mission and OBS reports only two aircraft shot down against the loss of a *Bf.109* (before 15.00).
It seems that on the same mission, Lt. Kalista (5./JG 27, W.Nr. 10125 Rote 11) was shot down by enemy fighters between Hakeim and Acroma, and went missing.

Lt. Van der Riet (40 SAAF, *Hurricane* Z4608) was out on a reconnaissance mission; it was his second mission of the day but its time is not available. He was jumped at 16000 feet by a *Bf.109* which wounded him with its first burst; afterwards he was unable to take effective evasive action due to his damaged aircraft. He was being chased all the way home when at 50 feet near the aerodrome, the *Bf.109* got in another burst which hit the *Hurricane* and caused it to crash in flames about a mile from El Adem.

Eight *Kittyhawks* of 2 SAAF Squadron were top cover for *Bostons* of 12 SAAF (12.00-13.20) with the other three squadrons of the wing. Just after the bombing (12.40), four *Bf.109s* attacked 2 SAAF but they were warded off (rounds: .50-38).

Boston (Bouwer)

In conclusion, it seems that 5./JG 27 clashed with Van der Riet and 2 SAAF and that a very lucky burst by a South African pilot down Kalista.

A Schwarm of 4./JG 27 was out on a frei Jagd in the Mteifel area (14.00-15.10). Fw. Stiegler (W.Nr. 8401, 100%) had to crash-land near Tmimi because of engine failure.

C) OBS reported the attack of twenty-three *Ju.88s* against tanks and motor vehicles to the west of El Adem, during which a *P-40* had been claimed by the bombers. Prien noted the escort of as many as thirty-one *Bf.109s*, eight of which of III./JG53, eight of II./JG 27 and the rest from I and II./JG 27 (17.00-18.05). Additionally, nine *Macchis* of 9° Gruppo (seven of 96ª Sq. and two of 97ª Sq.; 17.05-18.15) were close cover, led by Cap. Viglione.
The German fighter pilots reported the clash with many *P-40s* and with a single *Hurricane* (actually two *Hurricanes* were claimed); as many as nine enemy fighters were credited as shot down.
Lt. von Lieres u. Wilkau (2./JG 27), *Hurricane*, 20 km SW of Acroma (17.40);
Ofw. Alfred Schulze (4./JG 27), three *P-40s*, S of Gazala Bay (17.42 and 17.43); 2-3 km SE of Gazala Bay, 800-1000 m (17.58);
Uffz. Junge (9./JG 27), *P-40*, 5 km N of Meitfel Chebir, 2.500 m (17.44);
Oblt. Klager (7./JG 53) two *P-40s*, 17.40, 40 km NW of Bir Hakeim (17.50);
Lt. Quaritsch (8./JG 53), *Hurricane* (17.45);
Fw. Schmidt (7./JG 53), *P-40*, 25 km SE of Gazala Bay (17.58);
Oblt. Tangering (C.O. of 7./JG 27, W.Nr. 10132) had to make an emergency landing after a clash (10%), and so it might have happened in this occasion.
During the bombing, Malvezzi's patrol intercepted three enemy planes that had already been engaged by the Germans; Malvezzi himself fired at one (80 bursts).
All of 233 Wing was again up to intercept the enemy (directed by radar): seven *Kittyhawks* of 2 SAAF (18.10-19.30) were top cover with six others of 260 Squadron (18.10-19.15; two returned earlier); four *Tomahawks* of 4 SAAF (18.15-19.05), and six *Tomahawks* of 5 SAAF (18.15-

19.30) at 9000 feet. The weather was hazy.

At 18.45, there was a clash with at least ten *Ju.88s*, ten *Bf.110s,* and fifteen *Bf.109s* south-west of Knightsbridge.

The *Tomahawks* of 5 SAAF were lined abreast in three pairs and upon seeing the German fighters climbing towards the Wing, they attacked the bombers.

Lt. Van der Spuy (AK533 GL-Y) closed up to within fifty yards of a *Ju.88* that was lagging behind and fired three bursts; he saw the enemy aircraft shudder and dive. He was then attacked by the escort (possibly Malvezzi saved the bomber with his action) and broke off.

Lt. White (AN313 GL-X) was shot up and slightly wounded (Cat. II).

Maj. Frost (AM385 GL-W) was shot down, reportedly by anti-aircraft fire, but returned the next day.

Lt. Derham's plane (AN247 GL-K) was damaged and crashed upon landing (Cat. II).

    260 Squadron claimed four *Bf.109s* one *C.202* damaged, but two *Kittyhawks* were slightly damaged.

    2 SAAF reported that *"The sky was just full of enemy aircraft and a hell of a fight took place."* The Squadron was not able to reach the bombers. There were no casualties (rounds: .50-700).

    4 SAAF reported only heavy anti-aircraft fire.

At long last, the escort for the attacking formation was more numerous for the Luftwaffe had learnt from the beating of the two preceding days. The bombers were only slightly troubled by enemy fighters.

During the day Ofw. Braun (I./St.G.3) was reported kolled by fighters over Bir Hakeim. There are no encounters regarding Stukas so more likely the loss was due to anti-aircraft or it occurred in a diffent date.

.

Night of 5-6

Wellington IC Z9096 M of 70 Squadron attacked Martuba (take-off 0.25). It was hit by anti-aircraft fire and crash-landed in the desert. All crew members were taken prisoner.

Martuba was attacked and the Italians reported one dead, three wounded, three aircraft damaged; nails with four spikes were dropped. Presumably in the same occasion *Bf.109 F-4/Trop* W.Nr. 8580 (3./J.G.27) was destroyed.

6 June

Sandstorms continued to limit operations.

A) Ten. Mandolini was at the head of seven *Macchis* of 10° Gruppo (two of 84^a Sq., one of 90^a Sq., and four of 91^a Sq.) on a free sweep between Acroma and Bel Harmat (5.05-6.30). Weather conditions were poor. Before arriving over the objective at an altitude of 3500 m, Mandolini spotted a formation of about twelve enemy fighters 1000 m lower. It was attacked from behind and

Kittyhawk IA ET? of 112 Sqn. (San Diego Air and Space Museum)

the air-combat lasted five minutes. Two enemy planes were claimed shot down, one probable, and three damaged (780 rounds fired):
Mandolini (91ª Sq.) shot down a *P-40* and fired at one (80 rounds);
Ten. Alessandrini (90ª Sq.) fired at three Spitfires;
M.llo Bignami (84ª Sq.) fired at a *P-40*;

Eleven *Kittyhawk*s of 250 Squadron (one had returned before) were on a reconnaissance mission between Acroma and Knightsbridge (6.10-7.15). They came up against four *Bf.109s* and eight *C.202s*; they damaged two *C.202s* and a *Bf.109* without sustaining any damage.
P.O. Twemlow (AK921) was on top cover at 4500 feet flying right under the clouds. Proceeding west, he saw a single *C.202* coming out of the clouds and flying on his starboard slightly below heading east: it must have been a decoy that had not been attacked, and so the latter pulled up into the clouds. Immediately four *C.202s* (though their identity was not ascertained) came down approximately from the same position and attacked in pairs. The *Kittyhawks* made a turnabout and the attack was broken off. They then turned west again. Another attack of four *C.202s* followed and again the British pilots turned about. Twemlow saw a *Macchi* attacking a *Kittyhawk* and turned on him for a frontal quarter attack, hitting him on the fuselage. The *Macchi* turned and dived, presenting its belly; Twemlow delivered two more short bursts, seeing strikes on its underside, and the *Macchi* broke off the engagement, diving slightly. Following this, a general dogfight developed.
S.L. Judd (AL157) was flying at 3000 feet when enemy fighters were reported at 6 o'clock. He saw the engagement of the top cover and attacked a *Bf.109*, shooting from 400 yards with no visible effects. Then he was attacked from above by a *C.202* which followed him for two complete turns. Finally the *Macchi* dived, tightening its turn and opening fire, with its bullets going behind the Kitty's tail. As the *Macchi* straightened out, Judd turned the other way so the *Macchi* crossed

Cap. Ezio Viglione Borghese and S.Ten. Alvaro Querci, earlier period (Brancaccio-Chianese)

behind his tail. He got in a two second burst while he was climbing away almost vertically and was hit on the starboard wing. Then the *Macchi* entered the clouds.
The clash lasted only a short while and with a small number of rounds fired by the Italians, perhaps because of the poor visibility.

Nine *Macchis* of 9° Gruppo (three of 73ª Sq. and six of 97ª Sq.), led by Magg. Larsimont, were on a free sweep between Bir Hakeim and Bir El Harmat (7.15-8.40). A Spitfire attacked the last two planes of the formation over Bir Hakeim and then made off after a brief burst at the plane in the rear position. The other three aircraft of the formation also got away, flying into the sun.

They were three planes of 145 Squadron that were patrolling (8.40-9.30) to the south-west of El Adem and their pilots saw ten *Bf.109s* and attacked them, forcing them to break formation but without result.

B) Ten *Kittyhawks* of 112 Squadron were off for a bombing and reconnaissance mission over Bir Hakeim (10.15-11.40). They attacked four *Bf.109s* that were flying lower down near Bir Hakeim: three were shot down and one was claimed probable.
Sgt. Adye (AK988) destroyed one *Bf.109* and shared in the destruction of another;
P.O. Baker (AL107) destroyed one *Bf.109*;
P.O. Carson (AL211) shared in the destruction of one with Adye;
and S.L. Drake (AL161) probably destroyed one.

Two *Bf.109E-7* reconnaissance planes of 4(H)/12 were escorted by five *Messerschmitts* of II./JG 27, which had taken off at 7.30. They were attacked by enemy fighters and Uffz. Pickel was shot down. OBS reported an air battle with thirty *P-40s* near El Adem. The times do not match up but it seems possible to connect the two episodes.

During the day 4.(H)/12 suffered other losses: Lt. Hülle (*Bf.109 E -7*, W.Nr. 1299) was shot down by flak in area Acroma-El Adem-Gowi and lost his life; a third *Bf.109* (W.Nr. 762) for unknown reasons, flown by Ofw. Ritter that survived; and Uffz. Kanoldt (*Fi.156* W.Nr. 4449) went missing with his crew.

Ten *CR.42* of 50° St. bombed and strafed retreating enemy troops (10.20-12.00). 3 pilots were lost: S.Ten. Mario Ingino (387ª Sq., M.M.8467), Serg. Magg. Righetti (390ª Sq., M.M.8845), and Serg.Magg. Fiascaris (390ª Sq., M.M.8863), all probably victims of anti-aircraft fire. Ingino was killed while Fiascaris and Righetti were taken P.O.W.

At 13.00, Cap. Viglione (96ª Sq., M.M.7822) led nine *Macchis* of 9° Gruppo on a free sweep. After having roamed about in search of enemy planes, they picked out large concentrations of mechanized vehicles (they were then recognized as the British 7th Armoured Division). They attacked, strafing them. The heavy anti-aircraft fire hit Viglione, forcing him to crash-land. An attempt was made to rescue him with a Ca.164 protected by eight *Macchis*, but without success because of the intense fire from the ground. Viglione was therefore taken prisoner. In those days, 4° Stormo pilots were tempted into machine-gunning the ground. In fact Piccolomini (90ª Sq.) also did this once during the day while he was escorting the *CR.42s*. Perhaps this was owing to the fact that there weren't any adversaries in flight.

M.llo Stella (72ª Sq.) crash-landed during a test flight and destroyed his *C.202* (M.M.7792). The pilot was badly injured.

P.O. Asmuss of 238 Squadron was killed in an accident during a practice flight.

Bf.109 W.Nr. 8676 of I./JG 27 was damaged (40%) due to an error during a maneuver at Martuba.

Night of 6-7

Martuba was attacked: *C.202* M.M.7776 (81ª Sq.) was burned out and others were slightly damaged.

> 'RAF Casualties Middle East' reported the loss of a Hurricane and a Kittyhawk that was badly damaged during the day. 'Daily Resume of Air Operations' reported the loss of two Hurricanes in night operations.

7 June

6 RAF Squadron entered action with *Hurricane* IID tank-busters that were armed with two 40 mm cannons.
A) Eight *C.202s* of 10° Gruppo (two of 84ª Sq., three of 90ª Sq., and three of 91ª Sq.), led by Magg. Maddalena, were on a free sweep in the Sidi Muftach area (8.35-10.10). The Italian formation was divided into two sections: one at an altitude of 3500 metres with Maddalena and one covering at 4000 metres with Piccolomini. At 9.10, an enemy formation of about ten planes was

spotted heading east, 10 km to the west of Acroma. Maddalena informed the pilots by radio and headed towards it. It was then that he saw another formation of about twenty *P-40s* at almost the same altitude. He led the attack which lasted over twenty minutes and came to an end at a very low altitude. Five enemy aircraft were credited shot down along with one probable and fourteen machine-gunned (2658 rounds).
Maddalena (10°) shot down two *P-40s*;
Cap. Piccolomini (90ª Sq.) shot down a *P-40* and fired at two;
S.Ten. Squarcina shot down a *P-40*;
The pilots of (91ª Sq.) shot down a *P-40*;
Serg. Buttazzi (84ª Sq.) fired at four *P-40s*.

73 (9.30-10.50) and 213 Squadron (9.40-10.45) were on patrol over Acroma and Gazala, each with twelve *Hurricane IICs*. An aircraft of 73 Squadron returned earlier because of an oil leak.
73 Squadron was top cover at 11000 feet and flying south east (from Acroma towards Gazala) when (at 10.04) six *Bf.109s* were sighted at 12000 feet. While the Wing was manoeuvering to keep the enemy away from the sun, 73 Squadron was jumped by a further enemy formation of six *Bf.109s* that was coming away from the sun. A dogfight ensued and the RAF formation broke up. Altogether, twelve *Bf.109s* were met with some *C.202s* (total rounds: 204 ball, 87 HE/Inc.). There was no knowledge of any casualties inflicted on the enemy.

Cap. Ranieri Piccolomini Clementini Adami, C.O. of 90ª Sq. (Ufficio Storico SMA)

F.Lt. Cantrill (BH330) went missing; Sgt. Wiseman (BN375) made an emergency landing after losing the plane's propeller following the hits made on it by an unidentified plane; Sgt. Wilson (BL279) baled out. The rest of the Squadron then returned in groups of two or three.

213 Squadron, 10.05, 10000 feet, S of Acroma reported:

> "...Enemy formation sighted from W ... 1 flight of 73 500 ft above and behind, 1 flight 600 yds to port. EA formation consisted of 6 Me.109Fs 5000 ft above. EAs dived and whole formation went into tight defensive circles. Some Macchi 202s also appeared on the scene. Individual combats resulted. ... Combat broken off owing to shortage of petrol. All returned safely. ... 5 EA were attacked ... from 5000 to 15000 ft. ... Me.s generally attacked by steep dives, opening fire as they pulled straight out. The 202s dived down to the deck and pulled up on anybody who wasn't looking. No visible results. 1 AC received a strike in starboard mainplane."

S.L. Young (BN286):

> "... I saw a 109 diving down on the tail of a Hurricane. I followed it down and when I was within 300 yds, it pulled out of its dive and straight up. I struck to its tail and at 250 yds gave it a short burst, but with no results. ... The dog fight lasted about 20 minutes. 60 Ball, 60 He/Inc."

Hurricane IIC (Archivio di Stato)

F.Sgt. Lack (BE340):

"...after been warned, I saw one of them diving past me to starboard. It then pulled straight in front of me. I pulled my nose up and gave him a short burst of 30 rounds but with no luck. I saw a Macchi 202 slightly below me and heading in the opposite direction and prepared to attack it but then saw a 109 coming at me from starboard beam. I avoided this attack. Previously ... I saw 2 Hurricanes flying in line astern. The rear one pulled straight across to starboard, breaking off the tail of the leading Hurricane which spun down and crashed in flames. I saw nobody bale out. The other plane crash landed in the same area S of Acroma... 62 Ball, 63 He/Inc."

F.Lt. Temlett (BM981):

"... I saw them diving down through our formation, almost down to the deck, then pulling up straight. I dived down after one of them to 3000 feet but it pulled up and got above me. I climbed after it almost vertically, got within 250 yds range, gave it a short burst but with no visible result. 50-Ball, 50-He/Inc."

P.O. Wilson (BM983, 20 Ball, 20 He/Inc).
W.C. Wallace (BN139, 55 Ball, 55 He/Inc).

73 Squadron probably spotted Maddalena's section but it had then been surprised by Piccolomini emerging from a higher altitude. The formation of two echelons stepped at different heights, which was standard for 4° Stormo, appeared to be effective. And yet it is difficult to understand why the *Hurricanes* didn't fly at a higher altitude along with the *Spitfires* which were already in the theatre by then. The action appears to have been well led by Maddalena, helped, at long last, by the radio working well.

The noted collision does not match perfectly with the 73 Squadron report; in accepting it as good, it seems that Wiseman ran into Cantrill.

B) Nine planes of 24 SAAF attacked vehicles and tanks from 6000 feet at Pin Point 367401 (10.20-11.40). The escort, which was provided by all of 233 Wing, was quite strong: five *Kittyhawk*s of 2 SAAF (10.35-11.45) were top cover with another ten of 260 Squadron (10.40-12.00); eight *Tomahawks* of 5 SAAF were medium cover (10.30-11.40) and seven more of 4 SAAF were close cover (10.30-11.50).

2 SAAF was at 10000 feet when at 10.55 they were attacked by four *Bf.109s*, just as the *Kittyhawk*s had already headed for home.

Lt. Lindsay (AL173 DB-Q) stated:

> "...heard 'turnabout' .....saw an Me.109F about 1000 yards away diving towards me. His attack developed into head-on and he opened fire at about 500-600 yards. I held my fire until he closed to approximately 300 yards. ...he pulled away to starboard in a slight climb and so presented a good target. I gave him a long burst and whitish smoke poured from him as he disappeared behind me; I then lost sight of him....200 rounds expended."

The pilots of this unit complained about how they were systematically used as top cover and put to such high risks.

260 Squadron reported the clash with three *Bf.109s*, which slightly damaged one of their aircraft.

5 SAAF was at 7000 feet when eight to ten *Bf.109s* were observed.

Maj. Frost (AK or AM422 GL-B) described:

> "On return was attacked by 3 Me.109Fs. Turned towards one who came from the beam and got a head-on attack. Got in a good burst. The 109 then passed over me and was seen ... to pull up with clouds of white smoke (vapour)..... mingled with black smoke ....probably destroyed."

4 SAAF mistakenly noted not meeting up with enemy planes.

A *Bf.109* managed to find a gap in the escort and fired at a bomber but did not cause any damage. A machine-gunner fired 150 rounds at him.

A Schwarm of III./JG 53 was on a freelance when it attacked fifteen to twenty enemy fighters that were escorting twelve Bostons (also accompanied by fighter-bombers). Three fighters were shot down but were not confirmed because the places where they crashed were not precisely marked.

This was one of the few occasions in which the Axis fighters managed to get through to the bombers when the latter were escorted.

Axis fighters often clashed with the protected bombers formations. In some cases, this happened accidentally and so the number of the attackers was seldom above ten. In other cases, it occurred after a scramble on warning when the planes on stand-by were even fewer. Therefore the escorts managed to protect the bombers well almost always; even if they paid a high price, the bombers acted almost undisturbed.

The Axis air forces had the numbers to provide a force of aircraft in several groups of ten that would have been able to create serious problems for an enemy attacking formation even if escorted. What is more, the bombing missions practically went on for the whole span of a day and by then, radar guided the fighters. Clearly an operation of the type would have been to the detriment of others. Therefore, this leads to the conclusion that protection from bomb attacks was not considered a high priority by the Axis command.

At 11.00, a mission of 223 Squadron without escort was aborted because enemy aircraft were spotted. Again it should be noted that 223 Squadron continued to carry out missions without escort, even if they were normally in conjunction with a well covered attack formation (in this case the 24 SAAF).

F.Lt. Sabourin and Sgt. Spear in their Spitfires (145 Squadron, T852, B502, 12.25-13.25) were on a sweep at 20000 ft and spotted six *Bf.109*s 5000 feet below. They dived and from close range hit two enemy fighters. No results were observed.

C) At 12.45, four *Bf.109 Fs* of 6./JG 27 were escorting two *Bf.109Es* on a reconnaissance mission over El Harmat-El Adem. At 12.50 they were attacked by Italian fighters, driving them off (Shores). Later on, they were attacked by two enemy fighters and Uffz. Schwekutsch managed to shoot one down at 13.20. The enemy fighter belly-landed but was not confirmed because there were no witnesses.

Six *Hurribombers* of 274 Squadron were out to bomb enemy ground forces 10 miles east of Sidea (14.10-15.30). Cover was provided by six *Hurricanes* of the same squadron and six more of 33 Squadron. Three *Bf.109*s attacked them and Sgt. Eagle (274) fired a short burst at one, with no results observed. A *C.202* climbed through the formation of 33 Squadron and two *Hurricanes* chased him all the way to Gazala. The task of the bombers was not completed.

D) Eighteen *Ju.87s*, divided into two waves, attacked enemy motor vehicles near El Adem (III./St.G. 3: 15.15-16.45). They were escorted by thirteen *Bf.109s* of I./JG 27 (15.25-16.40), eight of III./JG 27, nine of III./JG 53, and others of II./JG 27 (15.35-16.30). III./JG 53 reported a clash with fifteen to twenty enemy fighters, claiming the destruction of a *P-40*; two more *P-40s* were claimed by Marseille:
Hptm. Belser (8./JG 53, 16.11);
Oblt. Marseille (2) SW of El Adem (16.10); 10 km NE of El Adem (16.13).
Two more were damaged by 8./JG 53, one by Lt. Quaritsch.
This was countered by the loss of Lt. Scheiter (8./JG 27) who was shot down; nevertheless, he baled out safely and returned to base.

This time eight *Kittyhawks* of 2 SAAF were close cover for *Bostons* of 24 SAAF (16.40-17.50; the mission was mistakenly recorded in the war diary as having taken place an hour later). The rest of the wing completed the escort. At 17.04, a formation of enemy bombers with a large fighter escort was seen at an altitude of 8000 feet over El Adem. The bombers were ordered to 'pancake' and 2 SAAF was attacked by ten *Bf.109s* (at 8000 feet, a low altitude). Possibly the unit had to cover the retreat of the bombers. Lt. Berrangè (AK628 DB-P) was shot down and reported killed while Lt. Frewan (AL193 DB-S) baled out and returned to his squadron after being badly damaged (18.20). He had been hit in the cockpit by a burst from a light gun, but even without the cloche the plane continued to fly straight. An attacking *Bf.109* dived and pulled up under Major Human (AL186 DB-G); the pilot didn't waste the chance of following it and fired a long burst from quarter astern and below, seeing the tracers bounce

Bf.109 F of 4./JG 27 (Gentilli)

off the cockpit. The enemy aircraft (most likely Scheiter) was confirmed destroyed (600 rounds).
The total rounds were: .50-1000.
233 Wing was moved to Baheira, its pilots happy to leave the dusty Gambut.

Fi.156/Trop W.Nr. 5587 (Wüstennotstaffel) was shot down (by Flak?) near El Cheima (60%).
Ju 87 D-1 W.Nr. 2176 (III./St.G.3) crashed at Derna-South due to technical problems (90%). All crew perished (Uffz. Krug).
Bf.109 F-4/Trop 8725 of 7./JG 27 (100%) was lost during the day because the engine broke down in the Acroma area.

Night of 7-8

Benghazi was bombed and two *Cant.Z.501s* were slightly damaged.

Eight *Ju.88* attacked Tobruk's harbour (2.30-5.46); *A-4* W.Nr. 140706 L1 + XL (I./L.G.1), was shot down by heavy AA with the loss of the entire crew (Lt. Alisch).

8 June

A) Forty-four *Ju.87s* attacked Bir Hakeim in three waves (St.G. 3: 5.00-7.00). They were joined by three *Ju.88s* (5.12-6.58) and 10 *Bf.110s* (5.27-7.00). They were covered by forty-four *Bf.109s* (5.43-7.07).
Also eight *Bf.109s* of II./JG 27 carried out a free sweep over Bir Hakeim (5.52-6.42) in combi-

2 SAAF Squadron Kittyhawk (Bouwer)

nation with the attack of the bombers. They clashed with twenty-five to thirty enemy fighters. The German fighter pilots claimed to have shot down three *P-40s*:
Ofw. Bendert (4./JG 27) (2): E of Bir Hakeim, 6.03; 6-8 km E Bir Hakeim, 1500 m (6.25);
Ofw. Schulze (4./JG 27), SE of Bir Hakeim (6.05).
Fw. Walchofer (6./JG 27, W.Nr. 8465) was shot down and landed on a minefield, killed by the explosion of a mine. This happened before 12.00, so it was possibly during this clash that some publications reported that he had been shot down by the Canadian ace Eddy Edwards. However, it appears more likely that 260 Squadron had clashed a little later with the *Macchis*.

Ten *Hurricanes IICs* of 73 Squadron took off from Gambut main to patrol Bir Hakeim (6.44-7.55) and were joined by twelve *Hurricanes IICs* of 213 Squadron (6.45-7.50) as top cover. At 7.17, 73 Squadron was flying at an altitude of 10000 feet near Bir Hakeim when it was attacked by approximately six *Bf.109 Fs*. A melee followed: one *Bf.109* was shot down and one was damaged. One *Hurricane* was damaged on its starboard aileron and wing by an explosive shell but returned safely. The enemies seemed to work individually (total rounds expended: 127 Ball, 127 HE/Inc).
During the fight they saw a large formation of sixteen to twenty *Ju.88s* heading east at a height of 12000 feet. There appeared to be two flights of eight *Ju.88s* each in line abreast. They were covered by about a dozen fighters positioned above and on the flanks. The *Hurricanes* were unable to engage that formation due to the large number of enemy fighters.
F.O. Selby (BE 568) saw five or six *Bf.109 Fs* in a loose circle at about 13000 feet:

> "I was between 10000 and 11000 ft, above a circle formed by 213 Squadron and watched a 109F that had a dirty look. It finally dived onto the aircraft below me. I stood on my tail as he came down and fired at about 50 yards range. He immediately emitted intermittent bursts of black smoke.

I stalled turned down onto his tail and gave him a long burst diving. ....saw him go right down....then a sudden burst of smoke came from the ground... 68 Rounds Ball, 69 Rounds He/Inc"

P.O. Coussens (BN280) turned inside two *Bf.109s* and hit one with a single burst (25 Ball, 25 HE/Inc).
213 Squadron noted that the formation was too tight and fell apart when attacked by the escorting 109s; instructions were given so that this tactical error would not be repeated.
213 Squadron also reported being attacked by *Bf.109s*, without a satisfactory outcome for either side, and that the enemy bombers managed to pass on towards their objective.
This time, the *Hurricanes* got the better of the *Messerschmitts*, even if the main objective — the bombers — escaped.

B) Ten. Malvezzi led seven planes of 9° Gruppo (six of 73^a Sq. and one of 97^a Sq.) on a free sweep between Bir Hakeim and Bir El Harmat (6.40-8.25). On the return trip at an altitude of 4000 metres, they met two formations of enemy planes: the higher one had reportedly thirty planes stepped up at different altitudes around 3000 metres while the lower one was positioned at about 500 metres and probably consisted of fighter-bombers. The *Macchis* at a higher altitude (as usual, there must have been two sections, one at 6000 metres with Malvezzi and another lower down at around 4000 metres) made good use of the height advantage and attacked the top cover. In total, four *P-40s* were credited shot down in addition to one probable and eight damaged (1111 rounds fired).
Malvezzi (97^a Sq.) shot down a *P-40* and fired at another two. He then landed at Tmimi because of a shortage of fuel.
A *C.202* was hit but managed to return.
  The whole of 233 Wing was on a free sweep when it encountered the enemy.
Ten *Kittyhawks* of 260 Squadron were top cover (8.20-9.30); they engaged five *Bf.109s* and Edwards shot down one of them. Evidence is provided from 'Kittyhawks Over the Sands':

> "Flying top cover with his fellows of 260, F.Sgt. Edwards watched as the l09s attacked from astern. Committing themselves to their attack pattern, the Jagdfliegern dared to come face to face with their Kittyhawk opponents before pulling skywards to repeat their routine. Eddie saw two of the Messerschmitts come, as anticipated, from behind the formation and start the expected dive. The Kittyhawk leader then called a turn-about, the usual defensive action, and together they changed direction. The lead 109 pulled up steeply at the unexpected move but his follower pursued the course just a little too long on Eddie's side. Quickly, the Canadian fired in front of him as far as he could. Within seconds, the well-aimed deflection burst hit the spinner and propeller of the 109 almost head on and Eddie watched as fragments splintered from the enemy aircraft right under the formation. Trailing clouds of black smoke, the Me 109 fell towards the earth. A few seconds later, Eddie and many of his comrades saw the plane blow to bits on the ground...."

'Springbok Fighter Fictory' reports:

> "2 SAAF (8.15-9.30), with 6 Kittyhawks, was top cover when bounced by about eight enemy fighters (109s or 202s) at 08h40 (7500 feet). Lt. McMaster (AK923? DB-V) damaged what was thought to be a Bf109E then had his own controls shot away and baled out. .....F/L Laubscher, the South African in the RAF seconded to 2, had seen two 202s attack and shoot down McMaster. The

Newly arrived Hurricane IID (Aviation Heritage Museum of Western Australia)

Squadron re-formed when a second attack commenced. Laubscher turned sharply to the right, meeting the Macchi in a quarter frontal attack. His tracers appeared to strike home. Turning back, he joined three Kittyhawks milling around, and they flew east, and then turned west. Laubscher saw a Bf109E low down and went after it. The enemy tactical fighter evaded his first attack by a steep climb and a stall turn. Captain Reynolds and Lt. Bryant then attacked. The Emil took the same evasive action. Laubscher gave chase again. The 109 zoomed up, Laubscher firing at close range, seeing his bullets strike it. A puff of smoke came off the cowling. The 109 dived away, Laubscher following until his guns jammed. Lt. Ismay, dicing with two 109s, lost the formation. He got in one good burst before they broke off."(1780 rounds were expended.)

Nine *Tomahawks* of 4 SAAF (8.30-9.30) were jumped by *Bf.109s* and *C.202s* (the number is not clear). Lt. Warden claimed a *C.202* damaged.

Four *Tomahawks* of 5 SAAF (8.15-9.25) were bottom of the formation at 6000 feet. At 9.00, they sighted an enemy formation of twelve *Bf.109s* at their same height north east of Bir Hakeim. The planes all attacked, and in the ensuing dogfight four enemy aircraft were damaged, respectively by Frost, Botha, Lindberg, and Stevens; no damage was sustained. And then the enemy broke off the fight and made west, for possibly the *Macchis* were at the limit of their range.

The remaining fifteen Commonwealth planes that flew lower could have been those of 3 RAAF and 450 Squadrons (8.55).

C) This time, seven *Macchis* of 10° Gruppo (three of them of 91ª Sq.), with Magg. Maddalena in command, were in action over the cauldron of Bir Hakeim (9.05-10.30). At 9.35, they were heading on a course of 180° at an altitude of 4500 when their pilots spotted a formation of twenty *P-40s* 500 metres further down on the left. The signal to attack was given over the radio and an air battle of about fifteen minutes followed. It ended at a low altitude a little to the east of Bir El

Harmat. There had probably been another mixed formation of *Hurricanes* and *P-40s* at around 500 m. that were also attacked.

A *Macchi* was damaged. Three *P-40s* and a *Hurricane* were credited shot down (482 rounds were fired; for unknown reasons only the three pilots of 91ª Sq. would have participated).

Twelve *Hurricane IIs* of 33 Squadron were top cover for twelve others of 274 Squadron on a free sweep over El Adem (10.15-11.20). The former unit was attacked by two *C.202s* and six *Bf.109s*:
P.O. Kallio claimed a *Bf.109* damaged but his own plane was damaged as well (Cat.I);
P.O. Merritt's plane (884) was badly damaged (Cat.II);
Sgt. Belleau fired at an attacker without results.

In its turn, 274 Squadron was attacked by two *C.202s* and Sgt. Eagle's aircraft was slightly damaged.

F.O. Brown of 208 Squadron (*Tomahawk* AN334) was on a reconnaissance mission over Bir Hakeim (11.15). He was attacked twice by two *Bf.109s*: the first time, over Bir Hakeim, he evaded them; the second time took place 10 miles east of Bir Hakeim while he flew low at ground level. He was hit but able to reach Sidi Rezegh where he crash-landed (12.15). Brown probably ran into the *Macchis* (considering some error in timing).

The lower-flying mixed formation that was spotted by the Italians could have been composed of 250 and 6 Squadrons and 3 RAAF engaged on a ground attack (10.40-11.45), but they didn't register any clashes.

Eleven *Kittyhawks* of 450 Squadron (11.22-12.20) covered another nine of 112 Squadron (11.15-12.20) in a strafing mission in the area of Bir Hakeim. Sgt. White (AL211, Cat II) of 112 Squadron was hit and had to make a forced-landing. 450 Squadron also came down to strafe and Sgt. James (AL146) did not return while another two planes were damaged.

Eight *Tomahawks* of 4 SAAF were escorting *Bostons* (11.45-13.05) on an attack against motor transports west of Knightsbridge. Three *Bf.109s* attacked the formation but were beaten off without results.

223 Squadron attacked Barce airfield (11.52): *Baltimore* II AG777 (Sgt. Saunders) was hit by anti-aircraft fire and exploded over the target with the loss of all its crew. AG285 was also hit, possibly by the explosion, and returned but was damaged beyond repair. The diary of Va Squadra reported that after being hit, the *Baltimore* crashed right on the airfield (12.30). Bad damage was inflicted on the ground: three tents were hit full on, causing the deaths of twenty-one people and the wounding of another nine. In addition, five Ca.311s and three *Cant.Z.1007bs* were badly damaged, three Ca.311s and three *Cant.Z.1007bs* were slightly damaged, and other material was destroyed.

Three *Hurricanes* of 6 Squadron (13.20-14.40), armed with 40mm guns, together with seven of 3 RAAF (13.15-14.23) attacked enemy vehicles near Bir Hakeim. The escort was provided by six *Kittyhawks* of 250 Squadron (13.25-14.35).
6 Squadron lost two aircraft. F.O. Morrison Bell (BN860) was shot down by anti-aircraft fire but returned the following day. F.Lt. Simpson (BN861) baled out from the burning plane after it had

Serg. Luciani Perdoni, 84ª Sq., in an earlier period (Perdoni-Chianese)

been hit by enemy action (without specification if it was from the ground or the air). P.O. Besly (BN844) was attacked by an unidentified enemy fighter.
Sgt.Hall of 250 Squadron (AK959) was hit and crash-landed.
Unfortunately the attacking fighters that might have been able to cause some losses cannot be identified. There is only confirmation of a free sweep of 9° Gruppo over Bir Hakeim (11.30-13.10) without any other relevant information.

D) Cap. Lucchini led ten *C.202s* of 10° Gruppo (six of 84ª Sq., two of 90ª Sq. and two of 91ª Sq.) on a free sweep over Bir Hakeim (13.45-15.10). At 14.20, a formation of fifteen *P-40s* was spotted lower down from an altitude of 4000 metres over Bir Hakeim. It was attacked and engaged in an air battle for ten minutes. In total, three *P-40s* were credited shot down, one probable, and ten machine-gunned (1507 rounds):
Ten. Giannella (84ª Sq.) shot down a *P-40*;
Serg. Perdoni (84ª Sq.) shot down a *P-40* and claimed a probable victory;
Cap. Lucchini (84ª Sq.) shot down a *P-40* in collaboration with other pilots and fired at three;
Ten. Berti (84ª Sq.) shot down a *P-40* shared with other pilots and fired at three;
Ten. Mandolini (91ª Sq.) shared a *P-40* with other pilots (60 rounds).
The *Macchis* would have met up with 233 Wing in action over Bir Hakeim.
  2 SAAF with four *Kittyhawks* was the leader squadron on a wing sweep (14.35-16.10). The planes were flying at an altitude of between 8000 feet and 6000 feet but they broke away from the formation and were not involved in the fight. Eight *Tomahawks* of 5 SAAF (14.45-16.00)

were top cover and were flying at 8000 feet. Eight *Tomahawks* of 4 SAAF (14.30-16.15) were medium cover.

4 SAAF reported over twenty enemy aircraft.
Lt. Kaufmann (4 SAAF) claimed a *Bf.109* damaged but the back of his plane's canopy was hit by a shell. This badly damaged the plane but the pilot was unhurt.

At 15.30, Lt. Lindbergh (5 SAAF, AN309 GL-O) was flying at 8000 feet when he saw seven *Bf.109s* attacking from above:

> "... I saw Me.109s attacking left-hand section of medium cover. I gave warning by R/T and turned towards the EA. At this moment I saw another 109 coming almost head-on and slightly below. I aimed a bit in front of him and fired. Almost immediately he started smoking from the top of its cowling, near the nose. ... I saw another 109, about 1000' below me climbing steeply. I intercepted his climb at my own level and fired a long burst, following him up. I saw the explosive ammunition hitting the 109's rudder and starboard wing. As I was turning away I had to take violent avoiding action to avoid another 109 on my tail. ... One Me.109 damaged."

Before the fight, Lt. Kemsley (5 SAAF) landed south of El Adem due to coolant trouble.
Capt. Bayly reported: *"Amounted to a good wing practice flight. But it was not helping the French."*

E) Nine *Macchis* of 6° Gruppo (three of 79ª Sq., two of 81ª Sq. and four of 88ª Sq.), led by Cap. Beggiato, were on a free sweep over the Bir Hakeim-Bir el Harmat area (14.55-16.20). At 15.30 they were flying at an altitude of 5000 m when they intercepted and attacked an enemy formation estimated to be twenty aircraft split between *P-40s* and *Hurricanes* (another source reported two formations of ten and fifteen aircraft at an altitude of 1000 and 6000 m, respectively).
Serg. Magg. Paroli (79ª Sq., 60 rounds);
Serg. Saiani (79ª Sq., 60 rounds);
Cap. Beggiato (81ª Sq.) believed that he damaged or probably shot down a *P-40* (140 rounds).
A section would have remained at a higher altitude as top cover while the formation below it dashed against the enemy.
S.Ten. Civetta (88ª Sq.) was the only one to intervene of the higher section. He fired at three enemy planes (335 rounds).
Ten. Palazzeschi (81ª Sq., M.M.7898) was shot down but managed to bale out safely and was taken prisoner. With five victories to his credit, he was one of the aces of 1° Stormo.

The clash would have taken place against nine *Hurricanes* of 33 Squadron that were escorting twelve *Hurribombers* of 274 Squadron on an attack of motor vehicles near Bu Amud, 10 miles east of Bir Hakeim (16.04-17.30). Two *Spitfires* flown by F.O. Sabourin (N321) and Sgt. James (L324) of 145 Squadron (16.00-16.50) were extra top cover for the *Hurricanes*.

The top flight of 33 Squadron was attacked by three *Bf.109s*. This caused Sgt. Menzies to make a forced-landing at Bu Amud (Cat.II), for he had presumably been hit by Cap. Beggiato. Only one pilot of 33 Squadron managed to get a good burst at the attackers.

274 Squadron was not attacked but saw C.202s below which they targeted: P.O. Keefer claimed a *C.202* destroyed while Sgt. Craggs claimed a second one damaged; no casualties were sustained by the squadron. The Macchis that were engaging the 33 Squadron were probably surprised by the pilots of 274 Squadron.

Spitfire Mk.V BR.390 of 145 Sqn. (later period, San Diego Air and Space Museum)

The two *Spitfires* attacked ten *Bf.109s* to the south-west of Tobruk and destroyed one. This was the first claim confirmed by Spitfire pilots in North Africa. As a result, Palazzeschi would have been shot down by these *Spitfires* or by Keefer. Both Sabourin and Keefer were at their third individual victory (George Keefer got it in this occasion while the Spitfire pilot just claimed half share) and both would go on to achieve ace status.

Keefer will end the war as a W.C., with his score at twelve while Joseph Sabourin will be KIA later in the campaign with his score at six and one shared.

Six *Kittyhawks* of 250 Squadron also operated in the same area (16.25-17.20). They were escorting eight planes of 3 RAAF (16.20-17.20) and seven of 112 Squadron (15.50-16.45) in bombing and reconnaissance action over Bir Hakeim. Just to the east of Bir Hakeim, 250 Squadron was attacked four times by fourteen enemy aircraft split between *Bf.109s* and *C.202s*; nevertheless, they managed to hinder the attack, allowing the fighter-bombers to proceed untroubled to the target.

F.O. Copeland (AL182) stated:

> "When approaching target I saw a standing patrol of 14 AC over B. Hakeim. They tried to attack 3 Sqn below us but I turned towards them with my formation of 5 ac and they climbed up behind us. They made another attack on 3 Sqn. and again we turned head on, and they climbed up above us. They then carried out two attacks on us and 3 Sqn. took this opportunity to bomb the target.
> … followed by 1 Me.109 who made two abortive attacks….The AC appeared to be MC.202 and Me.109."

3 RAAF pointed out that *Bf.109s* had engaged the escort.
Therefore it seems that 6° Gruppo had also come up against this formation.

Five *C.200s* of 8° Gruppo strafed motor transports and armoured vehicles (13.30-15.00). Cap. Marcovich (M.M.6700) was hit by anti-aircraft fire, force-landed east of Mteilim, and was taken prisoner.

There was another patrol by twelve *Hurricanes* of 213 Squadron - covered by two Spitfires (145 Squadron) over the Knightsbridge-Mteifel area (17.30-18.15). Two *Bf.109*s jumped the *Hurricanes* out of the sun without causing any damage. Instead an enemy fighter was seen with trailing white smoke, but no claim was made.
After having been warned, P.O. McKay (BN136) pulled up into the sun, seeing the enemy fighters pass by. And then, after a few tight turns, he sighted a *Bf.109* diving on a *Hurricane* just below, and so he pointed to him. The German pilot became aware of the danger and pulled up. The second Messerschmitt then got on McKay's tail and so he took violent evasive action. Again McKay saw another *Bf.109* in front of him at a far distance (700 yds), firing a burst but evidently without results.

During the day two *Bf.109s* crash-landed because of engine failure: Uffz. Pfeffer, 5 km east of Tmimi (3./Jg 27, W.Nr. 7397, 30%); at Martuba (7./Jg 27, W.Nr. 8695, 60%).

'RAF Casualties Middle East' reported that during the day there was lost a total of five single-engined planes in addition to the bad damaging of another seven. The Germans claimed to have shot down three and the Italians eleven; only three losses match the claims. Anti-aircraft fire should actually have accounted for as many as five, even if at least some of these aircraft had probably been involved in clashes with Axis fighters. The great effort made by the Commonwealth fighter-bombers to confront the Bir Hakeim crisis and the considerable losses they had to deal with should be highlighted.

Ju.88A-4 W.Nr. 2525 (I./K.G.54) belly-landed after having been damaged by Flak (20%).

Night of 8-9

Lt. Heschl (II./K.G.100, *He.111H-6* W.Nr. 7093, 6N + IG) went missing with his crew, presumably during a bombing.

9 June

A) Thirty-seven *Ju.87s* attacked the Bir Hakeim stronghold in three waves (St.G. 3: 6.25-8.15). The escort was provided by thirty-seven *Bf.109s* (6.55-8.15; fourteen of III./JG 53; one of JG 27 could not take off). The bombs hit their targets. There were clashes with enemy fighters and three of these were credited shot down:
Hptm. Franzisket (1./JG 27), *Kittyhawk*, SW of Hagfa El Beda (7.50);
Fw. Steinhausen (1./JG 27), *P-40*, S Mteifel Chebir (7.53);
Lt. Klager (7./JG 53), *P-40* (7.35). His victim was shot down in flames and then he claimed a second fighter damaged.
Uffz. Pfeffer (3./JG 27) was shot down 20 km north-east of Bir Hakeim (W.Nr. 8647 ge.9, 100%) and went missing.

Some time later five *Bf.109s* of II./JG 27 were escorting *Bf.110* reconnaissance planes over Bir El Gobi (7.33-8.37) when they came up against four *P-40s*. Two were claimed to have been shot down to the south-east of El Adem:
Ofw. Bendert (4./JG 27, 8.25); and Ofw. Schulze (4./JG 27, 8.26).

The whole of 233 Wing was also in this case scrambled to intercept the *Stukas*.

Six *Kittyhawks* of 260 Squadron (8.10-9.15) were top cover but did not take part in the clash. The other three squadrons were stepped at different heights: eight *Tomahawks* of 5 SAAF (8.10-9.30) were at 9000 feet, six *Kittyhawks* of 2 SAAF (8.00-9.20) were at 8000 feet, and lastly eight *Tomahawks* of 4 SAAF (8.05-9.30?) were at 7000 feet.

At 8.25, 2 SAAF was flying at 8000 feet when its pilots saw the bombing over Bir Hakeim along with eight *Bf.109s* in two groups of four at 10000 feet.
Lt. De Waal (AL126 DB-R) reported:

Magg. Larsimont, C.O. of 9° Gr. (Ufficio Storico SMA)

"The Me.s came down and attacked. Two 109s came in to attack, I shot at the leader and he broke off. The second came down to the formation leader but broke off into a climbing left hand turn. I followed him up and got in a good long burst from astern. I saw my tracers enter and dense clouds of greyish smoke left his machine. He went off west losing height, emitting clouds of smoke. One Me.109 damaged. .50:450 rounds."

At 8.30, 5 SAAF was flying at 9000 feet west of Bir Hakeim when its pilots sighted thirty *Stukas* in three squadrons and twelve *Bf.109s* as close escort. The Squadron dived to attack the bombers but was engaged by the escort coming from 4000 feet before they could reach them.
Lt. Hirst (AN309 GL-O) described the destruction of a *Bf.109*:

"...I picked up a 109F and closed in with plenty of speed in a fine quarter-stern. He pulled up steeply turning slightly. I followed and fired two bursts at close range and watched him fall away and eventually turned on his back low down, and crashed into flames."

Maj. Frost (AK or AM522 GL-B), one *Bf.109* probable;
Lt. Finlayson (AN 427 GL-D), one *Bf.109* probable;
Lt. Bidwell (AN415 GL-T) claimed one *Bf.109* probable. He recalled:

"... I got onto the tail of a 109F and fired one burst. He dived toward the West. I overboosted and fired two long bursts at about 100 yds range. What appeared to be golden flakes fell from the Me.109, which then dived very steeply and at great speed, making no apparent effort to pull out. I turned steeply towards two other Me.109s, which were attacking me from the rear. In the turn my aircraft was hit, the port elevator and rudder being badly damaged. It spun down out of control. My goggles came off and I was blinded by dust in the cockpit. I opened the hood and regained control, but the controls were ineffective and there was a tendency to flick when I attempted to turn. Frequent attacks were delivered by at least two 109s. My seat was hit and the cockpit was full of dust

Macchi Martinoli's C.202, 73-4, M.M.7764 (Gentilli)

and what appeared to be smoke. I was unable to see and me, and was very uncomfortable and rather unhappy. The engine was not behaving normally. Quite unintentionally I did a crash landing. A gunner from a Bofor gun about 100 yds away ran towards me. The gun team fired repeatedly at the enemy aircraft, driving one awey. The other Me.109 straffed us as we were running towards the Bofor gun, but he was chased away. The anti-aircraft gunners behaved magnificently, and certainly saved me before and after landed..."

4 SAAF also reported that *C.202s* formed a part of the enemy escort. They became separated by the clouds and were engaged by at least three enemy aircraft:
Capt. Bayly claimed a *Bf.109* destroyed (possibly Pfeffer) and a second shared with Lt. Kaufman (AN452 KJ-M) and Lt. Van Nus (AN377 KJ-B).
Capt. Bayly (4 SAAF, AN418 KJ-S):

"Due to dust and cloud we did not contact the Wing. Whilst patrolling the area west of Bir Hakeim (8.55, 7000 feet)... I saw a lone 109F heading west at about 4000'. I told my top cover to remain as such and took my No.2 with me to attack....No.2 turned back due to gun trouble....got a number of bursts from astern. Height was down to 500'. ...smoke poured out from the engine of the 109 which crash landed at high speed putting up a large cloud of dust...."

On the way home west of El Adem (9.30), 4 SAAF was attacked by two *Bf.109s* that were engaged by Van Nus (AN377 KJ-B) and Kaufman (AN452 KJ-M). The enemy engaged by the latter broke away. The other clashed with Van Nus and then flew out of sight. Van Nus's *Tomahawk* was holed in the starboard wing with damage to the hydraulic system, and so upon landing it flipped over (Cat.III).
This second clash can match the claims of the two pilots of 4./JG 27.

Replenishment of a C.202 of 1° Stormo (Archivio di Stato)

Unfortunately it is not clear how the escort of *Bf.109s* was set up. However, this time it was again numerous and prevented the attack on the *Stukas*. The clash of fighter against fighter seemed balanced, at least as far as losses were concerned. This was also because only 2 SAAF would have had the advantage of altitude. Clearly the task of the defence was made easier by the bad visibility that prevented 4 SAAF and presumably 260 Squadron from reaching the German attacking formation.

Seven *Bf.109s* of III /JG 27 were on a free sweep over Mteifel (around noon). They were targeted by anti-aircraft fire and Oblt. Klager 7./JG 53 was hit and had to make an emergency landing at Tmimi. The pilot was unhurt (W.Nr. 10179, 100%).

B) Magg. Larsimont, with fourteen *Macchis* of 9° Gruppo (six of 73ª Sq., six of 96ª Sq. and two of 97ª Sq.), was on a free sweep over Bir Hakeim (16.00-17.30).
The planes came up against three enemy formations at altitudes of 3000, 3500, and 4000 metres respectively over Bir Hakeim at 16.30. Their adversaries amounted to a total of thirty planes, split between *P-40s* and *Hurricanes* (a very precise estimate). The attack followed and six *P-40s* and two *Hurricanes* were credited shot down along with three *P-40s* and three *Hurricanes* probably shot down and nineteen machine-gunned (3839 rounds):
It was reported that Serg.Magg. Martinoli (73ª Sq.) easily shot down two *P-40s,* setting them afire in addition to damaging a third one; his plane was in its turn hit and slightly damaged. As

usual, the Italian ace flew at the top of the formation because of his outstanding eyesight.

Serg. Guerci shot down a *P-40* and fired at a second one from close distance. He saw a black trail coming from it. He did not follow it, engaged as he was in the midst of the dogfights. His plane was also hit and slightly damaged.

Ten. Squarcia fired at the tail of an enemy fighter at very close range but had to desist because his plane was in its turn slightly damaged.

Serg. Magg. Mechelli, who was following Squarcia, fired on another two aircraft, hitting the cockpit of one; he saw it heel over and then assumed an anomalous trim with the nose pointing down. He then followed it, hitting it again. But then he had to desist because another *P-40* was on his tail. S.Ten. Querci (73ª Sq.) shot down a *P-40* and fired at a second; his plane was in its turn hit, but not badly.

Ten. Annoni (96ª Sq.) fired at four planes;

Serg. Biagini (96ª Sq.) shot down a *P-40* and a *Hurricane* probably shot down;

Twenty-one year old Serg. Magg. Pasquale Rossi (96ª Sq., M.M.7822) did not return.

The enemy formations, on patrol over Bir Hakeim, were respectively: ten *Kittyhawks* of 260 Squadron (16.55-18.35) with 2 and 4 SAAF, but the first would break away from the other two; twelve *Hurricane IICs* of 213 Squadron (16.50-18.50) as top cover for another eleven of 73 Squadron (17.00-18.30), also on patrol over Bir Hakeim and searching for possible enemy bombers; four *Spitfires* of 145 Squadron (17.00-18.30) were top cover for the *Hurricanes* but probably were separated because nothing was reported.

The first to meet with the Italians was 260 Squadron who lost Sgt. Clark (missing).

Subsequently 213 and 73 Squadrons were engaged.

213 Squadron was on a course of 250° at 15000 feet when it saw a formation of *Kittyhawks* (260 Squadron) returning east,which warned the *Hurricanes* that bandits were heading south-east 20 miles south-east of Gazala.

And then ground control sent the warning that bandits were behind and to port 10 miles east of Bir Hakeim. The Commonwealth formation was at 15000 feet when it turned against twelve *Bf.109s* and *C.202s* in vic formation 500-1000 feet above.

Six peeled off in line astern and dived to attack the *Hurricanes*: individual combats followed with one *Bf.109* claimed destroyed and a *Bf.109* and a *C.202* damaged. Only two *Hurricanes* were slightly damaged: one received a strike in the petrol tank and another in the aileron. One *Bf.109* was seen going down in flames and hit the deck (Rossi) but no *Ju.88s* were sighted.

The *Hurricanes* formed into a defensive circle to the left, everyone weaving. The enemy aircraft practically attacked in a vertical dive and then pulled up. Four more enemy aircraft joined the fight.

F.Lt. Temlett (BM981, 100 Ball, 100 HE/Inc);

P.O. Henderson (BM128, 50 Ball,50 HE/Inc);

S.L. Johnson (BF272) stated:

> "I was leading the top flight of 213 Sqn…approaching Bir Hakeim at 13000 from the east (17.50) I saw 4-5 109Fs and 3 Macchi 202s 1500 ft above at 9 o'clock. I watched them begin to turn behind us no doubt preparatory to making an attack when suddenly I noticed that a Macchi 202 well in advance of the others had launched his attack and was nearly in firing distance of my No.2. I wheeled violently round and he broke off the attack and pulled up starboard. I followed him up, firing until I spun and saw a burst of glycol and smoke come from his engine. He staggered and fell away on his back. … on recovering became immediately engaged with 109Fs…One Macchi probable. 12 HE/Inc, 12 ball"

W.C. Fenton (BN157) led the eleven *Hurricanes IICs* of 73 Squadron; at 17.50 they were flying at an altitude of 12000 feet 10 miles west of Bir Hakeim when they were jumped by five to six *Bf.109s* and *Macchis* coming down from 3000 feet above.
F.Sgt. Joyce (BN156):

"...Our A flight was jumped by 5 Macchis and 109s. A mix up followed and I climbed to 14000 (from 10-11000). A Me109 dived on a Hurricane. I half rolled, losing my No.2 and pulled up waiting for him (the 109) to pull up, which he did about 300 yards in front of me, climbing on an angle of 45°. I fired and as I did, he turned slightly left. I changed my aim and blew about 2 square feet off his left wing. He went down in a vertical dive, left hand, and I watched him for about 5000 feet, when I was attacked by a Macchi 202. …. I then climbed to 15000 feet and made several attacks….I took evasive action and evaded an attack by an Me.109, which was coming from the sun, about 400 yards behind me.... There was one Kittyhawk (Clark), which belly landed about 10-12 miles east of Bir Hakeim. I claimed one probably destroyed. 53 balls, 52 He total 147-145."

The Italian formation was subdivided in two sections, one at 5000 metres with 96ª Sq. and another at 4000 metres. It was 260 Squadron that was met first, separated as it was from the South Africans, and it was briefly engaged (it is not known why it was not pursued). The *Macchis* then came up against the *Hurricanes* that, being in difficulty, formed a defensive circle. There must have been two separated clashes of the two squadrons with the two sections of 9° Gruppo. Notwithstanding the big battle and the difficulties of the enemy formations, the *Macchis* did not manage to do much damage and indeed lost a pilot, despite the large number of rounds fired by their Bredas and the large number of victories claimed.

Fl.Lt. Monk (145 Squadron, B502), force landed NNE of Gambut during an operational sweep (19.20).

C) Six *Hurricanes* of 274 Squadron with ten others of 33 Squadron as top cover were again out on an offensive patrol over Bir Hakeim (19.20-20.45). Another formation of 12 Kittyhawks of 3 RAAF and 450 Squadron followed after a few minutes (19.25-20.45).
  274 Squadron reported the attack by ten *Bf.109s* from 12000 feet. Sgt. Eagle got in a five-second burst on the leader and saw pieces break off the wings and fuselage; smoke poured from the aircraft which went into a dive (a probable victory was claimed). He also claimed a second damaged.
Sgt. Henderson got a burst on a *Bf.109* and saw glycol pouring out (it was claimed to be damaged).
  33 Squadron reported eight *Bf.109s* and one *C.202*. Many claims were made:
F.O. Wade one *Bf.109* destroyed;
P.O. Mac Challis one *Bf.109* destroyed;
P.O. McLarty one *C.202* damaged, while his aircraft was damaged Cat II.
Sgt. Allan recorded a probable *C.202* but did not claim it.
  The six *Kittyhawks* of 3 RAAF contacted seven *Bf.109s* ENE of Bir Hakeim. One was attacked by S.L. Barr (AL145 CV-Z) from front quarter and he saw 2 explosive bursts on the engine cowling, then the enemy fighter dived away steeply to the W and disappeared in the haze. Then the *Messerschmitts* broke off the engagement.
  450 Squadron was over the battle area when 'bandits' were reported several times. After having seen an escorted formation of Stukas, another formation of five *Bf.109s* was sighted below.

F.Sgt. Dyson and his No.2 dived on them and a short mix followed but with no results.

Sixteen *Bf.109s* of III./JG 53 with others of II./JG 27 covered *Stukas* again on Bir Hakeim (St.G. 3: 17.55-19.45). Enemy fighters were encountered and three *P-40s* were claimed shot down:
Lt. Müller (8./JG 53, 19.00, not confirmed);
Ofhr. Kientsch (Stab II./JG 27), NE of Bir Hakeim (19.05);
and Lt. Müller (8./JG 53, 19.10, not confirmed).
Prien took note of the sensation that the recognition of victories for III./JG 53 was much more rigorous than that of JG 27, which it was subordinate to.

Serg.Magg. Ruzzene (94ª Sq.) force lands with his *C.200* due to engine trouble.

OBS reported the loss of only one *Bf.109* during the day, when at least two were damaged 100%. We must assume that those that were wrecked on their return were not considered lost.

Night of 9-10

Up to four *He.111s* attacked aerodromes at Fuka and Sidi Barrani (19.30-2.25); Fw. Lenninger (II./K.G.100, *H-6* 6N + FH) was shot down by Flak over Qutaifiya. The crew was taken prisoner except one missing.

10 June

A) Twelve *Hurricanes IICs* of 73 Squadron (7.50) were top cover for twelve others of 213 Squadron (7.55-9.15) on a free sweep over Bir Hakeim to intercept expected *Stukas*. Two *Spitfires* of 145 Squadron (7.50-8.55) were extra top cover.

At 8.35, 213 Squadron was flying at 14000 feet 10 miles west of Bir Hakeim when it sighted fifteen to twenty *Ju.87s*. They were stepped up in vics escorted by over twenty *Bf.109s* in line astern slightly above, weaving gently, some circling in front about 6000 feet above. The *Hurricanes* altered course to come down out of the sun on the leading enemy flight, which was turning west; the squadron was attacked by some *Bf.109s*, but several *Hurricanes* managed to reach the *Stukas*.
F.Lt. Westlake (BE340) claimed one *Bf.109* probable and one *Ju.87* damaged:

> "...We were forming up to do a Squadron attack when we were jumped from astern by 6 109s. We were given duck and were milling round, when someone told us to go for the Stukas. Blue II and myself cut off the corner and went for two of the formation, I choosing one and closing from a quarter to dead astern, opened up at 250 yards range, with a short burst, then closing to 1000-150 yards for a longer burst, during which I saw strikes all along the starboard main plane from root to wing tip. There was some return fire. The 87 reared up and pulled to starboard. We were then jumped by 6 109s, the fire from which was very intense. I performed tight turns down to 3-4000', when 2 more dived on me. The second one went right across my line of sight, and when I opened up on him, he turned over on his back at about 2000' and with white smoke pouring from him, he went straight down into cloud...55 Ball, 55 He/Inc".

Marseille and his Bf.109 (Gentilli)

Two other *Ju.87s* were claimed damaged by P.O. Rehill (BN13955; 35 Ball, 35 He/Inc) and F.Sgt. Edwards (BE285; 23 Ball, 22 He/Inc)
F.O. Sowrey (BN562) fired at a *Ju.87* without seeing any results:

> "... My hood was open and I got all the dirt from the 87's return fire. This blinded me for a moment but I closed my hood and then another 87 climbed in front and I gave it a long burst full into his belly closing at about 50 yards. Dense smoke poured violently from its engine, and then it burst into flames. As I broke away to the right, it broke away from its own formation which was going round in a circle and plunged down to the deck in flames. An Me. then dived down on my stern, rearing up in front of me. I pulled my nose up and gave him a burst at 100 yards, observing strikes along left side of fuselage. He was still climbing away when I felt my own aircraft hit and immediately I went into an involuntary spin...I decided to bale out, but suddenly the machine righted itself...I went down to the deck, but soon had 4 Me.109s after me. They got my engine and set starboard aileron on fire and there was nothing for it but to crash-land..."

Then Sowrey returned unhurt.
Sgt. Jackson (BM159) went missing.
P.O. Hankok (BM966) hit a straggling *Ju.87* that dived to the ground in flames. He was then attacked by a *Bf.109* and was slightly wounded, and so he landed at El Gobi (Cat.I).
Officially only three *Ju.87s* were confirmed damaged, but at least five pilots made claims on them.
73 Squadron in its turn entered the fight engaging the escort:

> "'A' flight is jumped by 5 202s; the Hurricanes turn into them 3 times but the Italians won't stay to fight. Then two batches of 20 plus Stukas and 88s are seen heading west from Bir Hakeim, with AC of 213 Sqn. in hot pursuit. B Flight meets 3-4 109s and forces them up. PO Fraser sees an enemy belching black smoke, diving almost vertically with an ac following and shooting at him. FL. Scade has force landed but is safe, even if wounded (166 Ball, 167 He/Inc)."

S.L. Overton (145 Squadron, B502) destroyed a *Bf.109*.

Hurricane IIC with reduced armament (Aviation Heritage Museum of Western Australia)

In this case they came across a formation of forty-two *Ju.87s* that was attacking enemy positions at Bir Hakeim (St.G. 3: 6.25-8.20). They were protected by fourteen *Bf.109s* of I./JG 27 (6.50-8.05/8.20) and eight of II./JG 27, as well as more of III./JG 53. The *Messerschmitts* were credited with nine aircraft shot down:
Marseille (4), 5 km NW of Mteifel Chebir (7.35); 6 km NE of Mteifel Chebir (7.41); 6 km E of Mteifel Chebir (7.45); 6 km ENE of Mteifel Chebir (7.50);
Lt. von Lieres u. Wilkau (2./JG 27), N of Bir Hakeim (7.43);
Ofw. Mentnich (3./JG 27), N of Bir Hakeim (7.43);
Lt. Schroer (Stab I./JG 27), 5 km W of Bir Hakeim (7.49);
Lt. Quaritsch (8./JG 53) (7.53);
and Oblt. Götz (9./JG 53) (7.50). All claims were for *P-40s* except a Spitfire that was shot down by Götz.
Oblt. Sinner, C.O. of 6./JG 27 (W.Nr. 8492, ge.2+), was shot down over El Adem but returned safely. His score at the time stood at six confirmed victories; he would go on to end the war with the rank of Major and 39 kills to his credit. His victor was probably Overton, a Battle of Britain veteran that in this action achieved ace status.
During the day, Fw. Gromotka (6./JG 27) claimed a Hurricane without giving the place and time; "Star of Africa" reported it in this action together with the damaging of another four P-40s by II./JG 27.

Presumably in the course this mission Ju.87 D-1/Trop W.Nr. 2060 (III./St.G.3) was shot down by fighters.

This time the escort again seemed solid and the bombers were well defended and losses sustained had been moderate.

B) 1° Stormo carried out a free sweep over the Hakeim-Bir El Harmat area with planes of both Gruppi. Cap. Camarda led six Macchis of 6° Gruppo, two for each of the three squadrons (14.50-16.05). Meanwhile six other C.202s of 17° Gruppo (four of 72ª Sq. and two of 80ª Sq.) were led by Cap. Nioi (15.00-16.20). The small number of Macchis shows that by now their availability was low.

When they were flying at an altitude of 5000 m to the east of Bir Hakeim at 15.20, they came upon an enemy formation of about twenty P-40s and Hurricanes.

The 6° Gruppo pilots declared to have shot down six P-40s as well as fourteen machine-gunned (2625 rounds fired).
Cap. Camarda (79ª Sq.) shot down a P-40 and fired at five (500 rounds);
Serg. Benati (79ª) shot down a P-40 (180 rounds);
Ten. Falchi (81ª) fired at two planes;
Serg. Magg. Morosi (81ª Sq.) shot down a P-40 and fired at another six (81ª Sq., 795 rounds);
M.llo Baschirotto (88ª Sq.) shot down two *P-40s* and fired at three;
Serg. Magg. Borreo (88ª Sq.) shot down a *P-40* and fired at three (88ª Sq., 350 rounds).
Ten. Ghiglia and Serg.Magg. Bersani (72ª Sq.) shared a *P-40* shot down (72ª Sq. fired 420 rounds).

Cap. Clizio Nioi C.O. of 80ª Sq. (17°Gr., Ufficio Storico SMA)

Only four 17° Gruppo pilots reached the enemy:
Serg.Magg. Andrich (80ª Sq.) shot down a *P-40* and a second was shot down in collaboration with Cap. Nioi (80ª Sq.), Ten. Ghiglia (72ª Sq.), and Serg.Magg. Bersani (72ª Sq.). 1760 rounds were fired in total.
The air battle went on almost up to El Adem; all the *Macchis* returned to base undamaged. Andrich landed at Tmimi and then returned to Martuba.

The Italians came up against 73 and 213 Squadrons, which were again in action for a cruise over the Bir Hakeim area to protect the movements of their own troops.
Eleven *Hurricane IIs* of 213 Squadron (15.35-16.55.) were cover for another twelve *Hurricanes* of 73 Squadron (15.40-17.00).
During the flight, they were warned that more than twelve bandits were approaching.

At 16.20, twelve *Bf.109s* approached from astern at about 11500 feet while 73 Squadron was at 11000 feet, 10 miles south of El Adem. ''A'' flight was attacked from astern, notwithstanding the cover of 213 Squadron. And then the enemy pulled up 2000 feet above. Afterwards, ''B'' flight was attacked in the same manner.
Baker (BN402), 16.20, 8000 feet:

> "Formation was jumped by 12 109s and 202's. We did three turnabouts and waited until a favourable opportunity arose for a shot. As the enemy continued its tactics I took two snap shots, short bursts, as the EA pulled out of their dives. Then one 109F pulled straight up in front of me so I pulled straight up and fired a two second burst with about one quarter deflection. Observed 4 large holes appear in aircraft wings and machine reached top of climb and fell out in steep spiral with white smoke trail. I claim one probable. 76 ball, 75 inc."

P.O. Henry (BE372), 10500 feet, 16.20:

"...Heard a duck and pulled into a left hand climbing turn. One 109F came past with another in line astern. I fired at the second and saw hits register on tail plane and pieces fly off. Another 109F came down. I fired but all guns had stopped so I broke off … 8 ball, 7 inc he"

S.L. Ward (BN131) had a head on attack with a *Bf.109* when he broke off 500 feet above, exposing his belly at 50 yards. He saw explosions between the pilot and the tail. Then the *Bf.109* pulled up, waggling its wing and breaking away (61 Ball, 60 He/Inc).
Taken as a whole, 73 Squadron claimed a *Bf.109* probable and two damaged; this was counterbalanced with the loss of Sgt. Wilson (BE568) who was hit but baled out unhurt. (Total 295 Ball, 292 He/Inc).

213 Squadron was in its turn attacked by four reported *Bf.109s* (possibly four *Macchis* of 17° Gruppo). And the British claimed to have damaged an enemy plane as well as two probably damaged. However, one of its *Hurricanes* was slightly damaged.

Capt. Gordon Bayly, 4 SAAF Squadron (Bouwer).

213 Squadron was also flying at a height of from 10 to 11000 feet when it saw 73 Squadron, at the same level one mile ahead, being jumped by three *Bf.109s*. Then 'A' flight of 213 Squadron was jumped from astern by four other *Bf.109s*, employing the usual tactics. Individual combats followed. There was intense light flack over the area, which was being directed at the right position but 200 feet below.
P.O. Wilson (BM983 C) of 'A' flight, upon becoming aware of the attack, whipped into a steep left turn. Seeing a *Bf.109* climbing in front of him, he gave him a burst from 200 to 40 yards, seeing strikes hit home in front of the cockpit and along the cowling. Then he broke off the attack because a second *Bf.109* was diving on his tail (40 Ball, 40 He/Inc).
W.O. Wallace (BN139) of Black Flight noted that "A" flight went into a defensive circle, orbiting and weaving, when attacked. He also hit a *Bf.109* (60 Ball, 60 He/Inc).
P.O. Tomlinson (BN353 D) of Red Flight was hit while he was in the circle, but he also had a chance of hitting a *Bf.109*. Then he had to leave the fight because the cockpit was swamped with oil. He was also hit on the starboard wing. Cat. II (20 Ball, 20 He/Inc) (Total: 210 Ball, 210 He/Inc).

6° Gruppo would have attacked 73 Squadron and 17° Gruppo 213 Squadron, and this time there wasn't any stepping at altitude. The *Hurricanes*, as they often did, formed defensive circles. As usual, the Italians put the adversary in difficulty, expending many more rounds than the *Hurricanes* and claiming a large number of victories — but to scarce effect.

C) 33 Squadron was in as weep covered by 274 Squadron (17.10-18.40) in the same Knightsbridge area of the previous action. There were 24 *Hurricanes*, twelve for each squadron. Moreover, there was the cover of four Spitfires of 145 Squadron at 19000 feet. 33 Squadron was attacked by six Bf.109s and C.202s and a dog-fight ensued: one plane was badly damaged (Sgt. Menzies, Cat.II). Nevertheless, notwithstanding the identification of *Macchis* and the type of air-combat typical for the Italians, they should have clashed with *Bf.109s* given the time difference (OBS reports more than one clash during the day).

P.O. Norman (145 Squadron) was flying alone after having lost the formation when he spotted five *Bf.109s* 3000 feet above. He assaulted them and fired at one, but without results.

274 Squadron however did not report any clashes. It seems that visibility was not good because the rule was that the top cover would be the first engaged.

Wellington IC BB842 K of 108 Squadron was lost with all its crew over Crete (20.05), presumably shot down by anti-aircraft fire.

There was a very painful loss for 4 SAAF: Capt. Gordon Bayly (AM418 KJ-S) and Lt. Malcolm Ironside (AN236) collided while forming up after an evening scramble and lost their lives.

| DATE | AXIS TIME | \multicolumn{9}{c}{CLAIMS} | \multicolumn{6}{c}{CASUALTIES} | UNITS INVOLVED |

DATE	AXIS TIME	COMM. S	COMM. P	COMM. D	GER. S	GER. P	GER. D	ITA. S	ITA. P	ITA. M	COMM. S	COMM. D	GER. S	GER. D	ITA. S	ITA. D	UNITS INVOLVED
31	A 5.40-6.24	2A	1Bs 1A	1Bs 2A	4A								3A				II/JG 27, ?, Ju.87s, 5 SAAF Sqn
	B 6.58-7.42	2Bs	1Bs 1A	1A	10A						4A		2Bs				I/JG 27, III/JG 53, St.G.3, 4 SAAF Sqn
	C 10.50-11.50							2A									17° Gr, P-40?
	D 12.15-13.35	1Bs		1Bs							2A	1A					260 Sqn, ?
	E 17.15-18.25							4A	4A	?	1A	1A					9° Gr, Ju.87s, 274, 33 Sqn
	F 18.38-19.38				5A						7A						II/JG 27, III/JG53, 2, 4, 5 SAAF, 450, 3 RAAF, 112, 260 Sqn
	G 22.30-23.10				1B			1B			1B		1B				17° Gr, 7/ZG 26, 148 Sqn.
1	A 6.30-7.30			1B													1 SAAF Sqn, Ju.88 recco?
	B 6.45-8.00																1 SAAF Sqn, 205ª Sq
	C 15.20-17.00	1A			1A						1A						III./JG 53, 4, 5 Sqn
	D 16.30-17.30			1B 1A													145, 274, Bf.109?, Ju.88 recco?
	E 17.25-19.30	2A	1A	2B 1A2	5A						2A		1A				3 RAAF, 112 Sqn, I/JG 27, III/JG 53, III./ZG 26, I./KG 54
	F 2.48-?			1B													73 Sqn, Ju.88?
2	A 16.22-?				1A						1A						II/JG 27, 274 Sqn
3	A 5.40-6.35												1A				II/JG 27, 33 Sqn
	B 6.20-7.30							3A	1A	10A	1A	1A					6° Gr, 2 e 4 SAAF Sqn.
	C 11.32-12.52	10Bs 1A		1A	10A						5A		3Bs				2, 5 Sqn, JG 27, III/JG 53, 3/St.G 3
	D 15.05-16.00			1A													145 Sqn, Bf.109?

DATE	AXIS TIME	CLAIMS COMM			GER			ITA			CASUALTIES COMM		GER		ITA		UNITS INVOLVED
		S	P	D	S	P	D	S	P	M	S	D	S	D	S	D	
4 A	7.45-8.50	6Bs 1A	1Bs	2Bs 2A	2A			5A	3A	7A	5A		5Bs	1Bs			10°Gr, II/JG 27, I/St.G 3, 2SAAF, 4SAAF, 5 SAAF, 33, 274 Sqn
4 B	13.00-14.30							6A		8A							10° Gr, 33 Sqn
4 C	16.00-17.25	2A		2A					3A							2A	6°Gr, 50v St, 2 SAAF, 5 SAAF, 260 Sqn.
5 A	5.00-6.15							6A	2A	?							17° Gr, 274 Sqn.
5 B	11.15-12.15				2A						1A		1A				II/JG 27, 2 SAAF, 40 SAAF Sqn
5 C	17.05-18.15					1B 5A	9A			1A	2A	4A					9°Gr, I, II/JG 27, III/JG 53, Ju.88, 2 SAAF, 5 SAAF, 260 Sqn
6 A	5.05-6.30				3A			2A	1A	2A							10°Gr, 250 Sqn
6 B	9.15-10.40	3A	1A										1A				112 Sqn, 4(H)/12
7 A	8.35-10.10							5A	1A	14A	3A						10° Gr, 73, 213 Sqn
7 B	9.20-10.40					1A	1A	2A				1A					2 SAAF, 5 SAAF, 260 Sqn, III./JG 53.
7 C	12.45-13.45					1A											II/JG 27, ?
7 D	15.30-16.30	1A				3A		2A			2A		1A				I, III/JG 27, III/JG 53, St.G. 3, 2 SAAF Sqn
8 A	5.33-7.07	1A				1A	3A						1A				II/JG 27, St.G.3, 73, 213 Sqn
8 B	6.40-8.25	1A				6A		4A	1A	8A	1A	1A					9° Gr, 2, 4, 5 SAAF, 260 Sqn
8 C	9.05-10.30					1A		4A			1A	3A					10° Gr, 33, 274, 208 Sqn
8 D	13.45-15.10					2A		3A	1A	10A	1A						10° Gr, 4, 5 SAAF Sqn
8 E	14.55-16.20	2A	1A					1A	4A	1A						1A	6° Gr, 274, 33, 250, 145 Sqn

DATE	AXIS TIME	CLAIMS COMM. S	CLAIMS COMM. P	CLAIMS COMM. D	CLAIMS GER. S	CLAIMS GER. P	CLAIMS GER. D	CLAIMS ITA. S	CLAIMS ITA. P	CLAIMS ITA. M	CASUALTIES COMM. S	CASUALTIES COMM. D	CASUALTIES GER. S	CASUALTIES GER. D	CASUALTIES ITA. S	CASUALTIES ITA. D	UNITS INVOLVED
9 A	6.55-8.15	2A	4A	1A	5A						1A		1A				I/JG 27, II/JG 27, III/JG 53, 2 SAAF, 4 SAAF, 5 SAAF Sqn
9 B	16.00-17.30	2A	2A					8A	6A	19A	1A	2A			1A		9° Gr, 73, 213, 260 Sqn
9 C	18.20-?	2A	2A	3A	3A								1A				33, 274, 3 RAAF, 450 Sqn, II/JG 27, III/JG 53
10 A	6.50-8.05	1A	1A	5Bs	10A		4A				3A		1Bs 1A				I, III/JG 27, III/JG 53, St.G.3, 73, 213, 145 Sqn
10 B	15.00-16.20		1A	3A				8A		14A	1A	2A					6°,17° Gr, 73, 213 Sqn.
10 C	16.15-16.30												1A				33, 145 Sqn, Bf.109s ?
TOT		19 Bs 24A			1B 75A			1B 61A			1B 46A		11Bs 11A		4A		

LEGENDA

S - SHOT DOWN P - PROBABLE D - DAMAGED M - MACHINE GUNNED

A - SINGLE ENGINE FIGHTER A2 - TWIN ENGINE FIGHTER B - BOMBER Bs - STUKA T - OTHER TYPES

Chapter 6
KNIGHTSBRIDGE (11-18 June)

The rest of the three Armoured Brigades, along with the 201st Guards B the strongholds around Knightsbridge.

On June 12th, the 21st and 15th Panzer Divisions attacked but they had been worn out by the fighting. It was not until the following day, when the Ariete and Trieste Divisions joined the combat, that the battle was won.

On June 14th, Auchinleck authorised Ritchie to withdraw from the Gazala line. The defenders in the El Adem and two neighbouring boxes held firm and the 1st South African Division was able to withdraw along the coastal road. They were harassed by the Axis air forces but otherwise practically intact. The road could not accommodate two divisions, and so the remaining two brigades of the 50th (Northumbrian) Division had to find an alternative. They could not retreat directly east because of the presence of Axis armoured forces, and so instead they attacked south west, breaking through the lines of the Italian Brescia and Pavia Divisions and heading south into the desert before turning east and returning to friendly territory.

At about the same time, all the strongpoints west of Tobruk were evacuated.

Ritchie ordered the Eighth Army to withdraw to the defensive positions at Mersa Matruh, which were about a hundred miles east of the frontier. Tobruk was left to hold out and threaten the Axis lines of communication in much the same way as in 1941.

During this period, the opposing air forces in Africa were engaged in attacking actions and conversely in escorting the convoy that had to reach Malta from Alexandria (Operation Vigorous).

11 June

A) F.O. Mc Gregor (208 Squadron, *Tomahawk* AK567) was on a reconnaissance mission over Bir Hakeim at 16.40:

> "...I was attacked by 4 Me.109Fs. They caught me unawares coming out from the sun...hit my port wing but did no appreciable damage and I took evasive action...I pulled my nose up and gave him a ring and a half deflection, with a three second burst....black smoke coming from his engine....The Ea continued to make attacks in line astern but by turning towards them I managed to evade most attacks.....however, bullets smashed all instruments....over El Adem EA came under heavy AA,...with aircraft burning I decided to make a forced landing."

The attackers were four *Bf.109s* of 1./JG 27 on a freelance (15.02). Uffz. Timmermann claimed a *Kittyhawk* north of Sidi Rezegh (15.45).

B) Eleven *Hurricanes* of 274 Squadron (top cover, 17.00-18.05) scrambled with eleven others of 33 Squadron and headed for El Adem to search for enemy bombers.

When the formation was five miles south of El Adem, twenty-four to thirty *Stukas* were seen flying west at 7000 feet while at least six *Bf.109 Fs* were approaching from the north-west at 13000 feet (33 Squadron reported over 70 bombers and fighters leaving the area). 274 Squadron attacked the *Messerschmitts* head on:

Hurricane I Z4896; this type was used by 208 Sqn. along with Tomahawks (Aviation Heritage Museum of Western Australia)

P.O. Walsh attacked the leader whose plane burst into flames in addition to damaging a second *Bf.109*.

P.O. Persse and F.Sgt. Neil were attacked by two *Bf.109s*. Neil fired a three-second burst without results. The two *Bf.109s* turned away but three others attacked: Neil again fired at the leader and shot him down in flames with a three-second burst. Neil was again attacked by two *Bf.109s* and expended his last ammunition, without observing results. Persse was shot down and killed. It seems that also the close escort of *Stukas* (recognized as *C.202s*) climbed up to join the fight.

In its turn, 33 Squadron reported the attack of over twelve *Bf.109s* and *C.202s*; P.O. Challis (4953) damaged a *C.202* but his plane was damaged in its turn (Cat.II). Sgt. Allen hit a *Bf.109* with a long burst, seeing smoke trailing from it, and claimed a probable victory. Several other pilots got in bursts but no other claim was made. P.O. Wade (239) was reported to have been hit by anti-aircraft fire and force-landed at El Adem (Cat.II), but it seems more likely that he was shot down by fighters.

P.O. Marsh's plane developed an oil leak that covered its windscreen, reducing his visibility. Four *C.202s* were on his tail but were scared off by his companions.

They came up against a formation of twelve *Ju.87s* that were attacking concentrations of motor vehicles north-west of El Adem (15.50-17.00, OBS). The latter were escorted by eight *Bf.109s* of I./JG 27, nine of III./JG 27, thirteen of III./JG 53, and others of II./JG 27 (15.45-16.45); these engaged enemy fighters and claimed four shot down:
Oblt. Marseille (2), *P-40*, SW of El Adem (16.25); *Hurricane* II, 18 km NW of El Adem (16.35);
Lt. Harder (7./JG 53), *Hurricane* (16.25);
Ofw. Stumpf (9./JG 53), *Hurricane* (16.40).

Eight Jabos attacked the railway near Bu Amud (13.10-14.10). Uffz. Zeller (10.(J)/JG 27, W.Nr. 8539 gn.5+) was shot down over Acroma in air combat and went missing. Meanwhile, a second aircraft of the same unit (W.Nr. 7477) crash-landed at Martuba, 75%. The times do not match up but it seems that they were involved in the above-mentioned clash. They were probably computed as escort provided by III./JG 27.

Bf.109 of II./JG 27 (Gentilli)

Macchis should not have been present in this case as well.

Sgt. Adye (AK988) and Sgt. Greaves (AK937) of 112 Squadron were shot down during a bombing mission (20.10) and went missing.

12 June

At 6.20, twelve *Kittyhawks* of 3 RAAF attacked concentrations of lorry borne troops. Anti-aircraft fire was intense. Sgt. Bray (AK176) was hit, landing in a minefield with the tail of his aircraft blown off (Cat.III), but luckily the pilot himself was uninjured. Sgt. Stevens (AL187) was also hit by flak and his undercarriage was damaged. He subsequently crashed in the dispersal area upon arrival back to base with the unexploded bomb still attached. His plane, however, was written off (Cat.III). Sgt. Finlayson was also shot up (AL208, Cat.II).
F.Sgt. Cassell (112 Squadron, AL149) was shot down by anti-aircraft fire at 10.00. But he got away safely.
Undoubtedly, ground attack missions could be extremely dangerous.

F.O. Barlow (*Hurricane* IIA Z5330) of 208 Squadron was also shot down by anti-aircraft fire (6.30-8.00, Cat.II).

A) Ten *Kittyhawks* of 260 Squadron (8.55-9.45) and one of 2 SAAF were escorting six *Bostons* of 24 SAAF (8.45). They ran into six *Bf.109s* (some publications also report *C.202s*): one *Kittyhawk* (260 Squadron) was destroyed (Cat.III) and the injured pilot went to hospital. 24 SAAF reported that top cover was engaged by four *Bf.109s*.
  In the morning, six *Messerschmitts* of III./JG 53 ran across a number of twin-engined bombers and clashed with the escort: many hits were scored but no claims were made.

Bofors 40mm AA guns (Bouwer)

In another escort, three *Kittyhawks* of 2 SAAF (9.15-10.00) reported two enemy aircraft, possibly *C.202s*, that had no intention of attacking the bombers or the close cover. It is likely that they came up against the same German formation.

Twelve *Hurricanes* of 213 Squadron were patrolling at 12000 feet over El Adem (9.00-10.10) when they were jumped by two *Bf.109s*; there was evasive action but no combat.

Sgt. Halliday of 450 Squadron was attacked by a Spitfire south-east of El Adem (9.28-10.05). Possibly it was P.O. Norman of 145 Squadron.

B) Fourteen *C.202s* of 10° Gruppo (six of 84ª Sq., four of 90ª Sq., and four of 91ª Sq.; 9.20-10.40) were to escort indirectly for twelve *Ju.87s* (9.40, OBS), attacking vehicles in the Acroma area. The formation, which was led by Magg. Maddalena, was subdivided into two groups, one at an altitude of 4500 metres with Cap. Lucchini and the other at an altitude of 4000 metres with Cap. Piccolomini. The *Macchis* reached and went beyond the *Stukas* and their escort over Menelao. Halfway between Gazala and Acroma, the last patrol of 84ª Sq. was surprised by two *Spitfires* and broke up formation even if there was no damage; only Serg. Magg. Veronesi managed to fire at an attacking plane.
   The two attacking *Spitfires* belonged to 145 Squadron on a patrol (10.00-11.00) during which Sabourin (M339) claimed a *Bf.109* shot down (intelligence report notes damaged).
Lucchini, who remained alone with Veronesi and Serg. Buttazzi, continued the mission and came up against an enemy formation of about twelve planes divided between *Spitfires* and *P-40s* near El Adem (another source alternatively reports that there were about thirty divided between *P-40s* and *Hurricanes*). These were attacked and one was shared destroyed by the three pilots while some others were machine-gunned.

Ju.87 (Gentilli)

Eleven planes of 73 Squadron (10.15-11.25, one had returned earlier) were on a sweep southeast of El Adem. Three *Bf.109s* attacked but made off quickly. Sgt. Wilson's plane (BN372) was hit on the wing; it seems that it was the fighter credited to Lucchini's section.
The history of 4° Stormo ("Quelli del Cavallino Rampante") reported:

> "...the 90ª with Piccolomini, Vanzan and Taverna counterattacked and thwarted the action of the Spitfires, but in the meantime the formations were scattered. Piccolomini spotted a P-40 that was heading for Tobruk over Acroma and made for it followed by his two wingmen. The P-40 didn't notice the threat and the three Macchis were on its tail and opened fire when they arrived at a distance of some tens of metres. Taverna was with the others up to over Tobruk but all of a sudden Vanzan didn't see him any more. The P-40 stood up to all the bursts and continued its flight heading towards the east. Vanzan was hit by anti-aircraft fire beyond Tobruk but managed to get back to Martuba. Piccolomini followed the enemy fighter up to Gambut where it landed without lowering the undercarriage under the bursts of the Macchi."

Serg. Gregorio Taverna (M.M.7937) was shot down by the South African Bofors of Gambut, as was witnessed on the ground by 40 SAAF. The pilot baled out at 100 feet but was badly injured and did not survive.
The two *Macchis* took a little longer over the return to machine-gun motor vehicles.
In total, two *Spitfires* were claimed to have been shot down in the various clashes and eleven other fighters machine-gunned (1750 rounds fired).
Despite the detailed witness report by 40 SAAF of Piccolomini's section, the fighter pursued over Gambut has not been identified.

C) Two *Kittyhawks* of 250 Squadron with auxiliary tanks were on a patrol (9.50-12.05). Sgt. Stuart (GL182) attacked a *Ju.88* for as long as forty minutes. Material was thrown out of the *Ju.88*, presumably to lighten the plane, and it was able to escape.

D) Eleven *Hurricanes* of 274 were off for a sweep over El Adem (11.35-13.05). After being warned of ten enemy aircraft approaching Acroma from Gazala, they saw three *Ju.88s* and one *Ju.87* that were bombing motor transports thirty miles west of El Adem. The escort consisted of six *Bf.109s* and two *C.202s*. The Squadron attacked:
P.O. Brown hit a *Bf.109* in the fuselage with a five-second burst, seeing black smoke coming from the enemy aircraft that was diving, apparently out of control (probable).
Sgt. Henderson also hit a *Bf.109* with a five-second burst, seeing pieces fly off and glycol pouring out. The enemy aircraft then went into a vertical dive (probable). Henderson also damaged a second *Bf.109*.
Sgt. Thomson fired a six-second burst at a *Bf.109*, seeing smoke pouring out from the enemy aircraft that entered a vertical dive (probable).
P.O. Hunter attacked a *C.202* and fired two bursts, the aircraft turning over and slowing up before falling away apparently out of control (probable).
Sgt. Marsh attacked a *Bf.109* from a distance of between 70 and 200 yards, spraying it with a fifteen-second burst. Pieces flew off and the aircraft dived down to 20 feet and then pulled up with the undercarriage dropping down (probable). At this time, enemy anti-aircraft fire began to be directed at Marsh and produced a 6" hole in the propeller and minor damage to the engine cowling.
P.O. Buckley damaged a *C.202* but his plane was in its turn badly damaged by another *C.202*. He managed to return safely, however.

The British Squadron came up against fifteen *Bf.109s* of III./JG 53 that were close escort for *Ju.87s* [possibly fifteen attacking motor transports west of El Adem (11.15-?, OBS)]. They encountered ten *Hurricanes* and Ofw. Stumpf (9./JG 53) claimed one at a low altitude west of El Adem at 11.30.
During the fight, Oblt. Gotz lost contact with Fw. Heinz Herkenhoff, his No.2 (9./JG 53, W.Nr. 8586 ge. 9 + 1), and did not see him again. Obfw. Stumpt witnessed the crashing of a *Bf.109* with a parachute entangled on its tail 5 km west of El Adem. Herkenhoff lost his life with at least six victories to his credit. Probably also 2./JG 27 was present (11.02-12.08).
Also in this case there were no *Macchis*.

Sgt. House (AK749) of 450 Squadron was compelled to make an emergency landing while performing a ground attack (12.55). He had presumably been hit by anti-aircraft fire.

E) During a reconnaissance mission (18.55), P.O.Young (AL107) and Sgt. Beste (AL165) of 450 Squadron reported coming up against enemy fighters before going missing.
They would have come across three *Bf.109s* of 5./JG 27 on a free sweep. Their pilots claimed to have shot down two *P-40s*:
Uffz. Gierster, SSE of El Adem (18.15);
Ofw. Clade, S of El Adem (18.20).

F) In the evening, a mass attack by Luftwaffe bombers was carried out. Twenty-three *Ju.87s* attacked motor vehicles and troops 20 km west of El Adem (St.G. 3: 17,50-19.45) while seventeen *Ju.88s* attacked vehicles five km east of Acroma (it was the only *Ju.88* bombing of the day, more or less the target of the *Stukas*). The escort was provided by eight *Bf.109s* of I./JG 27 and ten of

III./JG 27, but III./JG 53 was also probably present; it had been escorting *Ju.88s* during the day. In view of the different typology of planes, it must have been two distinct formations, each with its own escort. Shortly before this time, two 4° Stormo formations were also in action; this was evidently to clear the way.

Three claims were made by the Germans:

Oblt. Franzisket (1./JG 27), *Hurricane* II, El Adem (18.50);

Fw. Steinhausen (2) (1./JG 27), *Hurricane* II, west of El Adem (19.03); *P-40*, SSW of El Adem (19.14).

As many as four *Hurricane* units scrambled to intercept the Axis formation that was estimated as 100 planes strong: the first to take off from Gambut West were 73 Squadron with twelve *Hurricane IICs* (19.35-20.30) and 213 Squadron with twelve *Hurricane IICs* (19.35-20.30) as top cover. 274 covered by 33 Squadron followed later at 19.42 (mistakenly some sources also mention the presence of 238 Squadron).

12 and 24 SAAF were over the same area on their return flight, accompanied by a strong fighter escort.

213 Squadron was south-east of El Adem when it was warned that the enemy formation was approaching from 20 miles away. The pilots, who were at 10000 feet, sighted it 10 miles away at 7000 feet: there were fifteen *Stukas* stepped in vics covered by the same number of *Bf.109s*. The *Hurricanes* turned into the *Messerschmitts* while they were trying to come up from the sun. At the same time, the *Stukas* dropped their bombs right in front of them (it is not clear if this was over the target or to get rid of the bombs). Then six *Bf.109s* came down on them and a general dogfight ensued for fifteen minutes, during which individual combats took place. Two aircraft were seen burning on the ground.

Flt. Lt. Westlake (BN117) destroyed a *Bf.109 F*:

> "....about 3000' below were about 15 Stukas stepped up in vics, escorted by about the same number of 109s mostly in line astern to port and starboard. EA then flew E for a while, then turned right round to face into the sun, flying SW. We turned into them and as they came round across our track the Stukas dived. We were turning to starboard and as we flew over them, about 6 109s came down on us. I stayed milling around with our formation, performing figures of eight and weaving, trying to gain height into the sun. Then I saw a dogfight to the west where two snappers were jumping 5-6 of our planes. I started to stalk them, gaining height on them to about 12000'. Saw a Me109 diving down on my No.2. He took evasive action but was too late and the Me got him underneath. 24 Ball, 24 He/Inc."

W.C. Wallace (BN139) destroyed a *Bf.109 F* south of Bir Hakeim (34 Ball, 34 He/Inc);

F.Sgt. Stephenson (Z3507; 120 Ball, 120 He/Inc);

P.O. Sissons (BE336; 160 Ball, 160 He/Inc);

P.O. Swinden (BE340; 40 Ball, 40 He/Inc);

F.Sgt. Edwards (BN285) was shot down in flames between Knightsbridge and Acroma, but baled out;

F.O. Edmunds (BN276) was missing.

213 Squadron claimed to have destroyed two *Bf.109s* in total.

73 Squadron was, in its turn, flying at 10000 feet eight miles south east of Acroma at 19.55 when it sighted a formation of twenty *Ju.87s* and twenty *Ju.88s* flying east with a strong escort of

Bf.109s. The *Stukas* then turned south and dive bombed in mass formation. They pulled out at 1500 feet and 73 Squadron attacked, confident in the knowledge that the *Messerschmitts* were engaged by the top cover.

F.O. Irwin (BN363) claimed a probable victory (40 Ball, 40 He/Inc);

P.O. Coussens (BN165) destroyed a *Ju.87*, was then engaged by a *Bf.109* (45 Ball, 45 He/Inc), and was finally damaged by anti-aircraft fire;

Sgt. Wiseman (BN183) claimed a *Ju.87* as a probable victory (23 Ball, 22 He/Inc);

F.O. Chatfield (BN560) was hit by anti-aircraft fire and a *Bf.109*'s cannon shell and was slightly wounded (Cat.I);

a pilot who was flying at 10000 feet saw two *Macchis* fighting *Hurricanes* below.

F.O. Chatfield evaded two enemy fighters and attacked a *Ju.88* which was leading the rear of the enemy formation. Strikes appeared between the starboard engine cowling and cabin, and then the enemy aircraft dived steeply to the ground followed by black smoke from the starboard engine. Then, Chatfield was mistakenly attacked by another *Hurricane*.

Sgt. Baker (BN402) reported:

> "...the majority of Ju.87s split up, one of which I followed, gaining quickly until I was about 1000 yards astern. Ju.87 then proceeded to play and we turned and twisted for about 3 minutes, I was unable to get in a shot. The Ju.87 was out-turning me when I pulled up intending to drop down on him. As I dropped back the Ju.87 pulled up in a steep climb turn and stall-turned at the top, in which position I was able to give him a good burst of about 3 seconds from quarter. Engine came away and Ju.87 plunged into ground in cloud of dust and smoke....a Me.109 did a beam attack but I was not hit. 30 Ball, 30 He/Inc."

Sgt. Hill (BN546) claimed a *Stuka* destroyed:

> "...I followed them and fired at two. I saw flashes on each of them ... , but these were probably return fire. I picked out another and stuck to him until I got in a long burst at about 150 yards which blew his starboard wing off at the root .... 144 ball, 144 He/Inc."

P.O. Henry (BN156) claimed a *Ju.87* probable (54 ball, 54 He/Inc);

Sgt. Jones (BE570) claimed a *Stuka* destroyed (43 ball, 42 He/Inc);

Sgt. Goodwin (BN357) claimed a *Ju.87* probable (29 ball, 29 He/Inc). He saw two *Macchis* fighting *Hurricanes*.

In total, 73 Squadron claimed five *Ju.87s* and one *Ju.88* shot down, four *Ju.87s* as probable victories, and one damaged (471 Ball and 469 He/Inc).

In the meantime, 33 and 274 Squadrons joined up and headed for the area five miles north-west of El Adem (19.42).

The pilots of 33 Squadron (at least nine) were top cover and reported a large dogfight where F.Lt. Cloete claimed two *Bf.109s* as probable victories; P.O. Woods, P.O. Mc Donald (?968), and P.O. Inglesby (?168) each claimed a *Macchi* probable. F.Lt. Aldridge (?5318) was shot down but he parachuted safely. Sgt. Hall (?917) and Sgt. Cameron (Z5143 RS-C) went missing.

This unit, similarly to 213 Squadron, had just engaged the escort, claiming that it had probably shot down five enemy planes in total.

The eleven *Hurricanes* of 274 Squadron attacked more than twelve *Stukas* along with the re-

C.202 of 84ª Sq. in Sicily (Archivio di Stato)

lated escort of *Bf.109s*. The Squadron dived to attack and shot down two *Bf.109s* in flames (unnamed P.O. and Sgt. Dodds). The enemy fighters turned to confront the attack, leaving the way open to the *Stukas*. P.O. Samuels shot down a *Ju.87*.
Dodds attacked a second *Bf.109 F*, seeing strikes on it;
P.O. Keefer damaged a *Bf.109 F*;
F.Sgt. Parbury claimed a *Bf.109* probable;
Sgt. Presland damaged a *C.202*.
In total it was claimed that one *Stuka* and two *Bf.109s* were destroyed, one *Bf.109* was probably so, and three other fighters were damaged.
Only one plane of 274 Squadron was slightly damaged. The unit mainly clashed with the escort, even if it managed to get through to the *Stukas*.

Finally, P.O. Glenn (*Hurricane* IIA BG691) of 208 Squadron also participated in the air-combat; shortly after take-off he spotted the formation of about forty *Stukas* and attacked one. He claimed that he had probably shot it down (19.40-20.15).

It seems that also six *Spitfires* of 145 Squadron were present as extra cover (19.40-20.30) and that they claimed a *Bf.109* damaged.

The attacks and victories were very well detailed, but nevertheless the loss of only one *Stuka* was admitted to: Fw. Loeper (3./St.G.3 F, 87 R-4/Trop W.Nr. 6227, S7 + DB) was shot down over Acroma; the crew managed to return home.

It can be concluded that 213 Squadron had only clashed with *Bf.109s* of 1./JG 27, which would have come away from acting as top cover. Therefore Franzisket and Steinhausen would have shot down two pilots lost by 213 Squadron. Steinhausen's second claim south-south-west of El Adem (19.14) must have occurred subsequently against one of the other units present.

73 Squadron's pilots managed to concentrate on the bombers with little interference from the escort. Therefore it must be thought that the close escort had been engaged by 33 and 274 Squadrons. In short, the escort of the German bombers would have again been insufficient to protect them, bearing in mind that the *Macchis* were not exactly on escort.

As we said, a short time before, 4° Stormo had sent two formations over the area to clear the way for the German attacking formation.

Magg. Larsimont led seven *Macchis* of 9° Gruppo (four of 73ª Sq. and three of 97ª Sq.) on a free sweep over Bir Hakeim (18.15-19.30). These probably joined in when the battle between German and British fighters was already in progress.

Serg. Guerci claimed a *Hurricane* probably shot down and fired at three more;

Larsimont fired at a *P-40*.

The *Macchis* probably engaged the second enemy formation, that is to say 33 and 274 Squadrons, firing a few rounds (700). Nevertheless, the enemy claims would make us think of a considerable involvement of Italian fighters.

In view of the large number of *Hurricanes* lost, we can believe it highly probable that Guerci had shot down a *Hurricane*.

In short, it would have been a battle of a considerable size, for the most part split into separate clashes. The losses of the attacking fighters were heavy, but again the escort for the bombers did not seem very effective.

G) As we have seen, in the immediate vicinity an attacking formation of twelve *Bostons* of 12 and 24 SAAF (19.00-20.05) was on its way home.

The escort was formed of 4 and 5 SAAF (19.10-20.10) with 260 Squadron as top cover (19.10-20.25).

While the bombers returned accompanied by 4 and 5 SAAF, the eight *Kittyhawks* of 260 Squadron were engaged by enemy planes. The Commonwealth pilots spotted sixteen *Bf.109s*, ten *Ju.87s*, and four *C.202s*; F.O. Waddy claimed a *C.202* destroyed but Sgt. Wrigley went missing while a second pilot was shot down (Cat.III). The *Bostons*' crews observed the bombing by the *Stukas*.

The clash should have taken place against Maddalena's *Macchis*. The second formation of 4° Stormo was also on a free sweep above El Adem (17.45-19.30); it was composed of thirteen *Macchis* of 10° Gruppo (five of 84ª Sq., three of 90ª Sq. and five of 91ª Sq.). The group flew in two separate sections, that of Maddalena at an altitude of 4500 metres and that of Mandolini (91ª Sq.) covering at an altitude of 6000 metres. The latter lost contact and did not participate in the clash. At 18.20, Maddalena sighted the German attacking formation. After fifteen minutes he sighted another formation of enemy bombers (12 and 24 SAAF) protected by *Spitfires* a little to the west of El Adem. He gave the order to attack but then sighted a third enemy formation to the east at a higher altitude (260 Squadron covering). In response, he gained altitude and attacked that which he believed to be composed of escorting *Spitfires* and *P-40s*.

The claims are somewhat confusing: it can be deduced that Maddalena claimed two fighters destroyed, one of which shared, while he fired at three more (the 320 rounds totally fired appear to be few). Berti did not fire because his plane's guns were jammed.

260 Squadron would only have sighted the German attacking formation and it should only have clashed with the 10° Gruppo formation. And yet, an intervention by the Germans against 260 Squadron would appear to be improbable in view of the trouble they had against the *Hurricanes*.

Night of 12-13

Wellington II Z8592 Z (P.O. Shakelton) was bombing Benghazi (take-off 21.50). It was hit by anti-aircraft fire and crashed into the sea with the loss of the entire crew. The loss was reported in the 5ª Squadra diary.

The Long Range Desert Group attacked 4 aerodromes, this time without much success. Bengasi K.2, 3 aircraft are hit by bullets; Bengasi K.3, 5 aircraft are slightly damaged by explosives; Benina, 2 warehouse are burned out; and Barce, a "Carabiniere" was wounded. At Benina also *Ju.52* W.Nr. 5643 (K.Gr.z.b.V. 400) and *Bf.110E-3* W.Nr. 2446 (4.(H)/12) were destroyed.

13 June 42

On its way back from a mission, a *CR.42* of 50° Stormo (5.15-6.45) was attacked by an enemy fighter at ground level and was hit by some bullets. The pilot was able to fire back, however, and returned unhurt.

A) Twelve *Hurricanes IICs* of 213 Squadron patrolled the Tobruk-Gazala road (7.15-8.20), covering the evacuation of the South Africans.
North of Acroma, the formation was jumped by six *Bf.109s* and evasive action followed. P.O. Wilson's plane (Z5307) was seen crashing into the sea and F.Sgt. Halvorsen (BE340) baled out of his plane, suffering from burns.

Twelve *Bf.109s* of I./JG 27 were escorting a *Bf.110* on a reconnaissance mission over the Acroma-El Adem area (6.02-7.27). They came up against enemy fighters and claimed four shot down:
Lt. Körner (2./JG 27) (3), *P-40*, S of Fort Acroma (6.40); *Hurricane* II, N of Wadi Es Sahaae (6.50); *P-40*, Tobruk (6.53);
and Lt. Stahlschmidt (2./JG 27),*Hurricane* II, Tobruk (6.52).

B) Eleven *Hurricanes* of 73 Squadron were on patrol (10.15-11.15) along with six *Spitfires* of 145 Squadron (10.25-11.45). On the way back, ten *Bf.109s* attacked the *Hurricanes* while they were at an altitude of 8000 feet: eight attacked head on and two on the stern. P.O. Woolley (BM363) climbed to 13000 feet with his no.2, but the latter lost position and Woolley was attacked in succession by *Bf.109s*, which he evaded. Then, he engaged two *Bf.109s* which were in close formation and climbing steadily 100 yards away. He made allowances for a deflection shot and damaged both. Sgt. Wiseman's machine (BN183) was holed by a few bullets.
145 Squadron reported the clash with two *Bf.109s* but to no effect.

Curious accident in Sicily with a propaganda lorrie and a car (Archivio di Stato).

It was not noted what unit they came up against, though it was probably German.

C) Twelve *Ju.88s* were off to attack motor transports east of El Adem (Gross: 17.02-19.20). They had an escort of twelve *Bf.109s* of I./JG 27 (17.40-18.50). In combination with this action, five *C.202s* of 71ª Sq. together with another eight of 6° Gruppo were on a free sweep over the Bir Harmat-El Adem-Acroma area (17.40-19.00).

As many as four Commonwealth units scrambled to intercept them. Ten *Hurricane IICs* of 213 Squadron were hunting for Italian reconnaissance planes (18.55-19.40). Additionally there were three South African squadrons: six *Kittyhawk* Is of 2 SAAF (18.55-20.00), seven *Tomahawk* IIBs of 4 SAAF (19.00-20.25), and seven others of 5 SAAF.

Moreover, six *Kittyhawks* of 450 Squadron (19.04-19.20) had taken off to cover eight *Kittybombers* of 112 Squadron and attacked enemy aircraft in the Sidi Rezegh area (19.00-20.00). 450 Squadron sighted the enemy attacking formation (presumably thanks to the help of fighter control):

2 SAAF Squadron Kittyhawk AK658 (Bouwer)

"... course WNW height 4000 observed 12 plus Ju.88s course westerly, 1000' above, with 10 plus fighters stepped up 500' above and higher. Our leader did a steep right hand climbing turn and attacked bombers head on from below, and with one other of the formation dived through the bomber formation. Several hits were registered but no claims were made. Our ACs were then attacked by Me.109s, one Ac being shot up Cat.I. ... saw Kittyhawk burning on ground. Parachute open 5 miles N of El Adem. Sgt. Mc Farlane attacked by Hurricane over base."

Sgt. Halliday (AL117) and Sgt. Stone (AK958) failed to return; P.O. Osborne (AL106) crash-landed and another plane was damaged (Cat.I); finally, P.O. Edwards (AK778) of 112 Squadron was also shot down at 19.40.

213 Squadron was, in its turn, attacked by four *Bf.109s* to the north of El Adem without outcome.

The German fighters claimed five victories, as many as four of them the work of Marseille: Oblt. Marseille (4), *P-40*, 5 km W of El Adem (18.10); *P-40*, 3 km NE of El Adem (18.11); *P-40*, 2 km NNE of El Adem (18.14); *Hurricane* II, 3 km ENE of El Adem (18.15); Lt. Remmer (1./JG 27), *Hurricane* II, NW of El Adem (18.20).

The 450 Squadron attack appears to have been rather risky, even if it was courageous, and losses were heavy. It can be thought, taking into account a certain difference in the times, that the 112 Squadron pilots had also been victims of the *Messerschmitt* pilots.

D) It seems that the SAAF formation encountered only the *Macchis* of 17° Gruppo.
2 SAAF was attacked head on by two *C.202s* at 11000 feet: both were shot down and the two pilots were seen to bale out (720 rounds).
Lt. Lindsay (AL134 DB-H):

"(19.05) 25+ EA reported 5 miles W of El Adem. (19.19, 11000) Just W of El Adem we observed bomb bursts in the Acroma area but had no time to get there as the formation was attacked ¼ head on by two Macchi 202s. One turned slightly away about 75 yards ahead of me and he appeared to be firing wildly. I turned on to him and after a two second burst he appeared to be alight and poured black smoke. The pilot was then seen to bale out. 100 rounds."

Lt. Morton (AK926 DB-L):

"...We turned S and saw two Macchi 202s approaching at our own height from ½ head on. I turned head on to the Ea and gave him a 4 second burst starting at 1000 yards and closing to short range. I saw my tracers hitting the AC and shortly afterwards I saw black smoke and a parachute descending. Capt. Smith had a hand in the destruction of this AC. 400 rounds."

Capt. Smith (AL223 DB-F) fired 200 rounds. Smith and Morton shared the second *Macchi*. The somewhat hazardous manoeuvre of the two *Macchis* is hard to explain: the number of planes and their poor armament made a frontal attack inadvisable.
4 SAAF reported the encounter with at least six *Bf.109s*.

Maj. Hewitson:

"(19.30, 9000') As we approached we were vectored on to the bandit snappers S of El Adem. I sighted two Me.109s flying E 2000 ft. below and the O.C.Wing ordered my squadron to attack. I went down with my No.2 and we each selected a Me.109. As I got within range the 109 climbed, but owing to my superior speed gained in the dive, I was able to keep right behind him firing all the time. The 109's engine caught fire and it stopped. I had to turn away to avoid crashing into him. The enemy AC was reported to have crashed just E of El Adem aerodrome."

Lt. Van Nus (AN452 KJ-M), Hewitson's No.2, damaged the second *Bf.109*.
While diving on the two enemy aircraft, Lt. Kaufmann (AN400 KJ-V) and Lt. Robertshaw (AN428 KJ-K?) saw a third *Bf.109* at their same level flying at an angle of 45° across their noses. They both shot at him and claimed it destroyed.
Lt. Cohen (AN397 KJ-U):

"....I followed another Tomahawk which had dived down on two Me.109Fs which did not seem aware of our presence. As soon as they saw us on their tails they pulled up in a steep climbing turn to the left. I pulled my nose up and gave one a burst without seeing results; I was almost out of range. I then saw another Me.109 diving past me followed by two Tomahawks, I gave him a burst as he passed but again observed no results. ...I lost my squadron...while flying along the railway line at 500' SW of Gambut Main, I suddenly came across two MC202s at my own height, diving down on the railway line. I pulled in towards them and gave one a good burst and saw my tracers hitting him... 0.5-100tr, 500 ball, .303-500 ball, 500 AP."

Sgt. William Halliday of 450 Squadron (Aviation Heritage Museum of Western Australia)

Hurricane I of 'Alsace'; Blenheim IV in the back (Aviation Heritage Museum of Western Australia)

Cohen's plane was then badly damaged and belly-landed (Cat.II).
5 SAAF limited itself to witnessing the clash.
In total, the South Africans claimed four enemy fighters shot down and two damaged.
71ª Sq.'s diary reported that a formation of about ten enemy planes was intercepted and attacked in the midst of sand clouds. Five of them were machine-gunned and Cap. Ferdinando Vicentini and Ten. Sergio Morandi did not return (both went initially missing; M.M.7859, M.M.7732, in fact Morandi had been K.I.A. while Vicentini had been taken P.O.W.) while Ten. Bacchi (M.M.8349) was wounded but managed to land away from the airfield. However they should have hit Cohen (130 rounds had been fired by the two returning planes). The 6° Gruppo pilots did not participate in the clash, presumably because of the bad visibility.
This was to be the last and also the unluckiest combat of 17° Gruppo in Libya; possibly bad visibility played a role in the negative outcome of the fight. As scant consolation, the 71ª Sq. pilots had almost certainly avoided the attack of the SAAF units on the German attacking formation.

5 *Hurricanes* Is of 'Alsace', attached to 80 Sqn. were escorting convoy 'Expert' (19.30-20.45). Lt. Colin and S.Lt. Bessot were at 9000 feet when 2 *Ju.88* were sighted at 20000 feet on the seaward side of the convoy. One of them dived towards the ships so the two French pilots attacked him. S.Lt. Bessot made attacks from the rear, firing all ammunitions from a range of 400 yds, closing to 250. Lt. Colin fired a burst from starboard quarter. In both cases, strikes were not observed but black smoke appeared from the port engine. The rear gunner fired only a short burst. One of the *Hurricanes* followed the *Ju.88* 75 miles out on sea, and then returned. No claims were made. It seems that the *Hurricanes* were not fast enough to close up to the bomber and .303 bullets could not cause damage from that distance.

The 40 SAAF diarist noted the scarse effort by the Luftwaffe to the retreating columns.

Ju.87 (San Diego Air and Space Museum)

14 June

Battle over the Eastern Convoy.

During the day, the battle over the convoy that had to reach Malta from Alessandria began.

It was during the escorting of the convoy that two *Hurricanes* of 805 Squadron strafed the conning tower of a submarine forty miles from Sollum at 7.30.

P.O. Oram (V) of 238 Squadron baled out and was picked up by a vessel (8.10). Fl.Lt Jenkins (D) ditched in the sea and paddled back with his dinghy (7.40).
Five *Kittyhawk*s of 250 Squadron (9.55) were patrolling over the convoy to Malta. P.O. Creighton (AL 151) and Sgt. Webster (AK775) failed to return; they probably crash-landed due to a severe dust storm over the aerodrome. Afterwards, Webster was found safe while Creighton died.

A) Eight *Tomahawks* of 5 SAAF were on an interception patrol over the convoy (11.50-12.55) with seven of 260 Squadron (11.44-12.25). They sighted twenty-four *Ju.87s*, twelve *Ju.88s,* and twelve *Bf.109s* 1,000' above them, while flying at 10000 feet at 12.15. Before they could attack, the *Stukas* dived and bombed two ships about fifteen miles north of Tobruk, one of which was hit and set on fire. The *Stukas* were attacked while making off just above the sea. Single *Tomahawks* attacked the stragglers and were in turn attacked by numerous *Bf.109s*.
Major Frost (AK or AM422 GL-B) shot down a *Ju.87* and damaged a *Bf.109* near Tobruk.

Hudson (San Diego Air and Space Museum)

Lt. Van der Spuy (AK533 GL-Y) shot down a *Bf.109* and was then shot down himself but ended up safe in hospital.
Lt. Kemsley (AN345 GL-V) stated:

> "I attacked one ME109 without result and found myself alone. I then saw the first squadron of Ju.87s dive bombing the convoy and I flew as fast as possible to intercept the second squadron of Ju.87s before they started to dive. I arrived just as they started to dive and on sighting me they broke formation. I picked one straggler and gave him a long burst and it went into a steep diving turn. I broke away and engaged a second straggler and at the same time I saw the first one hit the water. Black smoke came out of the engine of the second Stuka but I was forced to break off the engagement as I was being attacked by three ME 109Fs one of which overshot me and I damaged it. The other two kept on attacking me and eventually I was forced to crash-land." (10 miles west of Gambut at 12.15, Cat.III).

The enemy broke off the fight and made west. In total, 5 SAAF claimed two *Ju.87s* and one *Bf.109* shot down in addition to one *Ju.87* probable and two *Bf.109s* damaged.
  260 Squadron engaged the enemy with no positive results.
  Nineteen aircraft of III./JG 53 together with others of I./JG 27 (10.02-11.27) provided cover for *Ju.87s* of III./St.G 3 (9.40-12.15) and *Ju.88s* attacking the convoy. They clashed twice with the escort and claimed five enemy fighters, two of which (*Hurricanes*) were claimed in the first clash:
Oblt. Götz (9./JG 53, 11.05);
Ofw. Stumpf (9./JG 53, 11.06).

Beaufighter (Gentilli)

In the second clash they claimed three *P-40s*:
Lt. Harder (7./JG 53, 11.25);
Hptm. Belser (8./JG 53, 11.45);
Uffz. Klötzer (7./JG 53, 11.47).
However, Lt. Karl-Heinz Quaritsch (8./JG 53, W.Nr. 10068 sw.9 + 1) was shot down by a *P-40* 3-4 km north of Tobruk and lost his life (presumably the work of Van der Spuy); he was last seen at 11.45. Quaritsch was credited with eight victories at the time of his demise.
Lt. Hilke (W.Nr. 8680 sw. < +1, 5%) was slightly wounded but returned normally. His plane had been hit by fifteen bullets.
Ofw. Pantel's plane (III./StG 3, S7+FR) was shot down by a fighter; he was killed along with his gunner.
While the second clash is well documented, there is no confirmation for the first. However, it must have been a clash against the escorting *Hurricanes*. If we want to risk a hypothesis, it could be that 238 Squadron was in perpetual service above the convoys; there were probably gaps in their documentation.
In the second attack the convoy should not have been hit.

During the attacks on the convoy, II./St.G 3 lost two planes that were reportedly shot down by anti-aircraft fire. Probably one of them was Staffelkapitän Oblt. Ostler (II./St.G.3, *Ju.87 D-1* W.Nr. 2482, S7 + HN), reported missing on the 15th.

B) Seven *Tomahawks* of 4 SAAF scrambled over their base (11.50-13.00) together with seven *Hurricane IIs* of 213 Squadron (11.50-12.55).

Kaufman (4 SAAF, AN452 KJ-M) claimed a *Bf.109* damaged:

> "(12.15, 8000 feet, 10 miles north of Gambut)...two Me.109s detached themselves and flew over the top of us, one attacked me, hitting me in the main plane. Whilst turning to avoid him I spun,....attacked by two 109s and was hit again, once in the engine and once in the mainplane. I then spun to 2000' and came home."

A *Hurricane* of 213 Squadron was also damaged.

During the morning, thirteen *Bf.109s* of the three I./JG 27 squadrons were escorting *Stukas* on the attack of the convoy of Operation Vigorous. On the return from one of these actions, Lt. Körner and Lt. Stahlschmidt of 2./JG 27, who had presumably broken away from their formation, attacked twenty *P-40s* above Gambut and claimed to have shot down three planes:
Körner (2), N of Gambut (11.05); NNW of Gambut (11.08);
and Stahlschmidt, N of Gambut (11.10).

C) At 14.30, three *Beaufighters* of 252 Squadron and three of 272 Squadron took off to escort the convoy. This time they were unaccompanied by the *P-40s*, which were by then outside their range of action. F.Sgt. Gael (T.4709) of 272 Squadron did not return. The 252 Squadron pilots only saw a twin-engined plane go down into the sea with an engine in flames.
The formation was met by a heavy barrage of fire from the ships, so it was thought that he was a victim of friendly fire. But he was possibly shot down by the *Ju 88 C* of I./NJG 2 flown by Lt. Wiedow that claimed a *Beaufighter* without giving the time of his action. Gael was flying well behind his formation.

D) The following escorting formation, which had taken off at 16.35 and consisted of five *Beaufighters* of 272 Squadron and one of 252 Squadron, was also met by heavy friendly fire. As many as three planes from the former unit did not return: they were Sergeants Cooper (T3291 A), Tedesco (T4841 R), and Truby (T4867 S) — nothing more was ever seen of them.
P.O. Twaites (252 Squadron) attacked a *Ju.88* twice but was outperformed by the German bomber that managed to escape. Nine *Ju.88s* of I./KG 54 attacked the convoy (14.35-16.25); Lt. Müller (*A-4* W.Nr. 140216, B3+TL) ditched ditched, presumably hit by anti-aircraft. These planes were part of a wave of 25 *Ju.88s*. It seems that Tedesco had a wing blown off by anti-aircraft fire while he was attacking *Ju.88s*. With them was a *Hudson* of 459 RAAF Squadron (V9022 M, taken off at 14.30) flown by P.O. Blackstock; it went missing.

The missing *Beaufighters* must have come up against ten *Bf.109s* of I./JG 27 (15.35) and eleven of III./JG 53, escorting II./StG 3. The *Messerschmitts* had moved to Derna in order to be closer to the convoy; their pilots claimed were:
Lt. Körner (2./JG 27), *Beaufighter*, NNE of Derna (17.05);
Lt. von Lieres u. Wilkau (2./JG 27), *Beaufighter*, NNE Derna, 17.08;
Uffz. Gläser (7./JG 53), *Hudson*, 17.05.
Lt. Hesse (7./JG 53, W.Nr. 10163 ws.6+1) was shot down 100 km north of Derna; this was possibly the work of one of the missing British aircraft. Hesse got in his dinghy and was saved the following day.
This time the convoy was heavily hit and a freighter was sunk.

E) In the evening, a Rotte of 8./JG 53 was searching for Hesse when again *Beaufighters* were met up with and Fw. Seidl claimed one (19.15). It could have been P.O. Rogers' plane (T4885), which was part of the formation of five aircraft of 272 Squadron (18.15). The crew believed that they had been shot down by W.C. Riley of 227 Squadron, who claimed the destruction of a *Ju.88*. In fact great confusion reigned above the ships, as it would be easy to imagine:

> "The fighter direction system was incapable of dealing with sections of more than two aircraft at a time; sections of six were fired on by blind barrage and often vectored on to each other."

Sgt. Tuckwell was credited with the probable destruction of a *Ju.88* in the same action; he returned shortly after midnight and his plane almost ran out of fuel.
During the day, Oblt. Brenner (L.G. 1, *Ju.88 A-4/Trop* W.Nr. 5542, L1 + CH) was lost with all his crew; his plane had been shot down into the sea. The crew perished after several days in the rough sea without the possibility of a sea landing being made by a rescue plane to save them.
Lt. Knothe (I./KG 54, B3+ML) was attacked by a fighter while returning to Crete and his plane was very badly damaged. Upon landing, the bomber crashed, killing the entire crew. It seems to match Tuckwell's claim. A second aircraft of *L.G.* 1 was damaged by enemy fire near Crete and crash-landed at Heraklion: Uffz. Fraunhofer lost his life.

Eventually the convoy had to give up and head back to Alexandria because of the opposition of the Italian battle fleet.

Land Battle.

F) Nine *Hurricane IICs* of 213 Squadron (9.00-10.15) were top cover for 73 Squadron on a free sweep. At 9.47 they were at 16000 feet over El Adem when they came up against six *Bf.109s* at their same level and six more below at 9000 feet. Combats ensued and a *Bf.109* was damaged by S.L. Young (BN286; 60 Ball, 60 HE/Inc). 73 Squadron did not report the clash. There is no mention of this action in the Axis document consulted.

Nineteen *C.200s* of 2° Stormo strafed motor transports on Via Balbia between Ain Gazala and Acroma (14.35-15.55). M.llo Sozzi (77ª Sq., M.M.5236) was hit and force-landed behind enemy lines; he was taken as a P.O.W.

Fourteen *CR.42s* of 50° Stormo bombed and strafed armoured vehicles and motor transports on Via Balbia, a junction of Acroma – Sidi Daud (17.10-18.40); S.Ten. Paolo Guillet (390ª Sq.) went missing (K.I.A.).

Ten *CR.42s* of 50° Stormo bombed and strafed armoured vehicles and motor transports north east of junction of Acroma -Gazala (17.40-19.00); Serg. Leo Panizzi (388ª Sq.) went missing (K.I.A.).

Fifteen *C.200s* of 13° Gruppo strafed motor transports on Via Balbia at the junction of Acroma-Gazala (18.05-19.15); Serg.Magg. Luigi Giannotti (82ª Sq., M.M.5346) went missing (his body was recovered on the 19th). During the day 2° Stormo carried out 48 ground-attack sorties.

Rescue aircraft Walrus L2207 (Bouwer)

Five *Bf.109s* of II./JG 27 attacked a British column on Via Balbia two km north-east of Gazala (18.31-19.04); Uffz. Gierster (5./JG 27, 8510 rt 9+-) was hit by anti-aircraft fire and baled out but went missing.

Twelve *Kittyhawk*s of 3 RAAF were on a sweep and reconnaissance mission for 450 Squadron (19.45-21.00). They experienced heavy anti-aircraft fire south-west of El Adem and F.Lt. Chinchen (AL215) was shot down and taken prisoner. Sgt. Biden force-landed on his return due to battle damage (AL208, Cat.II); he had been hit while flying at low altitude to ascertain Chinchen's position.

Other losses were registered by Luftwaffe during the day: Uffz. Küppers (II./St.G.3, *Ju.87 D-1/Trop*, W.Nr. 2463, S7 + QC,); Ofw. Pantel (III./St.G.3, *Ju.87 D-1/Trop* W.Nr. 2139, S7 + FR). Both crews went missing. Pantel reportedly was lost for unknown reasons, Küppers stangely by Flak over Derna, so possibly it is a mistake.

15 June

Battle over the Eastern Convoy.

A) Between 6.10 and 6.22, twelve *Beaufort* torpedo planes of 39 Squadron took off from Sidi El Barrani to attack the Italian fleet; after the attack the formation had reached Malta. It seems that the *Beauforts* were unescorted.

Shortly after 8.00, the Beaufort formation was attacked to the north of Derna by enemy fighters. In five minutes the enemy shot down two planes: AW352 (F.Lt. Thomas) and AW297 (P.O. Abram); then, F.O. Hooper's plane should have been hit (DD955), which was last seen heading for Malta. It ditched near the coast and the crew were taken prisoners.
Another four Bristols were damaged and two of them were lost. P.O. Grant's plane DD949, with members of the crew wounded, crash-landed at Sidi Barrani after the pilot had dropped the torpedo (Cat.III). Sgt. Daffurn's plane DD974 crash-landed near Sidi Barrani. F.Lt. Taylor's and F.O. Leaning's planes, respectively DD945 and DD976, returned because of fuel shortage (they had possibly been hit on the tanks).
The five surviving planes came through the fighter attack undamaged (presumably the *Bf.109s* had run out of ammunition or were at the end of their range) and reached the Italian fleet to carry on their attack.
S.L. Gibbs' and P.O. Marshall's planes (AW337 and DD975) were hit by anti-aircraft fire and crashed upon landing in Malta; the latter collided on the ground with another parked Beaufort and both caught fire.

Five planes of 8./JG 53 (take off at 6.30) were 130 km north-north-east of Derna and in the process of transferring to Athens.
The *Bf.109s* first surprise-attacked the Beaufort on the far left of the formation, which was broken in half behind the rear turret. Now aware of the danger, the *Beauforts* dived toward the surface of the sea, but the aircraft on the far right was also shot down. Proceeding with caution, the *Messerschmitts* attacked the remaining *Beauforts*.
Quite accurately, the German pilots claimed seven *Beauforts* and a *Beaufighter* (the third of Belser):
Hptm. Belser (3) (7.28, 7.31, 7.38);
Lt. Kasten (2) (7.28, 7.32);
Fw. Seidl (2) (7.29, 7.34);
Uffz. Göhmann (7.31).
Ammiraglio Iachino, commander of the Italian Battle Fleet, complained to the Luftwaffe Command about the poor protection provided by the German aircraft for the fleet. The Germans replied that they had slaughtered the *Beauforts*. Nevertheless, the interception had been a case of pure chance, which had only a remote connection with protecting the ships. As often happened, fate played a major role because the torpedo-bomber component of the attack formation was indeed crippled, probably saving the Italian battle fleet of major problems.

B) P.O. Corbisier and Sgt. Blessing (272 Squadron, T4869 and T4829) were off at 6.30 with their *Beaufighter s* to escort the convoy. They both went missing: it is believed that they had been intercepted by a pair of 9./JG 53 fighters, which were again searching for Hesse (who went missing in the sea the day before) and whose pilots claimed two *Beaufighter s* at low altitude 10 km north-north-east of Ras El Tin:
Oblt. Götz (6.16);
Oblt. Beckmann (6.17).

C) Ofw. Rosenberg (9./JG 27), still searching for Hesse, claimed a *Beaufighter* north-north-east of Derna (7.40).

On 15th June 12 of the 15 Beauforts took off from L.G.05 briefed to proceed to meet the enemy Battle fleet - to be homed to it by a Maryland of 203 Squadron. The 12 aircraft proceeded in 4 sub flights of 3 aircraft each. the first sub flight took off at 0610 hours, the remaining three at 3 minute intervals, departure from the aerodrome was at 0625. The flights were lead by W/CDR MASON, S/Ldr.GIBBS, F/Lt.TAYLOR and F/O.LEANING respectively. Between 0805 and 0825 the formation was intercepted by 4 or 5 ME.109's in the DERNA region (actual position of encounter was $33°25'N. 23°28'E$) As a result of the encounter F/Lt.THOMAS' aircraft and P/O.ABRAM's aircraft were shot down. All members of the crews are casualties (F/Lt.THOMAS, Sgt. FLOCKHART, Sgt.FOBISTER and Sgt BALLINGALL - P/O.ABRAM, Sgt.EDGE, Sgt.FOX, and Sgt.BURROUGHS). Other aircraft sustained damage. After the encounter 4 aircraft were forced to turn back (F/Lt.TAYLOR, F/O.LEANING, P/O.GRANT and Sgt.DAFFURN) In the case of the first two, excessive petrol consumption made it apparent that there would be insufficient endurance to strike and make MALTA. Both P/O.GRANT's and Sgt.DAFFURN's aircraft were injured by the encounter. All 4 aircraft reached BARRANI, P/O.GRANT crash-landed just off the aerodrome. His W/Op Sgt.WILLINS had a cannon shell wound and .303 calibre wounds. Sgt.PEARSON of Sgt.DAFFURN's crew had shrapnel wounds. P/O.HOOPER was seen to break away from the formation and head in the direction of MALTA. Nothing further has been heard of him and crew (P/O HOOPER, Sgt.STAINES Sgt .LUTY and Sgt.HAINING).

There were left 5 aircraft to proceed to the strike - piloted by W/Cdr.MASON, S/Ldr.GIBBS, F/O.JEPSON, P/O.MARSHALL and W.O. MORSE respectively).

The co-operation with the Maryland worked excellently and the 5 aircraft were led right on to the target. This consisted of 2 Battleships and 5 Destroyers. The attack was carried out on the Battleships, at least one hit was obtained P/O.Marshall thinks a hit was obtained on a Destroyer as well. Liberators attacked enemy units from high level. Liberator pilots as well as the Maryland pilot confirm the torpedo hit on the Battleship. The five aircraft after the attack, proceeded to and landed at MALTA. S/Ldr.GIBBS aircraft had been hit by splinters from medium calibre guns which damaged the undercarriage hydraulics. Aircraft made a belly landing. P/O.MARSHALL's aircraft was also hit and the rudder control cut away, and the elevator trimming control cut, notwithstanding P/O.MARSHALL flew the aircraft for 230 miles to MALTA. He was unfortunate when landing, after firing down the undercarriage, to develope a slight swing which could not be controlled. His aircraft wing tip fouled a crashed Beaufort of 217 Squadron near the runway. As a result P/O.MARSHALL's aircraft was wrecked and caught fire. None of the crew was injured.

F/O.JEPSON and W.O.MORSE flew back to Base from MALTA on 16th June. W/Cdr.MASON on 17th. S/LDR.GIBBS and crew and P/O.MARSHALL and crew returned in other aircraft. All the crews at BARRANI and the serviceable Beauforts returned to Base 16th June.

Bf.109 F Gelb 9 of 9./JG 5 (Goss).

His victim had probably been P.O. Gibson (227 Squadron, *Beaufighter* T4933) who went off at 7.15 to escort the convoy and ended up missing.

D) The Italian battle fleet was bombed by seven *B-24s* of the USAAF 376th Group and two planes of the 159 RAF Squadron that hit the Littorio with a 500 lb bomb.
After the bombing, the Liberators dived to sea level to avoid the attack of fighters. The Americans reported to have been attacked by several *Bf.109s* and *Bf.110s*, shooting down one of each type. The *Bf.109* was shot down when it was less than 200 yards away.
B-24 AL553 of 159 Squadron was hit and crash-landed (one gunner was killed).

They had been intercepted by another Rotte of 9./JG 27, which this time had finally found Hesse, and Oblt. Heinecke claimed the Liberator, 100 km south of Crete (9.40).

E) P.O. Cobley of 272 Squadron and Sgt. Knight of 227 Squadron took off at 9.00 and shot down a Ro.43 (spotter of the heavy cruiser Gorizia); Cap. Gastone Mezzetti and Ten. Vasc. Arnaldo Pannaria were both killed.
Sgt. Clegget of 272 Squadron (10.20) located the Italian fleet and shot down a *Cant.Z.1007bis* (171ª Sq., S.Ten. Odoardo Visentin and crew K.I.A.).

F) At 17.40, four *Kittyhawks* of 250 Squadron together with two *Beaufighters* of 252 Squadron (17.45, using aircraft of 272 Squadron) were the escort for the convoy. Two aircraft of 250 Squadron returned ahead of time, and so only P.O. Copeland (AK955) and Sgt. Hall (AL197) remained. The *Beaufighters* were already being targeted by fire from friendly anti-aircraft fire 20 miles from the convoy.
The *Kittyhawks* came up against nine *S.M.79s* 130 miles north of Gambut and shot down two of them, forcing another four to get rid of their torpedoes.

Liberator (San Diego Air and Space Museum)

Kittyhawk of 250 Sqn. (Aviation Heritage Museum of Western Australia)

CR.42 of 387ª Sq., 50° St. (Ufficio Storico SMA)

P.O. Copeland in particular distinguished himself. He had been flying for as many as four hours and claimed the shooting down of the two torpedo planes, a feat that was achieved even with several inefficient guns. At 20.00, Copeland, who was by then alone, returned to base, reaching it at 20.40. Hall damaged a third *S.79*.

Ten *SM.79s* (four of 204ª Sq. from Rhodes and six of 274ª Sq. from Libya) attacked the convoy between 17.17 and 17.50. The ships were in a scattered formation. The strong defence provided by the fighters was reported. In fact it was believed that only two torpedoes hit the target. The pilots of the planes from Rhodes reported the clash with enemy fighters, claiming to have shot down two *P-40s* and a third probable. Ten. Salvatore Annona's *SM.79* was reportedly shot down by two *Beaufighters* (pilot and crew K.I.A). This loss matches the claim for a SM.79 probably destroyed by P.O. Thwaites (252 Sqn., T.4831, airborn at 15.00).

G) During the day, twenty-one *Ju.88s* had been in 5 escort missions over the Italian fleet. One Maryland was claimed shot down (OBS). This seems to be the claim of Ofw. Sommer (2./NJG 2) for a twin engined aircraft (20.10).

This action matches a clash with an Australian *Hudson* (459 RAAF Sqn., D9052 D, P.O. Cowan-Hunt, 18.15-01.15) that was still protecting the convoy. The crew reported the encounter with two *Ju.88s* at 400 feet. One of these attacked the *Hudson* who fired back with the turret while the second one was attacked with the front guns. The *Ju.88* was hit and seen to burst into flames.

H) During one of the patrols, Sgt. Vickery (252 Sqn., T4828) claimed a *Ju.88* shot down, confirmed by the Navy.

Marseille's Bf.109F (Gentilli)

The land battle

I) Ten *CR.42s* of 50° Stormo attacked armoured and mechanized vehicles over Via Balbia and the adjacent Herouma and Gazala (8.10-9.25). Eight 50 kg bombs were dropped and 3300 rounds fired. Many motor vehicles were destroyed and others damaged. The formation was attacked by three fighters of an unrecognized type. Serg. Rivolta sighted a monoplane that was firing at the patrol leader; he attacked him and made him flee. Serg.Magg. Giuseppe Della Valle (391ª Sq.) was shot down by the enemy fighters and was K.I.A.
It is not clear if the Fiat biplanes were escorted, as at 8.25 fourteen *Macchis* of 4° Stormo were on a free sweep and escort to *CR.42s* and *C.200s*. However, their pilots did not report any clashes.
   33 and 274 Squadrons were off for an offensive sweep (9.05-10.15). The pilots of 274 Squadron saw three *CR.42s*, two *C.202s,* and two Henschel 126s at an altitude of 1000 feet fifteen miles east of Gazala, and so they attacked them. W.C. Fenton shot down a *CR.42* (Della Valle); Sgt. Dodds fired two bursts at a *C.202* and saw flames leaping up from the engine cowling. P.O. Conrad's plane was hit on the oil tank (presumably by Rivolta) and was slightly damaged. 33 Squadron presumably top cover at 12000 feet did not see the enemy planes.

Ten *C.200s* of 2° Stormo strafed armoured cars and motor transports blocked on the road in the Mrassas area (7.50-9.10). Cap. Mario D'Agostini (C.O. 93ª Sq., M.M.5111) went missing (his body was recovered on the 19th;). A highly respected and competent leader, he had been wounded in a previous action but had refused hospitalization to remain with his men. During his last mission he had continued to attack, even if three of his pilots had been obliged to abort after being hit by the heavy ground fire. To reward his activity over the North African front, he was granted a postoumous Medaglia d'Oro al Valor Militare.

The strafing attacks against the retreating Commonwealth columns during the last two days (often performed by Regia Aeronautica's units) were, in fact, quite effective. This was in part because the targets of the Axis attack planes were mostly soft skinned vehicles.
In the words of British historian Barrie Pitt (The Crucible of War volume two: Auckinleck's command):

> "...This road from Gazala to the Acroma Monument is relentlessly machine gunned and bombed. Trucks blaze. Men run: ambulances howl towards the hospital in Tobruk: dead men lie in blood and oil and broken glass."

South African historian James Ambrose Brown remembered in his classic "Eagles Strike":

> "...At the top of the escarpment (El Agheila Pass) we saw the chilling sight of a Bofors just knocked out by dive-bombing... two burnt ammo trucks and dead men hanging like rag dolls from the gun. At the foot where we waited to join the columns on the Tobruk road enemy bombing and machine-gunning was carried out vigorously but inaccurately by an assortment of planes... Fiats, Me 109's, Macchis... on the El Adem road we saw our first signs of air support when two squadrons of Tommies flew over amid cheers!" There is no basis for the assertion of various British historians, including the Air Ministry's Historical Branch, "that no enemy air attacks threatened the withdrawal". These sources gave a total British casualties as six men; yet the South African 1st light Anti-Aircraft Regiment alone lost one officer and eight men in one Stuka attack."

The same regiment recorded (during June the 14th alone) fourteen air attacks from 15.00 to 22.00 for a total of approximately 80 aircraft.

J) During a free sweep of 10° Gruppo (16.15-17.45), Piccolomini's section (four *Macchis* of 90^a Sq.) sighted what seemed to be enemy planes and moved away from the leading patrol. Therefore, to the south-west of Tobruk, they came up against a formation of enemy bombers covered by about thirty *P-40s* at an altitude of 2000 metres. The *Macchis* attacked and a *P-40* was shot down, credited to Serg. Magg. Monterumici. Four bombers were machine-gunned, two of which by Cap. Piccolomini.
The other two pilots who participated were Serg. Magg. Veronesi and Ten. Alessandrini. Strangely enough, it was reported that only 150 rounds were expended.
They met up with a formation of nine *Bostons* of 12 SAAF (17.35-18.40) detailed to attack motor transports and tanks from 7000 feet. Top cover was provided by eight *Kittyhawks* (four each from 2 SAAF and 260 Squadron) while four *Tomahawks* of 4 SAAF were close cover.
The faint-hearted attack of at least two *C.202s*, which were easily driven off, was reported by 2 SAAF flying at 7000 feet 4 miles west of Adem. 260 Squadron engaged a single *Bf.109* with no positive results. 4 SAAF noted that three *C.202s* jumped on the bombers from out of the sun, and then the *Tomahawks* closed in. And so the enemy aircraft went up and were engaged by 2 SAAF acting as top cover. 12 SAAF did not report any attack.

K) Twelve *Hurricanes* of 274 Squadron were on a free sweep between El Adem and Tobruk (17.59). On the return, F.Lt. Darwin, whose plane's undercarriage had already been lowered, saw a *Bf.109*F at 900 feet on a shallow dive going towards a depression. He retracted the undercarriage and pursued it. Then, at a distance of 300 yards, he fired a first burst of two seconds and then one of three, seeing pieces coming away. The *Bf.109* then accelerated and seemed to be going towards the ground. He claimed to have damaged it.

There were 24 Jabos sorties during the day. In one of these, two *Bf.109*Fs (18.10-?, OBS) attacked the airport of Bu Hania (Gambut) and Uffz. Panier (10.(J)/JG 27, W.Nr. 10039 gm8+) was shot down and taken prisoner.
Commonwealth intelligence reported the attack on Gambut main by four *Bf.109*s at 19.15: one man was killed, a second one was wounded and three *Hurricanes* were damaged.

L) Twelve *Bf.109*s of I./JG 27 were escorting *Bf.110*s on a reconnaissance mission in the area between Gazala and Acroma (17.30-18.35, OBS); the *Messerschmitts* came across and engaged about twelve *P-40s*, six of which were credited shot down:
Oblt. Marseille (4), 6 km NW of El Adem (18.01); 4 km NNW of El Adem (18.02); 8 km NE of El Adem (18.04); 3 km NNE of El Adem (18.06);
Lt. Schroer (Stab I./JG 27) (2), NW of El Adem (18.06, 18.11**)**.
Schroer remembered ('Star of Africa'):

> "We were in the middle of this large formation and suddenly I heard someone shout: 'Here I go!' and it was in fact Marseille. I rolled over to attack a fighter when Yellow 14 appeared in front of me. I pulled back and up and as I did, I saw a Curtiss, so I fired and saw smoke coming from the exhaust. He went down but I could not follow him. There were more around me, but as I rolled again I saw Marseille. He had entered this Lufbery and shot one down and when I banked back and rolled again, I saw another P-40 going down. When he pulled up and rolled I lost sight of him then and I managed to fire a leading deflection shot at another P-40, got hits and saw the canopy fly off. I did not see the pilot bale out but assumed that it was the man's intention. I could confirm two of Joechen's victories. I think Pöttgen probably confirmed the others."

They clashed with the 233 Wing's Squadrons escorting seven *Bostons* 24 SAAF (18.15-20.01) headed to attack Rommel's spearhead south east of El Adem. The bombers reported that the escort was attacked by six *Bf.109*s over the target, but the bombers were not intercepted.

Two *Kittyhawks* of 2 SAAF (18.20-19.30) were top cover at 8000 feet: after the bombing they were attacked from 9000 feet by ten enemy aircraft (*Bf.109*s and *C.202*s). A long fight (fifteen minutes) took place on the way back to El Adem and the *Boston* formation was lost sight of. The enemy aircraft were driven off with no casualties on either side.

Two *Tomahawks* of 5 SAAF were also top cover while three more were close cover (18.20-19.30); they also engaged six *Bf.109*s but to no effect.

Four *Kittybombers* of 260 Squadron (18.22-19.40) completed the escort. They engaged two *Bf.109*s with no positive results.
But F.Lt. Waddy has provided us with a long and detailed account (the date is not certain but it seems to match this mission):

> "Date: June 1942; place: Libya (during the great retreat from El Agheila to El Alamein often called the Bardia Handicap).
> The enormous tank battle at Knightsbridge on the Gazala-Bir Hacheim had been fought and lost and the squadron was engaged on dive-bombing and strafing the advancing enemy forces southeast of El Adem. Having completed our bombing we were returning to base at about 3000 feet when two Me.109Fs dived and shot down my number 2 who was on the extreme left of the formation. No one

had reported the bandits and the first I knew was when I saw the Kittyhawk, about 100 yards on my left, catch fire and dive away, followed by the two 109s. (The pilot subsequently baled out and was picked up unhurt.) The 109s were following the Kitty down. . . . is was as perfect a position as one could ever expect and having already shot down some 10 or 11 I was feeling pretty confident...
Or so I thought! I opened fire, but after a few rounds all my .50 machine guns jammed and I quickly became the hunted. . . . To understand the sequence of events one needs to picture the terrain. . . . On my left, a few miles to the north, was the Mediterranean. Not far inland three escarpments, about 150 feet high, ran roughly parallel to the shore. I was flying about 20 feet above the ground with my right wing tucked in as close as safety permitted to the third escarpment with the leading 109 about 300 yards behind me. His number 2 was about the same distance away on top of the escarpment. He could not get at me and number 1 had to be fairly careful of my slipstream. I was, I thought, in the safest possible position [under all the circumstances; but a continuous series of bangs and smacks kept me well aware that the number 1's 20mm cannon firing through the prop of his 109 was working very efficiently... My consternation was complete when suddenly the escarpment flattened out and there was I, 20 feet up, two Messerschmitts on my tail, no guns and nothing but flat ground ahead. Strangely, I was not afraid but bloody angry. (The fear came later.) Instinct made me do a left-hand climbing turn which evidently took both 109s by surprise. . . .. I then dived back to deck level, having gained a valuable 150 yards. The 109s followed me right back to my airfield. As I went over the top at about 10 feet they fired their last burst.
The squadron had landed and the CO had just stepped down from his aircraft when he saw me coming and a line of bullets kicking up the dust across the landing ground heading in his direction. I can see him now, diving face first into the dust which, because of constant use, had become as fine as powder and inches thick. The Bofors guns opened up but the 109s made off, apparently unscathed, except for a few holes I put in the number 2 at the beginning. I landed and it was found that the Kitty had 124 20mm and .30 bullet holes in it. All the perspex down the left side had gone; instruments were shattered; there were no flaps and a flat tyre. I was wet through with perspiration; one earpiece was missing from my helmet; there was a large hole through my flying suit under the arm and another through the suit behind my knee. I was unscratched but my ego had been badly dented...
I was sent for by the CO and given a good dressing down for bringing the 109s back to the aerodrome, though it was never explained to me where I should have led them...
The epilogue: my aircraft was temporarily repaired by the squadron fitters before beig flown back to the aircraft depot in the Delta for major repairs. It was later completely written off by the ferry pilot who executed an upside down landing when returning it to the Desert."

This time the bombers had probably broken away from the escort but the German pilots did not manage to make the most of this.
In view of the high number of German claims in combination with the fact that three *Kittyhawk*s 'ere reported lost while escorting bombers during the day ('RAF Casualties Middle East' and 'Daily Resume of Air Operations'), we would think that, during this clash, there could have been some losses, especially more of 260 Squadron whose diaries lack a lot of detail. We can also make the same hypothesis for the action against 10° Gruppo.
The evidence Schroer gives is interesting, however it is thought that it referred to a different action.

During the day, P.O. Lee of 6 Squadron was shot down by flak.

I./JG 27 was moved from Martuba to Ain El Gazala.

In the afernoon, two *Bf.109* bombed 'A' flight of 33 Squadron at Gambut. 3 *Hurricanes* were Cat.II. One airman was killed and a second one badly wounded.

Night of 15-16

Benghazi was bombed: one *Cant.Z.501* was slightly damaged.
Barce was bombed: one *Cant.Z.1007b* was badly damaged and one slightly so.

16 June

The attacks of 3 SAAF intensified; their aerodromes were now quite close to the front line.

F.lt. Spicer (2 PRU, Spitfire IV BP916) went missing during a reconnaissance mission over Sidi Barrani (6.15). Probably some accident occurred.

A) Six planes of 3 RAAF were out on a bombing mission (8.50-9.40) and were attacked by two *Bf.109s* four times: two *Kittyhawks* were damaged (Cat.I and II); Sgt. Ryan (AK838) reacted without visible results. There is no corroboration but Stab I./JG 27 and 2./JG 27 were on free sweeps over Gambut (7.10-8.35) and over El Adem (7.32-8.35), respectively.

Four *Kittyhawks* of 260 Squadron were escorting fighter-bombers (9.20-9.50) when they engaged a *Bf.109* but without any success.

B) Two Spitfires of 145 Squadron were on patrol over Gambut (11.40-13.00). F.O. Philips (T284) attacked and damaged a *Ju.88*. The two pilots also engaged two *Bf.109*s that were attacking Gambut, but with no results.

Ten 3 RAAF aircraft were involved in bombing and in escorting *Hurricanes* south west of Rezegh (13.35-14.15). Two were hit by anti-aircraft fire and were wrecked upon landing (Sgt. Bray, AK838, Cat.II; Sgt. Boardman, AK812, Cat.II).

C) Eleven *Hurricanes* of 274 Squadron were patrolling to the east of Tobruk (14.35) when while they were at 11500 feet, their pilots sighted five *Bf.109s* 2500 feet lower down. The Squadron attacked and the Germans dived for safety.
P.O. Conrad (leader) got three bursts on the leading *Messerschmitt* which streamed glycol and went into a steep dive over the sea (probable);
P.O. Keefer hit a *Bf.109* with a four-second burst (destroyed);
Sgt. Dodds attacked a third with a two-second burst from 100-20 yards and broke away to avoid a collision while pieces from the enemy aircraft were breaking off (damaged). He then attacked another *Bf.109* with a five-second burst from 300 to 30 yards. The enemy aircraft turned over and crashed to the ground, exploding.
In total, two planes were destroyed, one probable, and one damaged; there were no losses for the Squadron.

Junkers Ju.88 (San Diego Air and Space Museum)

Four *Bf.109s* of 8./JG 27 were on a frei Jagd (13.25) when they encountered twelve enemy fighters over El Adem: Uffz. Fahernberger (sw3+) was shot down near Sidi Rezegh but he baled out safely.

D) Six *Kittyhawks* of 3 RAAF were again bombing south-west of Rezegh (14.50- 15.25); they were attacked by four *Bf.109s*:
Barr (AK745) managed to get a long burst into one of them, seeing pieces of fabric fly off;
Sgts. Biden (AL145) and Chinchen (AK961) got good bursts but with no visible results.
   It is possible that they came across a Schwarm of 10.(Jabo)/JG 53s that clashed with some *P-40s* (time not reported) with no results.

E) Ten *Hurricane IICs* of 213 Squadron were on a free sweep east of Tobruk (15.30-16.45); this was probably the forerunner for the attack formation that followed.
F.Lt. Westlake (BN184) was at 8000 feet between Gambut and El Adem when he spotted three *Bf.109 Fs* 2000 feet below to the starboard. He dived on them followed by F.O. Briggs (BN367). The Germans dived to ground level but Westlake picked one out at 150 yards, carrying out a full beam turning to quarter astern attack. This was only 100 feet from the ground.
Westlake saw a large hole in his adversary's rudder with great damage to the tail unit and fuselage before he was blinded by dust. The wreckage, which was discovered later, confirmed its destruction.

Ju.52s and Go.242 transports (Gentilli)

Briggs hit a second one in the same way from 50 yards. This was also confirmed later by the wreckage.
Overall two *Bf.109s* were credited destroyed (232 Ball, 232 He/Inc).

The action was concomitant with that of 2./JG 27 that engaged the successive attack formation, but it could be said that it had also come up against 213 Squadron.

F) Six *Bostons* of 12 SAAF were on a mission to attack mechanized and armoured vehicles in the Sollum Tobruk area (15.25-16.20). Four *Kittyhawks* of 2 SAAF were top cover (15.35-16.35) while four *Tomahawks* of 4 SAAF were close cover. Four *Kittybombers* of 260 Squadron were also a part of the escort (15.40-16.25).
Bombers' crews reported that four to six fighters came out of the sun over the target but failed to break through the escort. Nevertheless they followed the formation home and attacked a *Kittyhawk* over L.G.140 without apparent results.

2 SAAF (at 8000 feet, 2000 feet higher than the bombers) noted down the attack of four *Bf.109s* after the bombing at 16.06, just after they had turned for the the way back.
Lt. De Villiers (AL126 DB-R) was shot up and crash-landed (Cat.III), but got away from the flaming wreck and returned in the evening.
Lt. Bryant was slightly wounded (AK926 DB-L, Cat.II).
260 Squadron was also engaged by two or three *Bf.109s* with no positive results according to the war diary.

Capt. John "Jack" Frost climbs into a Hawker Hurricane of No. 3 Squadron SAAF at Addis Ababa, earlier period (Bouwer)

4 SAAF, however, should not have been involved as it was near the bombers.

Four *Bf.109s* of 2./JG 27 were on a free sweep over Rezegh (14.20-15.55) when they came up against twelve *Kittyhawks*; two were claimed shot down:
Lt. Körner, E of El Adem (15.20) and Lt. Stahlschmidt, SW of Gambut (15.25).

Two Spitfires of 145 Squadron on patrol over Gambut engaged inconclusively two *Bf.109s* (16.00). They also probably ran into 2./JG 27.

Two Kittyhawks of 112 and two more of 450 Squadron had an inconclusive clash with *Bf.109s* (15.40-16.20).

Twelve *Kittyhawks* of 250 Squadron were top cover for 3 RAAF and 112 Squadron over Rezegh (15.55-16.30). They were also detailed to strafe: Sgt. Hannaford (AK839) was hit by anti-aircraft fire and force-landed fifteen miles east of Rezegh.

G) At 15.02, five *Messerschmitts* of III./JG 27 were on a free sweep when they ran into nine enemy fighters split between *Kittyhawks* and *Hurricanes*. Two *P-40s* were claimed shot down:
Oblt. Tangerding (7./JG 27), 15 km E of El Adem (15.35);
Fw. Fink (7./JG 27), 10 km SE of El Adem (15.37).

The clash took place with eight *Kittyhawks* of 3 RAAF that were in action bombing and strafing north-west of El Adem (16.20-17.05); these were in fact attacked by four *Bf.109s* but they managed to repel them after a brief clash. Nevertheless, two pilots were lost: Sgt. Biden's (AK745) plane was hit with the bomb still on board and crashed to the ground, the plane then exploding causing the death of the pilot; Sgt. Ryan (AL145) went missing. Moreover, Sgt. Donald (AK961) was slightly wounded by anti-aircraft fire. The amount of missions carried out by the Australian unit during the day was considerable.

H) And then it was the turn of a Schwarm of 5./JG 27s over Rezegh (16.20-17.32) where they came up against six *P-40s* and claimed to have shot down two:
Fw. Niederhöfer shot down one in flames at an altitude of 4000 metres, 5 km east of El Adem, at 16.40;

Ofw. Clade shot down the other at an altitude of 4400 metres over Bu Ahmed at 16.42, and it landed on its belly.

It seems that they clashed with eleven *Hurricane IIBs* of 33 Squadron (17.00-18.10), which were on patrol in area Tobruk- El Adem. Reportedly they engaged more than ten *Bf.109s* and *C.202s*. P.O. Schwartz's and P.O.Rolls' planes were badly damaged (Cat.II); the pilot of the former was also slightly wounded.

I) P.O. Norman (V412) and Sgt. Mahady (T284) of 145 Squadron were on patrol (17.10-17.45) when they chased a *Ju.88* and shot it down to the south of Sidi Rezegh.

Five *Ju.88s* attacked the convoy heading back to Alexandria (7.56-21.24): one aircraft was lost (OBS).

Five Ju.88s attacked the convoy heading back to Alexandria (7.56-21.24): one aircraft was lost (OBS).

It is possible that the Spitfires' victim was Ju.88 A-4/Trop W.Nr. 140713, L1 + CN, 5./L.G.1) that was reported missing near Alexandria (Lt. Edelhoff).

In fact also a second Ju.88 was missing during a mission over Alexandria, but probably some time later: Fw. Ölsner (A-4/Trop W.Nr. 140001, B3+VL, I./KG 54, take off around 18.00).

Six *Kittyhawks* of 250 Squadron (17.25-18.10) were top cover for seven *Kittybombers* of 112 Squadron and strafed the Rezegh area (17.45-18.25). Two pilots were lost, supposedly hit by anti-aircraft fire: P.O. Simpson's (250 Squadron, AL?65) crashed into the aircraft it was attacking and caught fire, resulting in the death of the pilot; P.O. Carson (112 squadron, AL175) went missing. Probably also six Kittyhawks of 450 Squadron were in the same mission (17.45-18.25); they were attacked by two *Bf.109* and returned to base with their bombs.

J) Twelve *Hurricane IICs* of 73 Squadron were patrolling over El Duda (17.30-18.40): these were assailed by *Bf.109s* and F.Lt. Robin (BN560) was shot down and went missing.

P.O. Glenn (208 Squadron, *Hurricane IIA* BG914) had taken off for a reconnaissance mission at the same time (17.30) and did not return. This makes us think that he was on a mission along with 73 Squadron.

These two losses cannot be corroborated.

K) Magg. Maddalena led eleven *Macchis* of 10° Gruppo (six of 84ª Sq., four of 90ª Sq., and one of 91ª Sq.) on a free sweep over El Adem (17.30-18.55). There had probably been two sections: the one with Maddalena at 4500 metres and the other with Cap. Piccolomini at 4000 metres.

There was poor horizontal visibility at 18.20 when a formation of seven *Bostons* escorted by twenty *P-40s* was sighted. The latter were at an altitude of 2500 feet. Both the bombers and the fighter escort were attacked: two fighters were probably shot down and four *Bostons* machine-gunned. Only six pilots would have participated in the air battle, perhaps because of the poor visibility: Piccolomini (90° Sq.) and S.Ten. Vanzan (90ª Sq.) shared a probable *P-40*;
Maddalena (10° Gruppo) fired at two *P-40s* and so did Ten. Giannella (84ª Sq.);
Ten. Berti (84ª Sq.) did not fire because his guns were jammed;
three *Bostons* were attacked for ten minutes and damaged, as they had been abandoned by the fighters; one of the bombers broke away from the formation and dived towards Bardia, followed by a white trail. The reported 515 rounds overall fired seems to be few.

Five *Bf.109s* of I./JG 27 were on a free sweep north of Gambut (17.50-19.10). It would seem that at first they had clashed with *Hurricanes*, in view of the two claims made for that type of plane:
Fw. Steinhausen (1./JG 27), E of El Adem (18.00);
Obln. Marseille, 17 km SW of El Adem (18.02).
Afterwards, Marseille and Steinhausen again claimed three *P-40s* each:
Marseille (3), 17 km SW of El Adem (18.02); 5 km E of El Adem (18.10); 5 km NNE of El Adem (18.11); 10 km N of El Adem (18.13);
Steinhausen (3), E. El Adem (18.10); SW of El Adem (18.14); and E of Gambut (18.20).

Again both the *Macchis* and the *Messerschmitts* would have come up against six *Bostons* of 12 SAAF Squadron attacking motor transports and tanks (18.25-19.25). Four planes of 4 SAAF were close cover (18.45-19.55; one returned earlier). Two *Kittyhawks* of 2 SAAF were the intermediate cover, four out of the six *Tomahawks* of 5 SAAF were top cover, and two were close cover (18.40-19.50); seven *Kittybombers* of 260 Squadron were also part of the escort. All bombs were dropped in the target area (6000 feet, 19.09) but no results were observed. The formation was attacked by fighters near El Adem and was followed by them onto the target and all way back to L.G.140. Nevertheless, the *Bostons* managed to remain tightly together. It appears that an enemy fighter came down, hit by the bombers or the escort. *Boston* T713 was slightly damaged by cannon fire. The report continued:

"...14 fighters from 233 Wing. One 109 F at 8000 breaking through fighter escort. 2 attacks from above and astern. Duration about 3 minutes. Pilot closed formation. Top gunner opened fire from 450 closing to 300. AC holed by cannon shell in aileron and inner tank on starboard side. After last attack enemy AC seen dropping back out of control, losing height and smoking. Seen hit deck and burst into flames (must have been a Kittyhawk). T713: .303-300, INC, tracer and ball in 8 short bursts. Port gun stopped after 50 rounds. Starboard gun had 3 stoppages cleared by ... K711: 300 rounds from both gunners no stoppages. Tracers seen lighting aircraft."

2 SAAF pilots sighted more than nine *Bf.109s* and *C.202s* at an altitude of 7000 feet. Just before bombing, they were attacked by five enemy aircraft from an altitude of 8000 feet. They then had to fight with them all the way to Gambut. They were over the base at 2500 feet when they were again jumped by four enemy aircraft. There were no casualties.

5 SAAF reported that top cover was attacked by four *Bf.109s* over El Adem but to no effect. At 19.30 they were again attacked directly over their base of Gambut by one or two planes while the others remained higher up. The anti-aircraft fire intervened and appeared to hit an attacker. Nevertheless, Major Frost (AM or AK 422 GL-B) and Lieutenant Derham (AK370) did not return: the former would be killed and the latter taken prisoner.

4 SAAF noted the dive and zoom attacks of six *Bf.109s*. And then, while the *Tomahawks* were getting ready to land, they were attacked by at least three *Bf.109s* which were orbiting over L.G.176. Two *C.202s* were also seen. Lt. Mc Gregor (AN300) was wounded in the face and landed with blood obscuring his vision.

260 Squadron reported no incidents; probably they became separated while they were busy with their dive bombing.

During the same timeframe, seven *Kittyhawks* of 112 Squadron were bombing (19.05-19.45) and Sgt. Newton's plane (AL195) was shot down (19.25?). He was slightly wounded but he baled out safely. The same time of the last German claim would lead us to think that he had been shot down by Steinhausen.

It is obvious that the bomber formation was attacked by the Italians (the two opposing descriptions of Vanzan's attack are identical) but also probably by the Germans. Putting together all the different facts, it would appear that the attack of the *Macchis* had taken place in the final phase when the escort was separated from the bombers. Therefore they also attacked the escort over Gambut. The Germans instead would have intervened in the initial phase, then again over Gambut shooting down Frost and Derham. It is probable that the two Axis formations had met during this action but it was not recorded.

It can also be speculated that Newton of 112 Squadron had been hit by the Germans. The tactic of following the enemy formation all the way back home, as had already occurred in the previous action, is noteworthy.

The loss of John Everitt 'Jack' Frost, who was at the time the best fighter pilot in the SAAF and veteran of many air battles, was painful. The last that was heard about him was his call to the Squadron on the R/T: "*form up chaps I'm heading north.*" Then, he and his wingman were hit. Only after the war was Denham able to confirm that the South African ace had gone down '*a flamer,*' but Frost was such a living legend among his comrades that for a long time his death was not accepted and tales of his capture and subsequent escape began to circulate. In fact, his body was never found.

With 14 individual and two shared confirmed victories, half of which were achieved in the last few weeks of operations, he remained the SAAF top scorer of the war.

L) Six *Kittyhawks* of 250 Squadron (19.25-20.15) were the escort for four of 3 RAAF (19.25-20.25) on the attack over the Acroma-El Adem area.

Shortly after the fighter-bombers had dropped their bombs, four *Bf.109s* attacked and Sgt. Hall (AL179) was immediately shot down by one; after a dive, he attacked Hall from beneath the tail. P.O. Cable (AK884), who was in a more advanced position, turned and managed to fire at the leader, damaging his plane and forcing him into a sharp dive. The dogfight with the *Messerschmitts* went on for fifteen minutes; it was difficult to make them out with the sun so low in the sky by then. Cable then lowered himself in altitude and skimmed just over the ground, heading towards home but continuously pursued. He was hit and his plane was wrecked upon landing. Cable was slightly wounded, but nevertheless he succeeded in damaging at least one *Bf.109*. P.O. Hopkinson and Sgt. Seabrook also fired a few bursts but without observing results. 3 RAAF would not have been involved in the battle.

The enemy formation would have been a Schwarm of 2./JG 27 on the usual free sweep (17.50-19.10). One of its pilots, Lt. Körner, claimed a *P-40* to the south-west of Gambut (18.50) which presumably was Hall.

During the day, 250 Squadron pilots were credited to have destroyed or badly damaged more than thirty motor vehicles and two troop transport vehicles.

Sgt. Callister (33 Squadron, *Hurricane IIB* Z5453) crashed about 10 miles SW of Sollum after it stalled flying at a low altitude. The fatal accident should have taken place in the evening during a transfer flight.

17 June

A) Twelve *Macchis* of 10° Gruppo (six of 84ª Sq., three of 90ª Sq., and three of 91ª Sq.), led by Magg. Maddalena, were on a free sweep over Rezegh (8.00-9.35). The planes of 84ª Sq. and Maddalena himself were at an altitude of 4000/4500 metres and the remainder served as top cover at 6000 metres. Nine bombers with a strong escort of twenty-five fighters split between *P-40s* and *Spitfires* (thirty-five according to another source) were sighted at an altitude of 2000 metres to the south-west of Tobruk at 8.55: the attack followed. At a certain point, a patrol of *Spitfires* that was at a higher altitude also intervened.

Four *P-40s* and a Spitfire were credited shot down while nine *Bostons* and nine *P-40s* were machine-gunned (2782 rounds fired):

Serg. Magg. Savini (90ª Sq.) shot down two *P-40s*;
Ten. Giannella (84ª Sq.) shot down one Spitfire individually and a *P-40* shared;
Ten. Mandolini (91ª Sq.) shot down a *P-40* (570 rounds);
Cap. Lucchini (84ª Sq.) shot down a *P-40* shared and fired at three *Bostons* and a *P-40*;
Ten. Alessandrini (90ª Sq.) shot down a *P-40* shared and fired at four;
Serg. Buttazzi (84ª Sq.) fired at a *Boston* and at four *P-40s*;
Magg. Maddalena (10° Gruppo) shot down a *Boston* and fired at two *P-40s*;
Serg. Ugazio (84ª Sq.) fired at three *Spitfires*;
Serg. Barbera took part in the battle even though his plane's guns were not working.

A Schwarm of 2./JG 27 was on a free sweep and also claimed two *P-40s* in the same area (east of Sidi Rezegh) and at the same time:

Lt. Körner (8.50);
Lt. von Lieres u. Wilkau (8.59).

Nine *Bostons* of 12 SAAF were in action attacking armoured vehicles and motor transports between Sollum and Tobruk (9.32-?). Their formation was of three vics of three at 8000 feet, while as usual the escort was provided by 233 Wing: three *Tomahawks* of 4 SAAF were close cover (9.40-10.40) and four *Tomahawks* of 5 SAAF were top cover (9.30-10.30) along with four *Kittyhawks* of 260 Squadron (9.35-10.15).

12 SAAF stated that at 9.55 the formation was attacked by six enemy fighters. They came down one by one from 6500/7000 feet, two of them penetrating the escort and attacking K.711 from starboard quarter five times for four or five minutes. Successive diving attacks from above on starboard quarter were followed by steep climbing turns to port. The pilot of the bomber kept height and formation, while the top gunner opened fire from 300 yards, closing in on 200 yards. The bomber was hit by a cannon shell and seven bullets; there were no casualties (.303-400).

The report by 12 SAAF continues on to say that:

> "... the Bostons were pounding away steadily at enemy transport in the Sidi Rezegh area, only 30 miles away, so close that from Baheira main it was possible to hear the bombs bursting from our main raids. The armourers at least had the satisfaction of hearing the results of their labour."

Close tight to the bombers, the three pilots of 4 SAAF sighted six enemy planes divided between *Bf.109s* and *C.202s*. At least four of these, upon coming out of the sun, attacked in the moment in which the bombers had reached their objective. The attacks lasted from 9.55 to 10.20 but they didn't manage to break up the formation.

Cant.Z.1007bis of 261ª Sq., other theatre (San Diego Air and Space Museum)

3 SAAF Boston (Bouwer)

Lt. Reinders (AN394 KJ-N) described:

"9.55. I was flying on the left of the Bostons on the way to the target when enemy ac were reported attacking us....approximately: 445408. We were then attacked from then onwards until we reached about 10 miles W of Bahira main. At 10.20, after warding off two attacks from behind the bombers I saw a MC202 coming in from 6 o'clock below me. I was then flying on the port quarter of the Bostons and above them; the 202 went straight for the bombers. I peeled off to the right and attacked him from his rear port quarter; I gave him a long burst and pulled up to the left. As he pulled up I came from dead astern and into the sun and gave him another long burst. Black smoke and pieces of 'something' flew off the a/c at the wing roots; I could then have been no more than 100 yards behind at this stage, facing dead into the sun. I peeled off on the left and rejoined the bombers. I did not see what happened to the 202 …. .50-200 ball, 50 tr, .3-500 ball."

The 5 SAAF cover was also attacked by eight *Bf.109s* twelve miles north-west of Gambit at 10.00. S.L. Botha (AK519 GL-A) and Lt. Morgan (AN309 GL-O), whose plane was shot down in flames, did not return.
Lt. Sommerville's plane (AN420 GL-P) was also shot down but he managed to return safely. No claims were made.
'Springbok Fighter Victory':

"5 Squadron had lost three commanders in 18 days. And, starved of replacement aircraft, was but a shadow of itself- down to one fighter and 11 pilots. The ground staff worked like Trojans throughout the day, and by 15h 30 had all remaining aircraft (all 3 or 4 of them) serviceable. 'Top cover of Tomahawks on Bomber escort would hardly appear to be a paying proposition' remarked the bemused 5 Squadron War Diarist."

Crash-landed Bf.109E, earlier period (Aviation Heritage Museum of Western Australia)

After the loss in action of three aces the previous days (Frost, Duncan, and Pare), command of 5 SAAF had been given to Capt. Botha, a twenty-two year old permanent officer that had been a flying instructor in the Union before joining 5 SAAF in April. Displaying skill coupled with an aggression similar to that of his commanding officer, Botha had been able to claim four individual and a shared victory in just a forthnight (according to certain sources he qualified ace), being awarded an immediate DFC.

Clearly, at this stage, in light of the heavy losses already suffered by his unit, his death was a tough blow.

It seems that about the same moment that 5 SAAF was attacked, 260 Squadron was also attacked by six *Bf.109s* but to no effect.

Two 145 Squadron pilots who were patrolling over the airfield were also involved (9.25-10.35). P.O. Weber pursued a *C.202* from Gambut up to Rezegh, and then he saw two *Bf.109s* near Anarid and fired at them but to no effect.

The section of *Macchis* at an altitude of 4000/4500 metres would have attacked the bombers and 4 SAAF, while the one higher up would have attacked 5 SAAF and presumably 260 Squadron.

Maddalena, Lucchini, and Buttazzi fired at the bombers, though with little success. In this case they should have managed to reach them due to the overall fragility of the 233 Wing escort. At a certain point the two *Spitfires* intervened.

It is more difficult to explain the involvement of the Germans, either because the Italian sources do not mention their presence or due to the number of Axis planes reported by the Commonwealth pilots that matches only the number of the Italian formation. Nevertheless we cannot rule out their presence possibly against 5 SAAF and 260 Squadrons.

There is also the significant discrepancy in the estimate of the planes encountered by pilots of 10°

260 Sqn. Kittyhawk (Bouwer)

Gruppo and the enemy fighters recorded. 2 SAAF did not report the time of the missions during the day, and so they could have been present even if the notes were limited to just seeing a *C.202*. It is within the range of possibility that the *Macchis* had sighted the Australian units mentioned in the subsequent action. In any case, it appears that the escort did not amount to much, in fact at different times fighter units started to show the effects of wear and tear owing to their exhaustive effort. Finally, one cannot help but admire how the attacking forces of the Commonwealth kept going and were ever present notwithstanding the retreat.

B) Five *Kittyhawk*s of 3 RAAF (10.00-10.40) and one of 450 Squadron were bombing between El Duda and El Adem with the same number of 450 Squadron planes as top cover (9.55-10.40, a sixth returned ahead of time).

3 RAAF noted how it had been attacked by three *Bf.109s* and had been forced to get rid of its bombs. P.O. Pfeiffer (AL101) fired a burst at the German fighters without observing results, while Sgt. Hooke (AK813, Cat.III) was shot down but returned. Finally two planes were damaged by anti-aircraft fire.

450 Squadron was in its turn attacked by four *Bf.109s*: F.Sgt. Glancy (AK934) was hit and seen to come down..His plane then caught fire on the ground and he went missing.

This time it was the work of a Schwarm of III./JG 27 that claimed three *P-40s*:
Fw. Bauer (7./JG 27), SW of El Adem (9.08);
Uffz. Junge (9./JG 27), 8 km SE of Bu Ahmud, 10 m (9.10);
and Oblt. Heinecke (9./JG 27), S of Bu Ahmud (9.13).
Junge's claim at ground level well matches the mission of the *Kittybombers*.

Marseille reaches his 100th victory (Gentilli)

C) Nine *Bostons* of 24 SAAF were on mission (10.52-11.37) covered as usual by 233 Wing and reinforced by 274 Squadron.
The eleven *Hurricanes* of the latter unit (10.55-12.30) were unable to catch up with the bombers and so they continued patrolling before getting back to base:

"When over base at heights varying from 8000' to 11500', 4 M.202s were seen at 10000'. 274 Sqn. top cover attacked while bottom cover climbed to position for attack. P.O. Keefer got in a three second burst on a M.202 from 100-50 yards and saw bullets hit EA. Damaged. Sgt. Lerche, who heard warning given by Sgt. Dodds, saw 4 M.202s 2000' below him. Lerche dived and got in two 4 second bursts 250-200 yards (no results) Lerche followed up and EA flew across his gun sights. He gave a third 4 second burst and saw De Wilde bullets hit EA behind cockpit, M.202 broke away. Damaged. Dodds attacked a M.202 from astern at 10000' and got in a 5-8 second burst at 100 yards. EA rolled over, dived into ground and exploded. Destroyed. Dodds then saw another M.202 on a Hurricane's tail with a second Hurry on the 202's tail. The 202 broke away, Dodds gave chase and got within range 10 miles E. of Sidi Rezegh. He got in a 3 sec. burst from 100-50 yards. EA burst into flames and hit deck. Destroyed. P.O. Conrad was shot up at 800' E of Bu Hamud by a 109 F and he made a wheel up landing. The 109 followed Conrad down and strafed him before he could get out of the cockpit and Conrad was peppered in both legs and the left arm by cannon shell shrapnel. The 109 turned to make another run and strafe again when an unidentified Kittyhawk appeared and shot down the 109 F. Conrad then walked for some distance until he was picked up by an Army unit...We were bombed and strafed by 109s during the afternoon, no damage to personnel or AC. At 18.00, the Squadron was ordered to move to Sidi Azeiz." Two C.202s were destroyed and two others damaged.

In the meantime the attack formation was returning and they observed the combat. 24 SAAF reported that an enemy fighter hit the deck and burst into flames at Pin Point 453412; a second fighter belly-landed at 450414 followed by another aircraft. It was then ground strafed and burst into flames.

Four *Kittyhawk*s of 260 Squadron were on escort (10.45-11.35) when F.Sgt. Edwards saw *Bf.109s* attacking a large formation of *Hurricanes*, reporting a 'pitiful dogfight' because it appeared that they were flying in a defensive circle.
Then the top section of his own formation was attacked by several *Bf.109s* and soon after also Edwards' middle section was attacked by others *Bf.109s* while turning; 260 Squadron's was split up. Therefore a confused dogfight followed with everyone turning madly. Finally Edwards had his chance: one *Bf.109* overshot him pulling up, and so the *Kittyhawk* pilot could fire on him from close range, seeing a resulting explosion in the engine area. He was then engaged by another *Bf.109*.
The fight faded out and Edwards alone was heading south-east towards home at 1500 feet when he saw a Messerschmitt flying near the ground with two or three above it. Maintaining his speed of 300 mph, in a shallow dive he attacked and fired a deflection shot at 60°, sending the *Bf.109* to the deck. Probably because of the speed, he left behind the other *Bf.109s* above and turned home. He only claimed a probable victory because he was afraid of not being believed, but it was confirmed by Conrad later.
274 Squadron would not have encountered *Macchis*, but only *Bf.109s*.
  A Schwarm of II./Jg 27 was off at 9.50 on a freelance over Sidi Rezegh; it attacked enemy fighters and claimed two shot down:
Oblt. Schultz (Stab II./JG 27), *Hurricane* II, E of Bu Ahmud (10.20);
Ofhr. Kientsch (Stab II./JG 27), *P-40*, E of Sidi Rezegh (10.25).
Then Schultz (W.Nr. 10271 SW.<+-) was shot down and killed.
  At about the same time (10.00), a Schwarm of 9./JG 53 that was also on a free sweep came up against four *Kittyhawks* over Gambut:
Lt. Schaller (9./JG 53, W.Nr. 10103 ge.6+1) was hit, forced into making an emergency landing and taken prisoner. However he was freed a few days later when Tobruk fell.
  It seems most likely that 274 Squadron jumped over Gambut the Schwarm of JG 27 and Schultz shot down Conrad, but it is possible that the *Hurricanes* also met with the second Schwarm of JG 53 in light of the claims of Sgt. Dodds. At least Edwards of 260 Squadron met II./JG 27 when Schultz was shot down. Taking into account Edwards' first claim, it is also possible that 260 Squadron too met the Schwarm of III./JG 53; therefore, even if the two claims of Dodds look more precise as he was apparently able to ascertain the final fate of his victims, it is difficult to determine who shot down Shaller.
It was a real aces' clash: the overconfident German pilots this time had met their match. In fact, among the relatively few enemy pilots fighting over Gambut, there were two of the top Commonwealth aces of the sector, namely Scottish Sgt. James Dodds and Canadian F.Sgt. James Edwards.
Dodds in this specific combat achieved his last two victories reaching a total of fourteen confirmed and six probables. At the age of twenty, he was to remain the highest scoring *Hurricane* pilot in North Africa. It was reported that *"whenever hostile formations were encountered, at once he climbed as high as possible, then hovered above the main engagement and picked-off chosen victims."*
Edwards, who had just turned 21, was an exceptional shot who will end the conflict with fifteen confirmed and three shared victories, thirteen of the former and two of the latter being claimed whilst flying *Kittyhawks*, thus making him the top scorer on the type in the Western Desert.
As other colleagues and adversaries, Schultz had the habit of finishing off his own victims straf-

ing them on the ground. Once his last victory was achieved, this practice cost him his life. He had fifty-one victories to his credit, second only to Marseille in the ranking of German Aces in North Africa, and was a Knight Cross holder.

It is interesting to note, from the report of Edwards, that the German ace was flying literally guarded by the rest of his Schwarm as was common practice in the Luftwaffe. The most talented pilot was left free to go for the kills while the other members of the formation had only to carefully cover his back, but this time, the tried and tested tactic failed. Also, Shaller was himself an ace who at the time he was killed one month later, had been credited with nine victories.

Again, the Jagdfliegern demonstrated great effectiveness often combined with true ruthlessness. It must be highlighted that Italian pilots displayed a different behavior during the war on average. Commonwealth documents often refer of Italian pilots who, after shooting down an enemy plane, would proceed to circle around the victim descending in his parachute until he reached the ground safely. These reports pair up with accounts of Regia Aeronautica rescue planes that risked crashing in rough waters to save ditched enemy pilots. These attitudes, coming directly from the background of chivalrous professionalism that pervaded the ranks of Regia Aeronautica all throughout the war, were openly praised by the armed force high commands at the beginning of the war and accepted with undisguised complacency from then until the end of the conflict.

These behaviours are in stark contrast with the practice of deliberately shooting the enemy pilots once they had been obliged to abandon their planes and jump with the parachute that, introduced by the Luftwaffe in spring 1941, was quickly followed by the Commonwealth air forces. It was a habit made acceptable by a concept of 'total war,' in which the defeated enemy if not killed could rise up again and fight another day.

Looking in hindsight to these different ways of approaching the adversary, one could guess that perhaps it was exactly because of this idea of 'total war' that the Italian pilots, on average, did not conform to it.

In the afternoon, 260 Squadron was landing when two *Bf.109s* attacked it, causing a lot of panic. But it seems that the only damage was a *Kittyhawk* landing up on its nose.

Eight *Kittyhawk*s of 112 Squadron were on a ground attack (11.20-12.40): F.Sgt. Drew (AK586) did not return from the ground attack -- he was last seen in the area near Sidi Rezegh. He was supposedly shot down by anti-aircraft fire.

D) Marseille's Schwarm (3./JG 27) engaged twenty *Kittyhawks* and ten *Hurricanes*.
Marseille shot down a *P-40* on his first dive 5 km west of Gambut (12.02); and then, while turning to avoid a fighter on his tail, he shot down the second 3 km west of Gambut (12.03). Afterwards he saw four enemy fighters arranged in a defensive circle around a parachute and shot down two more: a *P-40*, 4 km south-west of Gambut (12.05) and a *Hurricane*, 6 km south-west of Gambut (12.08). His score was then ninety-nine. He spotted a lone *Hurricane* 300 feet above Gambut airfield and shot him down in flames into an anti-aircraft emplacement, 2 km south of Gambut (12.09). The Schwarm reassembled and he saw two *Spitfires* high above him, believing them to be reconnaissance planes. He shot one down in a steep turn, south-east of Sidi Omar (12.12).

Twelve *Hurricane IICs* of 73 Squadron (12.25-13.10) were off as top cover for eight *Bostons* of 12 SAAF (12.30-13.10). On the way back, they were shadowed by three to six *Bf.109s*, and then while they were flying at an altitude of 12000 feet near West Gambut (base), two of these were surprise attacked by other *Messerschmitts* coming from a different position (Marseille?) at 13.00.
F.Lt. Badger (BN357) damaged a *Bf.109* with only one cannon working and using only a few rounds (30 Ball, 30 HE/Inc).
P.O. Coussens (BE401) hit a *Bf.109* firing for two or three seconds and observed holes in the wings: it was damaged or probably destroyed (37 Ball, 32 HE/Inc).
Four pilots were shot down: S.L. Ward (BN277) and P.O. Woolley (BN649) were killed; P.O. Stone (BN157) and Sgt. Goodwin (BN121) baled out and were injured, but returned.
At the time of his demise New Zelander Derek Ward had been already credited with six individual and one shared victories.

Three *Kittyhawks* of 260 Squadron were also on escort duty (12.25-13.20): they engaged two or three *Bf.109s* with no positive results.

At the same time (12.30-13.25), two *Spitfires* of 145 Squadron were on a free sweep over the airport when two *Bf.109s* attacked them and flew off at low altitude. Probably the latter were Marseille and his wingman.

The day after, with his score risen to 101 victories, Marseille was ordered to Berlin to receive the Schwerten (swords) to his Ritterkreuz. He had got the Eichenlaub (oak leaves) only twelve days before. He was the first German fighter pilot to have scored 100 kills exclusively against the Commonwealth air forces. Now he left Libya and took two months' leave.

E) 112, 250, 3 RAAF and 450 Squadrons mass attacked Gazala airfield (13.45-15.00). P.O. Garton (AK925) of 250 Squadron was a part of the escort but he also dived down to strafe. He caught a *Bf.109* that was taking off, hitting him with a long burst; he claimed it as a probable victory.

F) Nine *Bostons* of 24 SAAF (14.20-15.15) were pursued all the way back to base by enemy fighters but without any losses.
3 *Kittyhawks* of 260 were on escort (14.20-15.20) and clashed with 5 *Bf.109s*; one was claimed probably shot down. No records on the opposite side can confirm this clash, but more probably they were German aircraft.

G) Eleven *Kittyhawks* of 260 Squadron were out on an evening patrol (19.30-20.35). F.Sgt. Matthews was shot down (Cat.III) and wounded. Edwards ('Kittyhawks over the Sand'): *"Top cover jumped. F.Sgt. Bernier AC shot up. OK."* Bernier crash-landed.
'Kittyhawks over the Sand' again notes that Bernier was jumped by two *Bf.109s*, possibly a Schwarm of III./Jg 53 that recorded a fight with fourteen *P-40s*, but no claims were made. They caught sight of a *P-40* on the return flight; it had apparently crash-landed after an earlier combat and it was strafed and set on fire. During the day 260 Squadron would have clashed with the enemy as many as five times!

Just as it was coming in to land near Derna, Ofw. Swoboda (*Bf.110 F-2* W.Nr. 4545, 3U + DS, 8./ZG 26) was forced into a crash-landing and he lost his life with his gunner.

Serg. Vanello (13° Gr.) damaged the undercarriage his *C.200* during take off and subsequently crashed upon landing.

On this date *Ju.87 D-1 Trop* W.Nr. 2537 (II./St.G.3) was reported hit by enemy fighters and compelled to make an emergency near Acroma. Probably there a mistake in the date.

The number of *Hurricanes* available rose to ninety aircraft.

DATE		AXIS TIME	CLAIMS COMM.			CLAIMS GER.			CLAIMS ITA.			CASUALTIES COMM.		CASUALTIES GER.		CASUALTIES ITA.		UNITS INVOLVED
			S	P	D	S	P	D	S	P	M	S	D	S	D	S	D	
11	A	15.10-16.00				1A						1A						208 Sqn, I/JG 27
	B	15.50-17.00	2A	1A	2A	4A						1A	2A	2A				I/JG 27, III/JG 27, III/JG 53, 10(J)/JG 27, 33 Sqn, 274Sqn,
12	A	7.55-8.45										1A						260 Sqn, III/JG 53
	B	9.20-10.40							2A		11A	1A						10°Gr, 145, 73 Sqn, P-40 ?
	C	10.50-13.05			1B													250 Sqn, Ju.88?
	D	10.35-?	5A	1A	1A							1A	1A					274 Sqn, III./JG 53
	E	18.20-?				2A						2A						5/JG 27, 450 Sqn
	F	18.00-19.30	1B 6Bs 4A	4 Bs 6A	1Bs 4A	3A				1A	3A	5A		1Bs				St.G.3, Ju.88s, I/JG27, II/JG27, III/JG 53 9° Gr, 33, 274, 213, 260 Sqn
	G	17.50-19.30	2A						1A		3A	2A						10° Gr, 260, 145 Sqn
13	A	6.15-7.20				4A						2A						213 Sqn, I/JG 27
	B	9.25-10.00				2A												73, 145 Sqn, Bf.109?
	C	17.55-18.40				5A						4A						213, 450, 112 Sqn, I/JG 27
	D	17.40-19.00	4A		2A						5A	1A					3A	17° Gr, 2 SAAF, 4 SAAF e 5 SAAF Sqn.
14	A	10.50-11.55	2Bs 1A		2A	5A						2A	1A	1Bs 1A	1A			III/StG 3, III/JG 53, 5 SAAF, 260, Hurricanes?
	B	10.50-11.55			1A	3A							2A					2/JG 27, 4 SAAF, 213 Sqn
	C	13.30-?				1A						1A2						I/NJG 2, 272 sqn
	D	17.05-?	2B			1B 2A2						1T 2A2		1A				252, 272, 459 Sqn, I/JG 27, III/JG 53
	E	19.15-?				1A2						1A2		1B				III/JG 53, KG 54, 252, 272 Sqn
	F	8.00-9.15				1A												213 Sqn, Bf.109 ?

DATE	AXIS TIME	CLAIMS									CASUALTIES						UNITS INVOLVED
		COMM.			GER.			ITA.			COMM.		GER.		ITA.		
		S	P	D	S	P	D	S	P	M	S	D	S	D	S	D	
15	A	6.16-6.17			2A2						2A2						9./JG 53, 272 Sqn
	B	7.28-7.38				7B 1A2						5B	2B				39 Sqn, 8./JG 53
	C	7.40-?				1A2						1A2					9./JG 27, 227 Sqn.
	D	9.40-?	1A2 1A			1B						1B					376th Group, 159 Sqn, 9./JG 27
	E	8.00-9.20	1B 1T													1B 1T	272 Sqn, Ro.43
	F	16.40-19.40	2B	1B					2A	1A						1B	250, 252 Sqn, 204a
	G	20.10-?	1B			1B											459 Sqn, 2./NJG 2
	H	?	1B														252 Sqn, Ju.88?
	I	8.15-9.45	1A									1A				1A	391a, 274 Sqn
	J	16.15-17.45							1A		4B						10° Gr, Boston?, 2, 4 SAAF Sqn
	K	18.59-?				1A								1A			274 Sqn, 10.(J)/JG 27
	L	17.30-18.35				6A						1A	1A				I/JG 27, 2 SAAF, 5 SAAF, 260
16	A	7.50-8.40											2A				3 RAAF, ?
	B	11.40-13.00				1B											145 Sqn, Ju.88?
	C	13.35-14.40	2A	1A	1A									1A			274 Sqn, III/JG 27
	D	13.50-14.25				1A											3 RAAF Sqn, 10/JG 53?
	E	14.20-15.45	2A														213 Sqn, 2/JG 27
	F	14.35-15.35				1A			2A			1A	1A					2/JG 27, 2 SAAF, 260, 145 Sqn
	G	15.20-16.05							2A			2A	1A					III./JG 27, 3 RAAF
	H	16.00-17.10							2A				2A					5./JG 27, 33
	I	16.10-16.45	1B												1B			145 Sqn, 5./L.G.1?

DATE	AXIS TIME	CLAIMS COMM.			CLAIMS GER.			CLAIMS ITA.			CASUALTIES COMM.		CASUALTIES GER.		CASUALTIES ITA.		UNITS INVOLVED
		S	P	D	S	P	D	S	P	M	S	D	S	D	S	D	
16	J	16.30-17.40										2A						?, 73, 208 Sqn
16	K	17.30-18.55				8A				2A	4B	3A	3A					10° Gr, I/JG 27, 12, 2, 4, 5 SAAF, 260, 112 Sqn
16	L	18.25-19.25		1A		1A						2A						2./JG 27, 250 Sqn
17	A	8.00-9.35		1A		2A			5A	9A	9B	3A	1B					10° Gr, I/JG 27, 12, 4, 5, 260, 145 Sqn
17	B	9.00-9.40				3A						2A						3 RAAF, 450 Sqn, III/JG 27
17	C	9.45-10.35	4A			2A						1A		2A				II/JG 27, III/JG 53, 274, 260 Sqn
17	D	11.25-12.10				6A						4A						I/JG 27, 73, 260, 145 Sqn
17	E	12.25-?		1A														250 Sqn, Bf.109?
17	F	13.20-14.20		1A														260 Sqn, Bf.109s?
17	G	18.30-19.35										2A						260 Sqn, III/JG 53
18	A	5.45-7.10				2A						1A						9/JG 53, 208, 450 Sqn
18	B	7.55-8.45																450 Sqn, Bf.109s?
	TOT	9B 8Bs 1A2 23A 1T			10B 7A2 65A			11A			6B 7A2 45A 1T		2B 2Bs 9A		2B 4A 1T		

LEGENDA

S - SHOT DOWN   P - PROBABLE   D - DAMAGED   M - MACHINE GUNNED

A - SINGLE ENGINE FIGHTER   A2 - TWIN ENGINE FIGHTER   B - BOMBER   Bs - STUKA   T - OTHER TYPES

Chapter 7
TOBRUK AND EGYPT (18-30 June)

Acting Lieut. Gen. Gott (commander of the XIII Corps) had appointed Gen. Klopper of the 2nd South African Division as commander of the Tobruk garrison. In addition to the division's two South African brigades, he also had the 201st Guards (Motorised), 11th Indian Infantry Brigade, 32nd Army Tanks and 4th Anti-Aircraft Brigades under his command. Tobruk had previously withstood a siege of nine months before being relieved by Operation Crusader in December 1941, but this time the Royal Navy could not make a commitment to keep the garrison supplied. Allied leaders expected it to be able to hold out for two months. Auchinleck, however, viewed the defence of Tobruk as non-essential and had already told Ritchie that he did not intend to hold it at all costs. Furthermore, it was commonly known that the Army, Navy, and Air Force Commanders-in-Chief in Cairo had already agreed that Tobruk should not stand another siege. Given this and the subsequent emphasis on building up strength at the Gazala position for an attack (which had been forestalled by the Axis offensive), it is likely that the defences at Tobruk had not been maintained at first-rate condition.

On June 20th, Tobruk was surrounded and the attack began. Tobruk surrendered the following day with 35,000 Commonwealth troops.

The British defeat at Gazala and the loss of Tobruk led Churchill to press for changes: Auchinleck dismissed Ritchie on June 25th and assumed personal command of the Eighth Army.

The British losses from the battle were high but the Axis had sustained heavy losses as well. Consequently, the British were unable to hold the Marsa Matruh line and its open southern border while Rommel could not fully press home the advantage of his success.

With the capture of Tobruk, the Axis gained a large amount of British supplies and a port nearer the front line. The Panzer and Afrika Divisions moved into Egypt while Auchinleck fell back into defensive positions at El Alamein. However, he decided to fight a delayed action at Marsa Matruh.

The 10th Indian Division was to garrison Marsa Matruh, the 7th Brigade was placed to the south east, the 4th and 22nd Armoured Brigades to the south, the 2nd New Zealand Division to the south west, and the 69th and 151st Brigades to the east.

Italian Infantry Divisions moved towards the north in the direction of Marsa Matruh while armoured and mobile units moved towards the south.

The first contact was made on the evening of the 26th. The day after, all of the Axis units engaged the enemy and again confused fighting ensued. On the 28th the Eighth Army began retreating but the fighting continued.

The line of retreat along the coastal road was cut off. The units had to break out at night and head south to work their way around the German positions. They became entangled in a running fight and sustained significant losses.

Meanwhile Auchinleck had pulled the bulk of the Eighth Army back another hundred miles to El Alamein, merely sixty miles from the vital port of Alexandria. However, the further Auchinleck moved east, the nearer he approached his supply base. Furthermore, the steep slopes of the Qattara Depression blocked the possibility of an armoured attack sweeping around an open southern flank. The two forces drew up to face one another at El Alamein, where over the next four months three major battles would be fought.

Following the retreat of land forces, the Commonwealth's flying units also had to pull back so that Tobruk could be attacked from the air with hardly any opposition of defending fighters. Losses where suffered by the Axis bombers and fighter-bombers, but only due to AA.

A considerable number of aircraft were unable to fly and had to abandoned in their aerodromes as they were reached by the enemy.

But in a few days, as the Commonwealth's units were positioned in the landing grounds of the Nile's area. Thanks also to a good number of replacements, they again started a strong activity against the advancing enemy. Particularly strong was the 'shuttle bombing' of 3 SAAF Wing.

18 June

Having just arrived at Gazala, I./JG 27 suffered the damaging of three aircraft during an attack by fighter-bombers.

A) At 6.30, four *Bf.109s* of 9./JG 53 were out on a freelance over Gambut and Gasr El Arid, coming up against six to eight *P-40s*, two of which were claimed:
Ofw. Kronschnabel, 15 km S of Gambut, low level (7.10);
Lt. Munzert, 20 km SW of Gambut, 500 m (7.14).

P.O. Bezencenet (*Hurricane* IIA, BG862) of 208 Squadron was on a tactical reconnaissance from El Adem to El Duda (6.45-8.10):

> "… 3 miles E of El Duda, at 7.55, at 5000', I saw a shadow pass over plane. I took immediate evasive action in a steep left hand diving turn and saw tracers pass above my starboard wing. I then saw three AC coming out from the sun. As my guns were not firing, owing to insufficient pressure; I decided to make for our own lines,....I reached 0 feet without being hit. I then used rich mixture, fine pitch and emergency boost cut-out.... did not exceed 220 mph..."

He was hit once more and eventually force-landed (Cat.III) near a British armoured car.

Two *Kittyhawks* of 450 Squadron were out on a reconnaissance mission in the Gambut-El Arid area (7.55-8.45); they were over Gambut when a *Bf.109* attacked them, but F.Lt. Williams (AK636) managed to shoot it down.

It cannot be ruled out that the Australians also came up against the above-mentioned formation of 9./JG 53.

B) Another six planes of 450 Squadron carried out the very same mission (8.55-9.45). They were attacked by two *Bf.109s* that slightly damaged three *Kittyhawks*; however F.Sgt. Dyson (Al195) shot down a German fighter.

On the other side an escort to reconnaissance aircraft by 2./JG 27 is recorded (7.39-8.57).

Capt. Thompson of 40 SAAF was killed in an accident during take-off.
During the day *Bf.110 F-2* W.Nr. 4573 (III./Z.G.26) was reportedly was heavily damaged (80%) by Flak near Gambut.

Bristol Bombay (Marble Arch, other period; Gentilli)

19 June

Haupt. Helmut Belser, commander of 8./JG 53 (*Bf.109 F-4/Trop* W.Nr. 10278), was killed in an accident during take-off from Castel Benito. He had thirty-six victories to his credit.

A) P.O. Foskett (*Hurricane IIC*, BN405 EY-K) of 80 Squadron scrambled to intercept a *Ju.88* that was at an altitude of 14000 feet 80-90 miles out to sea at 7.55:

> "As I was closing very slowly in the climb, I dived steeply and attacked from below at extreme range. On my third long burst EA suddenly pitched and slipped violently to port as though hit. He recovered and opened up his engines and dived steeply away into haze...240 Ball, 120 H.E."

Ju.87 R-2/Trop W.Nr. 6141 (1./St.G.3) was destroyed due to an accident on landing at Tmimi.

Night of 19-20

Reportedly a Baltimore returning from a dusk attack on Tmimi L.G. crashed on landing and was destroyed killing three of the crew.

Wellington IC DV669 W (F.O. Kauter) attacked Benghazi. It was possibly hit by anti-aircraft fire as it was seen crashing near the target, resulting in the loss of the entire crew.
Two bombers were claimed by the anti-aircraft defence.

20 June

During the day there were 189 sorties of *Ju.87s*, 129 of *Ju.88s,* and 17 of *Bf.110s* against the strongholds of Tobruk. Three *Ju.87s*, three *Ju.88s,* and one *Bf.110* were lost (OBS), all due to Flak:
Oblt. Morgenroth (KIA, I./St.G.3, *Ju.87 R-4/Trop* W.Nr. 6236, S7 + LH, Tobruk);
(KIA, I./St.G.3 *Ju.87 R-2/Trop* W.Nr. 6075, S7 + KH, Tobruk);
Uffz. Danninger (missing, I./St.G.3, *Ju.87 R-4/Trop* W.Nr. 6220, S7 + BH, El Adem);
A fourth *Ju.87 D-1* (Gefr. Mitterdorf, W.Nr. 2043), crash-landed at Tmimi (40%).
Bf.110 F-2 W.Nr. 4544 (III./Z.G.26, 80%).III./JG 53 was serving as escort (6.10) when its pilots witnessed two hit by anti-aircraft fire and their subsequent collision; they both crashed. This day was the peak of German bombers' sorties.

CR.42s bombers of 50° Stormo carried out 43 sorties against the strongholds of Tobruk. Not all raids were stalked by the enemy's fighter units that were now moving eastward.

A) Six planes of II./JG 27 were on a free sweep over Tobruk (11.58). At 12.30, they ran across six *Hurribombers* escorted by fourteen *Kittyhawks* with auxiliary tanks: they attacked them and claimed to have shot down two *P-40s* sixteen km south of Gambut:
Fw. Steis (4./JG 27, 12.37);
Oblt. Vögl (4./JG 27, 12.40).
This is another of the 4./JG 27 Schwarm's cases of missing confirmations.

Reportedly Uffz. Enste (II./K.G.100, *He.111 H-6* W.Nr. 7223, 6N + LJ) went missing over El Daba. Possibly it occurred during a night bombing.

21 June

Four *C.200s* of 8° Gruppo strafed armoured cars and motor transports on the Bir el Gobi-Taieb el Esem trail (5.10-6.55): Serg. Giordano Casadio (94ª Sq., M.M.6692) was shot down and killed.

F.Lt. Leu (AK225) of 112 Squadron was shot down during a ground attack (8.25-9.25) and taken prisoner. Rudolf Morris Leu was an ace with six individual andf one shared victories to his credit. He ended the war in captivity being released in May 1945.

During an evening attack on Gazala,several *Bf.109* of III./JG 53 sustained heavy damage: W.Nr. 10143 (7, 60%), W.Nr. 10041 (7, 70%), W.Nr. 10011 (7, 70%), W.Nr. 8775 (8, 40%), W.Nr. 10172 (8, 100%), and W.Nr. 8779 (9, 80%).
Bf.109 W.Nr. 7353 (10./JG 53, 80%) was also put out of use because of undercarriage failure.

Lt. Doyè (II./JG 27) was hit during a ground attack by anti-aircraft fire and crash-landed ('Fighters over the Desert').

Other image of Bf.109 F-4 trop of 4./JG 27 (Gentilli)

Night of 21-22

Wellington IC ES990 S (W.C. Kerr, 148 Squadron) attacked Gazala, but upon being hit by anti-aircraft fire, the aircraft exploded. Only one member of the crew survived.

Benghazi was bombed by four-engined bombers. One *Cant.Z.501* was slightly damaged. One bomber was claimed shot down and a second one probably crashed into the sea.

22 June

I./JG 27, III./JG 27 and III./JG 53 moved to Gambut.

Sgt. Bailey (145 Squadron, T284) crash-landed during a patrol (11.00-12.40).

Ju.87 D-1 W.Nr. 2539 (II./St.G.3) was destroyed (100%) at Tmimi during a bombing.

23 June

Four *Hurricanes* of 238 Squadron were out on a reconnaissance mission (10.20-11.45). They met with heavy anti-aircraft fire over Sidi Omar: F.Lt. Collinette's plane (T) was hit on the radiator and engine and crash-landed; P.O. Holmes (X) and F.Sgt. Stein (V) went missing.

A) 274 Squadron reported:

> "At 14.50 hours, 12 ac carried out a bomber sortie on enemy transports at Libyan Omar. Just before reaching the target, 2 109s were seen above at 12000' and the Squadron formed a defensive circle while the pilots peeled off singly to bomb the target. 4 direct hits were scored. F.Sgt. Neil, P.O. Samuel and Sgt. Thomson attacked the 109s and Samuel damaged one. All our AC returned OK."

Lt. Schroer (8./JG 27) was on a freelance over Sidi Omar with his wingman (14.13-15.05) and claimed a *P-40* 10 km south of Sidi Omar (14.40).

Sixteen *Ju.88* bombers attacked aerodromes and the railway at Sidi Barrani (17.05-19.00); one aircraft was lost (OBS).
During the day Lt. Stange of II./K.G.100 was reported wounded, but his unit was mounted on *He.111s*.

24 June

A) Four *Bf.109s* of II./JG 27 were on a freelance when Oblt. Sinner (6./JG 27) started chasing a *P-40*. This lasted for a long time period during which he hit it but did not succeed in shooting it down. Shortly afterwards the Schwarm came up against seven *Hurricane IIs*; this time, Sinner shot down one 20 km south of Bir El Tholata (10.00). Sinner then had to force-land.
   Supposedly he had chased P.O. Doak of 208 Squadron (*Tomahawk I* AK385, 10.15-11.10) who was on a reconnaissance mission over the southern area of Buq Buq; the British pilot was attacked by three *Bf.109s* and his plane was wrecked upon landing at L.G.121. The aircraft was Cat.II but had to be abandoned.
   And then the Schwarm ran into the six *Hurricanes* of 213 Squadron that were on a reconnaissance South of Sollum (10.30-11.45), but these reported no losses.

Two *Hurricane IIBs* of 33 Squadron scrambled during the morning. P.O. Inglesby dived from an altitude of 17000 feet and did not return; no encounter with the enemy was reported.

Bf.110 E-2/Trop W.Nr. 4440 3U + HR of 7./ZG 26 was shot down into the sea by anti-aircraft fire near Sidi Barrani with the loss of the radio operator (OBS did not report any losses).

B) Four *Kittyhawks* of 3 RAAF were on a reconnaissance mission (11.05-13.15) 18 miles northeast of Maddalena. They were flying in fluid pairs at 3200 feet when they were attacked at 6 o'clock by six *Bf.109s* and four *G.50s*. After dive and zoom tactics by *Bf.109s*, *G.50s* came down and turned with the *Kittyhawks*.
S.L. Barr (AK756) was evading an attack from a *Bf.109* when he sights a *G.50* that, after having attacked Sgt. Fox, was steeply turning away right in front of him. Barr managed to shoot at the *G.50* that fell on the ground inverted. The plane was claimed destroyed.

Abandoned Kittyhawk and Italian M13 tank (Gentilli)

Sgt. Kildey (AL101) added:

"... I made several attacks on AC attacking other members of formation, with no results observed. I then attacked another 109F and succeeded in getting on his tail. I got in two good bursts from about 200 yards dead astern and above. Immediately smoke poured from his engine (claimed probable) ... two of the 109s attacking me for about 5 miles ... I observed 3 fires in the area which I am certain were AC fires." A probable victory was claimed.

Sgt. Boardman (AK961) claimed a second *Bf.109* which hit the ground vertically, bursting into flames. Sgt. Fox (AK806 CV-N) went missing.
Unfortunately there was no confirmation for this interesting battle, unless we make a hypothesis of a mistake in the times of 3 RAAF. This would make the action concomitant with that of 208 Squadron.
Moreover, a joint action of G.50s and *Bf.109s* was highly unlikely because the G.50s were not in the front line, besides the unbelievable difference in performance between the two planes. The involvement of the *C.200s* was also improbable.

During the day, three *Bf.110s* intercepted and damaged a *Beaufighter* over Derna (OBS).
  Two *Beaufighters* of 252 and two others of 272 Squadron were strafing the road between Derna and Tmimi when they had to break off because they were attacked by *Bf.110* (12.00). Sgt. Pien (272, C) returned with a few bullet holes.

Maryland AH312 abandoned, possibly in some landing ground in Egypt; the men shown are probably personnel of 88ª Sq. (Ufficio Storico SMA)

Kittybomber of 3 RAAF with 250 lb. bomb (Aviation Heritage Museum of Western Australia)

Night of 24-25

Wellington IC DV643 of 37 Squadron was lost with all its crew over Benghazi (F.Lt. Hallywell); this was possibly due to anti-aircraft fire.

V Squadra reported the bombing by thirty-eight enemy aircraft, some of them four-engined. There was damage and some casualties. One *Cant.Z.501* was slightly damaged.

C) There was a large night-time fighter attack of 73 Squadron. Sgt. Hill (BN146) destroyed a *Ju.88* (39 Ball, 39 HE/Inc.) at an altitude of between 3000 and 4000 feet at 01.00. P.O. Henry damaged a *Ju.88* at 1.20.

Eight *He.111s* were detailed to attack Fuka landing grounds and then to carry out free sweeps over roads and the railway (21.15-5.14); many aircraft were destroyed on the ground. Staffelkapitän Hptm. Gustavus (II./K.G.100, *H-6* W.Nr. 7201, 6N + DH) was missing with all his crew, possibly the work of Sgt. Hill.

25 June

9° Gruppo moved up to Sidi Barrani.

Uffz. Schwerkutsch of II./JG 27 baled out safely because of engine failure (7.12-7.35).
A) Six *Bostons* of 12 SAAF Squadron attacked poorly dispersed motor transports East of Oxford circle (12.39-13.44). *Boston* 691 W (Lt. Jones) was hit by anti-aircraft fire over the target; one shell exploded on the starboard engine causing the plane to burst into flames and spin to the ground. All of the crew apart from the top gunner (POW) went missing. 2253 and 2218 were slightly damaged. Two enemy fighters followed the formation on the way to the target and then attacked, scattering the formation. One *Kittyhawk* was seen going down in smoke followed by a *Bf.109*. It must be noted that in this case the bombers were attacking from 4500 feet, lower than usual, and possibly this was the reason for the heavier losses.

Eight *Kittyhawks* of 250 Squadron were escorting *Bostons* (13.05- 14.25); P.O. Hamilton (AK904) was shot down and taken prisoner:

> "...Immediately after bombing the target, on the return journey, I was caught in the slipstream of the Bostons und went into a spin, losing about 2,000 feet in height. As I caught up with the formation again, I was attacked by a Me 109, which blew a large piece of my left wing off. I did a steep turn to the right, which brought me directly into the Bostons' line of fire, and I crash-landed in the desert, in the vicinity of Sofafy."

He was probably shot down by Lt. Jenisch (5./JG 27), who claimed a *P-40* over Sidi Barrani (12.32). OBS reported two *P-40s* shot down during the day.

250 Squadron's war diary points out that the Germans seemed to be using quite a lot of captured motor transports.

Two aircraft of 272 Squadron were shot down by anti-aircraft fire:

Blenheim IV Z6425 abandoned (Gentilli)

"9 sorties aerodrome and road strafing. Results were quite good. FO McGill and Sgt. Summers are missing (18.15), believed killed when their Ac ''C'' was shot down and blew up hitting the ground. Sgt. Dils in ''L'' had an engine failure but force-landed safely near El Imayd. FLt Lane- Sansam's AC 'W' was hit by flak and crashed on landing. Cat.2 crew unhurt. (15.15-17.15)"

A third AC landed successfully in the desert with a single engine after being hit.
The dedication shown by 272 Squadron was admirable, especially in view of the heavy losses incurred.

B) Six Spitfires of 145 Squadron were on patrol North of Matruh (19.35-20.20) when they attacked six *Bf.109*s and chased them to LG.07. One Spitfire's pilot was missing. There is no corroboration except for the second P-40's claim reported by OBS.

Night of 25-26

C) As many as four *Wellingtons* were lost.
Wellington IC DV522 (Sgt. Medwin) of 70 Squadron took off from L.G.09 between 0001 and 0045. While it was 40 km south-west of Marsa Matruh, it was attacked by a *Ju.88* that fired a long burst from its guns. The aircraft belly-landed in the desert and its pilot and co-pilot were injured.
Wellington IC DV564L (F.Sgt. Stewart) of 70 Squadron took off from L.G.104 at 2140 to attack enemy forces around Marsa Matruh and Sidi Barrani. After a successful attack on an enemy convoy, the aircraft was attacked by a *Ju.88*, killing the rear gunner. Small fires were extinguished by the observer but the aircraft was so severely damaged that it landed off the flare path of its air-

field. Two more members of the crew were injured. One member of the crew baled out and lost his life.

They were both hit by Lt. Rökker of 1./NJG 2: the first was hit at an altitude of 400 m 50 km south-west of Marsa Matruh at 23.45, the second at 00.09.

Wellington II Z8572 N (104 Sqn.) was hit during a night bombing of the aerodrome at 20.31 just before taking off for a second sortie. Two members of the crew were killed, the rest wounded. At 21.15, *Wellington* IC DV646 A crashed during take-off because of engine failure; its crew was uninjured.

D) At 1.05, F.Sgt. Joyce of 73 Squadron was flying at an altitude of 2500 feet when he saw two exhausts pass 800 feet above. Following them, he picked up a *Ju.88* and closed to within 30-40 yards before firing two bursts. The enemy aircraft took violent evasive action while the rear gunner started firing. Joyce, who had only one of his cannons working, finally hit the bomber and it crashed in flames (162 Ball, 162 HE/Inc).

Eleven *Ju.88s* attacked the troop concentrations of the railway and landing grounds between Marsa Matruh and Fuka (21.10-23.10). The barracks and tents went up in flames and many aircraft were destroyed on the ground. One *Ju.88* was lost (OBS); it was probably Joyce's victim.

F.Sgt. Campbell (80 Squadron, BN119) was killed during a practice flight.

26 June

In the day, 3 SAAF Wing activity reached the peak of the month:

> "The tactical disposition of the enemy forces had not changed and large concentrations of M.T. and tanks were still moving east along the Matruh Railway line. The beginning of the bottleneck formed by the Qattara Depression and the roadless waste of land stretching nearly to the sea still left the enemy no alternative when moving east but of bunding his vehicles into a good target for the light bombers.
> The two Boston squadrons surpassed their previous day's record by making 13 hourly raids and completing 110 sorties in this one day. Again the two squadrons made alternating raids and allowed themselves a period of approximately two hours' intervals between raids. ...On six of the thirteen raids enemy fighters intercepted our formations but they did not prevent them bombing. ..."

223 Squadron carried out 4 missions.

50° Stormo with its *CR.42s* moved to Sidi Barrani.

A) F.Lt. Montagu (*Tomahawk* I AK565, 6.00-7.05) of 208 Squadron was on reconnaissance 4 miles NE of L.G.75 when he saw a three-engined aircraft, flying low and heading north. He made a quarter attack and started firing at about 200 yards. The Ju.52 rolled on its back, dived into the ground and burst into flames.

B) Magg. Larsimont led ten *Macchis* of 9° Gruppo (five of 73ª Sq. and five of 96ª Sq.) on a free sweep in the Bir Astor area (7.55-9.30). From an altitude of 4000 metres, he sighted nine *Bostons* with fifteen *P-40s* escorting and ordered the attack. All of the pilots took part in the battle. Two fighters were credited shot down, five were probable victories, and fourteen planes were machine-gunned (2665 rounds were fired; another source reported three planes shot down, one probable victory, and four machine-gunned).

Ten. Querci (73ª) probably shot down a *P-40*;
Ten. Annoni (96ª) fired at two *P-40s*;
Serg. Biagini (96ª Sq.) probably shot down a *Hurricane*.

Nine *Bostons* of 12 SAAF were at an altitude of 8500' when they attacked enemy columns (8.30-10.00). During the day the escorts were provided by 239 Wing, with its few remaining planes: four *Kittybombers* of 450 Squadron were close cover (9.10-10.03), three planes of 3 RAAF were medium cover (9.10-1000), and four planes of 250 Squadron were top cover (9.00-10.05). 12 SAAF noted: six *C.202s* and four *Bf.109s* had been seen at an altitude of 8500 feet. Enemy fighters dived out of the sun and astern at the formation for six minutes. They were in formation when they began their attack from above at a distance of 400 yards and opened fire at 100 yards. Six of the fighters engaged the enemy. All of the enemy planes lined up in single file for the attack, going in one by one. Four bombers were damaged and one was wrecked upon landing; it was subsequently repaired, but there were no victims. A *C.202* was claimed to have been probably shot down by the *Bostons*. One gunner fired 200 rounds and tracers were seen entering a *Macchi* which dived vertically, but its fate was unobserved. No results were observed due to evasive action (2000 rounds fired).

250 Squadron war diary stated:

> "...were attacked by 6 ME.109s and 3 or 4 M.202s at 8000'. F.Lt Marshall (AK921) put a long burst into a ME.109F, but did not see it go in. Sgts. Cormack (AK640?) and Stewart (AK932?) also had good bursts; Stewart seeing a strike on the wing root of the EA. 250 was again attacked on way home, an AC seen going down in flames by P.O. Whiteside. F.Lt. Marshall and P.O. Curtis: one ME.109F destroyed confirmed."

3 RAAF was at 7000 feet when it was attacked from above at 5 o'clock. Curtis (AL101) reported the attack of a *G.50* on the last *Kittyhawk* (3 RAAF) which was followed by six *Bf.109s* and a *C.200*. The *Kittyhawk* jettisoned his bomb and chased off an aircraft that was attacking the bombers. A *Bf.109* then attacked, firing at a *Kittyhawk* of 250 Squadron until it broke away. He fired again against another one from the front quarter and saw tracers bouncing from the engine cowling. Curtis was then attacked by *Bf.109s*. He shot at the second and entered a stall when his guns stopped working. Spinning out from the stall, he was hit by explosive shells on the rudder and fuselage but was able to bring his plane back home (Cat.I). He was credited with a *Bf.109* shared with F.Lt. Marshall. Sgts. Ward (AK992) and Alderson (AL128) also fired at the enemy. All of the *Bf.109s* had dark camouflage and a white nose. One *Kittyhawk* was inflicted with holes in the fuselage and main plane.

450 Squadron was at an altitude of 8000 feet and going at a speed of 160 mph when bombs were dropped by *Bostons* and *Kittyhawks*. Three *Bf.109s* attacked top cover from astern while a *C.202* flew across the *Bostons,* damaging one of them. F.Sgt. Dyson (AK951) fired at a *Bf.109*, chasing it away from the bombers. His plane was in its turn shot at but to no effect.

Lt. Somerville (*Tomahawk* I AK565) of 208 Squadron did not return from a reconnaissance mission (9.20); it is presumed that he was involved in the above-mentioned clash. The reconnaissance mission must have concerned the area attacked by the bombers.

Boston of 12 SAAF Squadron after a crash landing (Bouwer)

This time, the weak escort allowed the *Macchis* to get through to the bombers.
As had happened on the 24th, the presence of Italian fighters with radial engines was curiously reported by 3 RAAF.

C) F.Lt. Lane-Sansam (N) and P.O. Deppe of 272 Squadron:

> "...took off L.G.14 to strafe road from BugBug to Sidi Barrani. As the AC approached the coast, No.2, P.O. Deppe saw a Me.109F approaching from the port side and turning to get on his (Deppe's) tail. He commenced to take evasive action and suddenly saw another Me.109F carrying out a similar maneuver to get on Lane-Sansam's tail. Deppe let fly and hit the enemy AC with a two second burst of cannon in the belly and it crashed straight into the desert in a cloud of dust. He then concentrated on getting away from the enemy AC on his own tail and succeeded eventually in doing so but not before the AC had been riddled.... Cat.I ..."

Lane-Sansam did not return.
 This matches the claim for a Blenheim IV by Oblt. Götz (9./JG 53), 20 km east of Sollum and at a low altitude (10.30).

D) Nine *Bostons* of 12 SAAF (10.35-12.00, 6700 feet) were covered by eight *Kittybombers* of 450 Squadron as top cover (11.05-12.00) along with 3 RAAF and 250 Squadrons. 450 Squadron reported that three or more *Bf.109s* (two sighted by 12 SAAF) attacked them but were driven away without any combat. P.O. Jones (AL107) did not return.
 Oblt. Klager's claim (8./JG 53) for a *Hurricane*, 20 km south-east of Marsa Matruh (10.35), would match up with the loss of Jones.

E) Eight *Bostons* of 24 SAAF attacked enemy columns marching towards Marsa Matruh (11.25-

3 RAAF Squadron's Kittyhawks (Aviation Heritage Museum of Western Australia)

13.05, 7000 feet). Five *Kittybombers* of 3 RAAF were close cover (11.55-13.05) while seven *Kittyhawks* of 112 Squadron were top cover (12.05-13.00).

24 SAAF noted that four *Bf.109s* followed the formation to the target and engaged top cover. One *Kittyhawk* was shot down but the pilot baled out and landed safely.

At 12.20, P.O. Cuddon (ET526, 112 Squadron) was at an altitude of 8500 feet near Charing Cross. He engaged four or five *Bf.109* Es and Fs but nothing is known about the outcome; he was last seen at about 6835. Howevever, P.O. Whitmore (ET570) claimed a *Bf.109*E that was shot down in flames.

Shortly after bombing (12.30), S.L. Barr (ET873 CV-N) was attacked by two *Bf.109s* that both fired at him. One of them was attacked by Sgt. Bray and pulled away but the second continued firing at Barr from 100 yards behind. Following an explosion, the aircraft of the Australian commander went into a steep dive. Notwithstanding his wounded leg and the high speed, Barr managed to bale out and was taken prisoner — and so 3 RAAF lost its best pilot. Andrew 'Nicky' Barr was a New Zealander from Wellington though he grew up in Australia. He had been C.O. of 3 RAAF since the previous 28th of May and was to remain the top scorer of the unit, with eleven confirmed victories, for the duration of the war. After being captured by the Italians and brought to Italy, he was able to escape in 1943 and rejoin the Allied forces.

The attackers were nine *Bf.109s* of III./JG 27 which were escorting a *Bf.110* over Marsa Matruh (10.55-12.00). They ran into ten *Bostons* being protected by twelve fighters. The German pilots claimed to have shot down four enemy fighters:

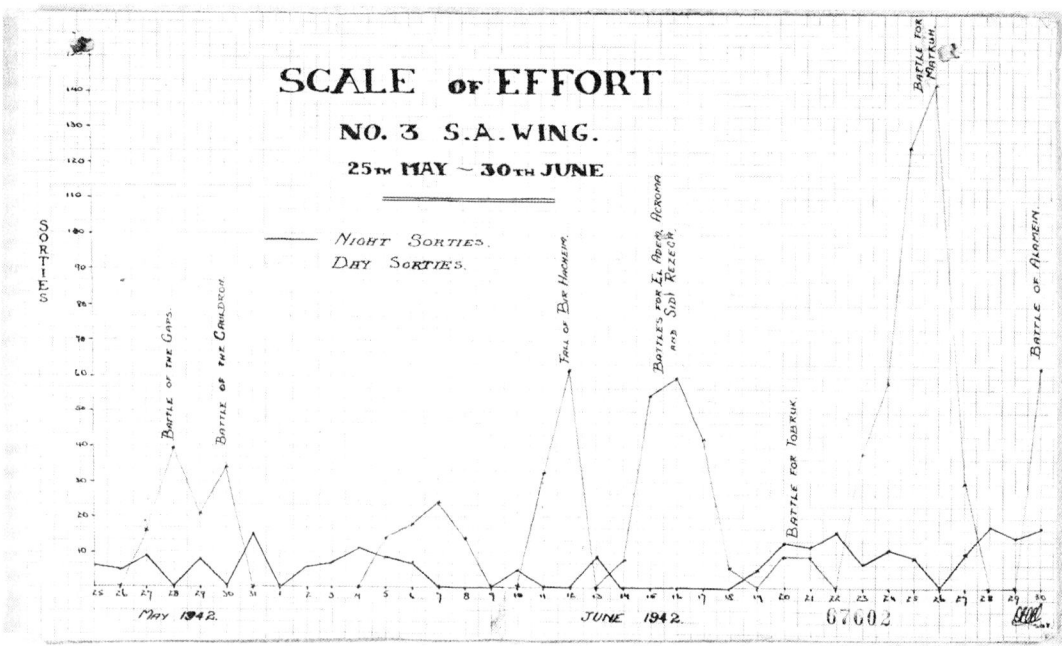

3 SAAF daily missions

Ofw. Rosenberg (9./JG 27), *P-40*, Marsa Matruh (11.42);
Fw. Kabisch (7./JG 27), *P-40*, Marsa Matruh (11.55);
Lt. Schroer (8./JG 27) (2), SW of Marsa Matruh, *P-40* (11.40); *Hurricane* (11.44).

F) At 11.25, six *Bf.109s* of I./JG 27 were patrolling over German armoured columns; they came across enemy fighters and claimed six:
Lt. Körner (2./JG 27) (2 *P-40s*) W of Marsa Matruh (11.48, 12.18);
Hptm. Franzisket (1./JG 27), *P-40*, SW of Marsa Matruh (12.12);
Lt. Stahlschmidt (2./JG 27)(3), *P-40* SW of Marsa Matruh (12.20); *Hurricane* II, W of Marsa Matruh (12.30); *Hurricane* II, 15 km SW of Marsa Matruh (12.27).

They probably first met with twelve *Hurricane IICs* of 213 Squadron which had scrambled up from their base (12.20-13.30) and were attacked by four *Bf.109s*; the *Hurricanes* reported no casualties or claims (Körner's first claim was at 11.48).

The Germans should have then come up against nine *Bostons* of 12 SAAF which were again on a mission (12.30-14.00) and heading west of Matruh. Top cover was provided by three *Kittyhawks* of 250 Squadron (13.00-13.55) with two of 450 Squadron while four more planes of the latter unit were close cover (13.10-14.10). Six enemy aircraft followed the formation to the target and two minutes before the bombing, they managed to break through the top cover from an altitude of 7000 feet at 13.30. Two *Bf.109s* engaged the *Bostons*, but one of them was shot down by a top gunner while a *Boston* was holed. Three more were put out of action by anti-aircraft fire. 450 Squadron reported:

"...Bostons dropped bombs from 6000'...Sgt. Lindsay (AK606) in top cover turned to attack 109

Bostons attack formation in line abreast (Bouwer)

which was firing at PO Jones M. (AK750) who went into a steep dive and baled out successfully. Lindsay rejoined Bostons and saw a further 3 109s being engaged by top cover 7 miles E. He was unable to join fight but was attacked from the rear, receiving no damage. PO Shaaf (AK636) observed Kittyhawk going into steep dive and smoke from the ground. He dropped bombs on four trucks. He then attacked 109 got in two bursts and claimed to have damaged it. He in turn was attacked and was hit several times but was unhurt and flew to base. Sgt. Wallace fired at a 109 attacking a Boston but no damage was observed. PO Parker was attacked but evaded and rejoined the Bostons. Sergeant Simpson observed 2 AC burning on the ground near the target area. 3 of our AC dropped bombs."

250 Squadron reported to have been attacked by *Macchis*:
Sgt. Wallis described how the *C.202* was able to turn inside him, forcing him to turn away and go down with holes in his plane's fin and wings.
Sgt. Seabrook (AK932) was attacked by a *C.202* or *Bf.109* and shot up; he landed at *L.G.* 91 with two flat tyres, the right aileron out of action, and the flaps not working.
F.lt. Copeland (AK921) went missing but was not seen going down. Two fires, however, possibly from exploded aircraft, were seen on the ground.
Finally, six *Hurribombers* of 274 Squadron were on a bombing mission. They were covered by four *Hurricanes* of 238 Squadron (13.15-13.55). Sgt. Lawrence-Smith of the latter was attacked by a single *Bf.109* and was injured on the leg (Cat II). Sgt. Thomson of 274 Squadron went missing; he was thought to have been hit by anti-aircraft fire.
Therefore, it is possible that I./JG 27 clashed for the third time with these *Hurricanes* and hit Thomson.
250 Squadron's scrupulous description of the clash with the *Macchis* would make us think that there were some gaps in the Italian documentation. In fact, at this time the *Macchis* had been engaged with 223 Squadron which was certainly in the vicinity.

G) Malvezzi led eight *Macchis* of 97ª Sq. on a free sweep over the Bir El Astar area (12.10-

13.20). As usual, the *Macchis* were in two sections: one at 6000 m. and the other at 4000. A formation of six Marylands was spotted and immediately attacked at an altitude of 4500 m. One was declared to have been shot down and five others were machine-gunned. These were all shared between the eight pilots (2507 rounds fired). Canfora and Frigerio were present as well as Malvezzi.

At 13.15, six *Baltimores* of 223 Squadron took off to attack Mtat, Pin Point 630330. At 13.45, the formation was at 16700 feet 8 miles north-west of Bir El Gallas when it was attacked by fighters shortly before reaching the target. The bombers jettisoned their bombs and headed home. The fighters attacked in the usual way, sweeping under the rear of the formation from the quarter halfway up and coming up on the other quarter. After ten minutes, the fighters broke away. At 14.02, the fighters were again reported well out of range. Sgt. Hewitt's plane (No.6, AG748) was badly damaged with the port air screw coming off. He therefore had to force-land it 25 miles west of base. AG.774 (P.O. Davies) crash-landed at the base (L.G.116); two of its aircrew were injured including Sgt. Dobson who ending up losing his life.

It is puzzling to notice a *Baltimores* action with no escort yet again, even though it would be the last. From the next day onward, fighters would always be present. The *Macchis* fired a large number of rounds but the bombers were not slaughtered as had occurred when the *Bf.109s* attacked unescorted bombers. The differing fire powers of the planes was probably one of the reasons for this.

Six *Hurricanes* of 274 Squadron bombed enemy concentrations. Sgt. Thomson went missing. The time of this action was not recorded.

At 14.26, *Bostons* of 24 SAAF bombed enemy columns; it seems that in this occasion, three Italian high ranking officers were killed. They were practically the head of XX Corpo: Gen. Ettore Baldassarre (the Corpo's commander), the Corpo's Artillery C.O. Gen. Piacenza, and the Engineers C.O. Col. Vittorio Raffaelli.

H) At 14.25, Sgt. Mahady (E322) and Sgt. Baily (T284) of 145 Squadron were off on a reconnaissance mission at low altitude (12000 feet). One was seen to bale out of his plane but neither returned.

Fw. Pöttgen and Fw. Mrosla (3./JG 27) were patrolling over the Sidi El Barrani aerodrome and claimed two *P-40s* east of Sidi Barrani (14.05, 14.10).

I) A great number of units seemed to have an appointment in the same area; this was at the heart of the land battle.

Five *Tomahawks* of 5 SAAF (14.55-15.50, one returned ahead of time) were to escort *Bostons* and patrol the Ishaila Rocks line as well as 20 miles further south. They had five more planes of 4 SAAF. Maj. Hewitson was piloting the first *Kittyhawk* (AK835) assigned to 4 SAAF. In fact it seems that they were ahead of the following attack formation, clearing the way and providing an umbrella at 14000 feet.

Six *Kittybombers* of 3 RAAF set off on an armed reconnaissance mission and to locate S.L. Barr (15.05-16.00).

Eight *Bostons* of 12 SAAF headed west of Charing Cross (14.44-16.11). The bombing took place from 5.600 feet at 15.43. Top cover was provided by six *Kittybombers* of 450 Squadron (15.19-

16.15); five other *Kittybombers* of 112 Squadron were close cover. The bombers reported that four enemy aircraft engaged the escort.

Twelve *Hurricane IICs* of 213 Squadron also took off from L.G.12 for a free sweep over Charing Cross (15.15-16.20). They possibly also coordinated with the attack formation.

Both South African Squadrons reported being attacked by four or five *Bf.109s* and two pilots were shot down:
Maj. John 'Gugu' Hewitson, who baled out and was taken prisoner;
and Lt. Popham (5 SAAF, AN241), who returned even though he was wounded.
After Duncan, Pare, and Frost now it was the turn of Hewitson. It was the destiny of the East African Campaign aces. He was the continuing nemesis of the East African Campaign aces. He had been appointed as CO of 4 SAAF after a distinguished service period in Italian East Africa and later in 5 SAAF, during which time he had amassed three individual victories and destroyed many enemy planes on the ground. He finally achieved aces status on June 13th. He would turn out to end the war as a POW, the second Desert Air Force's Squadron Leader to be lost to the Luftwaffe during the day.

3 RAAF was flying at 2500 feet when a pilot saw a descending parachute (15.30?) and circled around it. The pilot, supposedly Hewitson, was picked up by motor transports near an aircraft burning on the ground. After the bombing, two *Bf.109s* attacked Sgt. Kildey's plane (AK651) which was slightly damaged. Sgt. Jones (RT911) came to his rescue by making a frontal quarter attack on one of the *Bf.109s* and drew it away from Kildey (there were no claims).

450 Squadron released its bombs in the same area as the *Bostons*. Two *Bf.109s* dived toward the *Kittyhawks*. Sgt. Dyson (AL195) saw a *Bf.109* below him at 3000 feet. It was following a *Kittyhawk* and gaining height, and so Dyson fired a burst causing the *Bf.109* to stall. Before he could see any result, another *Bf.109* got on his tail. In total, four or five *Messerschmitts* were counted. P.O. Murdoch (AK990) went missing. ''Desert Warriors" describes the event:

> "Murdoch observed 5 109s attacking the formation. He stated that he had no time to report it. He dropped his bomb and climbed to engage the enemy. He claimed to have shot one down, but as the rest of the flight was initially unaware of the action he received no help. Four of his guns stopped working and were soon joined by the other two. His aircraft was hit and he lost height to avoid the enemy attacks, but to no avail. The aircraft caught fire and he crash-landed at 260 mph behind the enemy lines..."

112 Squadron dropped bombs from the same height as the *Bostons* but did not report the encounter with the enemy.

A Schwarm of 5./JG 27s was on a freelance south-west of Matruh (14.02-15.13). It came up against six *P-40s* and claimed to have shot down four (in fact also a *Hurricane* was claimed):
Lt. Jenisch (2), 30 km SW of Marsa Matruh (14.32); 600 m (14.43);
Fw. Fricke, *Hurricane* II, SW of Marsa Matruh (14.35);
Ofw. Clade, 35 km SW of Marsa Matruh, 20 m (14.50).
The timing of the claims seems to indicate that they were two different clashes: the first one was against the South Africans and 3 RAAF; the second one was against 450 Squadron at a low level. The number of enemies reported by the Germans does not match that of the enemies in the clash.

J) 213 Squadron was heading north-west between 19000 and 20000 feet when at 16.00, enemy aircraft were sighted below heading eastwards. Their white wing tips made them identifiable as eight *Bf.109s* which were flying in four pairs in echelon right formation at 14000 feet. The *Hurricanes* jumped the enemy, which turned 180° and climbed up into the sun.

P.O. Thomlinson (BN349):

"...as the Flight Commander dived down I followed him....he was preparing to attack the right hand ac of the leading pair, so I concentrated on the enemy's No.2 and closing to a very short range gave him a 2 second burst from dead astern. Just as I fired he pulled up almost vertically.....I saw several explosions on the tail, one on the fuselage....lost control...spinning down until it hit the deck....50 HE/I, 50 Balls."

Sgt. Ritchie (BN537): "...saw 4 109s closing into a defensive circle. I closed on one that was attempting a climbing turn to the left and delivered a beam attack on him at 1000 yards closing to 50. I saw his tail unit disintegrate and drop off, and then he rolled over on his back and plunged down to the deck in a spiral dive. 58 HE/I, 59 Balls."

Ten. Annoni, C.O. of 96ª Sq. (Ufficio Storico SMA)

F.Lt. Olver (BN139):

"...109s tried to evade by performing steep climbing turns to the left. I heard the CO say he was going down. I followed after him, pulling across the top of him and performing an aileron turn. I picked an Me109 out on the extreme left, just as it pulled up to get away from ''A" flight attack. I out climbed him and gave him a short burst as a result of which I saw bits flying off. He put his nose down and dived away to the ground..."

F.Lt. Temlett (BN349):

"...5000' above them....The 109s were flying in pairs in echelon right, and I selected the second from the end on the right. My sight wasn't much good, but I closed in to 20 yards and gave him a 5 second burst from dead astern. I saw strikes along the right wing from tip to root, then the wing crumpled up and fell away, whilst the AC burst into flames.... 50 Ball, 50 He/I."

P.O. Sissons (BM972):

"...I selected a 109 on the extreme left of the formation. My approach must have been observed for when I was 600 yards behind him and 500' above, he pulled into a steep climbing turn to the left. I turned with him and he ran through my line of sight at 200 yards. I put on deflection and from practically full beam, gave him a 2 second burst. I saw strikes along cockpit and bits breaking off, and then he went over on his back, barrelled out, and pulled up and again half rolled. ...I saw him hit the deck."

W.O. Wallace's plane was damaged (BN139, Cat.I): there were two strikes outboard of guns just behind the leading edge of port main plane and the port aileron was smashed.

Annoni led eight *Macchis* of 9° Gruppo (six of 96ª Sq. and two of 73ª Sq.) on a free sweep over the Bir Elastar area (14.00-15.30). After 14.30, they were at an altitude of 4000 metres when twelve *P-40s* attacked at the same altitude: three were claimed to have been shot down, one was a probable victory, and seven were machine-gunned (2080 rounds):

Ten. Annoni (96ª Sq.) fired at two *P-40s*;
Serg. Biagini (96ª Sq.) shot down a *P-40*;
Serg. Magg. Mechelli (73ª Sq.) shot down a *P-40*;
Serg. Magg. Martinoli (73ª Sq., M.M.7823) probably shot down a *P-40*; in his turn, however, he was hit and force-landed in the desert. His plane was badly damaged.

The description of the formation that was sighted by 213 Squadron matches well with that of 9° Gruppo. Therefore they probably clashed with the *Macchis*. For the first time, the *Hurricanes*, which had the advantage of height, troubled the *Macchis*. But it is hard to believe that some of the latter went into a defensive circle — this tactic only makes sense against aircraft with a bet-

The tombs of Larsimont and Golino (Gentilli)

ter performance. This time the Italian formation was probably not split into two sections at two different heights. In any case, it is possible that the Italians did not want to admit in the war diary that on this occasion they had had a hard time.

The *Hurricanes* would also in this case have had their weapons reduced to two cannons. We should therefore make a comparison with the *Macchi*'s weapons: they had more or less the same rate of fire, even if the fire-power was much different. And yet, the way the guns were placed on the *Macchi*'s nose increased the possibility of hitting the target.

There are several inconsistencies between the two versions of the clash that indicate that the Italians could also have come up against the *Kittyhawks* of the previous action, in view of how the place and time match up.

The pilots of 5./JG 27 had just landed at Sidi Barrani and so were still in their aircraft. They were involved in the bombing of the aerodrome and two aircraft were hit by splinters: Fw. Fricke (*F-4/Trop* W.Nr. 8466) and nine victory ace Lt. Kurt Jenisch (*F-4* W.Nr. 7417) were wounded, the latter fatally.

III./JG 53 was badly hit. Its aircraft were positioned close together to speed up refuelling and had their pilots by them: Lt. Beckmann (9./JG 53, *F-4/Trop* WNr. 10036, 95%) was fatally wounded; Uffz. Glaser (7./JG 53, F-4/Trop W.Nr. 8684) was badly wounded. Three more pilots were slightly wounded: Uffz. Manz (9./JG 53, W.Nr. 10111, 45%); Lt. Schaller (9./JG53, W.Nr. 8792, 50%); Lt. Lange (10(Jabo)./JG 53, W.Nr. 10140, 60%). Two more aircraft were badly damaged: *F-4 trop* W.Nr. 10114 (9./JG 53, 70%) and *F-4/Z* W.Nr. 7094 (10(Jabo)./JG 53, 80%).

The attack on L.G.05 was carried out by six *Baltimores* of 223 Squadron which were covered by 233 Wing (16.08-17.25). At 16.40 all of the bombs were dropped among poorly dispersed aircraft, leaving three of them burning.

The bombers caught everyone by surprise by coming from the sea. This was deadly for 9° Gruppo: Magg. Antonio Larsimont Pergameni, Magg. Ludovico Laurin (a former test pilot just arrived in the ranks of the Unit), and veteran Serg. Magg. Angelo Golino were killed.

Magg. Larsimont Pergameni was at the time one of the prominent individuals in the fighter force of Regia Aeronautica. A mature permanent officer (born in May 1912), he had already fought with great distinction during the Spanish Civil War. He was credited with four individual victories and granted three Medaglie d'Argento al Valor Militare for bravery during his period there. At the head of 97ª Squadriglia, he had fought during the first Libyan Campaign, earning an additional victory and one shared to became an ace. In that difficult period, he had also confirmed his reputation as a cool and gallant leader, gaining the unquestioning appreciation of his men for he always lead by example. He was a pilot with a strong technical knowledge, for back in Italy he had been assigned to follow the start-up of the then new *Macchi C.202*. This was a task that he accomplished thoroughly, requesting and obtaining more than two hundred changes in the pre-production machines. Returning to operations with the *Folgore*, he obtained two more victories over Malta. In the meantime, he had received two additional 'Medaglie d'Argento al Valor Militare'.

Sorrowly missed by everyone in his Stormo, he was remembered by his colleagues as 'Italy's finest fighter pilot'. He received the Medaglia d'Oro al Valor Militare as a reward for his overall activity.

The *Macchis* were also badly damaged: M.M.7920 FU, M.M.7914 and M.M.7936 RD (all three of the 73ª Sq.); M.M.7761 and M.M.7932 RS (of 97ª Sq.). CA.133 M.M. 6053 (73ª) RS.

Hurricane IIC HL887 of 213 Sqn.; note reduced armament, October (Aviation Heritage Museum of Western Australia)

K) Seven *Kittyhawks* of 2 SAAF (16.00-17.25) were top cover for *Baltimores* of 223 Squadron that were attacking L.G.5, which was three miles south of Matruh. Two *Bf.109s* made a quick attack coming out of the sun but did not persist and caused no damage.

This matches the claim Lt. Schroer (8./JG 27, 15.35-16.35) made for a *Hurricane* south-west of Marsa Matruh (16.10).

Lt. Colin of Alsace was attacked by two *Bf.109s* (16.30-17.30) but was able to take successful evasive action.

Four *Hurricanes* of 238 Squadron (17.30-18.20) were top cover for six fighter-bombers of 274 Squadron. They were attacked at an altitude of about 1800 feet by *Bf.109s* that caused no damage. 274 Squadron noted the attack of two *Bf.109s* against the top cover.

A *Cant.Z.1007bis* of 35° Stormo was on a reconnaissance mission over Siwa (6.20-10.25). It bombed and strafed a four-engined bomber but was badly hit by anti-aircraft fire. An airman was wounded. It then crash-landed at Tobruk.

L) Ten *Bostons* of 24 SAAF again attacked concentrations of motor transports advancing on Matruh (17.40-19.05). Eight *Kittyhawks* of 260 Squadron were top cover (18.15-19.30) while eight

Kittybombers of 3 RAAF were close cover. At 18.37, 12 SAAF reported that the top cover was attacked by enemy aircraft and an aircraft was shot down. Supposedly it was F/Sgt. Carlisle's of 260 Squadron, who went missing.
'Kittyhawks over the Sands' stated:

> "As they turned over their target two Me.109's attacked. As always, they came from nowhere. As F/Sgt. Edwards looked above to Sergeant Carlisle's aircraft he saw an enemy aircraft close behind, firing. The 109 made a hit seconds before Eddie was forced to turn for his chance at a second 109 about 150 yards away. The young Canadian fired a long burst and watched as the enemy aircraft shuddered. Pieces flew in every direction as it headed to the ground leaving behind it a stream of black smoke. Twisting and weaving, Eddie had just enough time to dodge two other attackers."

Edwards was credited with a *Bf.109* probable.
3 RAAF only observed the attack of two *Bf.109s*.
 The victor must have been Fw. Seidl (8./JG 53), who claimed a *P-40* (17.45).

M) Twenty-four *Ju.87s* of III./St.G 3 attacked motor vehicles, enemy positions, and the roads south-east of Marsa Matruh (17.35-20.10). The escort was provided by twenty-three *Bf.109s* (six of I./JG 27, 18.10-19.39, eleven of II./JG 27, 18.10-19.15, and six of III./JG 27). They clashed with about twenty-five enemy fighters to the south of Matruh and their pilots claimed to have shot eleven down:
Oblt. Sinner (6./JG 27), *Hurricane* II, SE of Marsa Matruh (18.40);
Lt. Körner (3) (2./JG 27), *P-40*, S of Marsa Matruh (18.42); Spitfire, Marsa Matruh (18.46); Spitfire, SE of Marsa Matruh (19.05);
Fw. Steis (4./JG 27), *P-40*, S of Marsa Matruh (18.55);
Ofw. Bendert (2) (4./JG 27), P-40, south-east of Marsa Matruh (18.55, 19.00; mistakenly the claim list reports these 'victories' the day after).
Fw. Stigler (4./JG 27), *P-40*, S of Marsa Matruh (18.57);
Oblt. Boerngen (5./JG 27), *P-40*, SE of Marsa Matruh (19.03);
Lt. Stahlschmidt (2./JG 27), *P-40*, SSW of Marsa Matruh (19.06);
Uffz. Beckmann (2./JG 27, +7) Spitfire, E of Marsa Matruh (19.12); ('Fighters over the Desert': *"this AC was first attacked by Körner, but escaped in a sharp turn, crossing in front of his wingman, Beckmann, who shot it down with 5 rounds of cannon and 10 of machine-guns"*. The pilot baled out.).
The *Stuka* attack appeared to have had a certain success, and in fact many fires were seen. With some mix up OBS notes the loss of 3 *Ju.88s* instead of *Ju.87s*. Lt. Lipsky (II./St.G.3, *Ju.87 D-1* W.Nr. 2530, S7 + EP) was reportedly shot down by fighters over Marsa Matruk (crew safe), and this certainly matches up this mission. Uffz. Wolff (II./St.G.3) reportedly was shot down by fighters over Bu Hania on the 27th, in which no clashes with Stukas occurred, so very likely he was the second casualty. Then is registered the loss of two *Ju.88s*: Uffz. Mader (I./L.G.1, *A-4/Trop* W.Nr. 4549, L1 + CK) also shot down over Marsa Matruk, all crew missing; Uffz. Hackhausen (I./N.J.G.2, *C-2*, W.Nr. 0752, R4 + LK) shot down near Fuka all crew KIA. But these seem to have occurred in different missions and the presumably were victims of Flak.
 The Commonwealth Command managed to put together more than thirty fighters to confront the German attack: twelve *Hurricane IICs* of 213 Squadron (19.30-20.05); four *Spitfires* of 145

Squadron (19.35-20.20, two had returned ahead of time because of overheating); five *Tomahawks* of 5 SAAF (19.40-20.10, one had returned earlier); three *Kittyhawks* of 2 SAAF (19.50-20.20); five *Tomahawks* of 4 SAAF (19.45-20.30); and five *Hurricanes IICs* of 73 Squadron (19.50-20.45).

The *Hurricanes* of 213 Squadron engaged twenty *Stukas*, claiming to have shot down three and damaging four. This was countered by F.Sgt. Lack (BN527) going missing.

2 SAAF attacked thirty *Stukas* that were about to bomb at an altitude of 6000 feet, five miles south of Matruh. In the ensuing dogfight Lt. Morton (AL186 DB-G) destroyed a *Stuka* (total 750 rounds).

Capt. Murray (4 SAAF, AK366 KJ-W) reported:

"...headed for Mersa Matruh at a height of 8000'... informed 15+ snappers were just East of Matruh heading in a SE direction...observed 30 plus 109s and Stukas about 9000 so we climbed towards them. The formation of enemy aircraft were then jumped by 6 Hurricanes and the Stukas started to peel off towards us to dive bomb a target on the Bagush-Matruh road. I gave the signal and dived down with the Stukas ...The tracers of my cannons were observed to enter the Stuka..."

Lt. Paterson (AK419 KJ-F) attacked four *Stukas* and claimed to have damaged three (they seem not to have been credited to him). But he was then attacked by a *Bf.109* and entered a spin before managing to regain control.

Lt. Kaufmann and Capt. Pierce shared a *Bf.109* damaged. Overall 4 SAAF claimed: a *Ju.87* destroyed and three damaged in addition to a *Bf.109* damaged.

At 19.50, 5 SAAF ran into the enemy formation and five minutes later they attacked from 8000 feet:

"Sighted about 30 plus Stukas with 8 Me.109s as top cover south of Matruh. Half of the Stukas dived from SE to NW and dropped their bombs, rejoining the other part of the formation afterwards. After dropping their bombs they were engaged by our AC. After flying NW for some time the Me.s came down and joined in the dog-fight ... The EA then broke the engagement."

Capt. Lacey (AK445 GL-A):

"...I attacked a Stuka in the middle of formation....he started smoking badly and lost height. I gave him another burst from dead astern and he went down in a low spiral. The rear gunner jettisoned his hood but I didn't see him jump. The AC hit the ground but did not burst into flames. I then attacked two more Stukas in quick succession but could not carry on the attacks as I was attacked by Me.s."

And then the *Bf.109* attacked but without results. (5 SAAF: one *Ju.87* destroyed and two damaged.)

The *Hurricanes* of 73 Squadron were attacked by *Bf.109s*:

P.O. Coussens (BE280) was shot down but baled out safely;

P.O. Fraser (BN570) was wounded but managed to return with the plane badly damaged.

Finally the four *Spitfires* of 145 Squadron that were on patrol dived down on three *Bf.109s* and followed them up to L.G.07; two *Spitfires* then followed a *Bf.109* towards the west. Sgt. Spear (AB 326) was lost in the subsequent clash (missing).

In total six *Ju.87s* were claimed destroyed and nine damaged, plus a *Bf.109* damaged.

Four *Kittyhawks* of 2 SAAF (19.10-20.20) were top cover for nine *Bostons* of 12 SAAF (with

Bf.110 night-fighter (Gentilli)

112 and 450 Squadrons) over Charing Cross. The bombers' crews reported the bombing by *Ju.87s*. Lt. Wilkinson was then jumped by four *Bf.109s* and shot down (AK900 Cat.III); he was slightly wounded. The rest of the escort did not report the attack. The Messerchmitt pilots escorting the *Stukas* had probably been Wilkinson's shooters. Given the scarcity of the documentation it is difficult to know how the clash developed. It appears that the Commonwealth units had correctly noted the number of *Stukas* except for that of escorting *Bf.109s*, unless they were divided into small groups. However, the bombers were attacked, the escort intervened too late, and it seems there were insufficient numbers. In short, it appeared once again to be a risky attack by the Germans. Even the diaries of the Commonwealth units do not allow us to establish the positioning of their own formation; it seems that they attacked with little coordination.

We can only assume that the top cover of the *Stukas* became engaged by 73 and 145 Squadrons while the other units managed to reach the *Stukas* easily. Finally, a part of the escort, presumably the top cover, also engaged the *Kittyhawks* of 2 SAAF, which were escorting the bombers. The escort shot down Wilson, which caused the continued weakening of the *Stukas*' protection. However, once again substantial forces were provided, gathered together from different quarters to confront the German attacking formations. This was never the case on the part of the Axis forces against the Commonwealth bombers.

S.L. Riley of 227 Squadron (attached to 272 Squadron) was shot down by anti-aircraft fire and returned after crossing the enemy lines on foot.

N) *Ju.86Ps* reconnaissance were able to carry out their daily missions without being harassed thanks to their high altitude. 103 Maintenance Unit stripped two *Spitfires* and overpowered them for the specific task of intercepting the German plane. During the the day the two *Spitfires* managed for the first time to damage a Ju.86P. One of the pilots was F.O. Genders.

Also during the day, 7 SAAF Squadron arrived at L.G.208 equipped with *Hurricane* Is.

OBS reported twenty-four *P-40s* shot down by Luftwaffe, two of which were probable victories.

Night of 26-27

O) *Wellingtons* were extremely active in night harassment. *Wellington* IC Z9028 V (Sgt. Gunn, 40 Squadron) was shot down by fighters and crashed near Halfaya station. All of its crew was lost. *Wellington* IC Z9102 A (Sgt. Clayton, 70 Squadron) took off between 21.20 and 23.15 on a mission over Daba. It was attacked by a fighter and shot down in flames. The crew baled out but the pilot and a second member lost their lives.
Wellington IC ES981 A (Sgt. Street, 108 Squadron) took off at 21.00 on a mission over Sidi El Barrani. It was attacked by a *Ju.88* and shot down in flames. Two crew members survived.
    These losses must be related to two claims made by *Ju.88C* pilots of I./NJG 2: Ofw. Köster (3./NJG 2), a *Beaufighter* (23.44); and Fw. Heyne (1./NJG 2), a *Wellington* (1.34).
It is unlikely that a *Beaufighter* was operating during the night.

Nine *He.111s* attacked the roads and railway in the Fuka-Burg El Arab area (00.23-3.23); Fw. Rohloff (II./K.G.100, *He.111H-6* W.Nr. 7214, 6N + BJ) was missing with his crew.

27 June

A) At 8.15, Lt. Sedgewick (*Hurricane* IIA Z.5412) of 208 Squadron took off for a tactical reconnaissance sortie (Bir Nasralla-Charing Cross) and did not return. He must have been shot down by Oblt. Klager (8./JG 53). The latter was on a freelance with his Schwarm (6.45) and claimed a *Hurricane* (7.35).

Kittyhawks of 260 Sqn. armed with bombs: the first one carries a 500 lb. bomb; the second a 250 lb. one (Aviation Heritage Museum of Western Australia)

B) At 8.22, six *Bf.109s* of I./JG 27 took off and attacked several *Martin 167s*, claiming two:
Hptm. Franzisket (1./JG 27), SW of El Daba (8.55);
Fw. Steinhausen (1./JG 27), WSW of El Daba (8.58).
They picked the *Baltimore IIs* of 223 Squadron, which had abandoned L.G.116 one by one for a transfer to another L.G; three of them were attacked by *Bf.109s* near Fuka. Two planes (AG771, F.Lt. Gidney and AG782, P.O. Davies) were shot down with the loss of their entire crews. The third one (AG774, Sgt. Carruthers) crash-landed at Wadi Natrum with two injured.

Two *Hurricanes* of 'Alsace' Squadron were patrolling in the vicinity of L.G.16 when they saw one the Baltimores being shot down by two Messerschmitts. The French pilots rushed on them but without results (9.45). It must be emphasized that 'Alsace' mounted *Hurricane* Is and the *Bf.109 F* was like an UFO compared with them.

1 SAAF's diarist, watching from the ground, also saw a *Bf.109* chasing a *Boston* at almost ground level near Daba; it was only 50 feet off the deck. The *Bf.109* swung off and came back attacking the road several times at a right angle, firing short ineffective bursts at the motor transports.

C) Four *Spitfires* of 145 Squadron were on a mission over Sidi Haneish (10.15-11.30). They were at an altitude of 20000 feet on their way up to 22000 feet when they were assailed by six *Bf.109s*: One Spitfire was damaged on the wing and aileron.

Five *Kittyhawks* of 112 Squadron took off on a tactical reconnaissance sortie (10.30-12.00). At 11.30, F.Lt. Walker (AK852) was shot down over the lines, possibly hit by anti-aircraft fire. He returned the next day.

D) Oblt. Vögl of 4./JG 27 claimed a *P-40* south-west of Fuka at 11.10. He was a part of a formation of five *Bf.109s* of II./JG 27 that was on a free sweep.

Three *Tomahawks* of 5 SAAF covered bombers to Charing Cross (11.30-12.25); Lt. Kemsley (AM392, Cat.II) force-landed at L.G.15 because of engine failure (they would not have met up with any enemy aircraft).

E) Nine *Macchis* of 88ª Sq. were at the end of a free sweep to the east of Marsa Matruk (11.35-12.55) when their pilots spotted *Hurricanes* that were strafing troops. The last section dived to attack and three pilots fired at four enemy planes, damaging one of them (195 rounds fired); the intervention would stop the *Hurricanes* from continuing their attack on the troops.

It could have been six *Kittyhawks* of 3 RAAF which had taken off for a reconnaissance mission over the roads in the area between Matruh, Charing Cross, and Siwa (12.45-13.50). Once the reconnaissance mission had been carried out, these planes were reported to have attacked three *Bf.109s* fifteen miles south-west of Matruh without any apparent results.

F) Nine *Bostons* of 12 SAAF were on a mission south of Marsa Matruh (13.10-14.30).
Eight *Kittyhawks* of 260 Squadron were top cover (13.35-14.40) while 4 SAAF was close cover. 260 Squadron was attacked by *Bf.109s* just after take-off but to no effect. Subsequently another six planes attacked the formation and in the battle that followed, two of them were claimed shot down and one probably so; one was the work of S.L. Hanbury as well as the probable victory and

Boston Z2302 of 3 SAAF abandoned in some landing ground (Archivio di Stato)

the second was the work of Sgt. Parrot.
12 SAAF reported the attack of five or six enemy aircraft but they did not break through the escort.
4 SAAF reported nothing.
   They had clashed with I./JG 27 when Lt. Stahlschmidt (2./JG 27) claimed a *Hurricane II*, 10 km south-east of Fuka (13.05).
Uffz. Beckmann (2./JG 27, rt. 7+) was taken by surprise while he was watching Stahlschmidt's Schwarm engaging *Hurricanes* 3000 feet below. His feet and shoulder were wounded but he managed to land at his airfield.

G) *Bf.109s* of 9./JG 27 were on a free sweep (13.55-15.10) when they came across two *Hurricane IIs* and three *P-40s*; both *Hurricanes* were claimed shot down:
Oblt. Heinecke, W of Fuka (14.45);
Ofw. Rosenberg, E of Haggag El Quasaba (14.48).
   Involved in the case were four *Hurricanes* of 'Alsace' (15.48), patrolling over the road Bagush-Fuka.
Tango Red Section (5000 feet):

> "Being attacked No.1 (S.Lt. Lafont) goes into a flat left hand turn. No.2 (S.Lt. Thiriez) turns facing the attack and opens fire on one Me.109. No.2 has its tail unit badly damaged and is obliged to land and in doing so is attacked a second time, being unable to control his AC he cannot take evasive action and is wounded by cannon fire. Crash-landed...
> No.1 avoids an attack coming from dead above, pulling strongly the stick backwards...avoids 2 further attacks by skidding turns...then attacked by 4 EA coming from cloud, astern right and left. Opens fire on EA attacking from above and ahead...possibly damaged.
> One shell burst into the cockpit, (wounded arm and leg) glycol tank and starboard petrol tank holed. Crash-landed and in ground strafed by one Me.109."

Probably Tango Blue Section (7000 feet) was unseen:

> "...see 4 Me.109Fs attacking Tango Red Section. Turned left to have the sun on the back and to be on position to attack. Enemy sees us and engage in dog-fight. No.1 (S.Lt. Louchet, Z4434) opens fire-long burst- on EA from 1/4 astern. EA dives vertically (Claimed as probably destroyed). No.2 (Lt. Brisdoux, X4708) opens fire with four short bursts on EA, while both on left hand turn. No.2 sees an EA attacking No.1, dives onto it and fires three bursts. EA dives and flies East on the deck. No.2 ...unable to catch up..."

Afterwards Heineke picked out an Albacore of 826 Squadron while it was taking off north-east of Haggag El Qusaba at 14.54, shooting it down.
P.O. Maclean (252 Squadron, *Beaufighter* T4831) was off on a long raid to Derna, Martuba, Tmimi, Gazala and Gambut , Fuka (15.15-20.10). A great number of enemy planes were claimed damaged. In fact at Sanyet El Scheterasat significant losses were suffered by the Luftwaffe due to bombing: *Ju.88 A-4* W.Nr. 5711 (6./L.G.1), it seems that also his pilot was killed; *Bf.110 E-3* W.Nr. 2315 (100%); *Bf.110 E-3* W.Nr. 2415 (60%).

H) Five *Bf.109s* of I./JG 27 engaged a group of *Hurricanes* around Fuka and five were shot down:
Hptm. Franzisket (1./JG 27), SW of Fuka (18.25);
Hptm. Maack (2./JG 27) over *L.G.* Fuka West (18.27);
Fw. Steinhausen (1./JG 27) (2) SW of Fuka (18.27, 18.30);
Lt. Körner (2./JG 27) hit a *Hurricane* which force-landed but did not claim it.
Once more 'Alsace' was attacked, again while patrolling over Bagush (19.10).
Tango Green (6000 feet): "*Saw 2 Me.109Fs ... faced the EA left hand turn. No.1 (Lt. Colin, Z4648) avoids an attack and turned sharp into the tail of one EA. He is then lost by No.2*". Colin lost his life.
S.Lt. Derville (No.2, Z4613) was engaged by two *Bf.109s* while three remained above. He was able to fire a long burst at the belly of an enemy aircraft and finally evaded flying at zero feet. He had been attacked for ten times.
Tango Yellow (6000 feet):

> "Top cover over Tango Green, saw 6 Me.109Fs above. Dived to warn Tango Green and turned sharp right facing the attack.
> No.1 (S.Lt. Louchet, Z4718) while turning is hit and takes fire. The pilot bales out but being but being wounded is unable to open his parachute and is killed.
> No.2 (S.Chef. Mailfert, Z4708) is then engaged by 4 EA and receives a few hits, causing very little damage. Reduced speed, opened flaps and takes violent evasive action. The EA are then unable to get into position.
> No.2 is hit by own Bofors gun. Big hole in port wing. Engine stops. Crash-landed. Pilot slightly wounded. Picked up by 5th Indian Division."

So in the afternoon two French pilots of 'Alsace' lost their life and five Hurricanes were shot down.

During one of the patrols over Daba two *Hurricanes Is* of 335 Squadron were attacked by two *Bf.109s* but they were able to evade them. F.Sgt. Soufrilias returned with a bullet hole through its port wing.

601 (*Spitfire Vs*) and 127 (*Hurricane IIBs*) Squadrons also arrived to the front line.

Uffz. Berben (3./JG 27, W.Nr. 8693, 100) crash-landed at Marsa Matruh due to engine failure (take-off at 18.49).

In the afternoon Oblt. Boerngen and Obfw. Clade of II./JG 27 clashed with enemy fighters and believed to have probably shot down two *P-40s*. The claims were not submitted for approval, however, because the two aircraft were not seen to crash.

During the day the Spitfires of 601 Squadron flew their first operational mission.

Night of 27-28

I) At 0.55, S.L. Johnston of 73 Squadron damaged a *Ju.88* (30 Ball, 30 HE/Inc).
F.O. Selby was at an altitude of 7000 feet over Fuka at 1.00:

> "I saw bombs on the road so manoeuvered to sea to endeavour to get EA in moon path on water. Succeeded and EA saw me at same time. A dog-fight ensued in which all forms of attack were carried out at a range of 50-100 yards. Both engines caught fire and at the same time the rear gunner, who had been keeping up rapid fire, was silenced by a burst from astern, 50 yards. EA a Ju.88 broke off the fight and dived steeply to sea ... Destroyed (50 Ball, 50 HE/Inc)."

It was the third individual success of John Selby who would go on to claim two more victories and become an ace (with three night victories). He would end the war as Wing Commander.
There were German losses in this period but the time and day do not match. Mistakes are possible so it cannot be excluded that some results could have been achieved by 73 Squadron.

28 June

272 Squadron was detailed to strafe reported Ju.52 at Derna. P.O. Wood (B) did not return (10.40). P.O. Delcur (G) and Sgt. Patterson (F) were off afterwards (11.25-15.50):

> "... AC 'G' hit two and probably a third Ju.52. AC raked a row of 3 Ju.52s, one of which emitted a puff of black smoke from the fuselage and finished off his ammo. on one of 5 Me.110s dispersed on the N.E. corner of the drome. The flak was intense, 'G' being hit in the main plane, the port engine cooling and the A.S.I. tube and both AC were hotly pursued out to sea by 2 Me.110 and 1 Me.109 but managed to shake them off."

Also 252 Squadron again raided enemy aerodromes. P.O. Gunnis was off (T4881, 9.40-14.05) when he was seriously wounded and Sgt.Wallis flew back the Beaufighter.
At Derna *Ju.88 C-6* W.Nr. 360231 (I./N.J.G.2) was strafed. Also Lufwaffe's personnel suffered casualties.

Macchi C202 of 88ª Sq. (Gentilli)

Seven Tomahawks of 4 SAAF on patrol (8.40-10.00) were attacked with no results by a Schwarm of *Bf.109*s.

A) Ten *Hurricanes* of 238 Squadron were up on a reconnaissance mission over the battle area around Sidi Haneish (12.00-12.45). At about 12.20 the formation was attacked by three *Bf.109s* diving almost vertically out of the sun. Four *Hurricanes* were shot down. One pilot was seen to bale out. And yet the British pilots believed that they had shot down a *Bf.109*. The *Hurricanes* reformed but were again attacked on the homeward journey by two *Bf.109s*. Another one was shot down. The pilots shot down were F.Lt. Collinette (T), F.Sgt. Cummings (G), F.Sgt. Lawrence Smith (H), F.Sgt. Doig (A), and F.Sgt. Purdy (X). Only Doig returned to base.

The attack was carried out by three pilots of 1./JG 27 on a freie Jagd (11.00-12.10). They went after twelve *Hurricane IIs* around Fuka. They claimed six of them, all south-west of Fuka:
Fw. Steinhausen (4) (11.25, 11.30, 11.31, 11.33);
Fw. Keppler (11.27);
Uffz. Timmermann (11.37).
There was another deadly attack by *Messerschmitts*: only three German fighters destroyed half of the enemy formation. The dive and zoom tactic was certainly effective but also the markmanship of the pilots must have been outstanding. The times of the claims would indicate that the *Hurricanes* would have been shot down one at a time -- this therefore makes the slaughter even more astonishing as usually the element of surprise would be ineffective after the first victory.
As the Italian pilots did not manage to obtain the same results with the identical tactic, it is necessary to understand the extent of the difference of fire power between the *Messerschmitts* and the *Macchis*.

B) Upon returning from a free sweep to the east of Marsa Matruk (10.45-12.20), Ten. Marchi, S. Ten. Sgorbati, M.llo Bladelli, and Serg. Host (88ª) sighted a *P-40* that was strafing motor transports. It was attacked and quickly shot down in flames (200 rounds). The victory was shared between the four pilots.

Presumably it was Lt. Bidwell (? 460) of 5 SAAF who did not return from an action; his plane came down fifteen miles from base (take-off 11.10). He was probably on the way back home.

Three *Bf.109* pilots would have observed the event as they had taken off in their planes specifically to intercept enemy fighters that were strafing motor transports towards Bir el Astas airfield ('Fighters over the Desert').

F.Sgt. Copping of 260 Squadron (*Kittyhawk* ET574) went missing during a delivery flight. The plane was found in the desert in 2012.

Night of 28-29

C) *Wellington* IC R1029 S (S.L. Jaclin, 108 Squadron) was attacking enemy positions at Marsa Matruh (take-off 21.50) when a *Ju.88* attacked it. The rear gunner responded to fire and claimed to have shot down the attacker in flames. But the bomber was badly damaged and was forced to crash-land; there were no casualties. Again the victor should have been Lt. Rökker (1./NJG 2), that claimed a Wellington, 60 km S.E. of Marsa Matruh (23.58).

D) Seven Liberators of the Halverston Detatchment bombed the harbour and shipping at Tobruk. One aircraft was attacked by a *Bf.110* nightfighter that caused damage, killing a member of the crew. The return fire was seen to strike the attacker that broke off diving.

Fourteen *Ju.88s* attacked Marsa Matruh (1.37-5.11); one aircraft was lost (OBS).
Reportedly the 29th two *Ju.88s* were lost: Lt. Rökker (I./N.J.G.2, *Ju.88* C-6 W.Nr. 360002, R4 + DH) was hit by Flak and compelled to force-land near Marsa Matruk (100 %); Ofw. Döring (4./L.G.1, *Ju.88* A-4 W.Nr. 5672, L1 + LM) went missing with his crew. It is more likely that Rökker was shot down in this occasion, while Döring in one of the clashes the following night.

29 June

A) Four *Macchis* of 9° Gruppo, led by Ten. Querci, were on 'caccia libera' (free sweep) to the south-east of Marsa Matruh (10.15-11.30). They sighted twelve *P-40s* at an altitude of 3500 m and attacked them. They were credited with two victories, a probable one, and several planes machine-gunned:
Serg. Biagini (96ª Sq.) shot down a *P-40* and fired at four more;
Serg. Magg. Martinoli (73ª Sq.) shot down a *P-40*;
S. Ten. Querci (73ª Sq.) probably shot down a *P-40*;
   Nine *Hurricane IICs* of 213 Squadron were on a free sweep over Marsa Matruh (11.45-13.45).
'A' flight was top cover at 10000 feet while 'B' flight was 6000 feet. At 12.40 an enemy formation was observed descending the escarpment five miles west of Fuka. Intense light anti-aircraft fire was experienced over Pin Point 782313. 'B' flight was heading west at 12.45 when it observed two *Bf.109s* diving down onto the port section; their attention was probably drawn because the *Hurricanes* were being aimed at by anti-aircraft fire. Two more *Bf.109s* then joined in and individual combats resulted. After fifteen minutes the engagement was broken off.

P.O. Bedham (BN139) reported the attack of three *Bf.109s* from an altitude of 10000 feet. He was attacked by one and went into a circle but the enemy aircraft gained on him, firing at a constant rate. He was down at 500 feet when the enemy aircraft overshot him, coming in within a 50 yard range. Unfortunately a gun began to fail after the first burst, shortly followed by the other two. Still he continued firing with the remaining final gun, seeing bits breaking off and the enemy aircraft diving straight to the deck, bursting into flames and blowing up. Bedham's plane sustained severe damage (Cat.II). There was a bullet behind the port petrol tank and one in the gravity petrol tank. A bullet struck the ammunition in the starboard wing but did not cause it to explode. The mirror was shot away. The airscrew was damaged by a bullet and needed to be replaced. As a result of all of this, the plane had to land at *L.G.*106 (rounds: 48 Ball, 47 He/I).
Olver (BN139) damaged a second plane (rounds: 40 Ball, 40 He/I).
BN117 (P.O. Chadwick) was Cat.I; an explosive bullet had struck the starboard tailplane. There was also damage to the trailing edge and stringers on the rudder as well as damage to the port main plane where a bullet had struck the cannon magazine. In this case the *Hurricanes* were armed with four cannons.

It is interesting to see that the Italians were sighted at the beginning of their attack, and so the RAF formation was warned by radio and able to avoid damage during the first bounce. A long dogfight then began during which the Italians, clearly numerically inferior, were unable to shoot down their opponents. Some of the *Hurricanes* received many hits but the damage was not enough shoot them down. This is a typical example of how combat often develops once the initial surprise is lost.

Lt. Warden of 2 SAAF was on an escort mission when he had to attempt a landing because of a sandstorm. He was killed in the process. He crashed on Blenheim IV Z7485 that was also destroyed.
Lt. Heald (40 SAAF) was taking off in ground mist (6.20). His Hurricane probably swung in, hitting a Beaufort loaded with a torpedo that exploded.

Bf.109 F-4/Trop W.Nr. 10156 (9./J.G.53) was heavily damaged (80%) during a bombing at Sidi Barrani.
Bf.109 F-4/Trop W.Nr. 8534 (4./J.G.27), was damaged (80%) in an accident at Sidi Barrani.
Bf.109 F-4/Trop W.Nr. 10165 (7./J.G.27), was damaged (70%) in an accident at Marsa Matruk.

<u>Night of 29-30</u>

B) Sgt. Baker of 73 Squadron (01.00-2.15, BN402) damaged a *Ju.88* at 1.45. After two bursts, only one cannon out of four was still working (rounds: Ball 50, HE/Inc 50).

B-24D (Capt. Nestor, 376th) was hit by flak over Tobruk and crashed. Four of the crew went missing.
Ju.88s night-fighters were spotted; hits on them were claimed by the gunners of two other *B24s*.

Ten *Ju.88s* attacked communication lines, motor transports, and tents at El Abu Dweis (20.38-01.38); one aircraft was lost (OBS). Possibly it was Rökker (see the previous night).

30 June

During a patrol a Spitfire of 145 Squadron (12.10-13.20) was reported missing. Sgt. Small (145 Squadron, E322) crash-landed at 16.00.

In the afternoon Lt. Warden (2 SAAF, AK753 DB-A) attempted to land at L.G.97 during a sandstorm. He crashed into a Blenheim and was killed.

Ju.87 D-1 W.Nr. 2476 (II./St.G.3), was damaged during a bombing at Abu Haggag (75%).

DATE	AXIS TIME	CLAIMS COMM.			CLAIMS GER.			CLAIMS ITA.			CAS. COMM.		CAS. GER.		CAS. ITA.		UNITS INVOLVED
		S	P	D	S	P	D	S	P	M	S	D	S	D	S	D	
19	A 8.55-?			1B													80 Sqn, Ju.88?
20	A 11.58-12.40				2A												II/JG 27, ?
23	A 14.13-15.05			1A	1A												8/JG 27, 274 Sqn
24	A 9.15-10.10				1A						1A						II/JG 27, 208, 213 Sqn
24	B 10.05-12.15	2A	1A								1A						3 RAAF Sqn, ?
24	C 0.00-1.00	1B		1B									1B				73 Sqn, II./K.G.100
25	A 13.39-14.44				1A						1A						250 Sqn, 5/JG 27
25	B 19.35-20.20										1A						145 Squadron, Bf.109s?
25	C 23.45-00.09				2B						2B						70 Sqn, 1/NJG 2
25	D 00.05-?	1B											1B				73 Sqn, Ju.88
26	A 5.00-6.05	1T															208 Sqn, Ju.52?
26	B 7.55-9.30	1A	1A					2A	5A	14A	1B 1A	3B 1A					9° Gr, 12 SAAF, 3 RAAF, 450, 250, 208 Sqn
26	C 11.25-13.40	1A			1B						1A2						III/JG 53, 272 Sqn.
26	D 10.05-11.00				1A						1A						12 SAAF, 450 Sqn., III/JG 53
26	E 10.55-12.00	1A			4A						2A						112, 3 RAAF Sqn, III/JG 27
26	F 11.30-13.00	1A			6A						3A	1B					I/JG27, 12 SAAF, 250, 450, 213, 238, 274 Sqn
26	G 12.10-13.20							1B		4B	2B	1B					9° Gr, 223 Sqn
26	H 13.25-?				2A						2A						145 Sqn, 3/JG 27
26	I 14.02-15.13				4A						3A	1A					5/JG 27, 3 RAAF, 4, 5 SAAF, 450 Sqn
26	J 14.00-15.30	5A						3A	1A	7A	1A				1A		9° Gr, 213 Sqn.
26	K 15.35-16.35				1A												8/JG 27, 2 SAAF Sqn

DATE	AXIS TIME	CLAIMS COMM.			CLAIMS GER.			CLAIMS ITA.			CASUALTIES COMM.		CASUALTIES GER.		CASUALTIES ITA.		UNITS INVOLVED
		S	P	D	S	P	D	S	P	M	S	D	S	D	S	D	
26	L 17.10-18.10				1A						1A						8/JG 53, 260 Sqn
	M 18.12-19.20	6Bs 1A		9Bs	11A						4A	1A	3Bs				I,II,III/JG 27, Ju.87s ?, 2, 4, 5 SAAF, 73, 213, 145 Sqn
	N ?			1T													103 Sqn, Ju.86?
	O 23.44-1.34				2B						3B						3./NJG 2, 40, 70, 108 Sqn
27	A 7.15 ?				1A						1A						8/JG 53, 208Sqn
	B 8.22-9.00				2B						3B						223, Alsace Sqn, I/JG 27
	C 9.15-10.30												1A				145 Sqn, Bf.109s?
	D ?-11.10				1A												4/JG 27, P-40s?
	E 11.35-12.55									1A							88ª Sq, 3 RAAF Sqn.
	F 12.35-13.40	2A	1A		1A								1A				I/JG 27, 260 Sqn.
	G 14.48-?	1A			2A 1T						2A 1T						9/JG 27, Alsace, 826 Sqn
	H 18.10-?				4A						3A						I/JG 27, Alsace, P-40s?
	I 23.00-0.55			1B													73 Sqn, Ju.88s?
28	A 11.00-12.10				6A						5A						1/JG 27, 238 Sqn
	B 10.45-12.20									1A	1A						88ª Sq, 5 SAAF Sqn
	C 20.50-23.45				1B						1B						108 Sqn., 1./NJG 2
	D ?			1B									1B				376th Group, Ju.88?
29	A 10.15-11.30	1A			1A			2A	1A	7A	2A						9° Gr, 213 Sqn.
	B 0.45-?			2B									1B				73 Sqn, 376th Group, 1./L.G.1
	TOT	2B 6Bs 16A 1T			8B 50A 1T			1B 8A			12B 1A2 31A 1T		5B 3Bs 1A		1A		

Chapter 8
CONCLUSIONS

The fall of Tobruk along with the rush of Rommel's Army toward the bottleneck of El Alamein ended the so-called 'Battle of Gazala'. As we have seen in detail, there was much harsh combat between the opposing air forces over the battleground. But what was the end result?

Was one of them able to gain complete control of the sky and therefore make a decisive impact on the operations on the ground below?

The ground victory of Rommel and his Italian ally coupled with the heavy losses suffered in the air by the Commonwealth air force could perhaps lead us to the conclusion that the Luftwaffe and Regia Aeronautica were able to gain some kind of aerial supremacy. Yet, while it is undeniable that certain relevant tactical victories of the Axis were helped by air support — above all the fall of Tobruk — it is also clear that no complete and durable superiority was achieved by any of the contenders.

German *Stukas* formations were often intercepted and sometimes mauled during their missions over the front line. It was no matter how heavy the losses suffered by the Commonwealth fighters were, as these were always made up for. Commonwealth bombers and fighter-bombers continued undeterred in attacking Axis troops and from time to time Axis airfields. The only time in which the Allied air force remained grounded — albeit for a short period — was in the days immediately after the breakthrough of the Gazala line when they had to relocate in airstrips toward

2 SAAF Tomahawk (earlier period); seemed damaged by a Bf.109: a considerable hole made by cannon shell and smaller damages made by 7,7 MG (Bouwer)

the rear. Yet, this was in no way due to the action of the opposing air forces but a direct consequence of the enemy's army advance.

It is always difficult to assess precisely the results of air operations over the battlefield and this campaign is no exception. However, in reading accounts of the land operations from both sides, the author senses that on the whole and with the notable exception of the conquest of Tobruk, air attacks had only a minor impact on those operations.

Thus the complete air campaign could be seen as a bloody and unresolved struggle for aerial superiority that had only the effect of wearing down the opposing air forces.

The heaviest losses, for operational but also non-operational reasons, were those suffered by the Commonwealth Squadrons. But these losses were bearable thanks to the extensive number of replacements already available in the second-line airfields in Egypt and the continuous flow of reinforcements arriving from the United States and the other countries of the Commonwealth. Losses on the other side of the front, on the contrary, were much more felt. The Luftwaffe was already overstretched, fighting a titanic struggle against the Soviet Union while at the same time defending its home country and facing the RAF and USAAF in France, Belgium, and Low Countries. Only relatively small efforts could be devoted to the war in the Mediterranean, also because of the strategic vision of OKW that saw the continental front in Russia as a priority. The Italian air force on the other hand, after two years of war, was already heavily reduced as a fighting force, chiefly for industrial reasons. When Italy had entered the conflict in June 1940, the idea was that the war was to last only a few weeks or months, and therefore no real conversion of the industry to military purposes had been carried out. In the following months, when it finally appeared that the war was not to finish so quickly, political reasons again prevented the beginning of this process, which finally began as late as the end of 1942. Thus, that summer the Italian industry, also hampered by a lack of raw materials, could supply the air force with a maximum monthly input of no more than 40 to 50 modern fighters and no modern bombers. This force had to be divided between the two main fronts of Malta and North Africa. The status in the field of aero engines, necessary to keep flying the planes already built, was even worse. The situation was so critical that in July when the moment came to equip 3° Stormo with the *Macchi C.202*, (although ageing was still last generation fighter), not enough *Folgores* were available. And so, half of the unit, its 18° Gruppo, had to remain mounted on *C.200s* which was at the time completely outclassed by its opposition. The rest of radial-engine fighters (*C.R.42s*, *G.50s*, and *C.200s*) could be profitably used in convoy escort duties or in point defence.

Ultimately the losses suffered by the Axis were much more difficult to replace, both in terms of material and in personnel. In hindsight, it is possible to say that the attrition that started in these early summer months laid the base for the defeat they were to suffer in late autumn over El Alamein.

In the following pages, some aspects of the air operations will be discussed.

Commonwealth Air Forces' Activities

As we can see from Appendix 3, the number of units is almost always constant. The longer the battle lasted, notwithstanding considerable reserves being available, the fewer the number of planes that there were 'in command' and 'serviceable.' This affected the *P.40s* (*Tomahawks* and

Kittyhawks) in particular as they were the planes mostly in use. As we have seen, there was a tendency for an increase in the number of planes, above all fighters, that were not able to complete their missions due to technical problems.

The number of sorties in the first week of the battle was almost double that of the week before. In particular the increase for the *P-40s* and *Bostons* was considerable. The number of sorties then went up to reach a peak in the third week. The data for the last two weeks show a drop for the fighters; nevertheless in the last week we can see that there was an huge increase in the number of sorties for the *Wellingtons* and *Bostons*.

Therefore with the exclusion of the escorts for the convoys and local defense, it is possible to estimate that Commonwealth fighters carried out about 5000 sorties over the front line.

The bombers carried out over 2000 sorties, considerably less than that achieved by the German units. The *Wellingtons* carried out the task of attacking at night at ports and the other logistic centers. The *Bostons* carried out more tactical missions, performing daylight attacks on airfields, enemy supply columns, other targets nearer the front line, and finally providing support during the battles. Their logistic capability was remarkable; after the collapse of the Gazala line, in spite of the retreat and the move of units back at new airfields, they were used more than twice as much as in the weeks before.

Luftwaffe's activities

It was estimated that the German *Bf.109* fighters carried out about 4700 sorties. While the bombers of every type carried out 2800, about 70% of them were by *Stukas* (estimated data). While at the start of the battle there had been about 100 serviceable German fighters in strength, by 10 June this number had already fallen to about 60. In view of this availability, the number of German sorties per aircraft a day was much higher than both that of the Italian fighters and that of the Commonwealth ones.

Regia Aeronautica's activities

The *C.202s* carried out about 2000 sorties in the period from 22 May-30 June with an effort that was practically constant throughout (1093 sorties during the first fifteen days of the offensive). There were about 80 serviceable *C.202s* at the start of the battle; on 30 June there were about 70 (App. 3). It seems that a considerably higher percentage of Italian fighter planes were efficient compared to those of the German ones. The number of sorties per aircraft a day was not as high as that of the Luftwaffe; nevertheless it was not smaller than that of the *Tomahawks* and *Kittyhawks*.

The activities of the level bombers were somewhat limited; however, they were also used as reconnaissance planes. The ground attack units of the 2° and 50° Stormi were also not used continuously. We should bear in mind that ground attacks were particularly costly in terms of planes and pilots, as the data show. Therefore an increased use of them would have led to the rapidly dwindling strength of those units. It was an offensive instrument that had much less of a capability in their hands than it had in those of the Germans and the Commonwealth. Therefore it seems that it was deemed more appropriate to keep it for more critical situations.

Bf.110 (San Diego Air and Space Museum)

In the period, the total production of the *C.202s* in the Macchi, Breda, and SAI Ambrosini assembly lines — limited by the low availability of engines – did not exceed a total of around 55 machines per month. In fact the units based in North Africa received only a couple of replacements in June; clearly it was necessary to make a careful use of them due to the lack of reserves and in particular spare engines.

The comparison between the activities of the Commonwealth and the Axis bombers is not simple. As we have seen, the *Wellingtons* exclusively carried out night attacks on logistic centres and this amounted to about 1000 sorties. And yet, there were the activities of the *Ju.88s* and *He.111s*, which were mostly at night and amounted to about 800 sorties (estimated data). Only a few sorties of Italian bombers were added. Therefore both parties flew a comparable number of sorties, even if the *Wellingtons* were capable of carrying a larger bomb load.

The *Bostons* and *Baltimores* usually carried out their activities during the daytime and these were mostly tactical, even if the attacks on the Axis airports were important and often deadly.

In this field, this was set against the about 1900 sorties of the Stukas (estimated figure). Obviously in one case the bomb load was much higher while in the other case the dropping of bombs was more accurate.

These activities were added to by the notably intense ones of the fighter-bombers (mostly of 239 Wing), which amounted to about 1800 sorties against the about 1300 sorties of the Axis fighter-bombers (700 German sorties, estimated figure; 600 Italian).

Commonwealth's fighters and fighter-bombers flew about 5000 sorties (excluding the escorts for the convoys and local defense) while the Axis' fighters flew about 8000 sorties, so the presence of Axis fighters over the battlefield was stronger than that of the Commonwealth's. What is more, the former flew on a greater number of missions because their formations were smaller than those of their adversaries. In fact, when the clashes took place, the numerical advantage was normally in favor of the Commonwealth. An overlook on the battlefield would have shown that it very often was covered by small patrols of German fighters, or to a much lesser extent by slightly more numerous Italian fighter formations. Instead, bigger Commonwealth fighter formations, with a least a couple of squadrons, showed up less frequently. Finally there would have been significantly large attack formations, with a strong fighter escort, on both sides.

Tactical considerations

The comparison between the numbers of sorties of the two opposing forces would indicate that they were pretty well matched in strength and would in the meantime indicate that the Commonwealth was better able to make good on its losses. Beginning with the fall of Bir Hakeim, we can see a certain crisis in the Commonwealth fighter sector. A representative case, 5 SAAF began with all its twenty planes ready for action and ended up with only one operational. Nevertheless, the crisis only lasted as long as it took the units to transfer from Libyan to Egyptian airfields, where they quickly became fully operational again using the reserves amassed there.

As for the bomber sector, the only uneasiness felt was due to moving back, which was moreover to last a very short time.

The Commonwealth light bomber formations mainly flew at medium-low altitudes. They generally operated under strong protection and thus were practically undisturbed by the enemy fighters.

In this context the result is particularly praiseworthy obtained by escort that was normally assured by 233 Wing;

NO. 5 SQUADRON, S.A.A.F.
WAR DIARY - JUNE, 1942.
GENERAL SUMMARY TO 30TH. JUNE, 1942.

	Brought forward	June, 1942	Total
Days in operations	87	24	111
No. of Sorties	1058	299	1357
Total Op. hours	1729.05	354.30	2083.35
Fuel expended (galls.)	60,159	14,792	74,941
S.A.A. "	175,500	54,109	229,689
AIRCRAFT:			
Average available	-	8.8	
Lowest no. "		1	
Serviceability percentage on available aircraft	87.2%	95.32%	91.28%
Wrecked by enemy action	4	11	15
" other causes	2	3	5
ENEMY AIRCRAFT:			
Destroyed	8	21	29
Probably destroyed	4	7	11
Damaged	13	11	24
PERSONNEL:			
Killed	2	3	5
Wounded	1	6	7
Missing	2	4	6
Admitted to Hospital	26	3	29
Average not available for duty	24	36	30
Number of Movements	4	5	9

CASUALTIES:

Killed:
103420 Lt. B.C. Thornhill-Cook - 4.6.42.
205417 Lt. K.C. Morgan - 17.6.42.
301467 Pte. C. Ross, Cape Corps - 22.6.42.

Missing:
203178 Lt. P.H. Saunders - 29.5.42.
103023 Major A. Duncan, D.F.C. - 31.5.42.
202945 Captain R. Pare, D.F.C. - 3.6.42.
P.102641 Major J.B. Frost, D.F.C. - 16.6.42.
103867 Lt. B.C. Denham - 16.6.42.
102722 Captain L.C. Botha - 17.6.42.
103215 Lt. W.N.L. Popham - 20.6.42. safe

30610

its *Tomahawk IIBs* (*P-40C*) were the close cover and its *Kittyhawk IAs* (*P-40E*) were the top cover. The Curtiss fighters were the first choice for the bomber escort role because they were the machines with the best performances at the heights to which the raids were carried out, while the Hurricanes were better at higher altitudes.

The more maneuverable *Tomahawks* could fly tightly linked to the bombers they were protecting. The *Kittyhawks*, however, with their heavy armament were favored to counterattack enemy fighters.

All considered, one of most significant results obtained by the Commonwealth Air Forces during this period was the development of escort formations that demonstrated near-impenetrability by the axis interceptors. Displaying tactical intelligence and discipline to the limit of self-sacrifice, the pilots of 233 Wing put in place a 'stepped' escort configuration that made them able to protect their charges with an effectiveness previously unseen on all the war fronts. The importance of this result, apparently not fully appreciated during the Gazala offensive period, showed all its relevance later that summer; this was when the Commonwealth employed over the front line a larger number of squadrons of modern medium bombers that were able to hit the enemy lines again and again, unhampered by the action of the enemy fighters that were kept at bay by the escort. The cost, in terms of fighter losses was high, but as already noted, at this stage of the war the American industry and the Commonwealth training command were able to make good without many problems.

In light of this success, critics focused on the use of unsuitable or outdated tactics that were from time to time moved to the Commonwealth fighter pilots of the sector, revealing them to be totally unfounded. These men, tasked to protect the bombers at all costs, had to fight in planes of dramatically inferior performances at all heights (until the arrival of the *Spitfire*). They performed their duty effectively because they were able to adapt their formations to exploit the few strong points of their mounts. The use of more advanced tactical configurations as the 'finger four' already adopted by the *Fighter Command* would probably not have fitted as well to their mission.

It cannot be explained how occasionally throughout this period formations of unescorted bombers were sent out: when intercepted, these suffered extremely heavy losses. 223 Squadron particularly so.

Nevertheless, it seems that the Axis Commands during this two months period did not show a great interest in countering these bomber formations, as never in the period were mass attacks ordered against them.

It is not clear how many tactical ground attacks were successful overall or how much they influenced the army's operations (at least up to the end of June), but at least some raids against the airfields proved deadly for the Axis units. And so their opposition should not have been considered of minor importance and the use of large numbers of *Bf.109s* and *C.202s*, guided by the radar, would perhaps have been able to put the enemy bomber formations into difficulty. But it is correct that this high number of fighters would have been only seldom available, and would have to give up other activities.

On the other side of the front, the Commonwealth readied large fighter formations to confront those of escorted *Stukas*. Even though there is no confirmation, one is led to believe that the intelligence service had played a part in the ordering of these actions. However the clashes between the Axis fighters and the escorting planes for the bombers were frequent and the Allied fighters were normally made to pay a high price.

Looking at the Axis attack formations, it seems that the *Bf.109s* had not always escorted the Stukas effectively. It is well known that planes with very different performances could not easily fly together and this was the case of the Messerschmitt and the Junker dive bombers. Yet from the analysis of the available data, it comes up that this was not a critical factor. The *Stukas* demonstrated vulnerability to the attacks of the enemy interceptors only when the number of escorting fighters was equal or inferior to that of the bombers escorted. It was not so when the escorts were sufficiently reinforced. But this problem was not definitely resolved, and the beatings were sometimes resumed. It seems probable that the number of combat-ready *Bf.109s*, despite the intensive use of these machines, was never sufficient to carry out the highly profitable 'frei-jagden' and at the same time make available large escort formations for the ground attack planes. Anyway, some doubts remain about the best use of those fighters. Italian planes, in particular the *Macchi C.200s* of 2° Stormo, were better able to follow the *Ju.87s* in the dive as well as able to cruise at a relatively lower speed. They could perhaps have been used as escort, providing a more effective protection to the *Stukas* when the *Messerschmitts* were too few.

It is important to highlight the role of the fighter-bombers: there was a large number of units specialized in ground attack.

The effectiveness of these units goes beyond this study, which focuses on the clashes between fighters. However, this must have been considerable especially taking into account the losses sustained. There is one thing well worth considering — the limited number of times these formations were intercepted by enemy fighters.

It was in this period that patrols of *Spitfires* of 145 Squadron started to appear over the front. They were to reinforce the bombers' formations, flying at high altitude. This began to create some problems for the attacking Axis planes. This tendency would increase and become more widespread in the following period, which will be the subject of the next study, and would bring about changes in the tactics of the Axis fighters. For certain, the *Spitfire* was less rugged than the *Curtiss* and *Hawker*, especially with regard to the type of undercarriage. And yet despite this, the question of why this plane was so late in being sent to the North African theatre has still to be resolved.

Moreover, it is not clear why the *Hurricane II* was only rarely used in the interceptor role at high altitude: it had lower performances than those of the *Spitfire*, but nevertheless both planes had similar engines and at high altitude the former was better than the two *P-40s*. Moving on to the clashes of fighter against fighter, there was a great difference in the performance between the two adversaries: the *Bf.109s* and *C.202s* were shot down on few occasions. So it must not have been easy for Commonwealth pilots to stand up against superior machines, especially in the cases in which they lost numerical superiority. There is little to add about the deadly attacks of the *Messerschmitts* though it is appropriate to highlight the different combat performance between these and the *Macchi C.202s* as the latter did not manage to obtain the same results as the Germans. As we have seen in previous studies, despite the fact that quite often the Commonwealth pilots tended to mistake the two types and were from time to time quite prodigal with compliments in regard to the maneuverability of the *Macchi*, the two planes were very different machines that belonged to two subsequent generations.

While the speed characteristics of the *Macchi* (albeit not up to those of the *Messerschmitt*) were enough to give them a clear edge over their opponents at medium and high altitude, its ever praised maneuverability was mostly a 'defensive' feature. It was able to enhance the chances of survival of the plane when under attack but was not very useful when it came to obtaining an aerial kill.

On the other side, the armament of this fighter always left much to be desired in terms of lethality, rarely permitting full use of the positional advantage gained during a dogfight. This drawback had been clear since the combat debut of the *Folgore* but in view of the insuperable technical constraints making it impossible to install a centrally mounted cannon, the only option remained to the Italians was to add a couple of rifle caliber guns in the wings of their *C.202s*. All of the Commonwealth fighters had by then installed plenty of amour plates to protect the pilot. Considering that and the fact that self sealing tanks were growing widespread in use, the added low caliber firepower did not help too much and often the Italian pilots ordered to remove the 7,7 *SAFAT* in the wings, gaining back some maneuverability.

These technical aspects, added to the inefficient radio communication system, have been seldom considered a primary cause of the inferior effectiveness showed by the Italian fighters when compared with those of the Luftwaffe. The tactics used were much more similar to those of the *Jagdfliegern* ('dive and zoom' methods against their slower and lower flying adversaries) as statements on this aspect are present in many contemporary combat and intelligence reports of the Commonwealth. This is clearly visible in the paragraph on the *C.202* present in the training manual of the Desert Air force published in spring 1943 and based on the experience of the previous year of war. When it comes to the tactics in use by the enemy, the manual states: *"The Macchi usually work in pairs (...). Tactics used by the MC202 very much like the Me 109 F or G except that they are more maneuverable and are prepared to stay down and dogfight more than German fighters"* The only difference (though it was not small) was the approach to R.T. communication, as the *Macchis* particularly after the arrival of 4° Stormo had barely begun to profitably operate it in action. Meanwhile the Germans were accustomed to it since the days of the Spanish Civil War and had fully developed its tactical use. This was noted also by the Allied pilots as told by Sqd. Ldr. Neville Duke: *"They* (the Italians) *appeared to have many problems with inter-aircraft communication in the air and were consequently easier to bounce"*[1].

On the opposite side R.T. was considered of vital importance, as recommended by American Spitfire ace F.O. Tilley: *"If your R.T. packs up near base, go back; ... A fighter pilot without R.T. is a liability to himself and his squadron. Never take-off with a faulty R.T."*

Regarding the impact of gunnery training, it is undeniable that cost constraints meant that this fundamental aspect of the formation of the fledgling Italian pilots would be underdeveloped. But it is also true that in every air force, more than half of the kills are usually obtained by the so called 'aces' — the pilots most gifted in particular in the field of marksmanship. This is also clearly shown by the Luftwaffe in North Africa, where only fifteen pilots claimed 674 of the 1300 victories credited to the *Bf.109* units within the end of 1942[2]. For these individuals, shooting ability is much more an instinctive skill than one arising from proper training. Therefore, even if the average Italian pilot came out of the flying school poorly prepared in this field, a fair number of 'natural' sharpshooters should have been present in the ranks of *Regia Aeronautica* and in particular of the elite *Stormi* deployed in North Africa. However, it is probably not best to overestimate the effectiveness of this aspect of training for the *Luftwaffe* pilots of the time, at least if one believes the account of ace Werner Schroer when he was interviewed after the war by British historian Christopher Shores: *"I believe that our armament (...) was better than the armament of the Hur-*

---

1 'Fighters over the Desert' P.224
2 ibidem P.220

ricanes (...). But you must hit – and that was the problem. How often I have missed, because accurate deflection shooting was not taught at training schools or during practice flight."

It is a matter of fact that, still in February 1941, the top scorer among the fighter pilots (whether considering the victories confirmed by enemy sources or just the claims) serving in the African and Mediterranean fronts was not coming from the air forces of the Commonwealth, but an Italian: Mario Visintini, an ace that was fighting in Eastern Africa an area where the Italians could rely on a certain technical superiority. It has to be highlighted that in the majority of cases aces mounted machines with superior performances.

In conclusion, although tactics and training probably played a role in the quite different combat performance displayed by the two Axis fighter forces, one is led to believe that absolutely critical in explaining this disparity was the different quality of their planes and in particular of the weapons with which they were equipped.

The vulnerability of the Axis aircraft on the ground should also be highlighted: they were badly damaged much too often by the enemy air attacks and sometimes by the intruders of the Long Range Desert Group. It is true that to better defend the aerodromes, a greater logistic cost would have been required, such as the use of advanced landing grounds. Also, Axis airmen on the ground suffered heavily from air attacks.

Final results

The sources leave out much that still needs to be discovered about the losses of the Commonwealth Air Forces. As we have seen, documentation is often lacking; particularly that relating to losses leaves much to be desired (again with the exception of some units: e.g.: 73 and 213 Squadrons).
'RAF Casualties Middle East' reported the casualties in operational missions, making a distinction between those due to enemy action and those because of accidents (therefore not including the losses for other accidents or the planes destroyed on the ground) and then between the planes totally lost from those badly damaged. The planes shot down and then salvaged were considered only as damaged. However, such criterion was valid also for their adversaries.

Very often these summaries do not match up with the units' diaries; sometimes they showed greater casualties, other times casualties are not reported, such as the two Beaufighters lost the 25th of June. Certainly there are some mistakes (e.g. losses of *Baltimores*) so there must have been some mix up. It is also possible that many aircraft lost to accidents were reported as lost to enemy action.

We can be fairly sure, however, about the losses in the Italian documentation; those are also backed up by a fortnightly review of the aircraft situation. Thanks to Genst.Gen.Qu.6.Abt. Luftwaffe Loss Microfilms (provided by Andreas Brekken and Andrew Arthy) detailed German losses seem fairly exhaustive.

As in earlier works, owing to the need to draw on some statistics, the author considered aircraft shot down that had damage done by enemy action and did not reach a friendly base, reached it but were wrecked on landing, or when they were declared damaged beyond repair, even after a successful landing in their own airfields. In many cases, fighters were lost during ground attacks (carried out mainly by 239 Wing), without reporting the encounter with enemy aircraft. Flak was deadly and made many victims, but in the cases where there was a pilot's claim that matched the loss, it seemed more correct to assign it to aerial combat rather than to anti-aircraft fire. The same criterion has been followed for night-fighter pilots' claims.

Going back to 'RAF Casualties Middle East' (Table 1), in this period 260 aircraft were reported totally lost (of which 213 fighters) during operations due to enemy action, while 140 were heavily damaged (110 fighters). Of the latter, many had to crash or force land but were salvaged. Also the number of aircraft lost to anti-aircraft fire is considerable (Table 2).

RAF CASUALTIES MIDDLE EAST				
'GAZALA'				
	A	B	C	D
HURRICANE	72	3	43	11
SPITFIRE	6	0	1	1
TOMAHAWK	30	3	21	5
KITTYHAWK	92	3	44	9
BEAUFIGHTER	13	0	1	0
TOT. FIGHTERS	213	9	110	26
WELLINGTON	26	6	7	5
BLENHEIM	4	2	0	3
BOSTON	4	2	16	3
BALTIMORE	3	0	4	1
BEAUFORT	7	0	2	0
OTHERS	3	0	1	0
TOT. BOMBERS AND OTH.	47	10	30	12
GRAND TOTAL	**260**	**19**	**140**	**38**
'CRUSADER'				
TOT. FIGHTERS	204	8	77	35
TOT. BOMBERS AND OTH.	99	26	50	20
GRAND TOTAL	**303**	**34**	**127**	**55**

TABLE 1. A – destroyed by enemy action, B – destroyed because of accidents, C heavily damaged by enemy action, D – heavily damaged because of accidents. Are excluded those destroyed in the ground or accidents not during operations. Source 'RAF Casualties Middle East' (AIR22/401)

On the contrary the losses on the ground admitted to by the Commonwealth are insignificant: a *Hurricane* destroyed, two *Kittyhawks* and a *Beaufighter* badly damaged, and two aircraft as well as 'some' others slightly damaged. The logistic efficiency of this sector was a determining factor in containing these types of losses; nevertheless they appear to be much too small, also considering the far from negligible number of attacks on the airports.

A total of 82 Commonwealth bombers were documented to have been lost in the course of operational missions in the period ('R.A.F. Bomber Losses in the Middle East & the Mediterranean').

Therefore this was with the exclusion of other activities such as transfers or others. 18 of these were attributed to enemy fighters while another 14 were to anti-aircraft fire. Therefore more than half of the losses had occurred because of flying accidents during operational activities. In many cases these were connected to night-time flights, which were in themselves very risky and practically represented the entirety of the activities of medium bombers. 7 *Beauforts* of 39 Squadron should be added to the total as they were lost in the action against the Italian battle fleet on 15 June. 5 of them were shot down by German fighters. There were, instead, many fewer bombers lost compared with Crusader. The Commonwealth in particular lost around half the number (26 against 48). They would have been almost none if the latter had not continued to throw 223 Squadron into the fray without escort and this was due to the effectiveness of the escorts.

The book Shark Squadron notes about 112 Squadron: *"May and June 1942 saw the highest loss of aircrew (12) and, naturally enough the highest losses of aircraft. 39 in May and 47 in June."* These latter numbers seem too high, but the book along with the details of 19 losses (6 in May and 13 in June) lists 40 *Kittyhawks* (17 in May and 23 in June) no more on charge without apparent reason.

This gives an idea of the heavy attrition the air forces were submitted to.

The Commonwealth fighter pilots made fewer claims than they had in the period of the previous offensive. This descended directly from the inferior occasions of scoring they experienced, faced ever by an enemy flying on superior machines and retaining the initiative.

	CLAIMS AND CASUALTIES IN AIR COMBATS					
	CLAIMS			AIRCRAFT LOSSES		
	COMMONW.	GERMAN	ITALIAN	COMMONW.	GERMAN	ITALIAN
BOMBERS (TWIN-ENGINED)	16	25	4	24	8	2
STUKAS	35				18	
FIGHTERS	83	260	109	179	28	14
OTHERS	2	1		2		1
TOTALS	137	285	113	205	54	17
CASUALTIES DUE TO ANTI AIRCRAFT FIRE						
BOMBERS (TWIN-ENGINED)				16	27	1
STUKAS					16	
FIGHTERS				42	17	21
OTHERS					4	
TOTALS				58	64	22
TOTAL CASUALTIES						
TOT. BOMBERS				40	69	3
TOT. FIGHTERS				221	45	35
TOT. OTHERS				2	4	1
GRAND TOT.				**263**	**118**	**39**

Considering the confused clashes in which they were involved, those pilots showed a fair degree of accuracy, claiming to have shot down 137 enemy planes against the 66 detailed lost;

During 'Crusader' they claimed 230 enemy aircraft against 114 reportedly lost, showing practically the same accuracy.

During 'Gazala' Axis pilots claimed 399 enemy planes (379 fighters) against 205 (179 fighters) detailed lost. The Germans claims summed up to 285 enemy aircraft, matched by 160 documented losses. The Italians claimed 113, compared to 32 detailed losses. Some 13 other victories have to be shared between the two allies.

It is interesting that the claims for bombers match the reported losses almost perfectly.

The reduced losses of Commonwealths bombers during 'Gazala' confirms the greatly improved tactics and quality of the bomber-aircraft adopted.

It is immediately visible that the ratio corroborated victories/claims drops considerably for both Germans and Italians (365 fighters claimed against 179 lost) when compared with that obtained during 'Crusader' (228 claims, 132 Germans and 96 Italian against 154 Commonwealth losses; of these 83 credited to the German pilots, 39 to the Italian ones, 32 shared). So the accuracy of Axis claims during Gazala seems to be heavily deteriorated. Taking into account 'RAF Casualties Middle East' ('Gazala', column A) it is possible that the actual fighters' losses were considerably higher than those reported in the chronology. But this would only confirm the insufficient documentation of several Commonwealth units.

The *Bf.109* fighters' units displayed a greater effectiveness than *Macchi C.202* units, considering a similar strength. We have seen that the *Bf.109* was a better war machine, but we have to consider also that the Italian units flew less than half as many sorties. While noting this difference, mostly due to the limited resources available to Regia Aeronautica (in particular the scarse production of German licence engines stretched the time between overhauls), the reader should not forget that — as already noted — the sorties per aircraft performed by the *C.202s* were similar to those performed by the P-40s.

Quite obviously Marseille was the star and was credited with as many as thirty-seven fighters shot down as well as two bombers. The enemy confirmed his claim for 19 fighters and the 2 bombers shot down. It can be assumed that in his case there was the maximum accuracy possible in the recording of events. In view of the large number of witnesses present in his actions, this can make up for the hypothesis of some gaps in the enemy reporting of its losses. Marseille was practically the only one of his own Staffel to score victories, as the remaining pilots were credited with only another seven victories.

The great difference in the 4./JG 27 between the big number of victories credited and the very few that find corroboration is significant. As is known in unit circles, there has long been gossiping about four pilot components of a Schwarm. The estimated statistics would seem to confirm the gossiping (TABLE 3).

Even when taking into consideration some possible dishonest claims for victories, the German system for confirming victories appears to be rigorous.

In conclusion, the period of the struggle in the air did not see a definite winner. The Axis obtained more points in the air, but the losses they suffered on the ground must not be forgotten. A notable number of mistakes seem to have been made by the opposite air forces, but not at a level that compromised the results. Neither side was able to reach a definite supremacy, therefore the credit for the outcome of the land battle should mainly go to the ground forces.

LUFTWAFFE CLAIMS AND COMMONWEALTH LOSSES IN SUPPORT		
UNIT	CLAIMS	SUPPORTED
Stab I./JG 27	7	5
1./JG 27	29	21
2./JG 27	37	21
3./JG 27	46	26
Stab II./JG 27	15	7
4./JG 27	30	5
5./JG 27	25	15,5
6./JG 27	8	5
7./JG 27	5	3
8./JG 27	4	1
9./JG 27	10	8
Stab III./JG 53	1	1
7./JG 53	14	7
8./JG 53	26	13
9./JG 53	16	10
others III./JG 53	1	4
No claims		4
Total Bf.109 units	274	155
7./ZG 26	5	2
I./NJG 2	6	6
II./St.G 3	0	2
Ju.88 units	1	1
Total units	286	167

Appendix 1
FROM SIDI EL BARRANI TO EL ALAMEIN 1940 – 1942, A STRATEGIC OVERVIEW

From a historical point of view and with the hindsight of many decades of studies, the whole North African campaign, at least until the final battle of El Alamein, could be considered nonsensical.

When Italy declared war on June 10th 1940, a total of 221,395 men, including all of the services, were present in Libya. By December 10th 1940, the number had increased to about 235,000 including police and custom guards (1). The British Army had a total of about 64,300 men stationed in the area between Egypt, Palestine (one day's railway journey from Cairo), and Cyprus in June 1940; this number became 85,000 in July 1940 and was later constantly increased by an average of more than 55,000 soldiers monthly until December 1940. Another 239,000 men arrived between January and July 1941, and in August 1941 more than 600,000 men were in that theatre of war (2); this is without taking into consideration the garrisons in Malta and Gibraltar and the remaining British and Imperial troops in Sudan, East Africa, Aden, Iraq, and Iran. In July 1942, Churchill, difficult to satisfy as usual, grumbled at great length. He wrote to General Auchinleck about the 750,000 people idle in the Middle East. Most of them were of course not combat troops. But with a strict comparison of numbers available and judging from the factors taken into account in war games or in the board game Risk, it was clear that since October 1940 any possibility the Italians had of invading the Middle East had long gone. The reality was that the Western Desert could not be crossed without motor transport and that the Regio Esercito, the Italian Army, had only 8,000 motor vehicles available (a big total which included cars and fire brigade trucks) in Libya in June 1940. In 1940 the harbour cranes and pontoons in Tripoli and Benghazi could only cope with a few hundred lorries monthly. And, the roughly 1,500 new trucks sent out there until 31 December 1940 were only to replace the ones worn out in that sand ridden area. Even with the stripping of the V Armata in Tripolitania, which had been ordered since late June 1940, the X Armata in Cyrenaica which was to benefit was unable to parade more than 4385 vehicles (3). In the face of these odds, Marshal Italo Balbo encountered the opposition of his staff, foremost of whom was his own chief of staff, General Giuseppe Tellera. Nevertheless, he managed to devise a plan for a swift and resolute advance of a week up to Marsa Matruh by a single motorized corps. It would be formed of two Libyan divisions, an armoured brigade group, a mixed Libyan and Italian infantry brigade group, and an autonomous artillery reserve force. The large number of about 23000 men had to be totally motorized with the lorries still available in Cyrenaica. However, the pugnacious Air Force Marshal was then killed when his aircraft was shot down by friendly machine-gun fire on the part of the Regia Aeronautica upon landing at an airport in Tobruk on 28 June 1940. His much more prudent successor, Marshal Rodolfo Graziani, decided to increase his forces by adding two further corps (XXI and XXIII) to the Army in Libya so that it had a total of about 64,000 men, almost all on foot, when the advance began in Egypt. Graziani's Force covered 114 kilometres, marching over the desert when it came to a stop due to the onset of a full logistical crisis after three days on 16 September. He asked the authorities in Rome for more time to build up his forces before covering the remaining 150 kilometres to get to Marsa Matruh. He postponed the advance in September and October 1940, and so this delay amounted to three months. In the end, it was the British who would meet up with his forces at Sidi el Barrani. Graziani's goal

Rommel at Bardia in 1941 (Cernuschi)

was, in any case as with Balbo, limited to the bottleneck at Marsa Matruh and El Alamein. The Regia Aeronautica bombers, operating under the protection of the Italian Air Force short-ranged fighters, would from there have been able to induce the Mediterranean Fleet to quit Alexandria, as it had with Malta before, and make its way to Gibraltar under the gauntlet of the Sicilian narrows. This vast area lacked any warship facilities beginning with docking between Suez, Bombay, Ceylon and Tanganyika, and could simply not be covered adequately by a battle fleet (4).
The succession of Italian disasters up to Beda Fomm in February 1941 is well known. The simultaneous halt of the British advance due to exhaustion (5) combined with the sudden appearance of the German troops acting under the orders of General Erwin Rommel opened a new phase in the desert war.
The most famous German general of World War II was actually not and never to become a favourite of the Reich Army's staff. Upon making a strict comparison between the logistical facilities in Libya and Tunisia and those available in Egypt, the top brass in Berlin had immediately come to the conclusion that there was no chance of an offensive in that war theatre. The front could only be made to endure with a defensive strategy — nothing else. This was in fact the original task given to the single German division which disembarked in Tripoli in February 1941. It was the newly formed 5 Leichte Division entrusted to hold up the enemy advance. Rommel was, in any case, a military genius who was born on the field and well aware that psychology predominates in battles if not in war itself. In October 1917 as the commander of two companies at Caporetto, he captured more than 9,000 Italians and 80 guns within fifty hours. In Spring 1940,

leading the 7th Panzer Division, he took more than 100,000 prisoners of war, including those from the 51st Highland Infantry Division. These enterprises would never happen in a war game and yet he managed them. The odds were against him, and so from the beginning he decided to discount them. What happened next from the first offensive in March 1941 up to the triumph in Tobruk on June 21st 1942 and the following advance into Egypt is a testimony to his military virtues and those of his German and Italian soldiers. In Summer 1941, these had amounted to 164,000. Therefore about 250,000 soldiers, including those from Libya, managed this astonishing feat in June 1942, despite all the difficulties and odds stacked up against them. And yet, miracles do not last. By July 2nd 1942, the Axis forces' hope for further breaches amongst the enemy troops which would open up the gates of Alexandria, Cairo, and Suez to them did not materialise. They foundered at El Alamein with the recovery and resolution of the 1st South African, 2nd New Zealand, and 1st Armoured Divisions, facing about 10000 exhausted soldiers (2000 of them German), 125 tanks (55 of them of the Deutsche Afrika Korps), and 530 guns. The three near fatal British and Imperial counterattacks that were unleashed on 10/11, 14/15, and 21/22 July 1942 were all repulsed and the El Alamein front, at least, held steady for a while. It was by then time for both sides to build up their strength to be ready for the next offensive of which the goal was, once again, the seizure of the Suez Canal. It would be, at least according to the Italian and German view of the conflict, virtually the end of the struggle in the Mediterranean or more probably of the war itself.

Enrico Cernuschi

German troops at Bardia 1941 (Cernuschi)

Italian troops at Bardia 1941 (Cernuschi)

NOTES

[1] Emilio Faldella, "Le forze italiane all'inizio del conflitto", Storia Illustrata, March 1970, page 76; Emilio Faldella, "Guerra in Marmarica", Storia Illustrata, December 1970, page 70.

[2] Andrew Mollo, The Armed Forces of World War II, ed. Military press, N.Y., 1987, page 121.

[3] We can draw a comparison with the 9,000 vehicles which enabled the 11th and 12th African and 1st South African Divisions to invade Italian Somaliland in February 1941 and reach Addis Ababa on 6 April 1941. Anyway, by late March 1941 this very same Corps was going through a severe logistical crisis and forced into difficult decisions like a bloody bayonet charge by the Transvaal Scottish Regiment because of a shortage of bullets at Combolcià on 23 April 1941. This was done to rescue the Royal Natal Carabineers who had surrendered shortly before for the same reason. Douglas Porch, The Path to Victory, ed. Farrar, Straus and Giroux, N.Y., page 134. Jacques Maignon, « Les uniformes de l'Armee Sud-Africaine 1939 – 1945 », Militaria, n. 102, January 1994.

[4] This very plan was conceived by the then Italian Army deputy chief of staff General Alberto Pariani in 1935 and had been pursued since then. Fortunato Minniti, "Il nemico vero gli obiettivi dei piani di operazione contro la Gran Bretagna nel contesto etiopico (maggio 1935 – maggio 1936)", Storia contemporanea, August 1995. Dorello Ferrari, "Il piano segreto di Balbo", Studi storico – militari, ed. Ufficio Storico dell'Esercito, Rome, 1984.

[5] In February 1941 the British commander of the Western Desert Force, General Sir Richard O'Connor was asked to gather together all of the available air, naval, and logistical support in the Middle East to back up his remaining armoured forces (about fifty tanks, most of them light MK VI ones, and forty armoured cars] and make an advance on Tripoli. This was to happen in conjunction with a decisive landing by a British group of brigades in the Libyan capital. The proposal was immediately rejected, the more so because the three large Infantry Landing Ships Glengyle, Glenearn and Glenroy necessary for such an operation had still on 31 January 1941 to set sail for the Cape route, as it was considered much too dangerous to go by the way of the Sicilian Narrows, and they would not get to Suez until at least March 7th, 1941.

[6] In spite of the improvements made with the arrival of slow convoys of tugs and pontoons from Italy during Summer 1940 and later on of the large, similar logistical reinforcements the French passed to the Germans and the Italians in 1941, the loading capacities of the Libyan harbours remained ten times smaller than those achieved by the British at Suez. The lack of a railway line between Tunisia and Tripoli, then, would have hampered the flow of materials to Rommel's Army anyway, even if Bizerta and Tunis had been available. The proof of this statement is the limited use (only a big total of about 5000 t) of "secret supplies," named Trasporti Gamma and Trasporti Beta, delivered by the French between December 1941 and April 1942 from France to Tripoli through Tunisia. Further shipments were stopped as the expenditure of oil for the trucks delivering the materials from the end of the railway in Tunisia to Tripoli was simply too much.

Most of the facilities were then reserved for the German supplies. Since Spring 1941 the Regio Esercito's mobile forces had remained so limited to a single corps while as for the lorries the Italian Army in North Africa still had in its charge around 9000 motor vehicles in Summer 1942. Meanwhile the DAK alone had three divisions containing 12000 vehicles.

Appendix 2
FIGHTERS COMPARED

In the recollections of the leading Australian ace Clive Caldwell, the *P-40 C Tomahawk*, though obsolescent, was still a fairly effective fighter: *"The Tomahawks were the best the RAF had in the Middle East and I was glad to be flying them, liked their flush-riveted clean lines and the aircraft itself. They were waiting in performance but the Allison engine was honest, hard-working and reliable. The aeroplane handled and turned well, gave a fair warning of the approaching stall, recovered from a spin without fuss, and in general had little vice. In service they proved strong and rugged and would stand up to a lot of punishment from opposing fire as well as from violent aerobatics. They picked up speed quickly in a dive, but at steep angles of dive at high speed, considerable strength of arm and leg and/or a lot of activity with the trim gear was needed to keep control. While inferior in performance, particularly at altitude, to the Bf.109 and the elegant C.202 Folgore, which latter aircraft appeared in the desert toward the end of 1941 and excited my admiration if not my approval, the Tomahawk seemed to hang on to them well in a steep or vertical dive and, operating within its own altitude limitations, performed creditably in a dogfight. The Tomahawk's lack of comparable performance left the initiative mainly with the opposition and it was usual to accept their initial attack in order to engage at our best height. We rarely caught them below us. The armament was adequate. The two .50-caliber guns firing through the airscrew were especially useful at close range, and the four .30 wing guns were changed over to .303 to take advantage of the more sophisticated ammunition then available"* [0].

According to the official trials, the *P-40 C Tomahawk*, tested on 27 August 1942 (presumably at a weight of some 7,500 lbs), had a maximum speed of 342 m.p.h. at 14,400 feet [1]. The maximum speed of the *P-40 E Kittyhawk*, tested on 25 September 1941 at a weight near to 8,100 lbs, was 342 m.p.h. at 11,400 feet. Despite the different engine, the two planes had the same performances because the increased power and better aerodynamics were only enough to balance the increase of weight. Not surprisingly, according to the witnesses, there was no noteworthy difference in performance between the *Tomahawk* and the *Kittyhawk*: *"The E [...] had no improvement in service ceiling and only slightly more speed. Climb performance was infinitesimally better"* [2]. In practice, even the slight advantage in speed was obliterated by the presence of the air cleaners (sand filters). The American tests with experimental filters, specifically carried out in 1942, prove this: the Tomahawk reached 323 m.p.h. at 9,400 feet at 3000 rpm with 1,090 hp, while the Kittyhawk achieved 317.5 m.p.h. at 11,250 feet at 2,900 rpm [3]. The Australians had faced the same problem: *"Early in 1942 the R.A.A.F. became very worried about the excessive wear occurring in aero-engine cylinders, not only in operational areas but also on training airfields. Losses from this source grew to such proportions that it was almost impossible to keep up with replacements. The trouble was discovered to arise mainly from the entrance of dust into the engines"* [4]. Many experiments were carried on, but *"The work was exceedingly slow and laborious"* [4]. The first official document which attests the introduction of a sand filter seems to be the 'Curtiss - operation, maintenance, and installation instructions for carburator air filters - P-40 E, P-40 E-1, P40 K series and P-40 M' [5]; hitherto, the aircraft had been shipped with provisional cleaners. This led to worried complaints in North Africa: *"The Kittyhawk arrived with an air filter that made it much slower than the Tomahawk. We have taken the filter off but it still leaves the aircraft with an inferior performance which is not countered by the increased hitting power. The Kittyhawk alone will not do for this front"* [6].

According to the South Africans, *"There were continual disappointments with new aircraft. (...) Fighter Squadrons had similar difficulties. Fine sand which penetrated everything (protective covers were issued to protect engines and guns) made engine changes necessary; engines frequently cut out on take-off, sometimes with fatal results"* [7].
It appears that some fighting units flew their *Curtiss* without air cleaners, while others tried and develop their own ones, as Australian pilot Robert 'Bobby' Gibbes (3 RAAF) recalls: *"Before the use of FO Abicair's filter, engines rarely lasted longer than forty hours: use of new filter doubled this period"* [8]. According to Canadian pilot Joe Crichton (No 112 Sqn), *"The Allison engine sure was not made for the sand conditions... We were lucky to get 30-50 hours out of the engines"* [9]. It was a common opinion that *"Despite various modifications and attempts made by the mechanics, the Kittyhawk was not fit for operating in the desert. Sand and dust caused break-downs very easily. Even more so than in the case of Tomahawks. Their engine installation life reached a maximum of 60 hours. Then a team of five men had to change them. This cost 12 hours of work."* [10]. The short life of these engines [11] was likely to be due not only to sand and dust, but also to the abusive high boost levels which were imposed to fight the *Messerschmitts*. The *Kittyhawk*'s new -F3R Allison engine (V-1710-39) gave 1,150 Hp at some 11,000 feet with a manifold pressure (boost) of 44 in.Hg (46 in.Hg for take off), but soon the pilots began to overboost the engines [12]. Many a South African pilot was thus blamed for "absolute carelessness", even though it was admitted that *"The fault lay in lack of adequate replacements, to make up for combat attrition and also to replace worn aircraft. These were vulnerable to malfunctions under the trying desert conditions, which could cause loss of pilot confidence in them"* [13]. With all its limits, the *Kittyhawk* was appreciated over the *Tomahawk* (older 1,090 Hp at 13,200 feet engine) due to its better protection and heavier armament, which in the latter was *"not very reliable. There were two .30-caliber guns in each wing, and two .50s firing through the propeller. All of them had mechanical cable rechargers, which was fortunate because jamming varied between often and systematically"* [2]. On the contrary, the guns of the *Kittyhawk* *"performed extremely well"* [2], *"these were superb weapons, and very reliable. They gave the aircraft, which was a very stable gun platform, a hell of a punch"* [14]. However the weight of the six .50s Browning with 1,410 rounds was entirely located in the wings (which were consequently loaded with 681.1 lbs more than those of the Tomahawk); this was a major factor in the sensible worsening of the maneuverability of the *P-40*, above all the roll rate [15]. In particular, *"snap rolls [...] in the P-40 always seemed to be harbingers of some forthcoming structural failure, as I would hear strange murmurs throughout the airframe. The aircraft seemed to resent the maneuver"* [16]. In effect *"there were restrictions on rolls; depending on the P-40 version no snap roll over 140 to 180 m.p.h. IAS* (indicated air speed) *and no slow or barrel rolls over 260 to 310 m.p.h. IAS were to be performed"* [15]. As for maneuverability on the vertical plan, *"Looping commenced around 250 miles per hour at 5,000 feet and would gain about 3,000 in the ensuing arc [...] but much rudder was needed all the way round"* [16].
Generally speaking, the *Kittyhawk* required more counteraction than the *Tomahawk* during speed changes: *"In a dive, as speed increased, more and more left rudder trim had to be added; slowing down in a climb some right rudder trim was needed [...] Every power and speed change brings and immediate trim change which the pilot must either counteract or trim out [...] A very significant dive characteristic was the strong right yaw tendency requiring more left rudder as speed increased. As one P-40 B pilot put it 'The need for constant attention was dramatically illustrated during strafing runs; the aircraft had a tendency to skid' [...] Pilots had to keep hard on the left*

rudder pedal to avoid skidding. The rudder required excess pedal pressure in a dive and, as noted earlier, rudder tab action was too slow to completely alleviate the pressure during steep dive bombing attacks. With the significant design changes making up the P-40 E model, major faults in directional stability and control came to the fore. As a NACA test report put it *'Difficulties were experienced in P-40 series aircraft in dive demonstrations, and there were inadvertent entries into spins in service operations'. Yawing led to snap rolls and then to spins"* [15].

The Kittyhawk was *"fairly good on acceleration [...] and reasonably responsive in heavy-G maneuvers. The normally light ailerons became quite heavy in high-speed dive"* [16]. The P-40 E and K *"would go straight down and hang together at speed of over 450 miles per hour (with both feet on the left rudder pedal). Also, their speed would bleed off much less quickly at lower altitudes after levelling off than would that of later series"* [2]. *"Though maximum allowable dive speed of a P-40 was about 480 m.p.h.* [actually 485 m.p.h. IAS], *pilots occasionally dove as fast as 510 m.p.h."* [15]. The *Bf.109 "could initially dive more quickly [...], but in a long dive a P-40 would catch a Me-109"* [15]. *"The minimum safe altitude to start pullout from this* [dive] *speed* [485 m.p.h. IAS] *was 7,100 to 8,000 feet depending on model. This was because dive acceleration was rapid and initial pullout stick force was inclined to be heavy"* [15]. *"The cooling system of the P-40 was much less vulnerable to gunfire than that of the P-51 C because it was concentrated in the nose area rather than extending aft to a rear cooler location as in the latter plane"* [15]. *"The P-40 was the hardest to land of any of the US World War II fighters"* [15]. According to the October 13 1941 'Report on combat trials of various pursuit aircraft' (which expressly did not take into consideration the armament of the airplanes), in the attack on fast bombers (*B-25, B-26, A-20 A*) operating at 10,000 feet - 15,000 feet, the *P-40 E* bested the *Hurricane* (*"in the case of the Hurricane it is impossible to catch the bombers in level flight"*) but was worse than the *Spitfire*. The *Kittyhawk*, when tested against *B-17 C* flying at 25,000 feet, *"because of its low rate of climb and speed"*, proved to be poorer than both the *Spitfire* and the *Hurricane* (the latter being anyway handicapped *"because of its low speed"*). The radius of turn of the *P-40 E* was worse than those of the Spitfire and, above all, of the Hurricane, which *"has the shortest radius of turn of any of the pursuit airplanes tested and therefore has the advantage over the others if the combat is permitted to develop into tight turns. The Spitfire has the next shortest radius of turn, being superior to the [...] P-40 E [...]. The Hurricane can easily turn inside the P-40 E and was able to continue turning after the P-40 E had stalled. With the P-40 E on the tail of the Hurricane it was possible for the Hurricane to tighten the circle and within 720°* [i.e. two 360° turns] *be in shooting position again. The P-40 E squashes on turns, whereas the Hurricane does not. The P-40E can outdive the Hurricane and is faster in level flight up to approximately 20,000 feet. The Hurricane can outclimb the P-40 E at any altitude for short periods of time, but sustained high power climb cannot be made in warm weather due to excessive coolant temperatures. Due to the higher critical altitude of the engine in the Hurricane, it gets better as the altitude increases compared to the P-40 E"* [17]. Slower than the *Hurricane* above 20,000 feet, the *P-40 E* was also considered a much worse combat airplane than the *Spitfire*, which *"has a shorter radius of turn, better rate of climb and higher speed at altitude"* [17]. *"The Spitfire and Hurricane are easier for inexperienced pilots to fly than the American pursuit airplanes. The automatic boost control is a big help in that respect"* [17]. Concerning the field of view, *"for locating or approach on the target, the P-40 E airplane is the best [...] Hurricane fair, and Spitfire poor. The Spitfire is also bad for landing in this respect. Another disadvantage was that the British engines after having* been flown for a short time at high power, throw so much oil that the windshield is covered and visibility poor; distortion when looking through windshield side panels is also bad. Most of the pilots like the British jointed control stick grip better than the Air Corp [i.e. American] stick for combat, and like the toe brakes in preference to the British stick control brakes. Landing gear and flap controls of the Hurricane and Spitfire were preferred to those of the [...] P-40, but cockpit arrangement of controls and instruments was not considered to be as good. The British safety belt restricts movement of the pilot and is therefore tiresome to wear, but provides better protection in case of a crash landing. Use of soft webbing in the harness similar to that of the P-40E would make it more satisfactory"* [17].

Tested against the U.S. Army Air Force version of the *Douglas SBD Dautless*, called *A-24 Banshee* (roughly comparable to the Stuka), *"the Hurricane was the best airplane for attack against the A-24 because of its maneuverability, also its low speed compared to the other pursuit airplane was an advantage, since the A-24 when dive-bombing has a slow diving speed. Although the Hurricane was the best pursuit airplane for attacking the A-24, it was difficult to get good shots because of the sharp turning of the A-24, its slow diving speed and the higher speed of the Hurricane. In turning, the Hurricane has a slight advantage over the A-24"* [17].

In October 1941 *Hurricane II B* Z3564 (Merlin XX, 1,255 B.H.P. at 10,000 feet, 2,850 R.P.M. and + 9 lb. boost, 7,397 lb. flying weight) was tested at Boscombe. The plane reached its maximum speed of 330 m.p.h. at 20,800 feet. Many authors state that the *Hurricanes II's* maximum speed was of 342 and 340 m.p.h. respectively for the *Mk.II B* and the *Mk.II C*. Probably these values were otained correcting the results of the aforementioned test. In fact there is a curve of max. speed 'calculated' of a *Hurricane IIA/B* brought up to 342 m.p.h. at 22,000 feet.

The same authors report the max. speed of the tropicalized version of *Mk.IIB* and *C* (armed with four 20 mm cannons with only 90 r.p.g., at he normal load condition of 7,707 lb.) at 22,000 feet respectively at 324 and 320 m.p.h.. It appears that the *Hurricane* suffered consistently from the tropicalization, so these values are probably the most correct. Meanwhile the often reported 301 m.p.h. should refer to the maximum speed at a lower altitude (moderate supercharging); it took 11.9 min to climb to 20,000 feet. The *Hurricane II B*, armed with 12 rifle-caliber machine guns (with 3,988 rounds), was marginally faster both in climb (11.6 min to 20,000 feet) and horizontal speed (324 and 310 m.p.h. respectively). It is worth noting that the temperate (i.e. not tropicalized) fighter-bomber variant of the *Mk.IIB*, at a normal weight of 7,733 lb., had a maximum speed (clean) of just 301 m.p.h. at 15,000 feet and needed 12 min to reach 20,000 feet. Loaded with 2 x 250 lb. bombs, the *Mk.IIC* had a maximum speed of 275 m.p.h. at 15,600 feet [19].

The agile *Macchi C.200 Saetta* was an obsolete fighter mainly employed as a ground attack plane. Equipped with an armoured seat, a receiver set and an additional internal fuel tank, it weighed some 5,732 lb. Its maximum speed (clean) was therefore limited to 298 m.p.h. at 14,764 feet [20]. Note that the Fiat A.74 R.C.38. radial engine gave only 960 metric Hp at 9,843 feet in emergency [21]. The armament was poor: two 12.7 mm Breda-SAFAT guns fired 370 r.p.g. through the propeller arc at an average rate of 600 r.p.m. Bombs carried under the wings would be added in the following period. A strength of this aircraft was the outstanding field of view, since the cockpit was placed on the "hump" of the fuselage and not totally enclosed. The Macchi 200 was a sturdy fighter: thanks to its ultimate load factor of 15.1, it could dive as fast as 500 m.p.h. TAS (true air speed).

The modern *Macchi C.202 Folgore* had a license-built DB-601Aa engine (1,100 metric Hp at 12,139 feet, in emergency for 5 minutes). The performances of this fighter (367 m.p.h. at 19,685 feet, 6,475 lb) refer to M.M.9486 during an acceptance test in 1942. Although it is not known if tests have been made with machines operating in Africa, it is likely that the perfomances of the 'African' *C.202*, similarly to all other planes, were consistently reduced.

According to an Italian pilot (Ten. Bertolaso), the engine began to lose power above 6,562 feet whenever the compressor was driven through low quality oil.

Italian pilots several times reported that the maximum speed was more or less equivalent to that of the tropicalized *Spitfire V*.

Besides its speed, considerable for the engine power available, the main assets of Castoldi's fighter were ruggedness (the ultimate load factor was 15.8, which enabled a true dive speed of some 530 m.p.h. TAS), maneuverability and rate of climb. According to British wartime pilot, Squadron Leader D.H. Clarke, D.F.C., A.F.C., *"Sleek, supremely fast [...] the 202 was capable of [...] out-turning our P-40s with ease; but the majority would pull away effortlessly into a climbing roll or a roll off the top when things became at all hectic. There is nothing more exasperating, when you are caning fifty-four inches of boost out of an engine, than to see your enemy indulge in carefree aerobatics [...] Their aircraft was superior to ours on all counts"* [22]. The armament, on the contrary, was rather modest, as it was still based on the usual two synchronized 12.7 mm Breda-SAFAT guns; the good supply of rounds (400 r.p.g.) assured some 37 seconds of fire (average R.O.F. was 650 r.p.m., slightly better than in the radial engined *Macchi C.200*). Opinions on the *C.202* as an opponent of the *P-40* differed: *"Clive Caldwell, who scored victories against them in his P-40, felt that the Folgore would have been superior to both the P-40 and the Bf.109, except that its armament of only two or four machine guns was inadequate. Other observers considered the two equally matched, or favored the Folgore in aerobatic performance, such as turning radius. Glancey wrote that the Folgore was superior to the P-40, noting the difference in turning radius. Aviation historian Walter J. Boyne wrote that over Africa, the P-40 and the Folgore were equivalent"* [23]. It is interesting to see that pilots' opinions sometimes are not reliable: in no way the Macchi's flying performances could be equivalent to the *P-40*, which was slower and heavier, and so to the *Bf.109 F*, which was much more powerful.

The *Messerschmitt Bf.109 F-4/Trop.* was an excellent fighter for its time. Its outstanding speed and climb performance was due to the 87 octane DB-601E engine, stretched to the very limit of its development: it performed 1,450 metric Hp at 6,890 feet, and 1,320 at 15,748 feet, in emergency for few minutes (1.42 ATA, 2,700 R.P.M.); the time between overhaul for a DB-601 is reported to have been around 50 hours [24]. The armament was not impressive: it was equipped with two synchronized rifle-caliber 7.92 mm MG17s with 500 r.p.g. and one Mauser MG 151/20 20 mm cannon firing through the spinner with 150 or more likely (sources differ) 200 rounds; this was however effective against fighters and medium bombers. Armour for the pilot had been increased and the plane weighed some 6,614 lb. In February 1942 pressure limitations were raised: 1.30 ATA for 30 minutes, 1.42 for few minutes: its maximum speed was almost incredible 335 m.p.h. at s.l. and 416 m.p.h. at 20,327 feet [25]. Even though it was not particularly nimble, this aircraft was undoubtedly the best fighter of the campaign.

Michele Gaetani

NOTES

[0] quoted in Geoffrey G. Pentland, The P40 Kittyhawk in Service, Kookaburra Technical Publications, Melbourne, 1974.

[1] *P-40 C No. 41-13377,* test 27 August 1942; *P-40 E* No. 40-384, test 25 September 1941.

[2] Bruce K. Holloway, 'The *P-40'*, in Robin Hingham (ed.), 'Flying American Combat Aircraft of WWII', Stackpole 2004.

[3] *P-40 C* No. 41-13377, test 27 August 1942 mentioned above; *P-40 E* No. 40-633, test 6 June 1942, but *"the propeller governor would not permit the engine to turn up military rated R.P.M. of 3,000"*. These data might seem too conservative: different flight tests of the *P-40 E* indicate a maximum speed of 332 - 335 m.p.h. for aircraft with sand filters (*P-40 E* ET-573 and perhaps *P-40 E* AL-229) and of 342, 344 and 348 m.p.h. without (again *P-40 E* No. 40-384 and *P-40 E* ET-573, and perhaps *P-40 E* A29-129 RAAF). On the other hand, comparative tests carried out in Australia among the Boomerang, the Aircobra and the Kittyhawk, show that the maximum speed of the latter was indeed 320 m.p.h. at 10,000 feet (280 m.p.h. at ground level and 310 m.p.h. at 20,000 feet); source: see note 4.

[4] 'Australia in the War of 1939–1945'. Series 4 – Civil, Volume V – 'The Role of Science and Industry', (1st edition, 1958), Chapter 18, 'The Aircraft Industry', p. 399-400.

[5] 'War department - Headquarter of the Army air Forces, Washington, Technical Order No. 01-25C-7', dated October 29, 1943; the instruction for accomplishing the installation were contained in Curtiss Service Bulletin 490-23, 530-7, revised February 2, 1943.

[6] Letter 10 December 1941 from Coningham to Tedder, in AIR 23/1345, AHB catalogue number II J1/183/146(B), 'Western Desert Operations'; the premise a few lines before had been: *"We must stop England thinking that 2nd class aircraft will do out here. [...] Air Ministry must reply to the German re-inforcement of the African front with equal re-inforcement of the best aircraft and personnel from England"*. Two days later Tedder wrote to C.A.S., London (AOC 429): *"Preliminary experience of Kittyhawk shows very little improvement of Tomahawk, except hitting power"* (ibidem).

[7] James Ambrose Brown, 'Eagles Strike, the campaigns of the South African Air force in Egypt, Cyrenaica, Libya, Tunisia, Tripolitania and Madagascar 1941-43'; Purnell, Cape Town, South Africa; 1974, p. 135.

[8] Russell Brown, 'Desert Warriors, Australian *P-40* pilots at war in the Middle East and North Africa 1941-1943'; Banner Books; Maryborough, Queensland, Australia; 2000; p. 99

[9] Michael Lavigne & W/C James F. Edwards, 'Kittyhawks over the sands, the Canadians and the RCAF Americans'; Lavigne Aviation Publications, Victoriaville, Quebec, Canada; 2002; p. 191.

[10] Andre R. Zbiegniewski, 112 Sqn 'Shark Squadron, 1939–1941'. Lublin, Poland: Oficyna Wydawnicza Kagero, 2003, p. 90.

[11] In order to fully understand how deadly for the engine was the desert, it should be borne in mind that the main overhaul for an Allison in temperate climate came after 186 hours in average, and that the engine could last another 168 hours thereafter (Lt. Col. Edward G. Kiehle, Acting Chief, Opns. Sec. Maint. Div., ASC, to Chief, Maint. Div., 24 June 1944, in TSAGD 452.031, 'Maintenance and Repair of Aircraft and Aeronautical Equipment in Army Air Forces Historical Studies': no. 51, 'The Maintenance of Army Aircraft in the United States, 1939-1945', August 1946, p. 126).

[12] Only towards the end of 1942 was higher boost (56 in.Hg) cleared and the maximum power (now called 'war emergency power' - WEP) rose to 1,470 Hp at sea level for 5 minutes; it is likely that such overboosting meant an increase of maximum speed at sea level up to 13% (in anal-

ogy to what happened with the Allison-equipped Mustang I, in England). There are also evidences of unauthorised boost as high as 60, 66 and 70 in.Hg for outputs of 1,590 - 1,780 Hp: R.M. Hazen, Allison Division Chief Engineer, 'Service Use of High Power Output on Allison V-1710 Engines, December 12 1942'; it was also reported that *"The British have operated* [the Allison] *at full throttle at sea level (72" Hg) for as much as 20 min. at a time without hurting the engines"*: E-GEH-16, Headquarters Northwest African Strategic Air Force, APO 520, 26 August 1943, Subject: 'British Army Cooperation Tactical Employment of the Mustang I' (P-51); in some instances, boost of even 108 in.Hg (three yards!) is reported: Holloway. No conclusive evidence has been found of the employment of such boost levels in Western Desert at the time of Gazala, but severe misuse in order to trade engines' life (and reliability) for higher output (and thus aircraft speed at low altitude) cannot be excluded.

[13] M. Schoeman, 'Springbok fighter Victory vol.3, Victory over North Africa 1940-1942', African Aviation Series No. 24, p. 63.

[14] Billy Drake with Christopher Shores, 'Billy Drake Fighter Leader', Grub Street, London, 2002, pag. 44.

[15] Francis H. Dean, 'America's Hundred Thousand: U.S. Production Fighters of World War II', Schiffer Military/Aviation History, 1996.

[16] Donald M. Marks, *P-40 Kittyhawk*, in Robin Hingham (ed.), 'Flying American Combat Aircraft of WWII', Stackpole, 2004.

[17] 'Memorandum Report' PHQ-M-19-1307-A October 13, 1941.

[18] Most likely only after Gazala was the +14 and +16 boost allowed for 5 minute emergency outputs of, respectively, 1,460 Hp at 6,500 feet (moderate supercharging) and 1,430 Hp at 11,000 feet (full supercharging).

[19] Francis K. Mason, 'Hawker Aircraft since 1920', Putnam, 1991; John Dibbs and Tony Holmes, 'Hurricane, A Fighter Legend', Osprey, 1995.

[20] Sebastiano Licheri, 'L'arma aerea italiana', Mursia, 1976-2000.

[21] Ministero dell'Aeronautica, Direzione Generale delle Costruzioni e degli Approvvigionamenti, 'Motore FIAT A74 RC 38 e derivati, Istruzioni per l'uso', C.A. 400, 1938-1941, p. 6. A metric Hp is 735,49875 Watt, whilst an imperial or U.S. customary Hp measures 745,69987 W; therefore 1 metric Hp = 0.98632 Hp; 1 Hp = 1.01382 metric Hp.

[22] D.H. Clarke, 'What were they like to fly', Ian Allen, 1964, p. 91-92.

[23] Fighters and Bombers of World War II plus the Grumman Cats, http://en.wikipedia.org/wiki/Book:Fighters_and_Bombers_of_World_War_II. Quoted sources are: Gunston, Bill. 'Gli aerei della 2a Guerra Mondiale'. Milan: Alberto Peruzzo Editore, 1984; Ethell, Jeffrey L. and Joe Christy. 'P-40 Hawks at War'. Shepperton, UK: Ian Allan Ltd., 1979; Boyne, Walter J. and Michael Fopp. 'Air Warfare: An International Encyclopedia', Santa Barbara, California: ABC-CLIO, 2002; Snedden, Robert. 'World War II Combat Aircraft'. Bristol, UK: Factfinders Parragon, 1997; Glancey, Jonathan. 'Spitfire: The Illustrated Biography'. London: Atlantic Books, 2006.

[24] O. Marchi, 'Aeronautica Militare, Museo Storico, Catalogo Motori', Pàtron, 1980, p. 130; A. Curami, 'Tecnologia e modelli di armamento', p. 174, in V. Zamagni, 'Come perdere la guerra e vincere la pace', Il Mulino, 1997.

[25] http://www.beim-zeugmeister.de. According to a test carried out in June 1943 to investigate the effects of sand filter on the later *Bf.109 G-6*, the air cleaner slowed the *Messerschmitt* of some 1.5-2% and lowered the full throttle height of 3%.

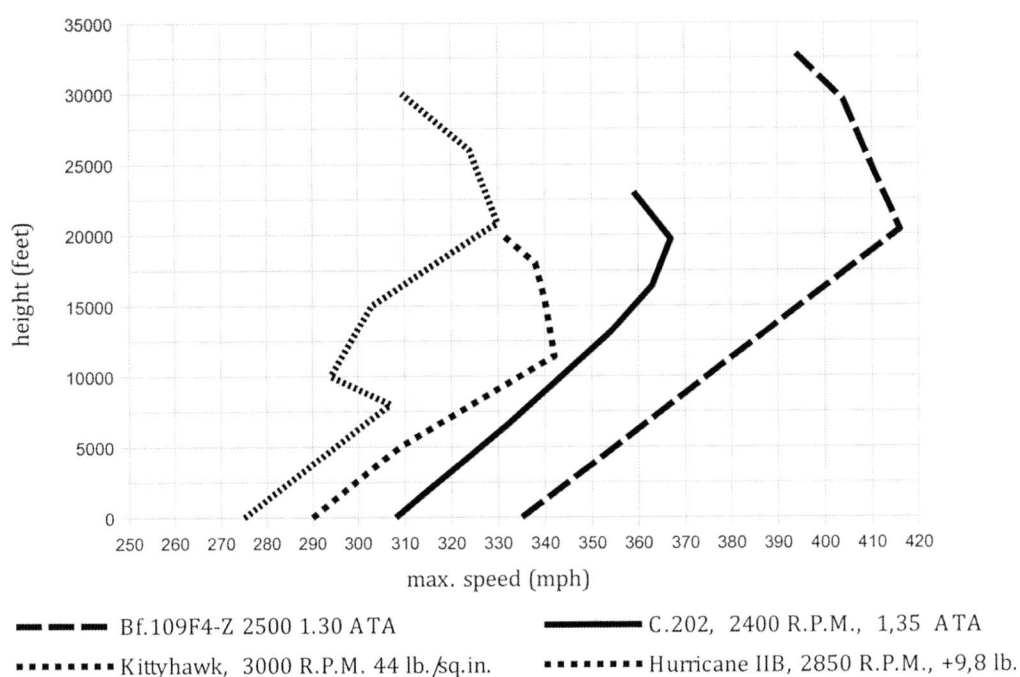

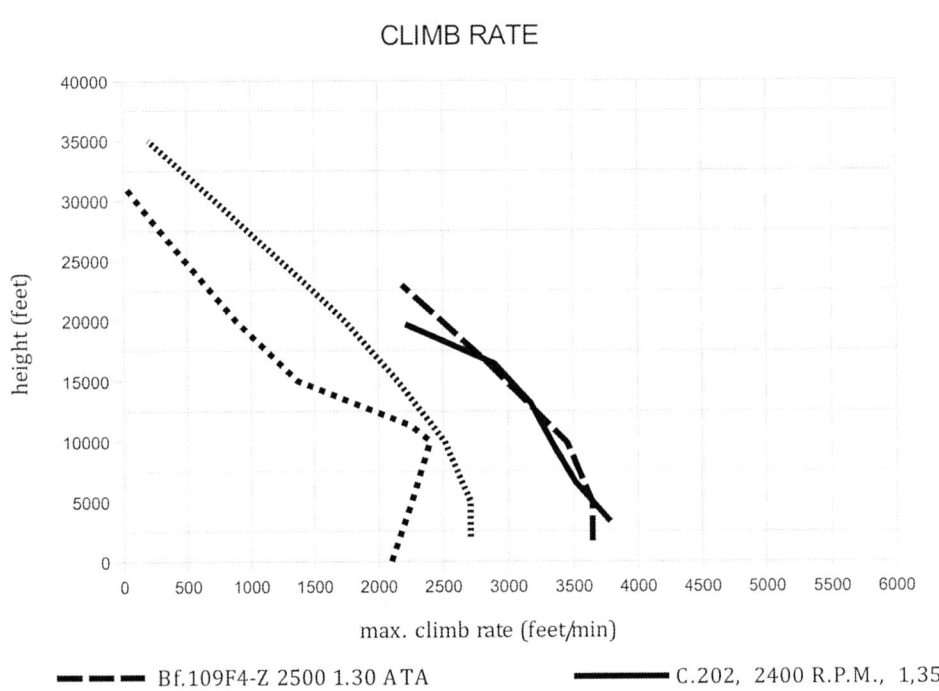

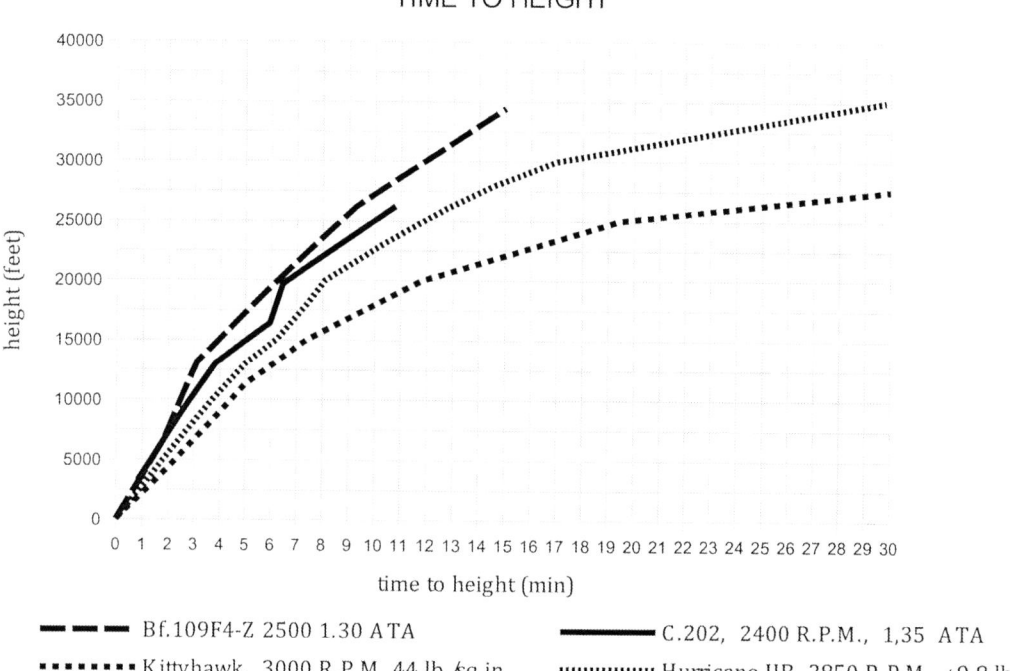

Appendix 3
AIRCRAFT SITUATION

NUMBER OF COMMONWEALTH OPERATIONAL SQUADRONS						
	17-24 May	24-31 May	31 May-7 June	7-14 June	14-21 June	21-28 June
FIGHTERS						
HURRICANES	10	10	10	11	11	11
HURR./TOM. ARMY COOP.	2	3	3	3	3	3
TOMAHAWKS	3	3	3	3	3	3
KITTYHAWKS	6	6	6	6	6	6
SPITFIRES	0	0,5	0,5	1	1	1
BEAUFIGHTERS	4	4	4	4	4	4
BOMBERS						
LIBERATORS	0	0,5	0,5	0,5	0,5	0,5
WELLINGTONS	7	6,5	6,5	6,5	6,5	6,5
BLENHEIMS	0	0	0	1	1	1
MARYLANDS	0	2	2	2	2	2
BOSTONS	2	2	2	2	2	2
BALTIMORES	1	1	1	1	1	1
BEAUFORTS	1	1	1	1	1	1
RECONNAISSANCE						
HUDSONS	1	1	1	1	1	1
SUNDERLANDS	1	1	1	1	1	1
OTHERS	5	5	6	6	6	6
TOTALS	43	46,5	47,5	50	50	50

Source: Weekly statistical analysis (AIR 22/165)

COMMONWEALTH AIRCRAFT IN COMMAND						
	17-24 May	24-31 May	31May-7June	7-14 June	14-21 June	21-28 June
FIGHTERS						
HURRICANES	519	543	504	512	474	453
TOMAHAWKS	130	125	118	108	91	75
KITTYHAWKS	334	356	329	278	261	250
SPITFIRES	22	29	37	46	47	41
BEAUFIGHTERS	79	85	87	93	91	92
BOMBERS						
LIBERATORS	3	3	3	3	2	3
WELLINGTONS	239	235	272	276	290	258
BLENHEIMS	249	245	246	225	222	219
MARYLANDS	40	40	40	39	39	39
BOSTONS	84	87	84	72	75	85
BALTIMORES	175	181	192	194	199	196
BEAUFORTS	28	26	31	30	34	31
RECONNAISSANCE						
HUDSONS	16	25	24	25	32	34
SUNDERLANDS	6	7	7	7	7	7
OTHERS	134	131	126	119	132	132
TOTALS	2058	2118	2100	2027	1996	1915

Source: Weekly statistical analysis (AIR 22/165)

COMMONWEALTH SERVICEABLE AIRCRAFT						
	17-24 May	24-31 May	31May-7June	7-14 June	14-21 June	21-28 June
FIGHTERS						
HURRICANES	275	273	267	280	281	254
TOMAHAWKS	52	59	46	29	30	21
KITTYHAWKS	159	137	104	82	97	71
SPITFIRES	8	16	15	10	16	18
BEAUFIGHTERS	27	34	42	46	49	39
BOMBERS						
LIBERATORS	2	3	3	2	1	2
WELLINGTONS	96	108	120	122	116	108
BLENHEIMS	96	90	89	94	87	74
MARYLANDS	17	17	17	19	22	16
BOSTONS	49	51	45	46	48	54
BALTIMORES	21	24	20	24	21	26
BEAUFORTS	5	4	3	7	13	3
RECONNAISSANCE						
HUDSONS	2	6	6	13	12	13
SUNDERLANDS	3	6	6	6	6	5
OTHERS	75	78	70	65	66	67
TOTALS	887	902	850	845	865	771

Source: Weekly statistical analysis (AIR 22/165)

COMMONWEALTH SERVICEABLE AIRCRAFT WITHIN 14 DAYS						
	17-24 May	24-31 May	31May-7June	7-14 June	14-21 June	21-28 June
FIGHTERS						
HURRICANES	114	83	109	100	90	93
TOMAHAWKS	40	29	31	28	17	12
KITTYHAWKS	34	34	47	35	34	32
SPITFIRES	4	2	3	13	15	13
BEAUFIGHTERS	24	16	18	20	17	21
BOMBERS						
LIBERATORS						1
WELLINGTONS	68	44	54	57	56	41
BLENHEIMS	56	52	55	55	60	77
MARYLANDS	10	12	13	17	14	20
BOSTONS	18	15	24	14	13	16
BALTIMORES	17	21	29	25	21	16
BEAUFORTS	8	9	8	11	9	18
RECONNAISSANCE						
HUDSONS	11	12	12	5	4	10
SUNDERLANDS	3	1	1	1	1	0
OTHERS	38	33	36	33	36	36
TOTALS	445	363	440	414	387	406

Source: Weekly statistical analysis (AIR 22/165)

		LUFTWAFFE AIRCRAFT SITUATION										
		AC AVAILABLE				AC SERVICEABLE		LOSSES MAY		LOSSES JUNE		REPLACEMENTS (NEW AC)	
Unit	Aircraft	10 May	31 May	10 June	30 June	10 May	10 June	Enemy	ACC.	Enemy	ACC.	May	June
S.E. Fighters													
Stab / JG 27	Bf.109 F-4	0	0	0	0	0	1	0	0	0	0	0	0
I. / JG 27	Bf.109 F-4	30	34	31	26	21	16	1	1	6	7	6	8
II. / JG 27	Bf.109 F-4	33	26	24	21	27	16	7	2	9	0	4	6
III. / JG 27	Bf.109 F-4	29	26	25	21	15	13	3	4	4	7	6	6
Jabo. / JG 27	Bf.109 F-4/B	8	10	11	9	8	3	0	1	3	1	0	0
III. / JG 53	Bf.109 F-4	39	24	34	17	25	12	1	6	20	5	2	5
Jabo. / JG 53	Bf.109 F-4/B	12	10	8	5	6	5	0	2	3	1	4	4
TOTAL		151	130	133	99	102	66	12	16	45	21	22	29
T.E. Night Fighters													
I. / NJG 2	Ju.88 C-6	9	36	35	26	5	14	2	0	3	1	12	12
Twin-engined Fighters													
7./ZG 26	Bf.110	12	?	?	?	5	?	?	?	?	?	?	?
Dive-Bombers													
Stab/St.G 3	Ju.87	2	2	3	5	0	2	0	0	0	0	0	0
I./St.G 3	Ju.87	41	37	30	28	28	16	5	1	2	0	0	0
I./St.G 4	Ju.87			30			17	?	?	?	?	?	?
I./St.G 5	Ju.87			38	26	36		13	5	5	8	1	0	0
Long-range Bombers													
12./LG 1	Ju.88	11	15	15	14	11	7	1	3	0	1	6	0
Stab/LG 1	Ju.88	1	1	1	2	1	1	0	0	0	0	0	1
I./LG 1	Ju.88	26	30	26	27	16	16	6	0	15	3	7	0
II./LG 1	Ju.88	31	25	31	29	15	15	7	1	7	6	5	17
I./KG 54	Ju.88		29	28	17		19	5	2	6	4	9	3
II./KG 100	He.111	25	23	25	28	12	12	2	2	5	0	14	10
Tactical Reconnaissance													
4.(H)/12	Bf.110, Bf.109 E,F	17	20	25	23	7	17	1	5	2	2	2	3
Long-range Reconnaissance													
1.(F)/121	Ju.88, Bf.109F	10	14	14	12	9	12	1	0	1	1	5	3

Losses of Bf.109s units in May are referred to the period 22-30 May. Losses indicate AC taken off of charge from the units, so include AC badly damaged. Serviceability of Bf.109s seems lower than that of C.202s.
Source: http://www.ww2.dk

REGIA AERONAUTICA AIRCRAFT AND PILOTS AVAILABILITY

UNIT	AIRCRAFT C.202								PILOTS							
	15 May		31 May		15 June		30 June		15 May		31 May		15 June		30 June	
	A	B	A	B	A	B	A	B	A	B	A	B	A	B	A	B
79ª	8	8	8	7	7	7			14	14	14	14	14	14		
81ª	7	4	5	5	5	5			12	12	11	11	10	10		
88ª	9	9	9	6	6	5	14	10	12	12	12	12	12	12	18	18
71ª	8	7	8	6	5	4			13	12	13	12	9	9		
72ª	9	8	6	5	5	5			12	12	12	11	10	10		
80ª	8	5	6	4	6	4			11	11	10	10	10	10		
Tot. 1° Stormo	49	41	42	33	34	30	14	10	74	73	72	70	65	65	18	18
73ª	11	7	10	9	9	9	9	9	9	7	9	9	8	8	8	8
96ª	9	6	9	9	8	7	11	9	10	10	9	9	8	8	8	8
97ª	11	3	9	7	9	9	11	9	14	12	13	12	13	12	11	10
84ª	12	7	10	8	10	8	11	11	15	14	15	14	13	11	13	11
90ª	9	8	8	4	8	4	11	10	12	11	12	10	11	10	11	11
91ª	10	8	9	0	9	2	12	12	12	12	13	13	12	12	14	14
Tot. 4° Stormo	62	39	55	37	53	39	65	60	72	66	71	67	65	61	65	62
Tot. 1° and 4° St.	111	80	97	70	87	69	79	70	146	139	143	137	130	126	83	80

A - available at the unit; B – combat ready. Data of 96a Sq. for 30 6 are estimated

	OTHER FRONT LINE UNITS											
	AIRCRAFT						PILOTS					
	31 May		15 June		30 June		31 May		15 June		30 June	
UNIT	A	B	A	B	A	B	A	B	A	B	A	B
159° Gr. (CR.42)	30	10	20	9	21	18	17		24		26	
158° Gr. (CR.42)												
8° Gr.(C.200)	30	22	29	13	25	24						
13° Gr. (C.200)	31	17	27	18	27	26						

It can be estimated that 158° Gr. had the same number of AC of 159° Gr.

	OTHER SERVICEABLE A.C.		
	31 May	15 June	30 June
C.200	22	23	23
C.R.42 (estim.)	10	10	10
G.50	24	26	24
S.79	23	20	18
Cant.Z.1007bis	22	12	13
Ghibli	24	41	42
Ca.311	13	5	9

Appendix 4
SORTIES

COMMONWEALTH WEEKLY SORTIES

FIGHTERS SORTIES BY TYPE OF AC

	17-24 May	24-31 May	31 May-7 June	7-14 June	14-21 June	21-28 June	24 May-28 June
HURRICANES	414	599	628	962	671(+)	424(+)	2340
TOMAHAWKS	83	200	137	233	107(+)	44(+)	1665
KITTYHAWKS	187	809	491	692	579(+)	555(+)	3126
SPITFIRES	0	0	46	61	52	72	231
MARTLETS	47	36	22	62	28	?	148
BEAUFIGHTERS	30	32	7	20(+)	55(+)	67	181
TOTALS	761	1676	1331	1968	1492	1162	7691

Source: Weekly statistical analysis (AIR 22/165). The day begins and ends at 18.00 hrs.

BOMBERS SORTIES BY TYPE OF AC

	20-26 May	27 May-2 June	3-9 June	10-16 June	17-23 June	24-30 June	20 May-30 June
LIBERATORS	0	0	0	0	15	50	65
WELLINGTONS	120	145	95	139	148	456	1103
BLENHEIMS	0	0	8	9	11	30	58
BOSTONS	35	114	67	204	119	372	911
BALTIMORES	6	0	5	7	23	65	106
BEAUFORTS	0	0	5	16	31	9	61
TOTALS BOMBERS	161	259	180	375	347	1000	2322

LIBERATORS included American aircraft. Sorties seem to be underestimated. Source: "Report on RAF operations in battle for Egypt 26.5-6.7", AIR 23.1180

FIGHTERS SORTIES BY TYPE OF MISSION

	20-26 May	27 May-2 June	3-9 June	10-16 June	17-23 June	24-30 June	20 May-30 June
OFFENSIVE SWEEP	169	297	291	596	357	106	1816
GROUND ATTACK	71	140	72	46	0	69	398
GROUND ATTACK WITH BOMBS	0	231	313	409	81	374	1408
BOMBER ESCORT	111	173	152	339	142	268	1185
RECONNAISSANCE ESCORT	92	33	68	22	5	6	226
PARTIAL	443	874	896	1412	585	823	5033
SHIPPING PROTECTION	445	297	291	596	357	106	2092
LOCAL DEFENCE	416	421	283	218	204	221	1763
TOTALS	1304	1592	1470	2226	1146	1150	8888

Source: "Report on RAF operations 26.5-6.7", AIR 23.1180

LUFTWAFFE MONTHLY SORTIES		
	May (1-31)	June
BOMBERS		
attacks on ground targets	1250	2225
attacks on ships	30	180
reconnaissance	110	60
convoy escorts	105	140
FIGHTERS		
offensive sweeps, defensive patrols, escorts	2060	3410
attacks on ground targets	155	550
land reconnaissance	180	235
TOTAL	**3890**	**6800**
REGIA AERONAUTICA MONTHLY SORTIES		
	May (1-31)	June
BOMBERS AND RECONNAISSANCE		
attacks on ground targets	60	80
attacks on ships (including torpedo bombers)	3	34
reconnaissance	65	80
convoy escorts	193	182
FIGHTERS		
offensive sweeps, escorts	475	1255
aircraft escorts	230	370
convoy escorts	470	400
defensive patrols	590	330
scrambles on warning	90	40
attacks on ground targets	300	400
OTHERS	100	150
TOTAL	**2576**	**3321**

Source: Santoro

LUFTWAFFE DAILY SORTIES				
DAY	FIGHTERS (Fl.Fü.Afrika)	BOMBERS (Fl.Fü.Afrika)	BOMBERS (X.Fl.Kps)	RECONN.
22 May	72	14	9	17
23 May	90	0	11	33
24 May	54	0	10	18
25 May	?	?	?	?
26 May	94	39	64	12
27 May	208?	?	?	?
28 May	180?	?	?	?
29 May	176	156	50	9
30 May	183	125	?	24
31 May	156	69	0	30
1 June	176	118	45	19
2 June	78	0	0	23
3 June	177	134	19	24
4 June	142	33	22	16
5 June	141	33	22	16
6 June	92	47	0	27
7 June	93	17	0	29
8 June	195	120	0	60
9 June	118	83	17	45
10 June	180	196	0	30

LUFTWAFFE DAILY SORTIES				
DAY	FIGHTERS (Fl.Fü.Afrika)	BOMBERS (Fl.Fü.Afrika)	BOMBERS (X.Fl.Kps)	RECONN.
11 June	133	34	28	41
12 June	186	106	0	31
13 June	113	115	20	18
14 June	90	39	9	18
15 June	110	73	36	28
16 June	132	51	25	31
17 June	92	10	9	21
18 June	86	17	0	16
19 June	?	?	?	?
20 June	186	376	21	
21 June	58	31	5	24
22 June	?	?	?	?
23 June	37	48	15	
24 June	90	16	0	25
25 June	90	?	33	?
26 June	120	24	26	20
27 June	73	25	27	26
28 June	136	47	48	20
29 June	41	14	?	36
30 June	?	?	?	?

Bombers of Fl. Fü. Afrika are mainly Ju.87. Source: OBS. 15 June: fighters are excl. Bf.110 and JG 53.

R.A. FRONT LINE UNITS DAYLY SORTIES

DAY	C.202	C.R.42	C.200	BOMB.
22 May	25	0	0	0
23 May	39	0	0	5
24 May	10	0	0	0
25 May	18	9	0	0
26 May	120	10	8	14
27 May	93	25	38	7
28 May	74	20	30	7
29 May	91	25	5	13
30 May	87	9	30	10
31 May	56	13	0	5
1 June	44	9	24	7
2 June	26	9	8	0
3 June	66	0	5	6
4 June	97	18	5	3
5 June	51	0	33	0
6 June	67	10	20	0
7 June	34	0	10	2
8 June	97	0	25	2
9 June	54	0	35	0
10 June	110	10	10	2

R.A. FRONT LINE UNITS DAYLY SORTIES				
DAY	C.202	C.R.42	C.200	BOMB.
11 June	54	0	10	0
12 June	112	0	14	2
13 June	91	14	11	0
14 June	71	24	48	0
15 June	56	10	26	3
16 June	40	0	5	0
17 June	35	0	0	0
18 June	24	0	5	2
19 June	12	0	0	13
20 June	77	43	20	5
21 June	0	0	10	0
22 June	0	0	0	0
23 June	0	0	0	6
24 June	0	0	0	5
25 June	32	0	0	5
26 June	44	0	0	0
27 June	26	0	0	3
28 June	37	17	0	2
29 June	34	17	0	0
30 June	0	0	0	0
TOTALS	2004	292	435	129

C.202s sorties are mainly offensive sweeps (75%) and aircraft escorts (25%). Have been considered only ground attack sorties by C.R.42s and C.200s, which represented the main activity. Bombers sorties were carried out mostly during the night by Cant.Z.1007bis and S.82. Source: Diario Va Squadra.

Appendix 5
LOSSES

COMMONWEALTH AC SHOT DOWN IN AIR COMBATS

#		PILOT	SQN		AC	SERIAL NO.	DAM	ENEMY AC
1	22 May	Sgt. Williams	450	KIA	Kittyhawk	AK717	III	Bf.109
2	22 May	Sgt. Young	450	SAFE	Kittyhawk	AL131	II	Bf.109
3	22 May	Sgt. Quirk	450	KIA	Kittyhawk	AK634	III	Bf.109
4	22 May	F.O. Gundry	112	KIA	Kittyhawk	AK787	III	Bf.109
5	22 May	P.O. Rogerson	250	SAFE	Kittyhawk	AL116	II	Bf.109
6	23 May	F.Sgt. Scott	80	KIA	Hurricane	BE339	III	Bf.109
7	23 May	Sgt. Howard	80	KIA	Hurricane	BM974	III	Bf.109
8	23 May	F.Lt. Desmond Wade	33	KIA	Hurricane	5654	III	Bf.109/C.202
9	23 May	F.O. Bangley	223	SAFE	Baltimore	AG708	III	Bf.109
10	23 May	Sgt. Horsfield	223	SAFE	Baltimore	AG717	III	Bf.109
11	23 May	P.O. Leake	223	SAFE	Baltimore	AG703	II	Bf.109
12	23 May	W.O. Mc Clure	223	SAFE	Baltimore	AG762	III	Bf.109
13	25 May	Sgt. Comfort	80	KIA	Hurricane	BN413	III	Bf.109
14	25 May	Lt. Nicol	40 SAAF	KIA	Hurricane	4033	III	Bf.109
15	25 May	F.Lt. Playford	274	W	Hurricane		II?	C.202
16	26 May	S.L. Gibbes	3 RAAF	W	Kittyhawk	AK874	III	Ju.88
17	26 May	P.O. Knapik	112	SAFE	Kittyhawk	AK682	III	Bf.109
18	27 May	Lt. Paddon	2 SAAF	KIA	Kittyhawk	AL138 DB-R	III	C.202
19	27 May	Lt. Ford	2 SAAF	KIA	Kittyhawk	AK904 DB-H	III	Bf.109/C.202
20	27 May	Sgt. Wilcox	229	SAFE	Hurricane	Z4005	III	C.202
21	27 May	Lt. Finlayson	5 SAAF	SAFE	Tomahawk	AN427 GL-D	II	Bf.109/Bf.110
22	27 May	Lt. Woodliffe	4 SAAF	SAFE	Tomahawk	AK or AM414 KJ-L	II	Bf.109
23	27 May	Sgt. Norman	3 RAAF	KIA	Kittyhawk	AL183	III	Bf.109
24	27 May	F.Lt. Dickinson	112	SAFE	Kittyhawk	AL122	III	Bf.109
25	27 May	2/Lt. Stevens	5 SAAF	SAFE	Tomahawk	AN263 GL-V	II	C.202
26	28 May	F.Sgt. Wintersdorff	80	SAFE	Hurricane	BE706	III	Bf.109
27	28 May	Sgt. Ovenstone	250	KIA	Kittyhawk	AK877	III	Bf.109/C.202
28	28 May	Sgt. Lyons	33	KIA	Hurricane		III	Bf.109
29	28 May	Lt. Pare	5 SAAF	SAFE	Tomahawk	AN383 GL-N	III	Bf.109
30	29 May	P.O. Pearson	80	SAFE	Hurricane	BM991	III	Bf.109
31	29 May	F.Sgt. Campbell	80	SAFE	Hurricane	BN354	III	Bf.109
32	29 May	Sgt. Swire	80	SAFE	Hurricane	BE396	II	Bf.109
33	29 May	Sgt. Sykes	80	SAFE	Hurricane	BN547	II	Bf.109

		COMMONWEALTH AC SHOT DOWN IN AIR COMBATS						
		PILOT	SQN		AC	SERIAL NO.	DAM	ENEMY AC
34	29 May	Lt.Brown	2 SAAF	KIA	Kittyhawk	AK870	III	Bf.109
35	29 May	Sgt. Packer	450	KIA	Kittyhawk	AL163	III	Bf.109
36	29 May	Sgt. Dean	450	KIA	Kittyhawk	AK979	III	Bf.109
37	29 May	Sgt. Shaw	450	KIA	Kittyhawk	AK998	III	Bf.109
38	29 May	Lt. Slater	5 SAAF	SAFE	Tomahawk	AN433	II	C.202
39	29 May	Lt. Murrow	24 SAAF	SAFE	Boston	Z2176L	III	Bf.110
40	30 May	Sgt. Buckland	450	KIA	Kittyhawk	AK704	III	Bf.109
41	30 May	Lt. Harrison	2 SAAF	POW	Kittyhawk	AK841 DB-K	III	C.202
42	30 May	F.Lt. Wilie	260	KIA	Kittyhawk		III	Bf.109
43	30 May	F.Sgt. Copping	260	SAFE	Kittyhawk		II	Bf.109
44	30 May	P.O. Hale	260	KIA	Kittyhawk		III	Bf.109
45	30 May	2/Lt. Fulton	2 SAAF	POW	Kittyhawk	AK735 DB-E	III	Bf.109
46	30 May	F.Lt. Barr	3 RAAF	SAFE	Kittyhawk	AK889	III	C.202
47	30 May	Sgt. MacDiarmid	3 RAAF	KIA	Kittyhawk	AL153	III	C.202
48	30 May	Sgt. Devlin	250	KIA	Kittyhawk	AK648	III	C.202
49	30 May	Sgt.Jenkins	450	SAFE	Kittyhawk	?	?	C.202
50	30 May	Lt. Saunders	5 SAAF	POW	Tomahawk	AM495 GL-T	III	Bf.109
51	30 May	F.Sgts McBurnie	450	SAFE	Kittyhawk	AL206	III	Bf.109
52	30 May	F.Sgts Nursey	450	KIA	Kittyhawk	AL200	III	Bf.109
53	31 May	Capt. Bayly	4 SAAF	SAFE	Tomahawk	AN242 KJ-P	?	Bf.109
54	31 May	Lt. Hankok	4 SAAF	SAFE	Tomahawk	AH914 KJ-T	III	Bf.109
55	31 May	Lt. Jackson	4 SAAF	KIA	Tomahawk	AK509	III	Bf.109
56	31 May	2/Lt.Marillier	4 SAAF	KIA	Tomahawk	AN360	III	Bf.109
57	31 May	Sgt.Veysey	260	KIA	Kittyhawk		III	no claims
58	31 May	Sgt. Sheppard	260	SAFE	Kittyhawk		II	no claims
59	31 May	P.O. Ismay	274	KIA	Hurricane		III	C.202
60	31 May	Sgt. Lindsay	450	SAFE	Kittyhawk	AL190	III	Bf.109
61	31 May	Lt. Thomson	450	KIA	Kittyhawk	AK787	III	Bf.109
62	31 May	Lt. de Waal	4 SAAF	SAFE	Tomahawk	AL176	II	Bf.109
63	31 May	F.Lt. Hindle	260	KIA	Kittyhawk		III	Bf.109
64	31 May	F.Sgt. Carlisle	260	SAFE	Kittyhawk		II	Bf.109
65	31 May	Capt. Copeland	4 SAAF	SAFE	Tomahawk		III?	Bf.109
66	31 May	Maj. Duncan	5 SAAF	KIA	Tomahawk	AK523 GL-R	III	Bf.109
67	31 May	F.O. Astell	148	SAFE	Wellington	AD653 R	III	CR.42
68	1 June	Lt. Murray	4 SAAF	SAFE	Tomahawk	AK998	II	Bf.109
69	1 June	P.O. Wilson	3 RAAF	KIA	Kittyhawk	AL196	III	Bf.109

COMMONWEALTH AC SHOT DOWN IN AIR COMBATS

		PILOT	SQN		AC	SERIAL NO.	DAM	ENEMY AC
70	1 June	P.O. Edwards	3 RAAF	SAFE	Kittyhawk	AK907	II	Bf.109
71	2 June	Fl. Lt. Moriarty	274	KIA	Hurricane		III	Bf.109
72	3 June	Lt. McGregor	4 SAAF	SAFE	Tomahawk	AK524	II	C.202
73	3 June	2/Lt. Golding	5 SAAF	SAFE	Tomahawk	AN468 GL-J	III	Bf.109
74	3 June	Capt. Morrison	5 SAAF	SAFE	Tomahawk	AK421 GL-Z	III	Bf.109
75	3 June	Capt. Pare	5 SAAF	KIA	Tomahawk	AN384 GL-V	III	Bf.109
76	3 June	Lt. Muir	5 SAAF	SAFE	Tomahawk	AN262 GL-C	III	Bf.109
77	3 June	2/Lt. Martin	5 SAAF	SAFE	Tomahawk	AM401 GL-I	III	Bf.109
78	4 June	Lt. Burdon	2 SAAF	SAFE	Kittyhawk	AK611 DB-B	III	Bf.109/C.202
79	4 June	Capt. Morphew	4 SAAF	POW	Tomahawk	AN393	III	C.202
80	4 June	2/Lt. Lawler	4 SAAF	POW	Tomahawk	AN 461	III	Bf.109/C.202
81	4 June	Lt. Lane	4 SAAF	SAFE	Tomahawk	AN460	III	Ju.87
82	4 June	Maj. Meaker	5 SAAF	SAFE	Tomahawk	AN388 GL-N	III	Ju.87
83	5 June	Lt. Van der Riet	40 SAAF	W	Hurricane	Z4608	III	Bf.109
84	5 June	Maj. Frost	5 SAAF	KIA	Tomahawk	AM385 GL-W	III	Bf.109
85	5 June	Lt. Derham	5 SAAF	POW	Tomahawk	AN247 GL-K	II	Bf.109
86	7 June	F.Lt. Cantrill	73	KIA	Hurricane	BH330	III	C.202
87	7 June	Sgt. Wiseman	73	SAFE	Hurricane	BN375	II	C.202
88	7 June	Sgt. Wilson	75	SAFE	Hurricane	BL279	III	C.202
89	7 June	Lt. Berrangè	2 SAAF	KIA	Kittyhawk	AK628 DB-P	III	Bf.109
90	7 June	Lt. Frewan	2 SAAF	SAFE	Kittyhawk	AL193 DB-S	III	Bf.109
91	8 June	Lt. McMaster	2 SAAF	SAFE	Kittyhawk	AK923? DB-V	III	C.202
92	8 June	F.O. Brown	208	SAFE	Tomahawk	AN334	II?	C.202
93	8 June	Sgt. Menzies	33	SAFE	Hurricane	AN334	II	C.202
94	9 June	Lt. Van Nus	4 SAAF	SAFE	Tomahawk	AN377 KJ-B	III	Bf.109
95	9 June	Sgt. Clark	260	KIA	Kittyhawk		III	C.202
96	10 June	F.O. Sowrey	213	SAFE	Hurricane	BN562	III	Bf.109
97	10 June	Sgt. Jackson	213	KIA	Hurricane	BM159	III	Bf.109
98	10 June	FL. Scade	73	W	Hurricane	BN370	II	Bf.109
99	10 June	Sgt. Wilson	73	SAFE	Hurricane	BE568	III	C.202
100	11 June	P.O. Mc Gregor	208	SAFE	Tomahawk	AK567	?	Bf.109
101	11 June	P.O. Persse	274	KIA	Hurricane		III	Bf.109
102	12 June	P.O. Young	450	KIA	Kittyhawk	AL107	III	Bf.109
103	12 June	Sgt. Beste	450	KIA	Kittyhawk	AL165	III	Bf.109
104	12 June	F.Sgt Edwards	213	SAFE	Hurricane	BN285	III	Bf.109
105	12 June	F.O. Edmunds	213	KIA	Hurricane	BN276	III	Bf.109

COMMONWEALTH AC SHOT DOWN IN AIR COMBATS

		PILOT	SQN		AC	SERIAL NO.	DAM	ENEMY AC
106	12 June	F.Lt. Aldridge	33	SAFE	Hurricane	5318	III	Bf.109
107	12 June	Sgt. Hall	33	KIA	Hurricane	917	III	Bf.109/C.202
108	12 June	Sgt. Cameron	33	KIA	Hurricane	Z5143 RS-C	III	C.202
109	12 June	Sgt. Wrigley	260	KIA	Kittyhawk		III	C.202
110	12 June		260	SAFE	Kittyhawk		III	C.202
111	12 June		260	SAFE	Kittyhawk		III	Bf.109
112	13 June	P.O. Wilson	213	KIA	Hurricane	Z5307	III	Bf.109
113	13 June	F. Sgt. Halvorsen	213	SAFE	Hurricane	BE340	III	Bf.109
114	13 June	Sgt. Halliday	450	KIA	Kittyhawk	AL117	III	Bf.109
115	13 June	Sgt. Stone	450	KIA	Kittyhawk	AK958	III	Bf.109
116	13 June	P.O. Osborne	450	SAFE	Kittyhawk	AL106	II	Bf.109
117	13 June	P.O. Edwards	112	SAFE	Kittyhawk	AK778	III	Bf.109
118	13 June	Lt. Cohen	4 SAAF	SAFE	Tomahawk	AN397 KJ-U	II	C.202
119	14 June	Lt. van der Spuy	5 SAAF	SAFE	Tomahawk	AK533 GL-Y	III	Bf.109
120	14 June	Lt. Kemsley	5 SAAF	SAFE	Tomahawk	AN345 GL-V	III	Bf.109
121	14 June	F.Sgt. Gael	272	KIA	Beaufighter	T.4709	III	Bf.109
122	14 June	Sgt. Cooper	272	KIA	Beaufighter	T3291 A	III	Bf.109
123	14 June	Truby	272	KIA	Beaufighter	T4867 S	III	Bf.109
124	14 June	P.O. Blackstock	459	KIA	Hudson	V9022 M	III	Bf.109
125	14 June	P.O. Rogers	272	SAFE	Beaufighter	T4885	III	Bf.109
126	15 June	P.O. Corbisier	272	KIA	Beaufighter	T4869	III	Bf.109
127	15 June	Sgt. Blessing	272	KIA	Beaufighter	T4829	III	Bf.109
128	15 June	P.O. Gibson	227	KIA	Beaufighter	T4933	III	Bf.109
129	15 June	F.Lt. Thomas	39	SAFE	Beaufort	AW352	III	Bf.109
130	15 June	P.O. Abram	39	SAFE	Beaufort	AW297	III	Bf.109
131	15 June	F.O. Hooper	39	KIA	Beaufort	DD955	III	Bf.109
132	15 June	P.O. Grant	39	SAFE	Beaufort	DD949	III	Bf.109
133	15 June	Sgt. Daffurn	39	SAFE	Beaufort	DD974	II	Bf.109
134	15 June	Sgt. Wilson	159	SAFE	B-24	AL553	II	Bf.109
135	15 June	?	260	SAFE	Kittyhawk		III	Bf.109
136	16 June	Lt. de Villiers	2 SAAF	SAFE	Kittyhawk	AL126 DB-R	III	Bf.109
137	16 June	Sgt. Biden	3 RAAF	KIA	Kittyhawk	AK745	III	Bf.109
138	16 June	Sgt. Ryan	3 RAAF	KIA	Kittyhawk	AL145	III	Bf.109
139	16 June	F.Lt. Robin	73	KIA	Hurricane	BN560	III	no claims
140	16 June	P.O. Glenn	208	KIA	Hurricane	BG914	III	no claims
141	16 June	Maj. Frost	5 SAAF	KIA	Kittyhawk	AM or AK422 GL-B	III	Bf.109

COMMONWEALTH AC SHOT DOWN IN AIR COMBATS

		PILOT	SQN		AC	SERIAL NO.	DAM	ENEMY AC
142	16 June	Lt. Derham	5 SAAF	SAFE	Kittyhawk		III	Bf.109
143	16 June	Sgt. Newton	112	SAFE	Kittyhawk	AL195	III	Bf.109
144	16 June	Sgt. Hall	250	SAFE	Kittyhawk	AL179	III	Bf.109
145	16 June	P.O. Cable	250	W	Kittyhawk	AK884	II	Bf.109
146	17 June	S.L. Botha	4 SAAF	KIA	Tomahawk	AK519 GL-A	III	Bf.109/C.202
147	17 June	Lt. Morgan	4 SAAF	KIA	Tomahawk	AN309 GL-O	III	Bf.109/C.202
148	17 June	Lt. Sommerville	4 SAAF	SAFE	Tomahawk	AN420 GL-P	III	C.202
149	17 June	Sgt. Hooke	3 RAAF	SAFE	Kittyhawk	AK813	III	Bf.109
150	17 June	F.Sgt. Glancy	450	KIA	Kittyhawk	AK934	III	Bf.109
151	17 June	P.O. Conrad	274	SAFE	Hurricane		II	Bf.109
152	17 June	S.L. Ward	73	KIA	Hurricane	BN277	III	Bf.109
153	17 June	P.O. Woolley	73	KIA	Hurricane	BN649	III	Bf.109
154	17 June	P.O. Stone	73	SAFE	Hurricane	BN157	III	Bf.109
155	17 June	Sgt. Goodwin	73	SAFE	Hurricane	BN121	III	Bf.109
156	17 June	F.Sgt. Matthews	260	W	Kittyhawk		III	Bf.109
157	17 June	FSgt. Bernier	260	SAFE	Kittyhawk		II	Bf.109
158	18 June	P.O. Bezencenet	208	SAFE	Hurricane	BG862	III	Bf.109
159	24 June	P.O. Doak	208	SAFE	Tomahawk	AK385	III	Bf.109
160	24 June	Sgt. Fox	3 RAAF	KIA	Kittyhawk	AK806 CV-N	III	no claims
161	25 June	P.O. Hamilton	250	POW	Kittyhawk	AK904	III	Bf.109
162	25 June	?	145		Spitfire		III	Bf.109
163	25 June	Sgt. Medwin	70	SAFE	Wellington	DV522	II	Bf.110
164	25 June	F.Sgt. Stuart	70	SAFE	Wellington	DV564 L	II	Bf.110
165	26 June	?	12 SAAF	SAFE	Boston		II	C.202
166	26 June	Lt. Somerville	208	KIA	Tomahawk	AK565	III	C.202
167	26 June	P.O. Jones T	450	KIA	Kittyhawk	AL107	III	Bf.109
168	26 June	P.O. Cuddon	112	KIA	Kittyhawk	ET526	III	Bf.109
169	26 June	S.L. Barr	3 RAAF	POW W	Kittyhawk	ET873 CV-N	III	Bf.109
170	26 June	F.Lt. Lane-Sansom	272	KIA	Beaufighter	N	III	Bf.109
171	26 June	PO Jones M	450	SAFE	Kittyhawk	AK750	III	Bf.109
172	26 June	F.lt. Copeland	250	KIA	Kittyhawk	AK921	III	Bf.109
173	26 June	Sgt. Thomson	274	KIA	Hurricane		III	Bf.109
174	26 June	Sgt. Mahady	145	KIA	Spitfire	E322	III	Bf.109
175	26 June	Sgt. Baily	145	KIA	Spitfire	T284	III	Bf.109
176	26 June	Maj. Hewitson	4 SAAF	POW	Kittyhawk	AK835	III	Bf.109
177	26 June	Lt. Popham	5 SAAF	W	Tomahawk	AN241	III	Bf.109

COMMONWEALTH AC SHOT DOWN IN AIR COMBATS								
		PILOT	SQN		AC	SERIAL NO.	DAM	ENEMY AC
178	26 June	P.O. Murdoch	450	KIA	Kittyhawk	AK990	III	Bf.109
179	26 June	Sgt. Carlile	260	KIA	Kittyhawk		III	Bf.109
180	26 June	F.Sgt. Lack	213	KIA	Hurricane	BN527	III	Bf.109
181	26 June	P.O. Coussens	73	SAFE	Hurricane	BE280	III	Bf.109
182	26 June	Sgt. Spear	145	KIA	Spitfire	AB326	III	Bf.109
183	26 June	Lt. Wilkinson	2 SAAF	W	Kittyhawk	AK900	III	Bf.109
184	26 June	Sgt. Gunn	40	KIA	Wellington	Z9028 V	III	Bf.110
185	26 June	Sgt. Clayton	70	SAFE	Wellington	Z9102 A	III	Bf.110
186	26 June	Sgt. Street	108	KIA	Wellington	ES981 A	III	Bf.110
187	26 June	Sgt. Hewitt	223	SAFE	Baltimore	AG748	III	C.202
188	26 June	P.O. Davies	223	SAFE	Baltimore	AG.774	III	C.202
189	27 June	Lt. Sedgewick	208	KIA	Hurricane	Z.5412	III	Bf.109
190	27 June	F.Lt. Gidney	223	KIA	Baltimore	AG771	III	Bf.109
191	27 June	P.O. Davies	223	KIA	Baltimore	AG782	III	Bf.109
192	27 June	Sgt. Carruthers	223	SAFE	Baltimore	AG774	III	Bf.109
193	27 June	S.Lt. Lafont	Alsace	W	Hurricane		III?	Bf.109
194	27 June	S.Lt. Thiriez	Alsace	W	Hurricane		III	Bf.109
195	27 June	?	826	SAFE	Albacore		III	Bf.109
196	27 June	Lt. Colin	Alsace	KIA	Hurricane	Z4648	III	Bf.109
197	27 June	S.Lt. Louchet	Alsace	KIA	Hurricane	Z4718	III	Bf.109
198	27 June	S.Chef Mailfert	Alsace	W	Hurricane	Z4608	III?	Bf.109
199	28 June	F.Lt. Collenette	238	KIA	Hurricane	T	III	Bf.109
200	28 June	F.Sgt. Cummings	238	KIA	Hurricane	G	III	Bf.109
201	28 June	F.Sgt. Lawrence Smith	238	KIA	Hurricane	H	III	Bf.109
202	28 June	F.Sgt. Doig	238	SAFE	Hurricane	A	III	Bf.109
203	28 June	F.Sgt. Purdy	238	KIA	Hurricane	X	III	Bf.109
204	28 June	Lt. Bidwell	5 SAAF	SAFE	Tomahawk	?460	III	C.202
205	28 June	S.L. Jaclin	108	SAFE	Wellington	R1029 S	III	Bf.110

KIA - killed in action, POW – prisoner of war, W - wounded

GERMAN AC SHOT DOWN IN AIR COMBATS

	DATE	PILOT	UNIT	DAM	AC	W.Nr.	DAM	ENEMY AC
1	22 May	Uffz. Sdun	8./JG 27	W	Bf.109	10102	100%	250
2	23 May	Oblt. Obernhuber	II./KLG 1	KIA	Ju.88	5633	100%	213
3	23 May	Uffz. Gierster	5./JG 27	W	Bf.109	7390	100%	450
4	26 May	Fw. Liebsch	I./L.G.1	Miss	Ju.88	14215	100%	73
5	26 May	Oblt. Riba	I./L.G.1	Miss	Ju.88	5615	100%	73
6	27 May	Uffz. Frickmann	III./ZG 26	Miss	Bf.110	2195	100%	5 SAAF
7	27 May	?	III./ZG 26		Bf.110	2384?	80%	5 SAAF
8	27 May	Fw. Reuter	5./JG 27	POW	Bf.109	7369	100%	450
9	28 May	Fw. Lange	4(H)/12	KIA	Bf.109	3489	100%	5 SAAF
10	29 May	Lt. Von Fritsch	9./Jg27	POW	Bf.109	8575	100%	450
11	29 May	Haupt. Drescher	4./St.G 3	SAFE	Ju.87	2469	100%	450
12	29 May	Oblt. Olfermann	4./St.G 3	KIA	Ju.87	2450	100%	450
13	31 May	Oblt. Fluder	6./JG27	KIA	Bf.109	8660	100%	5 SAAF
14	31 May	Ofwb. Krenzke	6./JG28	POW	Bf.109	8774	100%	5 SAAF
15	31 May	Fw. Gromotka	6./JG29	SAFE	Bf.109	8548	100%	5 SAAF
16	31 May	Uffz. Kretschmar	I./St.G.3	W	Ju.87		100%	4 SAAF
17	31 May	Uffz. Daminger,	1./St.G.4	SAFE	Ju.87	6320	100%	4 SAAF/260
18	1 June	Lt. Quaritsch	8./JG 53	SAFE	Bf.109	10134	100%	3 RAAF
19	3 June	Lt. Jenisch	5./JG 27	SAFE	Bf.109	8677	100%	33
20	3 June	Lt. Hans Deibl	3./St.G.3	POW	Ju.87		100%	5 SAAF
21	3 June	Uffz. Nusswitz	1./St.G.3	Miss	Ju.87	6015	100%	5 SAAF
22	3 June	Uffz. Schneider	1./St.G.3	Miss	Ju.87	5869	100%	5 SAAF
23	4 June	Hpt. Eppen	I./St.G.3	Miss	Ju.87	6146	100%	4 SAAF
24	4 June	Uffz. Horst	1./St.G.3	SAFE	Ju.87	6163	100%	4 SAAF
25	4 June	Lt. Herritsch	2./St.G.3	?	Ju.87	6306	100%	4/5 SAAF
26	4 June	Uffz. Brandt	3./St.G.3	?	Ju.87	6043	100%	4/5 SAAF
26	4 June		2./St.G.3	SAFE	Ju.87	6205	60%	4/5 SAAF
27	5 June	Lt. Kalista	5./JG 27	Miss	Bf.109	10125	100%	2 SAAF
28	6 June	Uffz. Pikel	4(H)/12	Miss	Bf.109	6414	100%	112
29	7 June	Lt. Scheiter	8./JG 27	SAFE	Bf.109		100%	2 SAAF
30	8 June	Fw. Walchofer	6./JG 27	KIA	Bf.109	8465	100%	73
31	9 June	Uffz. Pfeffer	3./JG27	KIA	Bf.109	8647	100%	5 SAAF
32	10 June	Oblt. Sinner	6./JG27	SAFE	Bf.109	8492	100%	145

		GERMAN AC SHOT DOWN IN AIR COMBATS						
		PILOT	UNIT		AC	W.Nr.	DAM	ENEMY UNIT
33	10 June		III./St.G.3		Ju.87	2060	100%	213
34	11 June	Uffz. Zeller	10.(J)/JG 27	KIA	Bf.109	8539	100%	33
35	11 June		10.(J)/JG 27	SAFE	Bf.109	7475	75%	33, 274
36	12 June	Fw. Herkenhoff	9./Jg 53	KIA	Bf.109	8586	100%	274
37	12 June	Fw. Loeper	3./St.G.3	SAFE	Ju.87	6227	100%	73?
38	14 June	Lt. Quaritsch	8./JG 53	KIA	Bf.109	10068	100%	5 SAAF
39	14 June	Ofw. Pantel	III./StG 3	KIA	Ju.87	2139	100%	238?
40	14 June	Lt. Hesse	7./JG 53	KIA	Bf.109	10163	100%	272?
41	14 June	Lt. Müller	I./KG 54	KIA	Ju.88	140216	100%	272?
42	15 June	Uffz. Panier	10.(J)/JG 27	POW	Bf.109	10039	100%	274
43	16 June	Uffz. Fahernberger	8./JG 27	SAFE	Bf.109	sw3	?	274
44	16 June	Lt. Edelhoff	5./L.G.1	Miss	Ju.88	14713	100%	145?
45	17 June	Oblt. Schultz	Stab II./JG 27	KIA	Bf.109	10271	100%	260
46	17 June	Lt. Schaller	9./JG 53	POW	Bf.109	10103	100%	260/274
47	24 June	Hptm. Gustavus	II./K.G.100	Miss	He.111	7201	100%	73
48	25 June				Ju.88		100%	73
49	26 June	Lt. Lipsky	II./St.G.3	SAFE	Ju.87	2530	100%	2, 4, 5 SAAF
50	26 June	Uffz. Wolff	II./St.G.3	W	Ju.87	?	100%	2, 4, 5 SAAF
51	26 June	?			Ju.87		100%	2, 4, 5 SAAF
52	27 June	Uffz. Beckmann	2./JG 27	W	Bf.109	rt. 7	100%	260
53	29 June	Ofw. Döring	4./L.G.1	Miss	Ju.88	5672	100%	73/376th

		ITALIAN AC SHOT DOWN IN AIR COMBATS						
		PILOT	UNIT		AC	SERIAL NO.	DAM	ENEMY UNIT
1	25 May	Serg.Magg. Modesti	155ª Sq	POW	CR.42		DES	73
2	28 May	Serg.Magg. Bottazzi	94ª	SAFE	C.200	M.M.6674	DES	40 SAAF
3	29 May	S.Ten. Massa	73ª	KIA	C.202	M.M.7824	DES	5 SAAF
4	30 May	M.llo Magli	72ª Sq	KIA	C.202	M.M.7735	DES	2 SAAF
5	30 May	Serg.Magg. Meneghetti	81ª	KIA	C.202	M.M.7881	DES	3 RAAF
6	4 June	Serg.Magg. Marcati	390ª Sq	KIA	CR.42	M.M.8572	DES	260
7	4 June	Serg. Magg. Bartolozzi	388ª Sq	SAFE	CR.42	M.M.5059	DES	5 SAAF
8	8 June	Ten. Palazzeschi	81ª	POW	C.202	M.M.7898	DES	274
9	9 June	Serg. Magg. Rossi	96ª	KIA	C.202	M.M.7822	DES	213
10	13 June	Cap. Vicentini	72ª	POW	C.202	M.M.7859	DES	2 SAAF
11	13 June	Ten. Morandi	72ª	KIA	C.202	M.M.7732	DES	2 SAAF
12	13 June	Ten. Bacchi	80ª	W	C.202	M.M.8349	H. Dam	4 SAAF
13	15 June	Cap. Mezzetti	Gorizia	KIA	Ro.43	M.M.27186	DES	272
14	15 June	S.Ten. Visentin	171ª Sq	KIA	Cant.Z.506		DES	272
15	15 June	Ten. Annona	204ª Sq	KIA	S.M.79		DES	252
16	15 June	Serg.Magg. Della Valle	391ª Sq	KIA	CR.42		DES	274
17	26 June	Serg. Magg. Martinoli	73ª	SAFE	C.202	M.M.7823	H. Dam	213

DES - destroyed, H.Dam – heavily damaged

COMMONWEALTH AC SHOT DOWN BY ANTI-AIRCRAFT

		PILOT	SQN		AIRCRAFT	SERIAL NO.	DAM Cat.
1	22 May	F.Sgt. Ward	38		Wellington	BB484X	III?
2	25 May	P.O. Beaumont	73	KIA	Hurricane	BD774	III
3	26 May	P.O. Samuel	274	SAFE	Hurricane	?	II
4	27 May	Sgt. Thomas	3 RAAF	SAFE	Kittyhawk	AK965	II?
5	27 May	Sgt. Clabburn	3 RAAF	SAFE	Kittyhawk	AK806	III
6	27 May		12 SAAF		Boston	AL773?	II
7	28 May	F.Lt. Dikinson	112	KIA	Kittyhawk	AK829	III
8	28 May	Lt. Ismay	2 SAAF	SAFE	Kittyhawk	AK747 DB-L	II?
9	29 May	Lt. Butler	24 SAAF	SAFE	Boston	AL673 W	III
10	30 May	Sgt. Halliday	450	SAFE	Kittyhawk	?	III?
11	30 May	Sgt. Burney	112	SAFE	Kittyhawk	AK770	?
12	31 May	P.O. Mitchell	112	SAFE	Kittyhawk	AK999	III
13	3 June	P.O. White	104	SAFE	Wellington	Z8385	II?
14	4 June	Lt. Thorhill Cook	5 SAAF	SAFE	Tomahawk	AN313 GL-X	III
15	4 June	P.O. Atkinson	112	SAFE	Kittyhawk	AL219	III
16	5 June	Sgt. Leach	70	POW	Wellington	Z9096 M	III
17	8 June	Sgt. White	112	SAFE	Kittyhawk	AL211	II
18	8 June	Sgt. James	450	KIA	Kittyhawk	AL146	III
19	8 June	Sgt. Saunders	223	SAFE	Baltimore	AG777	III
20	8 June	F.Lt. Gidney	224	SAFE	Baltimore	AG285	III
21	8 June	Morrison Bell	6	SAFE	Hurricane	BN860	III
22	8 June	F.L. Simpson	6	SAFE	Hurricane	BN861	III
23	8 June	Sgt. Hall	250	SAFE	Kittyhawk	AK959	III
24	10 June	F.Sgt. McRae	108	KIA	Wellington	BB842 K	III
25	11 June	Sgt. Adye	112	KIA	Kittyhawk	AK988	III
26	11 June	Sgt. Greaves	112	KIA	Kittyhawk	AK937	III
27	12 June	Sgt. Bray	3 RAAF	SAFE	Kittyhawk	AK176	III
28	12 June	Sgt. Stevens	3 RAAF	SAFE	Kittyhawk	AL187	III
29	12 June	F.Sgt. Cassell	112	SAFE	Kittyhawk	AL149	III
30	12 June	F.O. Barlow	208	SAFE	Hurricane	Z5330	II
31	12 June	Sgt. House	450	SAFE	Kittyhawk	AK749	II?
32	12 June	P.O. Shakelton		KIA	Wellington	Z8592	III

		COMMONWEALTH AC SHOT DOWN BY ANTI-AIRCRAFT					
		PILOT	SQN		AIRCRAFT	SERIAL NO.	DAM Cat.
33	14 June	Sgt. Tedesco	272	KIA	Beaufighter	T4841 R	III
34	14 June	F.Lt. Chinchen	3 RAAF	POW	Kittyhawk	AL215	III
35	14 June	Sgt. Biden	4 RAAF	SAFE	Kittyhawk	AL208	III
36	15 June	S.L. Gibbs	39	SAFE	Beaufort	AW337	III
37	15 June	P.O. Marshall	39	SAFE	Beaufort	DD975	III
38	15 June	P.O. Lee	6	SAFE	Hurricane	?	III
39	16 June	Sgt. Bray	3 RAAF	SAFE	Kittyhawk	AK838	II
40	16 June	Sgt. Boardman	3 RAAF	SAFE	Kittyhawk	AK812	II
41	16 June	Sgt. Hannaford	250	SAFE	Kittyhawk	AK839	III
42	16 June	P.O. Simpson	250	KIA	Kittyhawk	AL?65	III
43	16 June	P.O. Carson	112	POW	Kittyhawk	AL175	III
44	17 June	F.Sgt. Drew	112	KIA	Kittyhawk	AK586	III
45	19 June	F.O. Kauter	37	KIA	Wellington	DV669 W	III
46	20 June	F.Lt. Leu	112	POW	Kittyhawk	AK225	III
47	21 June	W.C. Kerr	148	KIA	Wellington	ES990 S	III
48	23 June	F.Lt. Collinette	238	SAFE	Hurricane	T	II?
49	23 June	P.O. Holmes	238	KIA	Hurricane	X	III
50	23 June	F.Sgt. Stein	238	KIA	Hurricane	V	III
51	24 June	F.Lt. Halliwell	37	KIA	Wellington	DV643	III
52	25 June	Lt. Jones	12 SAAF	KIA	Boston	691 W	III
53	25 June	F.O. McGill	272	KIA	Beaufighter	C	III
54	25 June	F.Lt. Lane-Sansom	272	SAFE	Beaufighter	W	?
55	26 June	Sgt. Thomson	274	KIA	Hurricane		III
56	26 June	S.L. Riley	227	SAFE	Beaufighter	?	III
57	27 June	F.Lt. Walker	112	SAFE	Kittyhawk	AK852	III
58	29 June	Capt. Nestor	376th	SAFE	B-24	?	III

"In the period are reported destroyed on the ground only two AC: 25 June, Wellington Z8572 N (Sgt. Sharpling, 104 Sqn.) by a bombing during take off; a Hurricane in the week 24-31 May at Gambut. "

		GERMAN AC SHOT DOWN BY ANTI-AIRCRAFT				
		PILOT	UNIT	AC	W.Nr.	DAM
1	22 May	Fw. Scharnowski	5./L.G.1	KIA Ju.88	5603	100%
2	24 May	Lt. Hetterich	1./L.G.1	Miss Ju.88	5553	100%
3	25 May	Lt. Riedlberger	I./N.J.G.2	W Ju.88	833	100%
4	26 May	?	III./St.G.3	Ju.87	2059	100%
5	26 May	Lt. Bruchner	III./St.G.3	W Ju.87	?	100%
6	26 May	Lt. Jänicke	1./St.G.3	KIA Ju.87	6333	100%
7	26 May	Uffz. Kochner	7./St.G.3	Miss Ju.87	2076	100%
8	26 May	Fw. Wittland	IV./L.G.1	POW Ju.88	5617	100%
9	27 May	Oblt. Bergfleth C.O.	9./ZG 26	KIA Bf.110	3797	100%
10	27 May	Uffz. Schneider	II./K.G.100	POW He.111	7218	100%
11	27 May	Ofw. Naifl	I./N.J.G.2	KIA Ju.88	360190	100%
12	28 May	?	9./JG 53	SAFE Bf.109	10108	100%
13	28 May	Uffz. Jordan	Wüstennotstaffel	KIA Fi.156	3489	100%
14	31 May	Fw. Kirner	I./St.G.3	W Ju.87		?
15	31 May	Gefr. Mayer	I./St.G.3	W Ju.87		?
16	31 May	Uffz. Krieger	3./St.G.3	W Ju.87	5995	100%
17	31 May	Fw. Kirner	I./KG 54	Miss Ju.88	B3+AH	100%
18	1 June	Lt. Wehmeyer	III./ZG 26	KIA Bf.110	2333	100%
19	1 June	Oblt. Bittner	III./ZG 26	KIA Bf.110	3U + US	100%
20	1 June	Ofw. Polenz	III./ZG 26	KIA Bf.110	4570	100%
21	1 June	Uffz. Holler	II./St.G.3	Miss Ju.87	2365	100%
22	1 June	Fw. Kirner,	I./K.G.54	Miss Ju.88	3678	100%
23	2 June	Hptm. von Kühlwetter	4.(H)/12	KIA Bf.110	4433	100%
24	3 June	?	8./Z.G.26	Bf.110	4652	80%
25	3 June	Hptm. Spangenberg C.O.	2/St.G 3	POW Ju.87	5967	100%
26	4 June	Lt. Hübel	II./St.G 3	Miss Ju.87	2465	100%
27	4 June	Lt. Blume	I./L.G.1	KIA Ju.88	0217?	100%
28	4 June	?	8./J.G.27	Bf.109		100%
29	4 June	?	Wüstennotstaffel	Fi.156		100%
30	6 June	Lt. Hülle	4.(H)/12	W Bf.109	1299	100%
31	6 June	Ofw. Ritter	4.(H)/12	SAFE Bf.109	762	100%
32	6 June	Uffz. Kanoldt	4.(H)/12	Miss Fi.156		100%
33	7 June	?	Wüstennotstaffel	Fi.156	5587	60%

GERMAN AC SHOT DOWN BY ANTI-AIRCRAFT

		PILOT	UNIT		AC	W.Nr.	DAM
34	7 June	Lt. Alisch	I./L.G.1	KIA	Ju.88	140706	100%
35	8 June	?	I./K.G.54		Ju.88	2525	20%
36	8 June	Lt. Heschl	II./K.G.100	Miss	He.111	7093	100%
37	9 June	Ltn. Klager	7./JG 53	SAFE	Bf.109	10179	100%
38	9 June	Fw. Lenninger	II./K.G.100	POW	He.111	7094	100%
39	14 June	Uffz. Gierster	5./JG 27	KIA	Bf.109	8510	100%
40	14 June	Oblt. Brenner	I./L.G.1	Miss	Ju.88	5542	100%
41	14 June	Lt. Müller	I./KG 54	SAFE	Ju.88	140216	100%
42	14 June	Oblt. Ostler	II./St. G. 3	Miss	Ju.87	2482	100%
43	14 June	?	II./St. G. 3		Ju.87		100%
44	15 June	Uffz. Panier	10.(J)/JG 27	POW	Bf.109	10039	100%
45	16 June	Fw. Olsner	I./KG 54	Miss	Ju.88	140001	100%
46	18 June	?	III./Z.G.26		Bf.110	4573	80%
47	20 June	Obltn. Morgenroth	I./St.G.3	KIA	Ju.87	6236	100%
48	20 June	Gefr. Schroer	I./St.G.3	KIA	Ju.87	6075	100%
49	20 June	Uffz. Danninger	I./St.G.3	Miss	Ju.87	6220	100%
50	20 June	Gefr. Mitterdorf	III./St.G.3	?	Ju.87	2043	40%
51	20 June	?			Ju.88		100%
52	20 June	?			Ju.88		100%
53	20 June	?			Ju.88		100%
54	20 June	?	III./Z.G.26		Bf.110	4544	80%
55	20 June	Uffz. Enste	II./K.G.100	Miss	He.111	7223	100%
56	21 June	Lt. Doyè	II./JG 27	SAFE	Bf.109		H Dam.
57	23 June	Lt. Stange	II./K.G.100?	W	Ju.88?		H Dam.
58	24 June	Hptm. Gustavus	II./K.G.100	Miss	He.111	7201	100%
59	24 June	Gefr. Kunke	III./Z.G.26	KIA	Bf.110	4440	100%
60	25 June	?	?		Ju.88		100%
61	26 June	Fw. Rohloff	II./K.G.100	Miss	He.111	7214	100%
62	26 June	Uffz. Mader	I./L.G.1	Miss	Ju.88	4549	100%
63	26 June	Uffz. Hackhausen	I./N.J.G.2	KIA	Ju.88	752	100%
64	28 June	Lt. Rökker	I./N.J.G.2	SAFE	Ju.88	360002	100%

ITALIAN AC SHOT DOWN BY ANTI-AIRCRAFT

		PILOT	UNIT		AC	SERIAL NO.	DAM
1	26 May	Serg.Magg. Antonicelli	8°	SAFE	C.200	M.M.5271	H Dam.
2	27 May	Serg.Magg. Poggi	13°	SAFE	C.200	M.M.5253	H Dam.
3	27 May	Cap. Cecchet	8°	SAFE	C.200	MM8337	DES
4	27 May	Cap. Tovazzi	154ª Sq (3° Gr.)	KIA	CR.42		DES
5	29 May		158° Gr.	SAFE	CR.42		H Dam.
6	30 May	Serg.Magg. Allevot	78ª Sq., 13° Gr.	KIA	C.200	M.M.8300	DES
7	1 June	Serg. Borgis	78ª Sq.	POW	C.200		DES
8	4 June	Cap.Antonelli Eugenio C.O.	391ª Sq.	KIA	CR.42	M.M.8528	DES
9	6 June	S.Ten. Ingino	387ª Sq	KIA	CR.42	M.M.8467	DES
10	6 June	Serg. Magg. Righetti	390ª Sq.	POW	CR.42	M.M.8845	DES
11	6 June	Serg.Magg. Fiascaris	390ª Sq.	POW	CR.42	M.M.8863	DES
12	6 June	Cap. Viglione	96ª Sq	POW	C.202	M.M.7822	DES
13	8 June	Cap. Marcovich	8°	POW	C.200	M.M.6700	DES
14	12 June	Serg. Gregorio Taverna	90ª Sq.	KIA	C.202	M.M.7937	DES
15	14 June	M.llo Sozzi	77ª Sq	POW	C.200	M.M.5236	DES
16	14 June	Serg. Giannotti	82ª Sq	KIA	C.200	M.M.5346	DES
17	14 June	S.Ten. Guillet	390ª Sq	KIA	CR.42		DES
18	14 June	Serg. Panizzi	388ª Sq	KIA	CR.42		DES
19	14 June	Serg. Giannotti	82ª Sq.	KIA	C.200	M.M.5346	DES
20	15 June	Cap. D'Agostini C.O.	93ª Sq	KIA	C.200	M.M.5111	DES
21	20 June	Serg. Casadio	94ª Sq.	KIA	C.200	M.M.6692	DES
22	26 June		35° St.		Cant.Z.1007bis		H Dam.

Appendix 6
MACCHI C.202S SERIAL NUMBERS (22 MAY - 30 JUNE)

SERIAL NO.	SQUADR.		DAMAGE	NOTES
M.M. 7709	80			
M.M. 7726	72		DES	26-27/5 BOMBING
M.M. 7732	71		DES	13/6 AIR COMBAT
M.M. 7735	72		DES	30/5 AIR COMBAT
M.M. 7740	80			
M.M. 7751	80		DES	13/6 AIR COMBAT
M.M. 7752	80		H.DAM	27/6? AIR COMBAT
M.M. 7754	80			
M.M. 7761	71	97	S.DAM	26/6 BOMBING
M.M. 7762	88	91		
M.M. 7764	79	73		
M.M. 7766	81			
M.M. 7767	88	91		
M.M. 7772	81		H.DAM	NIGHT 26-27/5 BOMBING
M.M. 7775	72			
M.M. 7776	81			to unit beginning of June
M.M. 7778	79			
M.M. 7779	72			
M.M. 7781	79			
M.M. 7782	88			
M.M. 7783	88		DES	26-27/5 BOMBING
M.M. 7785	80	90		
M.M. 7786	71	97		
M.M. 7787	80			
M.M. 7789	79	84		
M.M. 7790	91		H.DAM	26/5 COLLISION ON GROUND
M.M. 7792	72		DES	6/6 FLYING ACC.
M.M. 7794	91		S.DAM	29/5 BOMBING
M.M. 7795	80	90		
M.M. 7796	91		DES	29/5 BOMBING
M.M. 7797	84			

SERIAL NO.	SQUADR.	DAMAGE	NOTES
M.M. 7798	90		
M.M. 7799	91	S.DAM	29/5 BOMBING
M.M. 7801	90		
M.M. 7802	90	S.DAM	29/5 ACC
M.M. 7805	84		
M.M. 7806	90	S.DAM	4/6 BOMBING
M.M. 7807	97		
M.M. 7808	91	S.DAM	28/5 BOMBING
M.M. 7810	90	DES	28/5 BOMBING
M.M. 7812	84		
M.M. 7814	84	?	13/6 ACCIDENT DURING LADING
M.M. 7815	84		
M.M. 7816	73		
M.M. 7817	96		
M.M. 7819	97		
M.M. 7820	97		
M.M. 7821	96		
M.M. 7822	96	DES	6/6 AA
M.M. 7823	73	H.DAM	26/6 FLYING ACC.
M.M. 7824	73	DES	29/5 AIR COMBAT
M.M. 7827	73		
M.M. 7828	97		
M.M. 7829	97		
M.M. 7831	73	DES	9/6 AIR COMBAT
M.M. 7859	71	DES	13/6 AIR COMBAT
M.M. 7863	71	H.DAM	27/5 AIR COMBAT
M.M. 7864	88		
M.M. 7867	72		
M.M. 7870	71		
M.M. 7872	71		
M.M. 7873	81	H.DAM	26-27/5 BOMBING
M.M. 7878	79 73		
M.M. 7881	81	DES	30/5 AIR COMBAT

SERIAL NO.	SQUADR.		DAMAGE	NOTES
M.M. 7882	72			
M.M. 7883	72	84		
M.M. 7884	79			
M.M. 7886	88			
M.M. 7887	72			
M.M. 7887	81			
M.M. 7888	71		DES	24-25/5 BOMBING
M.M. 7889	79			
M.M. 7890	81			to unit end of May
M.M. 7892	80		S.DAM	27/5(?) AIR COMBAT
M.M. 7893	88			
M.M. 7896	79	84		
M.M. 7898	81			
M.M. 7900	81	90		
M.M. 7901	84			
M.M. 7902	91		S.DAM	28/5 BOMBING
M.M. 7903	88	91		
M.M. 7904	88		DES	25-26/5 BOMBING
M.M. 7905	79	84		
M.M. 7906	90			
M.M. 7907	91		S.DAM	29/5 BOMBING
M.M. 7908	73			
M.M. 7910	91		S.DAM	28/5 BOMBING
M.M. 7911	97		DES	24-25/5 BOMBING
M.M. 7912	96			
M.M. 7913	97			
M.M. 7914	73		H.DAM	26/6 BOMBING
M.M. 7916	97			
M.M. 7917	84			
M.M. 7919	84			
M.M. 7920	73		DES	26/6 BOMBING
M.M. 7921	90			
M.M. 7922	96			

SERIAL NO.	SQUADR.		DAMAGE	NOTES
M.M. 7924	96			
M.M. 7925	73			
M.M. 7926	73			
M.M. 7927	96			
M.M. 7928	84			
M.M. 7929	96			
M.M. 7930	90		S.DAM	28/5 ACC
M.M. 7932	97			
M.M. 7933	84			
M.M. 7934	91		S.DAM	28/5 BOMBING
M.M. 7935	91			
M.M. 7936	73		H.DAM	26/6 BOMBING
M.M. 7937	84	90	DES	12/6 AA
M.M. 7938	97			
M.M. 7939	97			
M.M. 7940	96			

Data of 96ª and 88ª Sq. regarding 30 June are missing. In June and July all AC of 1° St. were passad to 4° St. In the period only two replacements arrived. DES - destroyed, H.DAM – heavily damaged, S.DAM – slightly damaged

Appendix 7
INVESTIGATION OF "FIGHTER SQUADRON RESULT IN THE WESTERN DESERT AS AT 29TH JULY, 1942"

Investigation carried out by Squadron Leader HANBURY, D.F.C., for A.H.Q., W.D., as to the reasons for unsatisfactory fighter results at that time revealed the following points:—

MAIN REASONS

1. The main reasons for the bad standard then prevailing were summarised as follows:—

   (a) Insufficient training after joining the squadron.

   (b) Not enough interest is taken by pilots in air firing. They think that the all-important thing is to be able to fly, and they treat firing as a secondary matter. The most experienced pilots are much to blame for letting this spirit creep in, but squadron commanders are taking steps to right the matter.

   (c) A great contributory cause is that many new squadrons, especially the Kittyhawk squadrons, have so many new pilots that only about 1 in 10 knows what he is talking about, and wrong ideas on shooting are thus much more likely to get around unchecked.

   (d) The actual reasons for missing enemy aircraft in combat appear to be many, but the most numerous are as follows:—

   (i) Improper knowledge of deflection shooting.

   (ii) Improper knowledge of the principle of following through.

   (iii) Firing at too great a range.

   (iv) Taking absurd "squirts" at impossible angles instead of waiting for a decent opportunity.

   (v) Loss of head due to excitement.

SUGGESTED REMEDIES

2. The suggested remedies for the causes listed above are as follows:—

   (a) *Training Before Joining Squadron:* This does not concern this investigation.

   (b) *Insufficient Training After Joining Squadron:* Every wing and squadron commander with whom I have discussed this matter has agreed that pilots must have continuous practice at air firing if they are to maintain a high standard, and this applies to experienced pilots as well. Squadrons should be released for at least one day every fortnight for air firing practice alone, if possible once a week.

   The practice should be carried out as follows:—

   (i) One experienced pilot should take up three or four inexperienced pilots at a time for shadow firing and should fly along to one side and observe the results. If any pilot is shooting badly he should be given some tips by the instructor after landing and then be sent up again and again until he has mastered the knack of deflection shooting.

(ii) After shadow firing pilots should carry out dummy attacks from all quarters on the leader, who should watch them closely and tell them where their attacks go wrong.

(iii) Air to ground for ground strafing practice should be carried out against an artificial target, and all squadrons, especially those who do a lot of strafing, are very keen to have a butt and target erected near their aerodromes where they can take a short burst whenever the opportunity arises after a show.

(iv) It is not considered safe or practical in this area to indulge in shadow firing on return from a show as 109's have frequently followed us right back and if the pilots have their eyes glued on a shadow they will in all probability be " jumped."

3. Squadron commanders have agreed to appoint a member of the squadron as gunnery officer. He can be a flight commander, an experienced pilot, or even the C.O. himself, and his job will be to talk to the pilots, especially the inexperienced ones, at least once a week on deflection shooting and air fighting in general. He will promote discussions amongst the pilots and discuss the results of the previous week's combats. To this end it would help if we could obtain some model aircraft on sticks, such as were supplied to Fighter Command in England. Other suggestions include:—

(a) Rosters which show what a 109 looks like at a given range and angle, which should be framed to prevent tearing and hung up in the mess.

(b) Slogans printed and framed as above, such as, " DOUBLE YOUR DEFLECTION AND FOLLOW THROUGH," " ALWAYS SHOOT TO KILL." etc.

(c) A scheme tried out by Wing Commander Fenton, which would be most effective. This consists of a Me 109 raised off the ground with barrels, and distances marked off in circles round it. The pilot walks round with a reflector sight at these set distances and should get a good idea of what the enemy aircraft should look like in the air.

(d) As there is no doubt a shortage of crashed 109's in this area, would it be possible to mount one on an old lorry and have it sent round to each wing from time to time ?

STATISTICS

4. Statistics concerning the combat results of pilots in the Group when added up give an average of 7.5 combats for every enemy aircraft destroyed. " Probables " and " Damaged " have not been included. It will be interesting to take another census, in say, 2 or 3 months' time and see how much this campaign on shooting has raised it. It will be worth while if it is raised by only 5%.

GROUND STRAFING

5. Ground strafing is likewise most likely to improve by practice, and is a much simpler question altogether. The two outstanding faults with it at the moment, besides the inability to shoot straight, are:—

(a) Pilots try to shoot at several targets at once instead of one at a time.

(b) Not enough organisation amongst themselves before a show, which often results in several pilots firing at the same target.

Appendix 8
NAVAL WARFARE AND INTELLIGENCE ALONG THE NORTH AFRICAN COASTS, JANUARY – JUNE 1942

The Scenario

After the awful time between 9 November and 18 December 1941, when thirty-five Italian and German freighters sailed for Libya and only seventeen arrived, the naval war in the Mediterranean suddenly changed on 19 December. The losses suffered that day by Force K off Tripoli when the cruiser *Neptune* and the destroyer *Kandahar* foundered on a minefield laid in May and June 1941 by the cruisers and destroyers of the VII and IV Divisione [1], the serious damages suffered by the battleships *Queen Elizabeth* and *Valiant* at Alexandria, mined by the human torpedoes of the X Flottiglia MAS [2] and the safe arrival, after the brief First Sirte Action [3], of the four very important freighters of the "Convoglio L"escorted by the Italian navy's battleforce, dramatically altered the naval balance. The Mediterranean Fleet lost its fleet in being role against the Axis traffic in Eastern Mediterranean and the remaining surface strike force in Malta was forced to follow a more prudent strategy and did not molest the sea lanes between Europe and North Africa until December 1942.

The loss of Italian and German supplies bound for Libya in November 1941 had been, at 62.33 percent, the most severe in the entire North African campaign, but hard numbers dictated a different picture than the one later asserted by scholars basing their analysis upon wartime propaganda. Materiel shipped totalled 79,208 tons of which 29,843 arrived [4]. The losses of fuel (29,317 tons) had been balanced with the stocks available in Africa, which were sufficient, according to a Comando Supremo estimation of 1 November 1941, to supply the armed services and colony until January 1942. The other materiel lost, mainly food (16,263 tons), had been offset by the purchase of 20,000 tons of grain in French North Africa; fewer than three hundred trucks were lost at sea that month and these were replaced by hundreds of vehicles bought in Tunisia with French money that Vichy controlled banks were forced to loan. Italian and German weapons lost in ships sunk between 1 August 1941 and 18 January 1942 totalled twenty-five 20/65 AA guns, sixty-seven antitank guns, and twelve field guns, all smaller than 3.9 in. [5]. In fact what had been compromised during the November – December 1941 traffic crisis was the reconstruction of the Italian Infantry Division Sabratha, scheduled to be stationed in Tripolitania as a part of a force to being gathered invade Tunisia if necessary. In the event, the division was finally completed in the spring of 1942 in time to join Rommel's May 1942 offensive.

The build-up for the Italo-German attack against Tobruk and Egypt, anticipated by a mere forty-eight hours by the British and Imperial Crusader offensive, had actually been completed in September 1941 with the arrival in Libya of the motorized division Trieste; the subsequent delay had been imposed only by the late completion in November of the "Strada dell'Asse", a road constructed in the desert to allow motor traffic to bypass Tobruk beyond the range of British heavy artillery in that besieged town thus permitting the supply of forces larger than a single, small Corps along the Egyptian frontier.

Instead of the 50,000 tons of materiel sunk in November, what had actually been of major strategic relevance, despite their tiny amount, was the timely arrival of 217 tons of fuel and 6 tons of munitions, ferried to Bardia between 26 November and 2 December 1941 by the Regia Marina

Doria and Garibaldi seen from Abruzzi, during a convoy escort, spring 1942 (Cernuschi)

submarines *Cagni* and *Saint Bon* [6]. This was two days of fighting supplies for the starved 15th and 21st Panzer and the 90th Motorized divisions. This vital injection allowed these mobile divisions, cut off from the army since 25 November, to break their encirclement and counterattack joining again the Axis main body and reimposing, on 1 December, the siege of Tobruk. This critical delivery prevented the end, within that month or, at most, January 1942, of the North African war, which would have followed had these mobile divisions been forced to surrender.

On December 1941 the supply tonnage numbers returned to their normal balance: 47,680 tons shipped and 39,092 tons arrived (losses - 18 percent). Of personnel 1,748 men sailed and 1,074 landed in Libya (38.6 percent losses). On 1 January a golden period for Axis shipping commenced which lasted until 30 June 1942: 469,508 tons sent to North Africa of which 441,878 landed safely (5.9 percent losses compared to 10 percent scheduled). Of personnel 10,621 soldiers travelled by sea to Africa and 9,009 (84.8 percent) disembarked on the moles of Tripoli and Benghazi [7].

The Naval Sea Denial Effort

British sea denial efforts against Axis traffic, which originated mainly from Malta, had little impact. The cruisers and destroyers based in Grand Harbour until 8 April 1942, searched vainly for convoys sinking only the *Grongo*, 316 GRT, and the *Aosta*, 494 GRT, two motor fishing vessels on mail duty between Pantelleria and Lampedusa, on the night of 7/8 February 1942. After surface forces evacuated Malta the interception of convoys become the task of warships based at Alexandria. Earlier efforts of this sort had caused the loss of the battleship *Barham* and the cruisers *Galatea* and *Naiad*, all sunk by German submarines concentrated in the Eastern Mediterranean.

The sinking of *Naiad*, flagship of Rear Admiral Philip Vian, had been caused by a false air report of a crippled Italian cruiser. A similar and even more dramatic episode occurred on the afternoon of 10 May 1942. Courtesy of an ULTRA dispatch generated by the centralized decryption or-

Italian cargo head to head to Libya, spring 1942 (Cernuschi)

ganization based at Bletchley Park in Britain, the Royal Navy was aware that a convoy would sail from Italy to Benghazi. The origin of the information was, as usual, radio traffic generated by the German Air Force and enciphered by the supposedly unbreakable Enigma machine. The British plan was for the destroyers *Jervis*, *Jackal*, *Kipling* and *Lively* to attack the convoy off Benghazi. The small flotilla accordingly departed Alexandria at 2000 proceeding at high speed across the Eastern Mediterranean to make a predawn interception.

The convoy consisted of the steamer *Bolsena* escorted by the destroyer *Saetta*. It sailed from Taranto at 2200 on 9 May. The next day, at 0855, Italian navy codebreakers were able to read, within minutes, a RAF reconnaissance radio message which revealed that the convoy had been sighted [8]. At 1100 the Air Force informed Supermarina, the Italian Navy central command, that the minelayer *Welshman* had sortied from Malta. In the meanwhle a report from a Regia Marina floatplane flying unnoticed by the Britsh as it remained low on the horizon and below radar coverage, radioed that at 0900 that four enemy destroyers were sailing west at high speed south of Crete. The same aircraft provided updates at noon and 1300.

Supermarina's interpretation of the data was that a small British cruiser would join the destroyers to attack the convoy and therefore it immediately ordered the light cruiser *Montecuccoli* and destroyers *Camicia Nera* and *Aviere* to sail from Messina while the *Bolsena* and her escort continued on course until 1300 to set the trap. Because of recognized inferiority of Italian surfaces forces in night combat, a consequence of their lack of radar, the plan was to intercept one or both the enemy forces before dark.

In the early afternoon the Air Force advised that the *Welshman* was past Cape Bon while the British destroyers were running south; Supermarina then ordered the *Saetta* convoy to Augusta and recalled the *Montecuccoli* group as the enemy flotilla would be beyond its range. Taking care of the British force was a job for the Luftwaffe in Crete and the Regia Aeonautica bombers based in Africa.

German aircraft, homed in by Italian floatplanes which were broadcasting sightings the British were able to read only four hours later, sighted the four destroyers at about 1400. At 1634 eight

Ju.88s of I./LG 1 struck, each armed with two 250 kg bombs. The engagement lasted a quarter hour after which the Germans returned, appreciating correctly that all their bombs had missed. A few minutes later, a hundred miles northeast of Tobruk, six Cant Z 1007 bis bombers of the 35° Stormo B.T. from Barce attacked from out of the sun, benefiting from the fact that the British formation was scattered as a result of the just concluded attack. They dropped their bombs unseen from high altitude. One stick of twelve 100 kg bombs straddled *Lively*. She took a direct hit on "B" gun deck just abaft the gun that exploded at a lower deck level and several near misses occured abreast the "A" mounting. The vessel immediately settled by the bow listing heavily to starboard. A heavy explosion occured forward and the ship sank stern first within three and a half minutes. Seventy-seven of the ship's company were killed or missing They never knew what hit them.

The RAF escort, formed by a pair of just arrived *Beaufighters*, could not reach the three-engined Italian aircraft at 8,000 meters, moreover, with their bombs away and with tanks half empty [9]. At 1709 another German strike by nine *Ju.88* dive bombers combined with four high level *He.111s* of II./LG 1 arrived overhead. The ordeal of the destroyers lasted until 1733, but the three ships came through unscathed. The air escort, now four Beaufighters, continued to be ineffective. At dusk I./LG 1 attacked again with ten *Ju.88s*. This time the dives were held until 500 meters from the target and *Kipling* sustained one direct hit in the aft engine room. She flooded immediately and within ten minutes the ship sank by the stern. Another bomb penetrated *Jackal*, despite the 30 knots she was making during the attack, passing through the upper deck over the aft boiler room before exploding beneath the keel. She lost all steam and electrical power. Nearly nine hours later *Jervis* scuttled *Jackal* with a torpedo before returning to Alexandria crowded by the 630 survivors of the unfortunate flotilla.

To cover their codebreakers's abilities Supermarina leaked to the newspapers fake news that the British destroyers were carrying urgent supplies to Malta while the Germans claimed, as usual, all the successes to themselves. This catastrophe ended the Royal Navy's efforts to contest Axis traffic with surface warships, at least for the rest of the year.

Under the Sea ...

The accomplishments of British submarines against Axis traffic were likewise mediocre. Between January and June 1942 only four freighters bound to Libya (*Victoria* 13.098 GWT, *Marin Sanudo* 5.081 GWT, *Capo Arma* 3.172 GWT and the MFV *Maria Immacolata* 248 GWT) were sunk by British boats out of twenty-eight attacks made. Seven other freighters were sunk returning empty, except for cargos of Allied prisoners of war, with many human losses, and five along the coastal route to the frontline. The price paid was heavy: eleven British and Allied boats were sunk including four bombed at Malta, and fifteen damaged.

Interdiction of Axis coastal routes along Libya by Royal Navy and the RAF was ineffective. The only loss recorded by Italian and Germans shipping in January 1942 was an empty German landing barge (*PiLb* 1) sunk at Sollum on the 8th by the gunboat *Aphis* which was shelling that besieged town. There were no losses in February. Between March and June the losses, by all causes, mostly caused by the weather or stranding, totalled 2,509 tons of materiel, that is, 2.3 percent of the cargo sent to the front line in a total of 137 small vessels in ninety-six voyages escorted by Italian gunboats and German minesweepers of the "R" type (German fast coastal forces arrived in North

Africa in May 1942). In particular the many night raids by RAF bombers from Malta and Egypt against Libyan harbors proved ineffective despite the average loss rate of 1.5 – 2 percent of aircraft shot down by the Axis flak and the Regia Aeronautica's *Fiat CR.42* night fighters directed by search lights.

..and Over the Waves

The Italian Navy recorded thirty-six attacks against Axis traffic to Libya between January and June 1942 by aircraft based at Malta or Cyrenaica. These strikes resulted in one steamer, *Perla*, (5,741 GRT), sunk by four Albacores torpedo bombers on 7 January while she was returning to Italy. Three ships were damaged between 31 May and 21 June 1942 while in passage to Libya: the Italian motor ships *Gino Allegri*, 6,836 GRT, and *Reginaldo Giuliani* 6,837, and the German steamer *Reichenfels*, 7,744 GRT. The price paid by the attack aircrafts from Malta during this same time was heavy with forty-five aircraft lost to enemy action, twelve to accidents and an additional twenty gravely damaged due to action or accident.

What the Numbers Say

If history were a mere exercise in logistics, one could just compare the total supplies landed in North Africa by Axis forces in 1941 and 1942 (2,061,112 tons shipped, 1,727,136 tons, or 83.8 percent, arrived to Allied traffic to Suez during the same period (8,262,841 tons sent and 7,027,763 tons arrived) [10]. With Axis arrivals a mere quarter of Allied deliveries it would seem that the Desert War should have been no contest.
However, the face of battle contains a more profound truth than logistics as it involves categories beyond bookkeeping like will, psychology, cultural background and roots of peoples and, above all, their histories. Thus, the comparison of deliveries to the front and the fact that the campaign lasted nearly three years allows some nonconventional conclusions to be drawn. The first is the decline of Allied shipments to Egypt. Once we consider that since the end of the war in the Red Sea, on 10 June 1941, the United States sent never less than 1 million of tons of materiel to the Red Sea/Indian Ocean area as a regular component of its aid it is clear that the British-only war, unassisted by outside powers, in the Middle East was over after the failure of the Brevity and Battleaxe offensives of May – June 1941 being replaced, since late spring 1941, by an allied effort with a political price His Majesty's Government hoped to pay, as in the Great War, with lip service only. The end of the British Imperial Preference protetionist tariff imposed worldwide on 1931, was, moreover, a common goal of both the United States and Italy before and during the Second World War cemented by the two countries' complementary economic interests, which were opposed to British interests. The Italian economical leadership openly disregarded Il Duce's millennia programs for fascism after a famous speech made by Vittorio Cini, the Italian electrical industry baron, in the Senate in 1934, which rejected any dream of future changes in Italy's traditional, capitalistic and liberal framework.
Until the blind euphoria caused by victories in Russia between the summer of 1941 and the summer of 1942, the same German establishment's long term programs were for a future economic settlement with the United States based on a negotiated peace because only Washington could supply the capital and the technologies Germany needed for its development. [11].

Regia Marina HQ at Benghazi (Cernuschi)

However, in the case of Germany any bargain became impossible due to Hitler's visions, battlefield successes and crimes, imposing a policy based on the Reich's invasion, defeat and disarmament.

In such a perspective Italy had two options correctly appreciated by ber economical and naval leadership since 1934 and by the Comando Supremo's commander, Marshal Ugo Cavallero, since May 1941. The first was to win the war by the seizure of Malta and Suez, the second was to endure until shipping losses had bled Britain white. This would result in the passing of the leadership of the English speaking peoples from London to the more reasonable Washington. A compromise peace would then preserve Italy's economic progress and the economy's future prospects in a general free market of capital and trade like the one of the 1920s and provide relief from Britain's more recent protectionism over the sterling area of the British Empire. In such a scenario total German victory over the Soviet Union was unwanted, being that Moscow was one of the decisive counter balances needed to avoid German domination of the continent.

The second lesson concerns the failure of the tonnage war fought by the British in the Mediterranean between 1940 and 1943. The total of the materiel landed in North Africa between 1941 and 1942 was never affected by a lack of merchant vessels and provided the approximately 65.000 monthly tons of supplies the armed forces and colony needed, saturating in the process the capacity of the harbours [12]. Such a monthly level of delivery required only 200,000-250,000 GRT of shipping. Italy begun that war with 2,101,492 GRT of vessels bigger than 500 tons in the Mediterranean supplemented by an additional 203,512 GRT of German shipping.

Accounting for losses, new constructions, seizures, and merchant vessels entering the Mediterranean from the Black Sea or the Atlantic Ocean this grand total of 2.3 million GRT dropped to 2.17 million GRT on 31 December 1940, 1.82 million GRT on 31 December 1941 and 1.82 on 31 December 1942. After seizing French merchant vessels in France and Tunisia in November 1942 after the Anglo-Americans attacked North Africa the Axis shipping situation improved and on 8 September 1943, the day of the declaration of the Italian armistice, the total Axis tonnage in the Mediterranean was about 1.9 million GRT, plus an 100,000 GRT in the Black Sea. By April 1943 the British were aware that Axis tonnage would last at least until autumn 1944, notwithstanding the fantastic claims of enemy shipping losses they were broadcasting. In fact, even by the end of the war there was no shortage of shipping to service in the last surviving Axis sea lanes through the Tyrrhenian Sea and Upper Adriatic. The third and last appreciation regards the growing importance of Axis air transportation to North Africa between 1940 and 1942. Between June 1940 and January 1941 the few Italian aircraft available (about 200, almost all from the civilian airilines grouped in the SAS, Servizi Aerei Speciali and an half of them floatplanes or flying boats) transferred from Italy to Libya and vice versa, 11,600 people, civilians included, and 1,140 tons of mail and materiel. From February to December 1941 this traffic increased to 17,658 people and 2,177 tons from Italy to Libya and 23,030 people and 1,162 tons from Libya to Italy. The Germans were almost absent from this traffic except for some VIP missions.

In 1942 the Italian air transports, greatly reinforced after the conversion of some bomber groups to this new activity, totalled 142,786 soldiers, 43,969 civilians and about 12,000 tons of materiel. Between 10 February 1942 to 30 June 1942 German transports operating from Crete flew 28,200 soldiers and 4.400 tons of fuel and materiel, mainly munitions, to Africa and ferried back 10,700 wounded. Between 1 July 1942 and 19 November 1942, German to-

Torpedo-boat Calliope, in convoy-escort service (Cernuschi)

tals were 42,000 soldiers and 15,000 tons returning to Europe 9,000 wounded [13].
Thus, in 1943, in Tunisia, materiel that arrived from the air could effectively balance losses suffered on the sea lanes to Tunisia, with an average of 6-7,000 tons monthly delivered monthly.

Coastal Warfare

Returning, after this orgy of data, to the day-by-day chronicle of the war and intelligence at sea during the time covered by this book we must remember that in November 1941, Rommel's original plan to seize Tobruk by a swift *coup de main* included a diversionary double naval action: a brief shore bombardment of the fortress by the heavy cruisers of the III Divisione and a landing by the marines of the 3° Battaglione of the San Marco Regiment between Tobruk and Ain el Gazala from German navy F lighters.

The plan was proposed again in early May 1942. The naval shelling [14] was anyway cancelled soon as the Regia Marina was, since late-April 1942, in a deep oil crisis with only 14,000 tons of reserves scattered among more than one hundred depots and in the bunkers of its ships The Germans promised a supply, but only 5,000 tons arrived on May of such a low quality it had to be passed to civilian uses.

The landing remained and on 23 May 1942 the marines boarded three German F-lighters. The landing force also included four German landing barges towing four pontoons carrying three former British Crusader tanks and one Landwasserschlepper (LWS), a 13 ton amphibian tractor carring twenty German Brandemburger commandos, some of them English speaking. The plan, named Operazione Venezia, was intended to cause confusion behind the enemy lines and it was hoped to recover the force through the advance of the Axis mobile Corps. Given the importance Rommel put on this initiative Supermarina promised two Italian submarines to support and pilot the party. On 27 May, however, less than three days from the final "Go" delayed two days before for weather reasons, there was an engagement, at 0130 in the Gulf of Bomba between a German landing craft, *F 149*, and the British MTBs, *309* and *312*. In spite of the respective claims no damage was suffered on either side. The Royal Navy's fast coastal forces had been previously alerted by an ULTRA decrypt of the usual German Air Force Enigma about the planned landing and were patrolling accordingly. The British too, however, also talked too much over the airwaves and on 29 May, after 30 hours and 20 minutes of codebreaking effort, the Reparto Informazioni of the SIS, the Italian Navy Intelligence, read a Royal Navy wireless message crypted in the Naval Cypher No 4 intercepted on 28 May at 1015 which disclosed that the enemy was aware of the planned landing. The operation was immediately cancelled. A later, generic Italian Navy warning about the debatable security of the German codes (the Regia Marina guarded, in fact, its abilty to read the British codes and cyphers) was, as usual, dismissed as nonsense by the Mediterranean command of Field Marshal Albert Kesselring.

On 21 June 1942, at dawn, the German MTBs *S 34, 54, 55, 56, 58* and *59* attacked the small British vessels which were leaving the collapsing fortress of Tobruk. The drifter *Highland Queen*, the auxiliary MFVs *Eskimo Nell*, *Kheir-el-Dine*, *HDML 1069*, the whaler *Parktown* and the *LCT*-119 were sunk. *HDML 1039* and the *LCT-150* were seized.

On 27 June 1942, at h 08.50, the Regia Marina codebreakers were able to read, within a few minutes, the order issued by the Mediterranean Fleet to the surface vessels to leave the Mediterranean retreating through the Channel of Suez except for two cruisers at Haifa and a flotilla of Hunt destoryers. The game seemed over.

NOTES

[1] The cruisers *Aurora* and *Penelope* were damaged as well requiring, respectively thirteen and two weeks respectively to return to action.

[2] The destroyer *Jervis* wad damaged too needing one month of repairs while the tanker *Sagona* was out of service for the remainder of the war.

[3] The destroyers *Kipling* and *Napier* recorded splinter damage caused by the cruiser *Gorizia* and the destroyer *Maestrale*.

[4] The numbers for personnel are, on November 1941, 4,872 sent and 4,628 arrived.

[5] Lucio Ceva, *La condotta italiana della guerra, Cavallero e il Comando Supremo 1941/1942.* (Milan: Feltrinelli, 1975), 199.

[6] The German and Italian Air Forces, like the RAF at Tobruk during the siege, had been unable, due to a lack of airstrips outside the range of British artillery, to supply the Afrika Korps.

[7] The French delivered between January and April 1942 an additional 3,000 tons of supplies and ninety-two trucks through Tunisia. This Vichy courtesy (Code named "Trasporti Gamma" or "Trasporti Delta" according to the recipient if German or Italian) was in any case hampered by the lack of a railroad between the Tunisian frontier and Tripoli. The trucks burned too much fuel for the value of the cargos and this route was later abandoned confirming the solution of the impossible Libyan logistic situation, constrained from the beginning of 1940 by too few and poorly equipped harbors of that territory, could not be balanced by the availability of Tunisia ports.

[8] Fondo Supermarina, Azioni Navali, Rapporto 11 maggio 1942, Archivio dell'Ufficio Storico della Marina Militare, Rome

[9] Giancarlo Garello, "Il Cant Z. 1007 Alcione", Storia Militare May 1995 , and Posta, Storia Militare, Sept. 1995, 58.

[10] Rivista Marittima, "Marine mercantili, Egitto," October 1952, 182.

[11] Raffaele D'Agata, *Da Monaco a Bretton Woods* (Milan: Franco Angeli, 1989); Raffaele D'Agata, *La nemesi dei prestadenaro*, ed. Rubbettino, Catanzaro, 2001; Paolo Fonzi, *La moneta del grande spazio*, (Milan: Unicopli, 2011.

[12] Rommel'sudden request, on September 1942, for 180,000 tons of supplies a month was only a rough attempt to pass the blame for the recent failure in the sands of Alam el Halfa of his impossible North African campaign. It was a smoke screen that worked well during the suceeding years becoming a sort of mantra in popular history.

[13] Fritz Morzik, *Die deutschen Transportflieger in Zweiten Weltkrieg. Die Geschichte des FuBvolkes del Luft* (Frankfurt, 1966)

[14] The attack scheduled for May 1942 was to be carried out by the cruisers *Gorizia* and *Trento* sailing from Messina escorted by three destroyers of the Navigatori-class and two Spica-class torpedo boats, coming from Benghazi, minesweeping ahead. A contemporary raid by three light cruisers of the VIII Divisione and three destroyers would have to search for enemy coastal convoys between Tobruk and Alexandria going later to Suda and Leros. In any

case, the Regia Marina staff had concluded as early as 1937 that shore bombardments had, perhaps psychological effects, but little military utility. They paid much more interest in the raid. Fondo Supermarina, Azioni Navali, Rapporto 14 maggio 1942, Riferimento N. ro 224/42 del 12 maggio 1942, Archivio dell'Ufficio Storico della Marina Militare, Rome.

GLOSSARY

RAF - Royal Air Force
RAAF - Royal Australian Air Force
SAAF - South African Air Force
Luftwaffe - German Air Force
RA - Regia Aeronautica
OBS - Oberbefehlshaber Süd, High Command South

Aircraft damage categories
Cat.I - slightly damaged, repairable in the unit's workshop
Cat.II - heavily damaged, repairable by maintanance unit
Cat.III - written off
Luftwaffe reported damage in percentage of the aircraft loss, RA reported damage in the same way of Commonwealth.

Commonwealth ranks
W.C. - Wing Commander
S.L. - Squadron Leader
F.Lt. - Flight Lieutenant
Lt. - Lieutenant
2/Lt.- Second Lieutenant
F.O. - Flying Officer
P.O. - Pilot Officer
F.Sgt. - Flight Sergeant
Sgt.- Sergeant
W.O. - Warrant officer

Lufwaffe ranks
Oberstleutnant
Maj. - Major
Haupt. - Hauptmann
Lt. - Leutnant
Oblt. - Obleutnant
Stabsfeldwebel
Ofw. - Oberfeldwebel
Fw. - Feldwebel

Regia Aeronautica ranks
Gen.B.A. – Generale di Brigata Aerea
Col.- Colonnello
T.Col. - Tenente Colonnello
Magg. - Maggiore
Cap. - Capitano
Ten. - Tenente
S.Ten. - Sottotenente
M.llo - Maresciallo
Serg.Magg. - Sergente Maggiore
Serg. - Sergente

UNITS AND FORMATIONS
COMMONWEALTH
Squadron – base unit, with an operational establishment of 16 AC (fighters or bombers), up to 20 AC in command.
Wing – unit composed of several Squadrons
Group – unit composed of several Wings
Flight- formation composed by 4 AC.

LUFTWAFFE
Kette - formation composed by 2 AC.
Schwarm - formation composed by 4 AC.
Staffel - base unit, but usually part of a Gruppe, usually had an operational establishment of 12 planes
Gruppe - usually 3 Staffeln
Geschwader - usually 3 Gruppen
JG - Jagdgeschwader - fighter Geschwader
KG - Kriegsgeschwader high level bomber Geschwader
Stuka - Sturzkampfflugzeug - dive bomber
St.G - Stuka Geschwader
LG - Lehrgeschwader - multi-purpose geschwader operating fighters, bombers and dive-bombers.

REGIA AERONAUTICA
Sq. - Squadriglia - base unit , but usually part of a Gruppo. A fighter Squadriglia usually had an operational establishment of 12 planes (bombers squadriglia 5 planes).
Gr. - Gruppo - usually composed of three Squadriglie.

St. - Stormo - usually composed of two Gruppi.
Pattuglia - formation composed by 3 or 4 AC.
Coppia - formation composed by 2 AC.

OTHERS
Jabo - Jagdbomber - fighter-bomber
Hurribomber - Hurricane armed with bombs
Kittybomber - Kittyhawk armed with bombs
Freie Jagd / caccia libera- the terms were used by Luftwaffe and R.A. to indicate a fighter mission with the only scope to gain air superiority. In comparison commowealth used the term fighter sweep or offensive sweep.
L.G. - Landing ground - identified numerically
A.L.G. - Advanced landing ground, sometimes not attended
ORB - Operation Record Book- Commonwealth's units war diary. Composed by Form M.540 and Form M.541. The ORBs were completed by the appendixes that usually were the mission's reports

SOURCES

Commonwealth

1 SAAF Sqn., M.540, CFR
2 SAAF Sqn., M.540, M.541 (only June), CFR
3 RAAF Sqn., M.540, M.541, CFR
4 SAAF Sqn. M.540, CFR
5 SAAF Sqn., M.540, M.541, CFR, M.865
6 RAF Sqn., M.540
12 SAAF Sqn. M.540, Sortie Reports
14 RAF Sqn. ?
24 SAAF Sqn., M.540, Sortie Reports
33 RAF Sqn., M.540, M.541
39 RAF Sqn., M.540, M.541
40 SAAF Sqn., M.540, Appendices, M.865
73 RAF Sqn., M.540, M.541, CFR
80 RAF Sqn., M.540, Appendices
148 RAF Sqn., Appendices
112 RAF Sqn., M.540, M.541, Appendices
145 RAF Sqn., M.540, M.541
208 RAF Sqn., M.540, M.541, Appendices
213 RAF Sqn., M.540, M.541, CFR
223 RAF Sqn., M.540
238 RAF Sqn., M.540, M.541, Appendices
250 RAF Sqn., M.540, M.541, CFR
252 RAF Sqn., M.540, M.541, Appendices
272 RAF Sqn., M.540, M.541, Appendices
260 RAF Sqn., M.540, M.541
274 RAF Sqn., M.540
450 RAF Sqn., M.540, M.541, CFR
Alsace Sqn., AIR 23/6004
2 PRU, M.540, M.541
1437 Flight, M.540, M.541
3 SAAF Wing, M.540, Sortie Reports
243 Wing, M.540
'Report on operations during the withdrawal from Cyrenaica, 26 May- 6 July 1942' (AIR 23/6481), War Diary SAAF; Narrative of Operations in the Middle East.
AIR 22/365; Air Ministry; Daily Resume of Air Operations.
AIR 22/401; RAF Casualties Middle East
AIR 22/165; Weekly Statistical Analysis.

Luftwaffe
Genst.Gen.Qu.6.Abt. Luftwaffe Loss Microfilms
Oberbefehlshaber Süd (OBS) Daily Reports (USSMA)
Flight logs:
Karl-Heinz Bendert
Helmut Beckmann
Hans Gross
Werner Schroer

Regia Aeronautica (USSMA)
V Squadra, war diary (USSMA)
Stormi: 1°, 50°, war diary (USSMA)
Gruppi: 6°, 17°, 159°, war diary (USSMA)
Squadriglie: 71ª, 72ª, 79ª, 80ª, 81ª, 84ª, 88ª, war diary
Operational Reports (Relazioni Operative) V Squadra
Aircraft and Pilots Numerical Situation (fortnightly, 1° and 4° St.) (USSMA)
Operational Reports (Relazioni Operative) V Squadra (USSMA)
Aircraft and Pilots Numerical Situation (fortnightly, 1° and 4° St.) (USSMA)
Flight logs:
Alessandrini
Annoni
Barcaro
Bertolaso
Berti
Biagini
Bignami
Bondi
Buttazzi
Camarda
Canfora
Frigerio
Giannella
Lucchini
Maddalena
Malvezzi
Mandolini
Martinoli
Mecatti
Perdoni
Querci
Ruspoli
Stabile
Vanzan
Viglione

Publications

G. Bertolaso, Ricordi di un vecchio aviatore, 2010

J. Edwards, M. Lavigne, Kittyhawk Pilot, Turner-Warwick Publications, 1983

R. Brown, Desert Warriors, Maryborough, Banner Books, 2000

D. Gunby - P. Temple, R.A.F. Bomber Losses in the Middle East & the Mediterranean vol.1 1939-1942, Hinckley, Midland Publishing, 2006

A. Duma, Quelli del Cavallino Rampante, Roma - Editore Dell'Ateneo, 1981

M. Lavigne & F. Edwards, Hurricanes over the Sands, Victoriaville, Lavigne Aviation Publications, 2003

M. Lavigne & F. Edwards, Kittyhawks over the Sands, Victoriaville, Lavigne Aviation Publications, 2003

D. Minterne, The history of 73 Squadron part 2 November 1940 to September 1942, Dorchester, Tutor Publication, 1997

M. Palermo - L. Slongo, Wings of Africa, IBN, Roma, 2009

M. Palermo, North Africa Air Battles November-December 1941, IBN, Roma, 2011

J. Prien - G. Stemmer - P. Rodeike - W. Bock, Die Jagdfliegerverbande der Deutschen Luftwaffe 1934 - 1945 Teil 8/I Einsatz im Mittelmeerraum 1942, Eutin, Struve Druck Verlag, 2004

J. Prien - G. Stemmer, JG 27: Messerschmitt Bf 109 im Einsatz bei der Stab und I../JG 27, Eutin, Struve Druck Verlag, 2005

J. Prien - G. Stemmer, JG 27: Messerschmitt Bf 109 im Einsatz bei der II../JG 27, Eutin, Struve Druck Verlag, 2006

J.Prien - G.Stemmer, JG 27: Messerschmitt Bf 109 im Einsatz bei der III../JG 27, Eutin, Struve Druck Verlag, 2007

J.Prien, Jagdgeschwader 53, A History of the Pik As Geschwader Volume 2: May 1942 - January 1944, Schiffer Military History, 2004

M. Schoeman, Springbok Fighter Victory (Vol.II), Freeworld Publications

C. Shores - H.Ring, Fighters over the Desert, London, Arco Publishing Company, Inc., New York, 1969

C. Shores - B. Cull - N. Malizia, Malta The Spitfire Year, Grub Street, London

Internet Sites

http://www.ww2.dk
http://www.wwiiaircraftperformance.org
http://www.beim-zeugmeister.de
http://cecilgolding.yolasite.com
http://naa.gov.au
http://www.cwgc.org
http://www.quarry.nildram.co.uk/WW2guneffect.htm

ACKNOWLEDGEMENTS

I wish to thank Tenente Colonnello Massimiliano Barlattani, Maresciallo Pasquale Rubertone and Dottor Massimo Pasquali of the Ufficio Storico Stato Maggiore Aeronautica Militare for the most kind collaboration.
Special thanks go to Enrico Cernuschi, Michele Gaetani, and Ludovico Slongo.
Further, I thank Andreas Bierman, Marco Manni, and Eva Saltus for the considerable work done.
I would also like to acknowledge the Aviation Heritage Museum of Western Australia, Andrew Arthy, Stefaan Bouwer, Gabriele Brancaccio, Andreas Brekken, Craig Busby, Fulvio Chianese, Roberto Gentilli, John Krug, Giam Piero Milanetti, Daniele Moretto and Danilo Ventura for all the help and materials provided.

INDEX OF PILOTS

A

Abram	James	P.O.	39	87, 150
Adye		Sgt.	112	100, 131
Alderson		Sgt.	3 RAAF	81, 190, 136
Aldridge		F.Lt.	33	
Alessandrini	Italo	Ten.	90ª Sq.	99, 156, 166
Alexopulos		Sgt/P.	335	24
Alisch	Günther	Lt.	I./L.G.1	106
Allan		Sgt.	33	119
Allen		Lt.	2 SAAF	40, 59, 65, 130
Allevot	Giuseppe	Serg. Magg.	78ª Sq.	64
Amos	Frederick	Sgt.	272	?
Andrich	Alvise	Serg. Magg.	80ª Sq.	39, 59, 123
Annona	Salvatore	Ten.	204ª Sq.	154
Annoni	Emanuele	Ten.	96ª Sq.	73, 118, 190, 197, 198
Antonelli	Eugenio	Cap. C.O.	391ª Sq.	93
Antonicelli	Orazio	Serg. Magg.	8° Gr.a	38
Asmuss	Alan	P.O.	238	101
Astell		F.O.	148	77, 79
Atkinson	Eric	P.O.	112	95

B

Bacchi Andreoli	Vittorio	Ten.	80ª Sq.	96, 143
Bagnoli	Renato	S.Ten.	80ª Sq.	72
Bailey		Sgt.	145	183
Baker		Sgt.	73	100, 123, 136, 211
Baldelli	Italo	M.llo	81ª Sq.	84
Baldini	Edoardo	Cap.	81ª Sq.	25, 83
Bangley	Leonard	F.O.	223	28
Barbera	Livio	Serg.	84ª Sq.	88, 166
Barr	Andrew	S.L.	3 RAAF	22, 62, 63, 64, 81, 119, 160, 184, 192, 195
Barrie	Donald	F.Sgt.	73	66, 156
Bartesaghi	Luigi	Serg. Magg.	88ª Sq.	62, 64
Bartolozzi	Pietro	Serg. Magg.	388ª Sq	94
Baruffi	Pericle	Cap.	71ª Sq.	58
Baschirotto	Gian Lino	M.llo	88ª Sq.	32, 123
Bauer	Ludwig	Fw.	7./JG 27	169
Bayly	Gordon	Capt.	4 SAAF	71, 90, 112, 116, 124, 125
Beckmann	Erich	Oblt.	9./JG 53	150, 199
Beckmann	Helmut	Uffz.	2./JG 27	27, 201, 206
Beggiato	Guido	Cap.	81ª Sq.	112
Belec	Joseph	Sgt.	33	27
Bell		P.O.	274	55
Belleau		Sgt.	33	37, 110
Belser	Hptm. Helmut	Hptm.	8./JG 53	62, 71, 84, 105, 146, 150, 181
Benati	Amedeo	Serg. Magg.	79ª Sq.	24, 83, 123
Bendert	Karl-Heinz	Ofw.	4./JG 27	23, 26, 64, 107, 115, 201
Bergfleth	Johannes	Oblt.	9./ZG 26	44
Bernier		F.Sgt.	260	173
Berrange		Lt.	2 SAAF	59
Berti	Paolo	Ten.	84ª Sq.	111, 139, 163
Bertolaso	Giorgio	S.Ten	91ª Sq.	88, 89, 236
Bessot		S.Lt.	Alsace	143
Beste		Sgt.	450	134
Bezencenet		P.O.	208	180
Biagini	Bruno	Serg.	96ª Sq	118, 190, 198, 210
Biden		Col.	40 SAAF	28
Biden	Ross	P.O.	3 RAAF	149, 160
Bidwell		Lt.	5 SAAF	57, 115, 209
Bignami	Luigi	M.llo	84ª Sq.	88, 99
Bittner		Oblt.	III./ZG 26	81
Blackstock	William	P.O.	459	147
Bladelli	Alessandro	M.llo	88ª Sq.	209
Blauuw		Capt.	40 SAAF	28,
Blessing	Wilson	Sgt.	272	150
Blume	Karl	Lt.	I./L.G.1	95
Boardman	Lloyd	Sgt.	3 RAAF	81, 159, 185
Boerngen	Ernst	Oblt.	5./JG 27	65, 96, 201, 207
Bondi	Alvaro	Ten.	91ª Sq.	88
Bordin	Alfredo	M.llo	88ª Sq.	39
Borgis	Paolo	Serg.	78ª Sq.	81
Borreo	Anano	Serg.	88ª Sq.	61, 62, 123
Botha	Louis	S.L.	4 SAAF	85, 95, 109, 167, 168,
Brandt		Uffz.	3./St.G.3	88
Bray	Henry	Sgt.	3 RAAF	131, 159, 192
Brisdoux	Pierre	Lt.	Alsace	207
Brenner		Oblt.	LG 1	148
Brown		F.Lt.	112	45
Brown	Ivan	Lt.	2 SAAF	53, 54
Brown		F.O.	208	80, 110
Brown		P.O.	274	134
Bruchner		Lt.	III./St.G.3	38
Bruckshaw		Sgt.	274	74,
Bryant	Philip	Lt.	2 SAAF	26, 109, 161
Buckland	Graham	P.O.	250	58,
Buogo	Egidio	Serg.	71ª Sq.	96
Burdon		Lt.	2 SAAF	40, 65, 89, 28, 60,
Burney	Henry	P.O.	112	
Buttazzi	Piero	Serg.	84ª Sq.	102, 166, 168

C

Cable	William	P.O.	250	50, 58, 165
Cairns	David	Sgt.	250	58,
Callister	Norman	Sgt.	33	165
Camarda	Domenico	Cap.	79ª Sq.	32, 39,

				122, 123	Dickinson	Eric	F.Lt.	112	45
Cameron	William	F.Sgt.	33	136	Dils		Sgt.	272	188
Campbell	Duncan	F.Sgt.	80	53,189	Doak		P.O.	208	184
Cantrill	Charles	F.Lt.	73	102, 103	Dobson	Frank	Sgt.	223	195
Cappellini	Ottorino	Ten.	71ª Sq.	96	Dodds		Sgt.	274	57, 96, 137,
Carini	Mario	Ten.	72ª Sq.	46, 59					155, 159,
Carlisle	John	F.Sgt.	260	23,75,200,					170, 171
				201	Doig		F.Sgt.	238	208
Carruthers		Sgt.	223	205	Donald		Sgt.	3 RAAF	136, 162
Casadio	Giordano	Serg.	94ª Sq.	182	Döring	Werner	Ofw.	4./L.G.1	209
Cassell		F.Sgt.	112	131	Doyé	Hans	Lt.	Stab II./JG 27 51
Castellani	Bruno	M.llo	80ª Sq.	95	Drescher	Johann	Hptm.	4./St.G 3	54
Cattaneo	Angelo	S.Ten.	79ª Sq.	84	Drew	Roy	P.O.	112	172
Cecchet	Orfeo	Cap.	8° Gr.	46	Duncan	Andrew	Maj.	5 SAAF	70, 76,
Cella	Silvio		205ª Sq.	80					168, 196
Civetta	Alfredo	S.Ten.	88ª Sq.	32, 112	Dyson	Charles	Sgt.	450	37, 60, 75,
Clabburn		Sgt.	3 RAAF	36, 44					120, 180,
Clade	Emil	Ofw.	5./JG 27	134, 163,					190, 196
				196, 207	**E**				
Clark	Harold	Sgt.	260	118,119	Eagle	William	Sgt.	274	80, 105,
Clayton	Frederick	Sgt.	70	204					110, 119
Clegget	Noel	Sgt.	272	152	Edelhoff	Gottfried	Lt.	5./L.G.1	163
Cloete		F.Lt.	33	136	Edmunds		F.O.	213	135
Cohen		Lt.	4 SAAF	91, 142, 143	Edwards		F.Sgt.	213	135
Colin		Lt.	Alsace	143, 200,	Edwards	James	F.Sgt.	260	171, 172,
				207					173, 201
Collinette	Frank	F.Lt.	238	183, 208	Edwards	Felix	P.O.	112	141
Collovini	Giovanni	M.llo	81ª Sq.	49	Enste	Friedrich	Uffz.	II./K.G.100	182
Comfort	Alexander	P.O.	80	32	Eppen	Heinrich	Hptm.	I./St.G.3	87
Conrad		P.O.	274	155, 159,	Ermo	Carlo	Serg.	71ª Sq.	46
				170, 171	**F**				
Cooper	Alan	F.Sgt.	272	147	Facchini	Gino	Serg.	387ª Sq	73
Copeland		Capt.	4 SAAF	75	Fahernberger		Uffz.	8./JG 27	160
Copeland	Percy	F.Lt.	250	113, 152,	Falchi	Giorgio	Ten.	81ª Sq.	123
				154, 194	Faresi	Renato	Serg.	391ª Sq.	93
Copping	Dennis	F.Sgt.	260	60, 209	Ferrari	Pietro	S.Ten.	364ª Sq	30
Corbisier	Roger	P.O.	272	150	Ferrazza	Adelmo	S.Ten.	79ª Sq.	32, 39
Cormack	Desmond	Sgt.	250	24,53, 190	Fiascaris	Giacinto	Serg. Magg.	390ª Sq.	101
Coussens		P.O.	73	108, 136,	Fink	Walter	Fw.	7./JG 27	162
				173, 202	Finlayson		Sgt.	3 RAAF	81, 141
Craggs		Sgt.	274	112	Finlayson		Lt.	5 SAAF	115
Creighton	Francis	P.O.	250	144	Fluder	Emmerich	Oblt.	6./JG27	70
Cuddon		P.O.	112	192	Ford	Norman	Lt.	2 SAAF	40
Cummings	Michael	F.Sgt.	238	208	Fox		Sgt.	3 RAAF	184, 185
D					Franzisket	Ludwig	Hptm.	1./JG 27	23,114,
D'Agostini	Mario	Cap. C.O.	93ª Sq	155					135, 138,
Daffurn		Sgt.	39	150					193, 205,
Daminger	Johann	Uffz.	I./St.G.3	72					207
Darwin		F.Lt.	274	156	Freewen		Lt.	2 SAAF	89
Davies	Ian	P.O.	223	195, 205	Fricke	Siegfried	Fw.	5./JG 27	196,199
De Michelis	Pier Giuseppe	Ten.	174ª Sq.	87	Frickmann		Uffz.	III./ZG 26	41
De Villiers	Theodore	Lt.	2 SAAF	161	Frost	John	Maj.	5 SAAF	41, 42, 48,
De Waal		Lt.	4 SAAF	75, 89, 115					56, 70, 76,
Dean	John	Sgt.	450	54					85, 91, 92,
Deibel	Hans	Lt.	3./St.G.3	84, 85, 86					98, 104,
Della Valle	Giuseppe	Serg. Magg.	391ª Sq.	155					109, 115,
Derham		Lt.	5 SAAF	98, 164, 165					144, 162,
Derville	Raymond	Lt.	Alsace	207					164, 165,
Devlin	Lewis	F.Sgt.	250	62					168, 196
Devlin	Henry	Sgt.	450	57					

Fulton		2/Lt.	2 SAAF	60

G

Gael		F.Sgt.	272	147
Ganda	Bruno	S.Ten.	81ª Sq.	83
Ganes		F.Sgt.	229	40
Gaymans		Lt.	5 SAAF	85
Gerlitz	Erich	Maj.	Stab III./JG 53	74
Ghiglia	Giovanni	Ten.	80ª Sq.	59, 123
Giacomelli	Giuliano	Cap.	81ª Sq.	39, 62, 64, 83, 84
Giannella	Luigi	Ten.	84ª Sq.	111, 163, 166
Giannotti	Luigi	Serg.	82ª Sq.	148
Gibbes	Robert	S.L.	3 RAAF	233
Gibson	Douglas	F.O.	227	152
Gidney		F.Lt.	223	205
Gierster	Helmut	Uffz.	5./JG 27	84, 134, 149
Glancy	Alexander	F.Sgt.	450	169
Gläser		Uffz.	7./JG 53	147
Glenn	William	P.O.	208	137, 163
Glynn	James	Sgt.	80	82
Göhmann		Uffz.	8./JG 53	150
Golding	Cecil	2/Lt.	5 SAAF	42, 80, 84, 85, 86
Golino	Angelo	Serg. Magg.	9° Gr.	198, 199
Goodwin		Sgt.	73	136, 173
Götz	Franz	Oblt.	9./JG 53	122, 145, 150, 191
Grant	Frank	P.O.	39	150
Greaves		Sgt.	112	131
Grimes		Lt.	40 SAAF	47, 64
Grobler		Lt.	5 SAAF	75
Gromotka	Fritz	Fw.	6./JG 27	70,122
Gruber	Viktor	Uffz.	7./JG 27	51
Guerci	Mario	Serg.	73ª Sq.	55, 118, 138
Guillet	Paolo	S.Ten.	390ª Sq.	148
Gundry	Kenneth	F.O.	112	22
Gunn	Stanley	Sgt.	40 SAAF	204
Gustavus	Ewald	Hptm.	II./K.G.100	187

H

Hackhausen	Hermann	Uffz.	I./N.J.G.2	201
Hale		P.O.	260	60
Hall		Sgt.	33	136
Hall		Sgt.	250	111, 152, 154, 165
Halliday	William	Sgt.	450	60, 132, 141, 142
Halvorsen		F.Sgt.	213	139
Hamilton		P.O.	250	187
Handysides		Sgt.	80	53
Hankok		Lt.	4 SAAF	71, 121
Hannaford		Sgt.	250	62, 64, 162
Harder	Jürgen		7./JG 53	64, 74, 130, 146
Harrison		Lt.	2 SAAF	59
Heald	John	Lt.	40 SAAF	210
Heidel	Alfred	Fw.	4./JG 27	70
Heinecke	Hans-Joachim	Oblt.	9./JG 27	152, 169, 206
Henderson	Robert	Sgt.	274	118, 119, 134
Herkenhoff		Fw.	9./JG 53	41, 134,
Herritsch		Lt.	2./St.G.3	88
Heschl	Karl	Lt.	II./K.G.100	114
Hesse	Heinrich	Lt.	7./JG 53	81,147, 148, 150, 152
Hetterich	Karl	Lt.	1./L.G.1	31
Hewitson	John	S.L.	4 SAAF	142, 195, 196
Hewitt		Sgt.	223	195
Heyne	Werner	Fw.	1./NJG 2	204
Hill	Geoffrey	Sgt.	73	136, 187
Hindle	Thomas	F.Lt.	260	48, 73, 75
Hirst	Robert	Lt.	2 SAAF	115
Holler	Rudolf	Uffz.	II./St.G.3	81
Holmes	Norman	F.O.	238	184
Homuth	Gerhard	Hptm.	3./JG 27	28
Hooke		Sgt.	3 RAAF	169
Hooper		F.O.	39	150
Horne		Lt.	2 SAAF	92
Horsfield	Hugh	Sgt.	223	28
Horst	Michael	Uffz.	1./St.G.3	88
Host	Mario	Serg. Magg.	80ª Sq.	39, 40, 66, 79, 209
House	Edward	Sgt.	450	134
Howard	John	W.O.	80	24
Hübel	Robert	Lt.	II./St.G 3	87
Hughes		Sgt.	80	53
Hülle	Fritz	Lt.	4.(H)/12	101
Human		Maj.	2 SAAF	40, 65, 84

I

Ingino	Mario	S.Ten.	387ª Sq.	101
Inglesby	Herbert	Lt.	33	89, 105
Ironside	Malcolm	Lt.	4 SAAF	89, 90, 125
Ismay		Lt.	2 SAAF	52
Ismay	Wilfred	P.O.	274	52, 74, 109

J

Jackson	Rowan	Lt.	4 SAAF	71
Jackson		Sgt.	213	121
Jaclin		S.L.	108	209
James		Sgt.	145	80, 112
James	John	Sgt.	450	110
Jänicke	Arno	Lt.	1./St.G.3	38
Jenisch	Kurt	Lt.	5./JG 27	24, 32, 83, 187, 196, 199
Jenkins		Sgt.	450	54, 64, 144
Jones		Lt.	12 SAAF	187, 191
Jones	Thomas	P.O.	450	194
Jones	Michael	Sgt.	73	52, 136,
Jones		Sgt.	3 RAAF	196
Jordan	Rudolf	Uffz.	Wüstennot-staffel	52
Joyce		F.Sgt.	73	38, 119, 189
Junge	Hans-Günther	Uffz.	9./JG 27	97,169

K

Name	First	Rank	Unit	Pages
Kabisch	Helmut	Fw.	7./JG 27	193
Kaiser	Emil	Fw.	Stab I./JG 27	60
Kalista	Alexander	Lt.	5./JG 27	96,97
Kanoldt	Walter	Uffz.	(4(H)/12)	101
Kasten	Dietrich	Lt.	8./JG 53	150
Kaufmann	Graham	Lt.	4 SAAF	112, 142, 202
Keefer		F.Lt.	274	32, 90, 112, 113, 117, 159, 170
Kemsley		Lt.	5 SAAF	112, 145, 205
Keppler	Gerhard	Fw.	1./JG 27	59, 60, 208
Kientsch	Willy	Ofhr.	Stab II./JG 27	26, 87, 120, 171
Kildey	Edward	Sgt.	3 RAAF	22, 185, 196
Kirner	Ludwig	Fw.	I./St.G.3	76
Kirner	Theodor	Fw.	I./KG 54	79
Klager	Ernst	Lt.	7./JG 53	81, 84, 97, 114, 117, 191, 204
Klötzer		Uffz.	7./JG 53	146
Knapik		P.O.	112	37
Knight		Sgt.	227	152
Knothe	Herbert	Lt.	I./KG 54	148
Kochner		Uffz.	7./St.G.3	30
Konrad	Hugo	Uffz.	III./Z.G.26	38
Körner	Friedrich	Lt.	2./JG 27	45, 54, 139
Köster	Alfons	Ofw.	3./NJG 2	204
Krenzke	Erich	Ofw.	6./JG 27	40, 53, 70
Kretschmar	Dieter	Uffz.	I./St.G.3	72
Krieger	Johann	Uffz.	3./St.G.3	74
Kronschnabel	Josef	Ofw.	9./JG 53	53, 54, 180
Krug	Walter	Uffz.	III./St.G.3	106
Küppers	Julius	Uffz.	II./St.G.3	149

L

Name	First	Rank	Unit	Pages
Lacey		Capt.	5 SAAF	202
Lack	Walter	F.Sgt.	213	103
Laflamme		Sgt.	33	27
Lafont	Henry	S.Lt.	Alsace	206
Lane		Lt.	4 SAAF	71, 90, 93
Lane-Sansam	Ernest	F.Lt.	272	188, 191
Lang		Lt.	4 SAAF	43
Lange	Willi	Fw.	4(H)/12	48
Lange	Max	Lt.	9./J.G.53	199
Langerman		Lt.	4 SAAF	43
Larsimont Pergameni	Antonio	Magg. C.O.	9° Gr.	55, 100, 115, 117, 138, 189, 198, 199
Laurin	Ludovico	Magg.	9° Gr.	199
Lawler		2/Lt.	4 SAAF	90
Lawrence Smith	Michael	F.Sgt.	238	194, 208
Le Roux		Lt.	1 SAAF	79
Leake		P.O.	223	28
Lenninger	Heinz	Fw.	II./K.G.100	120
Lerche		Sgt.	274	170
Leu		F.Lt.	3 RAAF	81, 182
Liebsch	Hans	Fw.	I./L.G.1	38
Ligugnana	Mario	Ten.	72ª Sq.	46
Lindberg		Lt.	5 SAAF	56, 109, 112
Lindsay		Lt.	2 SAAF	104, 141
Lindsay	Gordon	Sgt.	450	75, 193, 194
Lipsky	Joseph	Lt.	II./St.G.3	201
Loeper	Rudolf	Fw.	3./St.G.3	137
Louchet	Bernard	S.Lt.	Alsace	206, 207
Lucchini	Franco	Cap. C.O.	84ª Sq.	48, 92, 93, 94, 111, 132, 133, 166, 168
Lui	Marcello	M.llo	71ª Sq.	59, 96
Lyons	Gordon	F.Sgt.	33	51

M

Name	First	Rank	Unit	Pages
Maack	Ernst	Hptm.	2./JG 27	54, 65, 207
MacDiarmid	Colin	Sgt.	3 RAAF	62
Maddalena	Paolo	Magg. C.O.	10˚ Gr.	
Mader	Adolf	Uffz.	I./L.G.1	201
Magli	Giuseppe	M.llo	72ª Sq.	
Mahady		Sgt.	145	163, 195
Mailfert	Maurice	S.Chef	Alsace	207
Malvezzi	Fernando	Ten.	97ª Sq. C.O.	
Mandolini	Orlando	Ten.	91ª Sq.	88, 89, 98, 99, 111, 138, 166
Manz	Walter	Uffz.	9./J.G.53	199
Marcati	Francesco	Serg. Magg.	390 Sq.	94
Marchi	Emilio	Ten.	80ª, 88ª Sq.	46, 59, 209
Marcovich	Riccardo	Cap.	8° Gr.	114
Marillier	Ronald	2/Lt.	4 SAAF	71
Marseille	Hans-Joachim	Oblt.	3./JG 27	7, 28, 58, 71, 81, 83, 84, 86, 87, 105, 121, 122, 130, 141, 155, 157, 164, 170, 172, 173, 226
Marsh		Sgt.	274	130, 134
Marshall		F.Lt.	250	150, 190
Martin		2/Lt.	5 SAAF	48, 70, 76, 85
Martinoli	Teresio	Serg. Magg.	73ª Sq.	54, 55, 116, 117, 198, 210
Massa	Mario	S.Ten.	73ª Sq.	55, 56
Matthews		F.Sgt.	260	173
Mayer	Josef	Gefr.	I./St.G.3	76
Mc Clure		W.O.	223	28
Mc Cormack		Sgt.	80	24, 53
Mc Farlane		Sgt.	450	141
Mc Gregor			208	129, 164
McBurnie	Donald	F.Sgt.	450	65

Surname	First Name	Rank	Unit	Pages
McDougall		Capt.	73	53
McGill	Thomas	F.O.	272	188
McGregor		Lt.	4 SAAF	84
McLeod		Lt.	2 SAAF	59
McMaster		Lt.	2 SAAF	108
McWilliam		Sgt.	250	58
Meaker		Maj.	5 SAAF	92, 93
Mechelli	Salvatore	Serg. Magg.	73ª Sq.	118, 198
Medwin		Sgt.	70	188
Meneghetti	Nello	Serg. Magg.	81ª Sq.	62
Mentnich	Karl	Ofw.	3./JG 27	28, 71, 122
Menzies		Sgt.	33	112, 125
Mezzetti	Gastone	Cap.	Gorizia	152
Mitchell	Stuart	P.O.	112	75
Mitterdorf		Gefr.	III./St.G.3	182
Modesti	Luigi	Serg. Magg.	155ª Sq.	33
Monk		F.Lt.	145	119
Montagu		F.Lt.	208	189
Monterumici	Amleto	Serg. Magg.	84ª Sq.	156
Morandi	Sergio	Ten.	72	46, 59, 96, 143
Morgan	Kenneth	Lt.	4 SAAF	167
Morgenroth	Eberhard	Oblt.	I./St.G.3	182
Moriarty	Patrick	F.Lt.	274	83
Morphew		Capt.	4 SAAF	90, 93
Morrison	Robert	Capt.	5 SAAF	42, 85
Morrison Bell			6	110
Morton	Robert	Lt.	2 SAAF	142, 202
Mrosla	Bernhard	Fw.	3./JG 27	195
Muir	David	Lt.	5 SAAF	42, 85
Müller	Wilfried	Lt.	I./KG 54	147
Müller	Rudolf	Lt.	8./JG 53	71, 12
Munzert	Hermann	Lt.	9./JG 53	53, 18
Murdoch		P.O.	450	196
Murray	Thomas	Capt.	4 SAAF	71, 80, 202
Murrow		Lt.	24 SAAF	57

N

Surname	First Name	Rank	Unit	Pages
Naiß	Anton	Ofw.	I./N.J.G.2	47
Neil		F.Sgt.	274	32, 47, 96, 130, 184
Neill	Garth	Sgt.	112	81
Nel		Capt.	40 SAAF	52
Nestor		Capt.	376th USAAF	211
Newton		Sgt.	112	164, 165
Nicol	Burton	Lt.	40 SAAF	32
Niederhöfer	Hans	Fw.	5./JG 27	32, 96, 162
Nietzke	Helmut	Uffz.	7./ZG 26	41
Nioi	Clizio	Cap.	80ª Sq.	94, 95, 123
Norman		P.O.	145	125, 132, 163
Norman		Sgt.	3 RAAF	47
Nursey	Ian	F.Sgt.	450	28, 54, 65
Nusswitz	Werner	Uffz.	1./St.G.3	84

O

Surname	First Name	Rank	Unit	Pages
Oakley	Edward	Sgt.	450	45
Oberholster		Sgt.	24 SAAF	57
Obernhuber	Otto	Oblt.	6./L.G.1	25
Ocarso	Dante	Cap.	88ª Sq.	39
Olfermann		Oblt.	4./St.G 3	54
Ölsner	Alfred	Fw.	I./KG 54	164
Olver		F.Lt.	213	197, 210
Osborne	Oliver	P.O.	450	141
Ostler	Anton	Oblt.	II./St.G.3	146
Ovenstone	Harold	Sgt.	250	50

P

Surname	First Name	Rank	Unit	Pages
Packer		Sgt.	450	54
Paddon	David	Lt.	2 SAAF	40
Palazzeschi	Antonio	Ten.	81ª Sq.	48, 49, 62, 112, 113
Panier	Karl Heinz	Uffz.	10.(J)/JG 27	157
Panizzi	Leo	Serg.	388ª Sq	148
Pannaria	Arnaldo	Ten.Vasc.	Gorizia	152
Pantel		Ofw.	III./StG 3	146
Parbury		F.Sgt.	274	32, 137
Pare	Robin	Capt.	5 SAAF	51
Paroli	Eracle	Serg. Magg.	79ª Sq.	32
Parrot		Sgt.	260	206
Paterson		Lt.	4 SAAF	95, 202
Patterson		Sgt.	272	208
Pearson	Philip	P.O.	80	53
Perdoni	Luciano	Serg.	84ª Sq.	94, 111
Persse	Charles	P.O.	274	130
Pfeffer	Erhard	Uffz.	3./JG 27	114, 116
Piccolomini Adami	Ranieri	Cap. (C.O.)	90ª Sq.	88, 93, 101, 102, 132, 133, 156, 163
Pickel	Hans	Uffz.	4(H)/12	100
Pien		Sgt.	272	185
Pierce		Capt.	4 SAAF	202
Playford		F.Lt.	274	32
Polenz	Otto	Ofw.	III./ZG 26	81
Polizzy	Piero	Ten.	79ª Sq.	48
Popham		Lt.	5 SAAF	196
Pöttgen	Rainer	Fw.	3./JG 27	81, 86, 157, 195
Presland		Sgt.	274	137
Pride		Lt.	1 SAAF	79
Pufahl	Wilfried	Oblt.	7./JG 53	58, 74
Purdy		F.Sgt.	238	208

Q

Surname	First Name	Rank	Unit	Pages
Quaritsch	Karl-Heinz	Lt.	8./JG 53	62, 81, 97, 105, 122, 146
Querci	Alvaro	S.Ten.	73ª Sq.	55, 100, 118, 190, 210
Quirk	Elston	Sgt.	450	22

R

Surname	First Name	Rank	Unit	Pages
Reinders	Sydney	Lt.	4 SAAF	167
Remmer	Hans	Lt.	1./JG 27	141
Reuter	Horst	Fw.	5./JG 27	24, 27, 37, 45
Riba	Hans	Oblt.	I./L.G.1	38
Riedlberger	Walter	Lt.	I./N.J.G.2	33
Righetti	Giorgio	Serg. Magg.	390ª Sq.	101
Ritchie		Sgt.	213	197
Ritter	Wilhelm	Ofw.	4.(H)/12	101

Rivolta	Pasquale	Serg.	159° Gr.	155		Slater		Lt.	5 SAAF	48, 57
Robertshaw		Lt.	4 SAAF	142		Small	Gordon	Sgt.	145	
Robin	Michael	F.Lt.	73	163		Smith	Eric	Capt.	2 SAAF	40, 59, 75, 142
Robottom		Lt.	4 SAAF	84						
Rödel	Gustav	Oblt.	Stab II./JG 27	26, 87		Somerville		Lt.	208	190
Rogers		P.O.	272	148		Sommer	Hermann	Ofw.	2./NJG 2	154
Rogerson		P.O.	250	23		Sommerville		Lt.	4 SAAF	51, 52, 70, 76, 167
Rohloff	Erwin	Fw.	II./K.G.100	204						
Rökker	Heinz	Lt.	1./NJG 2	189, 209, 211		Soufrilias		F.Sgt.	335	207
						Sowrey		F.O.	213	24, 121
Rose		F.Lt.	450	21, 22		Sozzi	Felice	M.llo	77ª Sq.	148
Rosenberg	Heinrich	Ofw.	9./JG 27	150, 193, 206		Spangenberg	Herbert	Hptm.	2/St.G 3	84, 134, 149
Ross		Sgt.	148	77, 79		Spear		Sgt.	145	105, 202
Rossi	Pasquale	Serg. Magg.	96ª Sq	118		Spicer	Frederick	F.Lt.	2 PRU	159
Russell	Edwin	F.Sgt.	250	38		Squarcia	Vittorio	Ten.	73ª Sq.	118
Ruzzene	Alessandro	Serg. Magg.	94ª Sq.	120		Squarcina	Mario	S.Ten	10° Gr.	102
Ryan	Frederick	Sgt.	3 RAAF	159, 162		Stabile	Natalino	Mar.	88ª Sq.	32, 39
						Stahlschmidt	Hans-Arnold	Lt.	2./JG 27	54, 139, 147, 162, 193, 201, 206
S										
Sabourin		F.Lt.	145	80, 105, 112, 113, 132						
Saiani	Renato	Serg.	79ª Sq.	39, 84, 112		Stammers	Leslie	F.Sgt.	33	29
Salmon		Lt.	1 SAAF	79		Stange		Lt.	II./K.G.100	184
Sands	Alwyn	Sgt.	73	47		Stein		F.Sgt.	238	184
Saunders	Peter	Sgt.	5 SAAF	57, 65, 110		Steinhausen	Günther	Fw.	1./JG 27	23, 48, 71, 114, 135, 138, 164, 165, 205, 207, 208
Savini	Angelo	Serg. Magg.	10° Gr.	166						
Scade	Thomas	F.Lt.	73	38, 52, 53, 121						
Schaller	Wolf	Lt.	9./JG 53	171, 199						
Scharnowski	Bruno	Fw.	5./L.G.1	24		Steis	Heinrich	Uffz.	4./JG 27	23, 182, 201
Scheid	Helmut	Lt.	III./Z.G.26	30		Stella	Andrea	M.llo	72ª Sq.	46, 101
Scheiter		Lt.	8./JG 27	105, 106		Stephenson	William	F.Sgt.	213	24, 25, 135
Schmidt	Erich	Fw.	7./JG 53	97		Stevens		2/Lt.	5 SAAF	46, 109, 131
Schneider	Karl	Uffz.	1./St.G.3	84		Stewart		F.Sgt.	70	188
Schneider	Leopold	Uffz.	II./K.G.100	47		Stewart		F.Sgt.	70	188
Schroer	Werner	Lt.	Stab I./JG 27	52, 60, 122, 157, 158, 184, 193, 200, 222		Stewart	Herbert	Sgt.	250	60, 62, 190
						Stewart		Sgt.	250	60, 62, 190
						Stigler	Franz	Fw.	4./JG 27	70, 201
						Stone		P.O.	73	173
Schultz	Otto	Oblt.	Stab II./JG 27	48, 49, 52, 57, 171		Stone	Roy	Sgt.	450	141
						Street	Paul	Sgt.	108	204
Schulze	Alfred	Ofw.	4./JG 27	48		Stumpf	Werner	Ofw.	9./JG 53	41, 62, 80, 130, 134, 145
Schwekutsch	Otto	Uffz.	6./JG 27	105						
Scott	William	F.Sgt.	80	24						
Sdun	Gerhard	Uffz.	8./JG 27	23		Summers	Geoffrey	F.Sgt.	272	188
Seabrook		Sgt.	250	23, 165, 194		Swan		Sgt.	33	74
						Swire		Sgt.	80	53
Sedgewick	Gerald	Lt.	208	204		Swoboda		Ofw.	8./ZG 26	173
Seidl	Alfred	Fw.	8./JG 53	148, 150, 201		Sykes	Harold	Sgt.	80	48, 53
Sgorbati	Roberto	S.Ten.	88ª Sq.	32		**T**				
Shaw	Raymond	Sgt.	450	54		Taddia	Ernesto	Serg. Magg.	13° Gr	76
Sheppard	Lionel	Sgt.	260	73		Talamini	Renato	Ten.		39, 66, 77
Shillabeer		Sgt.	450	45		Tangerding	Hermann	Oblt.	7./JG 27	162
Simon	Oskar	Oblt.	4./JG 27	52		Taverna	Gregorio	Serg.	90ª Sq.	133
Simpson		F.Lt.	6	110		Tedesco	Yves	P.O.	272	147
Simpson	Anthony	P.O.	250	163		Temlett		Lt.	213	103, 118, 197
Simpson		Sgt.	450	194						
Sinner	Rudolf	Oblt.	Stab I./JG 27	60, 71, 122, 184, 201		Thiriez	Daniel	S.Lt.	Alsace	206
						Thomas	Cyril	F.Lt.	39	150

Thomas		Sgt.	3 RAAF	44	Wein	Hans Wein	Fw.	7./ZG 26	41, 134,
Thomson	Donald	Capt.	40 SAAF	180	Westlake		F.L.	213	120, 135,
Thomson	Eric	Lt.	450	75					160
Thomson	Robert	Sgt.	274	134, 184,	Wheeler	William	Lt.	4 SAAF	91
				194, 195	White		Lt.	5 SAAF	98, 110
Thornhill-Cook	Basil	Lt.	5 SAAF	75, 92, 93	Whiteside		P.O.	250	190
Timmermann	Walter	Uffz.	1./JG 27	129, 208	Wiedow		Lt.	I./NJG 2	147
Tomaselli	Pio	Cap.	72ª Sq.	23	Wilcox		Sgt.	229	40, 41
Tovazzi	Giuseppe	Cap.	154ª Sq.	47	Wilie		F.Lt.	260	60
Troke		Sgt.	250	65	Wilkinson		Lt.	2 SAAF	203
Truby	Ernest		272	147	Williams	Arthur	F.Lt.	450	21, 23, 180
Tuckwell		Sgt.	272	148	Wilson		P.O.	3 RAAF	81
					Wilson	Alan	Sgt.	73	102, 124,
U									133, 203
Ugazio	Roberto	Serg.	84ª Sq.	166	Wilson		Sgt.	159	152
					Wilson	Peter	P.O.	213	103, 124
V					Wintersdorff		F.Sgt.	80	48
Van der Riet		Lt.	40 SAAF	96, 97	Wiseman		Sgt.	73	52, 102,
Van der Spuy		Lt.	5 SAAF	42, 98,					103, 136,
				145, 146					139
Van Nus		Lt.	4 SAAF	116, 142	Wittland	Albrecht	Fw.	IV./L.G.1	38
Vanderweert	Heinrich	Obgefr.	6./JG 27	51	Wolff		Uffz.	II./St.G.3	201
Vanello	Sergio	Serg.	13° Gr.	174	Woodliffe		Lt.	4 SAAF	43, 44
Vanzan	Virgilio	S.Ten.	90ª Sq.	133, 163,	Woolley		P.O.	73	139, 173
				165	Wrigley	James	Sgt.	260	138
Vatta	Glauco	Ten.	71ª Sq.	96	Wylie		F.L.	260	60
Veronesi	Mario	Serg.	84ª Sq.	132, 156					
Veysey	Clarence	Sgt.	260	73	**Y**				
Vicentini	Ferdinando	Cap.	72ª Sq.	96, 143	Young	Ivan	P.O.	450	22, 134
Vickery		Sgt.	252	154	Young		S.L.	213	102, 148
Viglione Borghese	Ezio	Cap.	96ª Sq	73, 97,					
				100, 101	**Z**				
Visentin		S.Ten.	171ª Sq.	152	Zeller	Fritz	Uffz.	10.(J)/JG 27	130
Vögl	Ferdinand	Oblt.	4./JG 27	48, 64, 70,	Zimmermann		Uffz.	1./JG 27	60
				182, 205					
von Fritsch	Erik	Lt.	9./JG 27	54					
von Kühlwetter	Huber	Hptm.	4.(H)/12	83					
von Lieres u. Wilkau	Karl	Lt.	2./JG 27	23, 65, 71,					
				97, 122,					
				147, 166					

W				
Waddy	John	F.Lt.	250	22, 23, 37,
				73, 95,
				138, 157
Wade	Desmond	F.Lt.	33	27
Wade	Lance	P.O.	33	51, 119, 130
Walchofer	Walchofer	Fw.	6./JG 27	107
Wallace	Robert	Sgt.	213	103, 124,
				135, 194,
				197
Wallis		Sgt.	250	194, 208
Walsh		Sgt.	274	47, 130
Ward		F.Sgt.	38	24
Ward	Derek	S.L.	73	82, 124, 173
Warden	JS	2/Lt.	2 SAAF	43, 109,
				210, 211
Webb		Lt.	40 SAAF	51, 57, 60
Webster		Sgt.	250	26, 144
Wehmeyer	Alfred	Oblt.	7./ZG 26	41, 57, 79,
				81

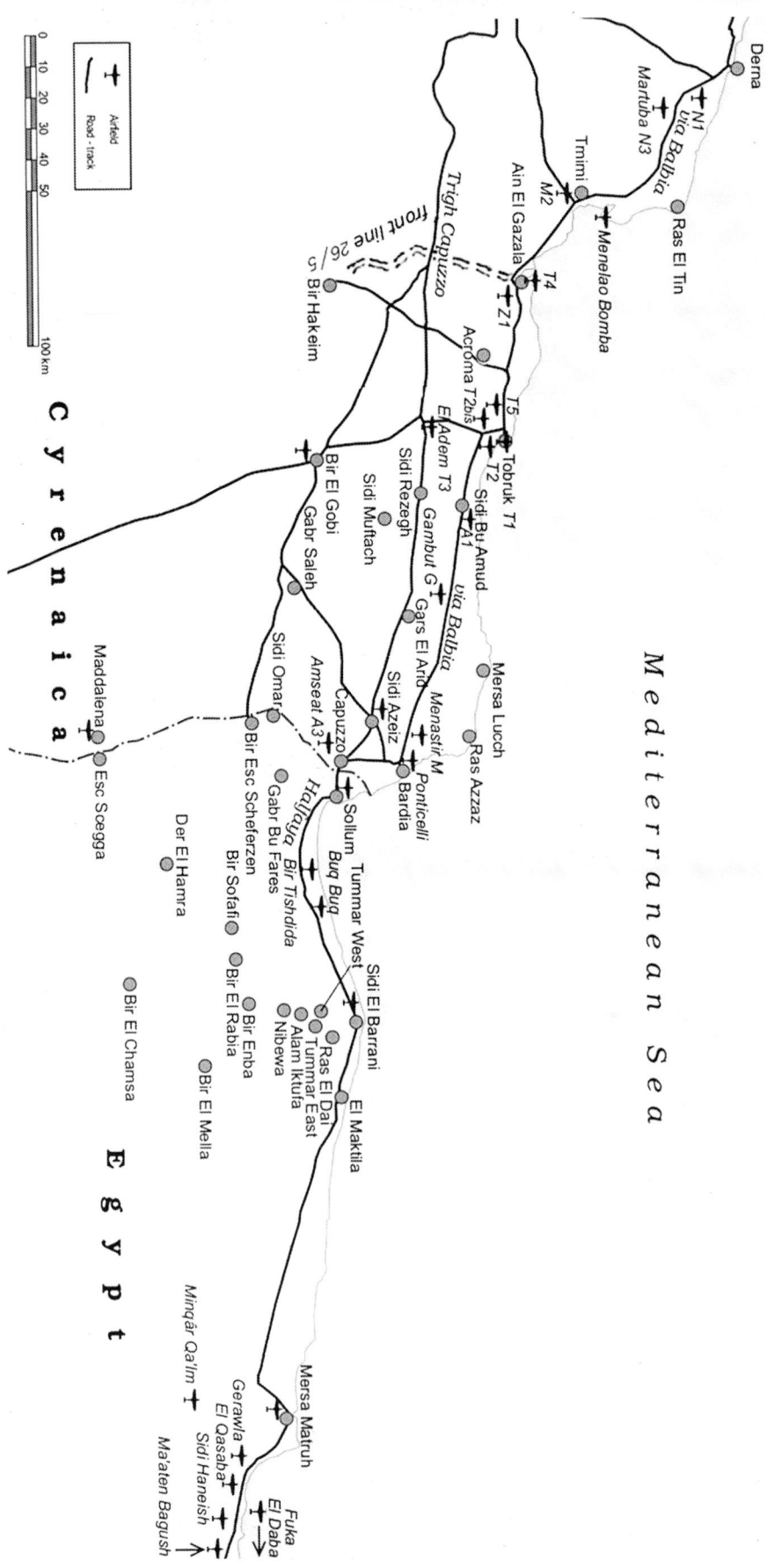